Suraiya Faroqhi is Professor of History at Bilgi University, Istanbul, and the author of *The Ottoman Empire and the World Around It*, *Pilgrims and Sultans* and *Subjects of the Sultan* (all published by I.B.Tauris).

LIBRARY OF OTTOMAN STUDIES

See www.ibtauris.com/LOS for a full list of titles

1. *The Sultan's Yemen:*
19th-Century Challenges to Ottoman Rule
Caesar E. Farah
978 1 86064 767 3

2. *Between Two Empires:*
Ahmet Agaoglu and the New Turkey
A. Holly Shissler
978 1 86064 855 7

3. *Lightning over Yemen:*
A History of the Ottoman Campaign
in Yemen, 1569–71
Clive Smith (ed. & trans.)
978 1 86064 836 6

4. *Rethinking Orientalism:*
Women, Travel and the Ottoman Harem
Reina Lewis
978 1 86064 729 1

5. *Frontiers of Ottoman Studies, Vol 1*
Colin Imber and Keiko Kiyotaki (eds)
978 1 85043 631 7

6. *Frontiers of Ottoman Studies, Vol 2*
Colin Imber, Keiko Kiyotaki and
Rhoads Murphey (eds)
978 1 85043 664 5

7. *The Ottoman Empire and the World*
Around It
Suraiya Faroqhi
978 1 85043 715 4

8. *Ottoman Reform and Muslim*
Regeneration
Weismann Zachs
978 1 85043 757 4

9. *Governing Property, Making the Modern*
State: Law, Administration and Production
in Ottoman Syria
Martha Mundy and
Richard Saumarez Smith
978 1 84511 291 2

10. *The Crescent and the Eagle:*
Ottoman Rule, Islam and the Albanians,
1874–1913
George Gawrych
978 1 84511 287 5

11. *Guarding the Frontier:*
Ottoman Border Forts and Garrisons
in Europe
Mark L. Stein
978 1 84511 301 8

12. *Ottomans, Turks and the Balkans:*
Empire Lost, Relations Altered
Ebru Boyar
978 1 84511 351 3

13. *Ottoman Propaganda and Turkish*
Identity: Literature in Turkey During
World War I
Erol Köroğlu
978 1 84511 490 9

14. *Ottomans Looking West?:*
The Origins of the Tulip Age and its
Development in Modern Turkey
Can Erimtan
978 1 84511 491 6

15. *Women in the Ottoman Balkans:*
Gender, Culture and History
Amila Buturović and Irvin Cemil Schick
(eds)
978 1 84511 505 0

16. *Innovation and Empire in Turkey:*
Sultan Selim III and the Modernisation
of the Ottoman Navy
Tuncay Zorlu
978 1 84511 694 1

17. *Artisans of Empire:*
Crafts and Craftspeople Under the Ottomans
Suraiya Faroqhi
978 1 84511 588 3

Artisans of Empire

Crafts and Craftspeople Under the Ottomans

Suraiya Faroqhi

LONDON · NEW YORK

Published in 2009 by I.B.Tauris & Co. Ltd
6 Salem Road, London W2 4BU
175 Fifth Avenue, New York, NY 10010
www.ibtauris.com

Distributed in the United States and Canada Exclusively by Palgrave Macmillan
175 Fifth Avenue, NY 10010

Copyright © 2009 Suraiya Faroqhi

The right of Suraiya Faroqhi to be identified as the author of this work has been asserted by the author in accordance with the Copyright, Designs and Patents Act 1988.

All rights reserved. Except for brief quotations in a review, this book, or any part thereof, may not be reproduced, stored in or introduced into a retrieval system, or transmitted, in any form or by any means, electronic, mechanical, photocopying, recording or otherwise, without the prior written permission of the publisher.

Library of Ottoman Studies: 17

ISBN: 978 1 84511 588 3

A full CIP record for this book is available from the British Library
A full CIP record for this book is available from the Library of Congress

Library of Congress catalog card: available

Typeset in Adobe Jenson Pro by A. & D. Worthington, Newmarket, Suffolk
Printed and bound in India by Replika Press Pvt. Ltd.

Contents

	List of Illustrations	vi
	Acknowledgements	vii
	Note on Transliteration	xi
	Introduction: Artisans of Empire	xiii
1.	Writing about Artisans	1

BEFORE THE 1670S

2.	Before and After 1500: How Artisan Organization May Have Emerged in the Ottoman Lands	23
3.	Services to the State	45
4.	Guildsmen of Istanbul and Cairo	65
5.	Provincial Craftspeople and Merchant Networks	87

FROM THE 1670S TO THE 1850S

6.	Changes in Istanbul Guilds	108
7.	Cairo: From Military Penetration of Artisan Guilds to the State Monopolies of Mehmed Ali Paşa	128
8.	Political Roles of Craftsmen	142
9.	Provincial Craftsmen: How Guilds Adapted to New Circumstances	160

AFTER 1850

10.	1850 to 1914: A Different State, a Different Economy and the Disappearance of the Guilds	186
	Conclusion: Characterizing Guilds Through Comparison	208
	Notes	221
	Bibliography	244
	Index	271

Illustrations

Map: Selected Manufacturing Centres in the Ottoman Empire
(Seventeenth–Eighteenth Centuries)   xii

Illustrations

Ottoman ornamented jug, late seventeenth to early eighteenth centuries	24
Leather purse once containing Ottoman letters	25
Ottoman silk fabrics, sixteenth and seventeenth centuries	81
Two cushion covers dating from before 1691	98
Cope used by an Orthodox priest, seventeenth century	99
Coffee cup from the Tophane manufacture, nineteenth century	126
A Bulgarian tanner from Berkovica	162
A workshop in the town of Travna manufacturing braid (*gaytan*)	166
Elaborately decorated model of the Church of the Holy Sepulchre	182
Ottoman factory in Sliven producing woollens	198

Figures

1. Real Daily Wage of Construction Workers: Istanbul, 1489–1914 (From Süleyman Özmucur, and Şevket Pamuk. 'Real Wages and Standards of Living in the Ottoman Empire, 1489–1914', *The Journal of Economic History* 62, 2 (2002), p 306)   76

2. Real Wage of Unskilled Construction Workers in European Cities, 1450–1913 (From Özmucur, and Pamuk, p 312)   78

3. Real Wage of Skilled Construction Workers in European Cities, 1450–1913 (From Özmucur, and Pamuk, p 313)   78

Acknowledgements

While working on this study, I have accumulated many debts, intellectual and otherwise. To begin with what is normally said at the end, obviously none of the people who have graciously helped me are in the least responsible for the final result. I can only hope that they will not be too badly disappointed.

The sources used in this book are largely from the Ottoman archives; for the most part they can be found in the Başbakanlık Arşivi-Osmanlı Arşivi in Istanbul. Among the many archivists and directors I have encountered over the years, I owe a special debt to my *hoca*, Midhat Sertoğlu, who first allowed me in. I also would like to pay tribute to the memory of my other *hoca*, Nejat Göyünç, as well as to that of Veli Tola. Other archival material was held in the National Library in Ankara, where the qadi registers of Turkey were housed in the 1990s, and in the İstanbul Müftülüğü, where I worked later on during the same decade. I am grateful to all the archivists and librarians who have allowed me to work on their precious holdings.

Most of this book was written during my last year at the Department of Near Eastern Studies at Ludwig-Maximilians Universität in Munich. Above all I salute Yavuz Köse: although himself in the last stages of writing a brilliant dissertation, he was invariably cheerful and ready to help; many computer problems could not possibly have been solved without him. I am also grateful for his willingness to share his knowledge of late Ottoman business history. Mehmet Hacısalihoğlu most kindly has produced the map. Elfie Semen has provided all manner of logistic support and when, as often happened, she has had to remind me of bureaucratic obligations that I had managed to 'repress' in order to work on this text, she has done so in a most charming manner. I am also grateful to Isabel Mayer-Nothafft for her help in getting the manuscript into a presentable shape and to Elif Şimşek for her efficient help with the index.

Certain chapters were written during a quarter as a guest professor at Dartmouth College in Hanover/New Hampshire during the late-arriving spring of 2007. This experience was novel and most thrilling: thanks to the initiative of Pamela Crossley, there was an opportunity to discuss similarities and differences between the Ching (Manchu) and Ottoman Empires;

this is a subject on which much more can be learned. The students of my undergraduate seminar, especially Elizabeth Terry and Henry Whitehead, asked challenging questions; and particular thanks go to Gene Garthwaite, Stephanie Taylor and Gail Vernazza for making it all possible. Time and again Alastair has provided comic relief.

Credit also goes to the participants in three conferences and one lecture discussion. The first of these (Munich, 2004), now about to be published, concerned traders on Ottoman territory and provided numerous insights into the ways by which artisans' products came to reach their final consumers. If I have been somewhat responsive to the 'demand' side of production, the participants in this conference have been instrumental: special thanks go to Olga Katsiardi-Hering, Katerina Papakostantinou and Vassiliki Serinidou. Secondly, there was a seminar specifically on artisans (Halle, 2004); here I am particularly grateful to my co-organizer Jürgen Paul and, among the participants, to Donald Quataert, Nalan Turna, Onur Yıldırım and Eunjeong Yi, who flew all the way from Korea to be with us. The third such occasion was the discussion that took place at the Great Lakes Ottoman Workshop (GLOW, Ann Arbor, 2007) organized by Gottfried Hagen; here the interest of Betül Başaran has been of special value. Last but not least, there were long and lively interchanges after a lecture at SUNY/Binghamton University (Binghamton, 2007); many thanks to the participants and, above all, to Donald Quataert for organizing the event.

When reviewing these gatherings, I understand even better that while writing is a solitary business, a book is of necessity a collective product, and the international community of Ottomanists has provided me with a great deal of support. It is good to see that 'ordinary subjects' of the Ottoman sultans and the workaday lives of both male and female craftspeople continue to interest a sizeable number of our colleagues: many thanks to Betül Başaran, Nalan Turna and Charles Wilkins who have made their very pertinent dissertations available to me. Özlem Sert kindly allowed me to see an unpublished article, and Eunjeong Yi made available two of her studies awaiting publication.

Much help has been given by people I have contacted either in person or through the internet. About Egyptian crafts, I have had to learn everything 'from scratch', and without Nelly Hanna, Febe Armanios and Siegfried Richter I would have been even more ignorant than I am at present. Minna Rozen graciously has provided information about Jewish artisans. At one point Erdem Kabadayı took time off to email me a large number of references on late Ottoman factories, while Nicolas Vatin generously lent out a much needed book. Albrecht Berger, Arsen Yarman and Tufan Karasu supplied publications I might not otherwise have seen. Most importantly Cemal Kafadar's generous hospitality has provided access to that well-defended citadel of knowledge, the Widener Library in Cambridge MA, while Ali Yaycıoğlu helped me out at a moment when I really needed help. Many thanks to them all.

A book on artisans needs illustrations and I am especially grateful to the people and institutions that have helped me find and contextualize them; I am also in their debt for the gracious permissions to reproduce them. My greatest debt is to Şevket Pamuk (University of the Bosporus, Istanbul), who allowed me to include the graphs from his and Süleyman Özmucur's work on Ottoman and Turkish wages (Özmucur and Pamuk (2002)). Jürgen W. Frembgen from the Völkerkundemuseum in Munich took me into the storage rooms of his institution and found the coffee cups manufactured in Tophane/Istanbul, and it was my colleague Hans Georg Majer who identified the sultanic 'signatures' (*tuğras*) adorning them as the decorative fakes by which goldsmiths sometimes embellished their handiwork. The Bayrische Nationalmuseum/Munich kindly provided the model of the Church of the Holy Sepulchre in Jerusalem. I also owe an enormous debt to the Abegg Foundation of Riggisberg/Berne and to its two helpful curators, Anna Jolly and Evelin Wetter: they not only provided the photographs of the Bursa textiles shown here but gave me a tour of their splendid museum that I will never forget.

When a manuscript is completed a number of colleagues are inconvenienced by a bulky package that lands on their desks or even a piece of work that as an uninvited guest makes room for itself by stealth on the receiver's computer. I am very grateful to the people who have given me their time and their comments: Lester Crook, Cem Emrence, Liz Friend Smith, Ipolya Gerelyes, Nelly Hanna, Marcel van der Linden, Donald Quataert, Giorgio Riello, Jürgen Schlumbohm and Onur Yıldırım. Good luck to our common project of establishing the lives and works of Ottoman artisans as a topic of study in a world historical context!

Suraiya Faroqhi
Department of History
Bilgi University
Istanbul

For Saadet Özen, Meryem Atlas, Djene Bajalan and my other students at the University of the Bosporus and Bilgi University, with affection

Note on Transliteration

Modern Turkish spelling has been used for all terms and names relevant to Anatolia and the Balkans. Those relevant to the Arab provinces have been transliterated according to the *International Journal of Middle East Studies*. Words that have entered the English language such as qadi or sheikh have been spelled as in standard dictionaries.

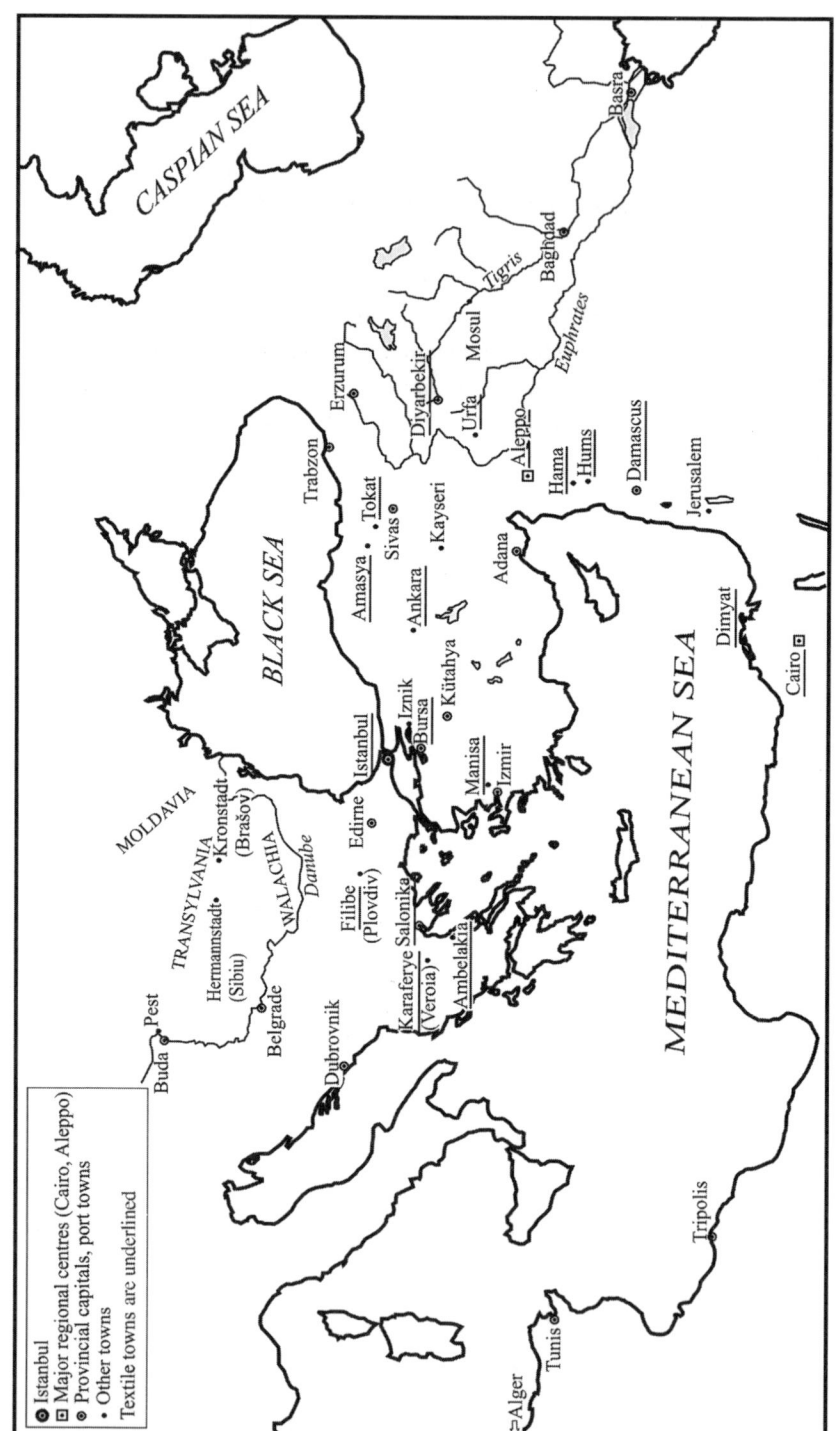

Selected Manufacturing Centres in the Ottoman Empire (Seventeenth–Eighteenth Centuries)

INTRODUCTION

Artisans of Empire

Situating the project

In the present volume we will try something rather unusual. It is our project to sketch the history of a largish segment of Ottoman urban society, namely craftsmen, and, as far as the sources permit, craftswomen as well. Studies to date of social groups active within the empire normally concern men involved with the government, especially religious scholars, but also officials with scribal training; most recently foreign residents also have come in for their share of attention.[1] Among Ottoman urbanites, merchants have been the most privileged in life as in scholarly research; and in the hierarchy of neglect, artisans rank just above peasants and nomads, the most numerous and least studied segments of the Ottoman population.

In addition, at least where the period before the nineteenth century is concerned, members of the subject population over lengthy periods of time have not often been investigated; for the most part available studies focus on a few years, decades or, in one or two exceptional cases, a single century.[2] Out of this situation comes the second challenge inherent in our project: we will follow the history of artisans over four centuries, from about 1500 to the years just preceding the First World War. As happens in most accounts dealing with long-term change, our story will tend to get richer and more detailed as we move closer to the present: for the 1800s and early 1900s more primary sources are available and more historians have been interested in discussing them.

On the other hand, my own work with primary sources concerns mainly the 1600s and 1700s, and as a result I have highlighted this period. About 40 years ago it was common enough to jump from the late sixteenth straight into the mid-nineteenth century; for the period of Ottoman florescence was deemed to have ended sometime after 1566. Until the campaign of state restructuring that began after 1839, known to historians as the Tanzimat (1839–76), people supposedly lived through a period described by the catch-all phrase 'Ottoman decline'. About this period little was known and moreover it was not considered worthy of serious study. But these days are behind us, at least where scholarly discourse is concerned, and hopefully the present study will show that this 'middle period' in Ottoman history is a fascinating topic in itself. For as we will see, it is during these two centuries that Ottoman artisan and shopkeeper guilds emerged as organizations with their own internal structures and a degree of bargaining power.

We will begin by drawing a map, or rather two different kinds of maps, concerning Ottoman artisans; for the term 'map' should be understood both in the literal and in the figurative sense. The literal meaning is relevant because the Ottoman Empire was enormous, and only for certain places do we possess the data that make detailed studies of artisans possible. Istanbul, Cairo, Bursa, Jerusalem, Aleppo and Damascus, and at a later date Ambelakia in Thessaly and certain Bulgarian towns, sometimes along with their hinterlands, were centres of craft production and are also reasonably well documented (see p xii). But other places may have been important as well, and in some cases usable documentation may have survived. However, as the relevant texts have not been studied to date, or at least there are no works in languages accessible to me, it is difficult to include them in a work of synthesis such as the present one.

As a result we will produce something resembling a sixteenth-century map: a few regions can be depicted with what hopefully is a reasonable degree of accuracy. But there are wide expanses of territory about which little is known and which European cartographers of that time liked to fill with mermaids and monsters. It would be foolish to deny that present-day scholars are never tempted to emulate Renaissance geographers: no one cares for maps with many blanks. Yet throughout this book we will do our best to avoid subterfuges of this kind.

At the same time, the term 'map' also is employed in the figurative sense: for like any other major historical topic, the study of Ottoman artisans cannot be separated from the historiography that has shaped our problematic. Our study as a work of synthesis can be interpreted as an attempt to organize the available information and relate matters that at first glance appear to be unrelated: if the enterprise succeeds the reader will be enabled to use it as a guide to our field.

The labour of men and women: the market, the state and artisan concerns

As present-day readers want to know the results of any particular train of thought before they are willing to follow it through in detail, I will begin with the conclusion of our discussion: Ottoman craftsmen were for the most part organized in such a fashion as to have their guilds defend the interests of the masters and, in addition, especially in the central provinces, transmit the demands of the state apparatus. Furthermore artisans served customers both close to home and further afield, and thus had to bring forth goods and services conforming to the expectations of consumers: the important role of the market becomes obvious especially from the eighteenth century onwards but must have been significant earlier on as well. State and market were not totally separate however: while the sultans' officials set the parameters within which sales took place, physical and social distances were great and the effectiveness of the central government in outlying towns was often limited. Market forces in many cases must therefore have crept into the socio-political setting more or less unobserved.

Previous scholarship, as we will see, has tended to emphasize either the demands of the Ottoman state or to a lesser degree, the attempts of the masters to make their own voices heard. Private consumers and thereby market demand have only entered the picture in recent years. But in my view it is necessary to pull these three factors together and study their interactions, just as 'real' artisans had to satisfy their customers, negotiate with their fellow guildsmen concerning craft regulations and at the same time play along with the demands of the Ottoman state whenever that seemed the most feasible course. Or else they might engage in passive or very occasionally even in active resistance. We will show how contexts in which artisans had considerable room for manoeuvre alternated with situations in which they had little choice.

While highlighting the guilds, the present volume also will discuss the contributions of non-guild workers, who might be in casual employment or even work at home. A special 'hobby horse' of the author is the textile crafts, attractive not only because they occupied a large share of the urban working force but also because in this sector women so often played an active role: in the 1550s, they spun the yarn that Ankara manufacturers made into mohair cloth, and by the 1800s women in Egypt wove cottons and linens for the market.[3] In addition slaves both male and female were employed in Bursa silk manufactures during the fifteenth and sixteenth centuries, while male slaves worked in the copper mines of northern Anatolia: two striking examples of non-guild and even unfree craftspeople in the Ottoman realm.[4]

Consequently we will try to depict a society of mainly urban working people who were both male and female and in a few instances at least, both slave and free. Our major concern will be with four issues: firstly – insofar as our sources permit – the workmen and workwomen as living people; secondly, the jobs they did and the organizations they formed; thirdly, consumer demand for craft goods and services; and fourthly, the relationships of artisans and their guilds to the Ottoman state apparatus.

Delineating Ottoman guilds and artisans

Such an approach must begin by delineating what is meant by the term 'guild'. Ottoman guilds had certain features in common with their much more fully researched counterparts in western, central and southern Europe. In both these places artisans attempted to limit the exercise of their crafts to those men – and in a very few places a small number of women – that they themselves had selected for membership in their associations.[5] To defend this right to regulate access to artisan life, the heads of guilds or perhaps even the entire group employed a whole array of social and economic pressures not excluding violence and sometimes used the state authorities to bring recalcitrant competitors to heel. In this respect there was no great difference between the guilds of Bologna, Amsterdam and Bursa.

Of course within this broad definition there was much scope for variation, and therefore classing Ottoman craft organizations as guilds does not mean that we will downplay the special characteristics of the latter. A short comparison with Safavid Iran will make this clearer. Safavid guilds have been defined as groups of people pursuing the same occupation, working in the same bazaar, guided by their own headmen and paying a particular tax to the state. While this definition does not mention the right of guilds to control access to a given craft it seems to me that this aspect is implicit.[6] In many Ottoman towns, by contrast, working in the same location perhaps was not as important as it seems to have been in the Safavid realm: certain artisans such as bakers could have shops outside the bazaar area and yet be members of the bakers' guild. Headmen and taxes were important in both cases, although, as we will see, in the Ottoman case it apparently took some time before recognized headmen emerged from among the senior representatives of certain crafts. Paying craft-based taxes along with a given guild, however, was at least in the 1600s a major prerequisite for being a member in good standing.

Probably owing to the loss of many Iranian archives from that period, we do not hear very much about Safavid guildsmen collectively going to court; Ottoman artisans, on the other hand, become visible particularly when they litigate and petition. Therefore I will propose a second and, I hope, more operational definition of the term at least for the Ottoman context. For the purposes of our study we will regard as guilds any associations of artisans capable of initiating court cases or petitioning the central administration in order to protect craft interests. In my opinion this second definition is helpful because of the trouble we often have in proving that Ottoman artisans actually were capable of preventing outsiders from exercising their crafts – in certain cases they were not able to do so, but then the same thing applies to many of their European counterparts as well.[7] On the other hand, groups of artisans applying to local courts or to the central administration are easy to pinpoint; in fact to the Ottomanist historian, this 'lobbying' often seems so prominent that concern with the actual work performed by artisans is pushed into the background.

This delineation, however, has the disadvantage of defining guilds in their relationships to representatives of the Ottoman state and not on the basis of actions that can be viewed as 'autonomous'. But I think that the corresponding advantage by far outweighs this defect: for if we focus on complaints and petitions, we concentrate on something that is empirically accessible; and at least at the present stage of our research I prefer the approach once recommended by Sherlock Holmes, namely to put 'facts' before 'theories'. Moreover in focusing on collective action we cannot avoid asking ourselves how craftsmen established a social cohesion within their groups that was strong enough to overcome the divisiveness that economic competition within a small community frequently must have engendered.

But what do we mean by 'artisans' and 'craftsman/craftspeople'? In the present study, incidentally, these two terms will be treated as synonyms. Most scholars who have dealt with artisans have not troubled themselves very much over the delineation of these terms: it has always seemed evident that silk weavers, fez makers, blacksmiths and barbers all qualify as craftsmen. On the whole, including people such as barbers, who provided services rather than produced goods, appears unproblematic. Yet complications do arise in certain cases. Thus it is more because of convention than for any more profound reason that we will exclude scribes working in state offices, who performed services both to the sultan and to the public by producing tangible items, namely documents. It would have been possible to include them, as it is known that their professional groups in certain respects functioned rather like guilds.[8] Yet on the whole our study will follow established precedent by focusing on groups whose products and services were on offer in the shops and on the markets of Ottoman cities.

The political framework

As is well known, within the limits of what was technically feasible and mentally imaginable in an age before trains and telegraphs, the Ottoman Empire in the sixteenth century achieved a high degree of political centralization. Moreover, even when decentralization set in during the late 1600s, a large share of the available documentation concerned cities such as Bursa and Istanbul, where the central government if anything was more involved in artisan affairs than probably it ever had been before.

Ottomanist historians have demonstrated many times over that the central authorities aimed for a stable market, in which prices were low so that wars and sultanic building projects could be realized at minimal cost.[9] There was a strong concern about protection of the urban consumer as well, especially where the large and potentially unruly capital city of Istanbul was involved: after all, discontent about scarcities was dangerous to rulers and viziers alike. This bundle of official concerns about ample supplies and low prices has been dubbed 'provisionism'. Craftsmen therefore were subjected to close control by the market supervisor and other officials. Precedent ruled, for whatever could be declared 'ancient custom' (*adet-i kadime*) had high prestige in the eyes of the sultans' officials. As the authorities themselves so often claimed to respect 'tradition', a leading historian has identified 'traditionalism' as the second guiding principle of Ottoman 'economic policy'. Last but not least, officials frequently were concerned about short-term state revenue even when, by our present-day understanding, it would have made sense to forego certain sums of money immediately collectable in the interests of fostering long-term economic expansion and thus increasing the volume of taxes in the future. This approach has been called 'fiscalism', and the triad of 'provisionism, traditionalism and fiscalism' as a convenient formula describes the officially determined parameters within which all economic activity in the Ottoman realm needed to take place.[10]

In eighteenth-century Istanbul or Bursa, state control was frequently desired by the guildsmen themselves, worried as they often were about unavailable raw materials and outsiders breaking into their limited markets. We therefore will encounter plenty of examples in which artisan groups actively embraced traditionalism and provisionism. Fiscalism of course was a different matter; and the interaction between artisans and government officials, out of which policy was ultimately shaped, is as yet an under-studied topic.[11]

In cities like Cairo or Damascus, however, the sultan's administration was far away and as a result had less of a say than in Istanbul, Bursa or Edirne. Here it was the local soldiery, admittedly a governmental organization in the wider sense of the term, that determined the conditions under which artisans lived and worked. However, military men were less concerned than civil officials with the legitimization of the sultans' rule by providing food and work for the urban population, although sometimes religious scholars could be mobilized to protest against the demands of the soldiery. Thus the paternalistic element that we can discern in the behaviour of the central government in Istanbul was largely absent in Cairo, especially during the late 1700s when elite military groups were engaged in a ferocious power struggle; probably under such circumstances artisans were forced to rely on whatever local allies they could secure for themselves.

The problem of historical change

Remarkably enough given the fact that change is the historian's meat and drink, Ottomanists seem to have had trouble freeing themselves of the notion that the Ottoman state and, more importantly, the society which it governed remained more or less immutable from the late fifteenth to the mid-nineteenth century – apart from a few disturbances due to official 'corruption'.[12] As a corollary, minimizing the importance of institutional change was common enough: in the 1940s and 1950s, İsmail Hakkı Uzunçarşılı, in his widely used reference works on the various branches of the Ottoman administration, was concerned with an 'eternal present' lasting from the late fifteenth to the late eighteenth century.[13] While few people have said so outright, it was long regarded as axiomatic that after the unfolding of a centralized state apparatus in the 1400s and 1500s, what followed could at best be stagnation and at worst 'decline'.

Accordingly mutations in artisan organization have come to attract scholarly attention only in the very recent past. However, as recent historians are putting a great deal of effort into 'restoring the Ottomans to history', these misconceptions are being laid to rest. Accordingly we will emphasize changes over time, in other words treat Ottoman guilds as social groups with a history that hopefully can be recovered.[14]

Sources – some new and others examined with a fresh eye

Our enterprise is beset with many difficulties, not the least of which is the low level of literacy among artisans and the resultant paucity of sources in which these people discussed their experiences. Such materials only become available, and that in very small numbers, towards the very end of our story, namely for the late 1800s and early 1900s.[15] We therefore will view artisans only 'through a glass darkly', with the aid of sources written by government scribes. With a degree of accuracy that we have no way of evaluating, these officials relayed what artisans had said to them: a sentiment of insecurity thus constantly accompanies the historian working on Ottoman craftspeople. But on the other hand, documents purporting to relay artisan claims and complaints are reasonably numerous, and the time has come to discuss the questions asked and to some degree answered to date and to formulate those that can be asked in the future.

Over the last decades our source basis has expanded. Thus the qadi registers (*sicil*) of Ottoman towns in the Balkans, Anatolia and particularly the Arab provinces are being studied in detail, and urban historians often have noted the prominent presence of both Muslim and non-Muslim craftsmen in the courts of the qadis. More recently the 'Registers of [sultanic] commands', instituted in the mid-eighteenth century, also have come under scrutiny; they are especially rich for Istanbul, which for this purpose was counted as a province in its own right.[16] Documents featuring Istanbul's craftsmen are numerous and easy to locate; as to the other cities, once the local qadi registers have been exhausted we often have to depend on chance finds. Anatolia unfortunately has produced few of the private archives that have survived in Syria and Lebanon today.

If the researcher has time and patience, rewarding items of information can be gleaned from the eighteenth- and nineteenth-century registers containing the commands of Ottoman sultans, deceased at the time of writing, that were confirmed by their successors on the throne. In earlier periods as well, holders of sultanic privileges had needed to submit their documents for review by newly enthroned rulers. Yet the habit of recording these sultanic confirmations in separate registers seems to have been an outcome of the growing bureaucratization of the mid-1700s. It is a daunting task to find commands relating to artisans in registers hundreds of pages long and without any kind of index. But documents not available elsewhere can often be located in these collections.

In addition, legal history presently is a developing sub-field, and scholars have studied the responses of Muslim juris-consults (*fetvas*) that have been collected and sometimes published, although many *fetva* compilations unfortunately remain in manuscript.[17] Contrary to what has frequently been assumed, many of these texts concern real-life issues and not problems invented in the schoolroom. In the best of cases such *fetvas* allow us a glimpse of the legal framework within which customers could obtain redress against artisans whose workmanship was shoddy, or who employed raw materials of poor quality. Disputes between members of different guilds, or between artisans and traders, are also treated in *fetva* collections, the work of Tahsin Özcan being especially relevant for these issues.[18] Similar information has occasionally been gleaned from Jewish court records and the *responsa* of prestigious rabbis. In these latter texts specialists in Jewish law and religion commented on legal questions in a manner that at least to the non-specialist shows certain affinities with Islamic practice. In addition, from the nineteenth century there survive a few records of the deliberations of Jewish guildsmen themselves, a rare and precious find.[19]

While our sophistication in dealing with these newly located documents is often not what it should be, important progress has been made through the recent efforts especially of legal historians.[20] We now know something about the strategies of ordinary Ottoman subjects when using the court, which included bringing the same issue to judgement several times over. In other words plaintiffs might return to the attack once the presiding judge had changed, to say nothing of mobilizing the 'influence' of powerful local inhabitants and sometimes outright financial manipulation. Certainly when learning about the numerous tricks and subterfuges used in the courts of the 1600s and 1700s just as they are today, it is easy to become discouraged, and some historians have doubted whether the judges' records have anything valid to say for Ottoman social history including artisan life. But in my view, it is important to not throw out the baby with the bath water. We need to determine the concrete limits within which the information provided by the court records is valid and formulate our conclusions with special prudence. And all the time, we will remain conscious of the fact that no matter how careful we are, at some later moment we may need to thoroughly revise our conclusions – or more probably, our colleagues and competitors will do it for us.

The scope of our project: time limits

Our story will begin around 1500, and for this early period the paucity of sources will make it necessary to focus on Istanbul, Edirne and Bursa. In this context we will discuss, among other things, the vexed question of how Ottoman guilds came into being. At first glance this may appear to be a non-issue, as one of those insoluble problems on which Europeanist historians long since have given up, viewing the search for 'origins' as no more than a nineteenth-century romantic aberration.

But I am convinced that it is impossible to approach any historical problem outside the discourse that has constructed it. If that is true, we need to confront the 'origins' of Ottoman guilds, for this question has formed the background to a good bit of speculation. Our situation somewhat resembles that of medievalist historians and social theorists who are confronted with a similar penury of sources and yet continue to struggle with the 'origins' of the Ottoman Empire – or else with the origins of towns and craft guilds in medieval Flanders or Italy.[21]

In our present case, the position concerning possible 'origins' is somewhat special, for some authors have contended that in pre-Ottoman Egypt and Syria guilds were unknown.[22] As a non-medievalist, I have no independent opinion on this issue, but even if some kind of artisan organization existed, it cannot have been very active. If the opposite had been true after all, the chronicles of the Mamluk period probably would have made some reference to guild demands. An Iranian historian has concluded that in Iran guilds existed from an early period, and he has found documents that show them operating in the fifteenth century; to what extent this observation is relevant to the Anatolian context remains unknown. Yet though their 'origins' remain doubtful, fully developed guilds did function in Cairo by the second half of the seventeenth century. So much for the Middle Eastern context: as to Byzantine craft corporations, what little is known about them pertains largely to the tenth century. Given the relative weakness of craft activity in the 1400s, the organizations of Constantinople's artisans, if indeed they existed, cannot have had much of an impact on post-1453 Ottoman practices. Thus the guilds of the early modern eastern Mediterranean can be viewed as an Ottoman 'invention', and this makes the question how they emerged worth discussing, even though the scarcity of sources makes any hard and fast conclusions impossible.

Our study will begin with a discussion of previous research, interlaced with short references to the socio-political context in which these products of twentieth- and twenty-first-century scholarship have emerged (Chapter 1). Such a discussion can be regarded as a mental map of the historiographical landscape of the last 70 or 80 years, at least where the small field of Ottoman studies is concerned. Down to the 1980s, craftsmen were not a topic much favoured by Ottomanist historians, and therefore we will find ourselves focusing on just a few names. But this situation recently has changed for the better, and we will take advantage of stimulating new studies that have appeared recently and continue to appear with increasing frequency.

In terms of time, our discussion will be organized in two main sections: the first (Chapters 2–5) will reach from the beginnings to the 1670s, and the second from the 1670s to the 1850s (Chapters 6–9). A separate chapter (Chapter 10) will deal with the end of the guilds, while the conclusion will attempt to situate our findings with respect to the work of Europeanist historians concerning artisans and guilds. As a dividing line the 1670s have been selected for the simple reason that the Ottoman traveller Evliya Çelebi (1611–after 1683), who was the son of a court goldsmith and, doubtless on the basis of familial experience, has provided us with extensive discussions of guildsmen in both Istanbul and Cairo, probably completed his work around that time.[23] His accounts allow us to draw a kind of balance sheet concerning the condition of artisans at the time when the Ottoman Empire had reached the end of its expansionary period. They thus provide a standard against which later changes can be measured.

As a possible alternative, the concluding years of the seventeenth century could have been selected; for it was during those years (1695) that lifetime tax farms (*malikâne*) were instituted, and over the following decades this novel mode of revenue collection profoundly changed the parameters within which Ottoman artisans had to operate. For when a permanently established tax farmer of high official rank could determine the locations of craft shops or control access to coveted raw materials, artisans could only stay in business if they established a viable relationship with such a powerholder, and their guilds needed to take this state of affairs into account. As things stand, these lifetime tax farms will be introduced as one of the hallmarks of the second period in Ottoman guild history.[24]

As to the end of the time-span discussed here, it will coincide with the decline and disappearance of artisan guilds. This development would not have been easily foreseen around 1800, when at least in the cities close to the Ottoman centre, guilds had reached the high point of their influence and elaboration. But in the following decades, guild marginalization occurred, partly due to the increasing prevalence of putting-out arrangements. But the final step, as observed earlier on, was due to official intervention: by decree of the Young Turk government, guilds were abolished between 1910 and 1912, depending on whether the city in question lay in the Balkans and Anatolia or else in the Arab world. As I am by no means a nineteenth-century specialist, this last chapter is based on the works of others, particularly Donald Quataert and John Chalcraft. Additional inspiration has come from an ethnologist dealing with the leather crafts of Safranbolu: Heidemarie Doğanalp-Votzi has focused on the mid-twentieth century but discussed artisan reminiscences going back all the way to the 1920s. As she has studied an 'old-style' craft after the disappearance of the guilds, her work has helped me broaden my perspective.[25]

The scope of our project: variety within a common framework

Rather ambitiously we will discuss a multiplicity of craft histories, both within and outside the guild framework. Enough information has by now accumulated that an attempt at synthesis is in order.[26] There already exist a considerable number of articles as well as a few monographs on Ottoman craftsmen. Istanbul, Egypt and Syria are especially well covered; time-wise many scholars have favoured the nineteenth century with its relatively abundant source base. In addition there are sections on crafts and guilds in many monographs on Ottoman cities.

In this very provisional synthesis we will try to show how within an overall framework determined largely by the central government, there was room for a great deal of local initiative and variation, especially if the town in question was not too close to Istanbul. In any event it is not a viable option to maintain, as has been done for a long time, that what happened in Istanbul was somehow normative, and that *nolens volens* the artisans and craft guilds of the provinces always conformed to the pattern set by the capital. On the contrary, apparently even in the eighteenth century, in some places craft organizations were of little importance: a detailed study of Mosul refers to markets and even to craftswomen, but has nothing to say about guilds.[27]

Thus the logic of our enterprise requires that we do not make guild membership a criterion for inclusion: the women silk spinners and slave weavers of Bursa were not guild members, but their labour contributed decisively to the city's famed silks and brocades. Therefore it would be a serious mistake to exclude them. In the same fashion the rural craftworkers, not normally guild members, who were of some importance already in the sixteenth century and gained a central position during the nineteenth, will be discussed to the extent that the sources permit. In general, shopkeepers have been included while long-distance merchants remain outside our purview. Yet a certain degree of fuzziness will remain, since many traders who brought in goods from remote places did not shy away from retailing when the opportunity presented itself. Moreover it is one of the more pervasive characteristics of artisan life that those who produce the goods also sell them, and in the Ottoman realm there were guilds consisting entirely of shopkeepers and other salesmen.

Throughout, the dialectic between common Ottoman-style norms and local peculiarities is one of the major points to be made in the present study. For this purpose, it is fortunate that a good deal of secondary work in French and English is available on the provinces of 'Greater Syria' (Bilād al-Shām) and also on Ottoman Cairo. For this latter city had an enormous array of crafts, comparable only to Istanbul; and taken all by itself, this abundance demonstrates that Cairo possessed a metropolitan character absent from other provincial cities. Therefore confronting evidence from Istanbul and Cairo will be a major concern of the present study.

Over the years my own research has focused on eighteenth-century Bursa and Istanbul, and the relevant sections will reflect my engagement with the primary sources. Yet any broadly based study needs to deal with regions unfamiliar to the author, and here the work of predecessors and the help of friendly colleagues are indispensable.[28] I regret that owing to considerations of space, the provinces that for the sake of brevity we might call 'Greater Syria' will be given relatively short shrift. For the same reason, Balkan artisans also make but intermittent appearances.

The scope of our project: people and things

Throughout, I hope to strike a balance between discussing artisans and their customers, and the material items produced. A balancing act between people and things is not an easy task, as the established traditions of our field have made artefacts into the domain of art historians and museologists, while historians are expected to concentrate on written sources and socio-political organization. Yet unlike wheat, barley or grapes, the objects produced by craftspeople could be meant for auto-consumption only to a very minor extent; these goods needed to possess certain intrinsic qualities pleasing to the customer and be available at competitive prices. Material qualities and socio-economic relations thus are closely intertwined, and we will treat relations between artisan producers, merchants and customers in conjunction with material culture.

As an inveterate museum-goer I have developed an 'extra-curricular' interest in objects and have experienced in person how much the historian can learn from them. To mention one striking example, it was only after having seen elaborate ecclesiastical embroideries dated to the sixteenth and seventeenth centuries and signed by Orthodox women living in the Ottoman realm that I realized that apparently female Greek embroiderers active probably in Istanbul might possess enough of a reputation that their work was in demand even in relatively distant provinces.[29] To my knowledge only a few surviving pieces of these craftswomen's handiwork demonstrate their art and even their very existence; seemingly the archival documents found to date do not refer to these women at all. Studying the numerous works of jewellery and silversmith's work, presented to the tsars by dignitaries of the Orthodox Church, also helps us gain a fresh perspective: in the 1600s the artisans who produced these precious goods were all subjects of the sultan. It is something of an eye-opener to realize that the sceptre and orb used by certain seventeenth-century tsars had been manufactured by Ottoman craftsmen.[30]

When we focus on the link between artisans and their work, on the one hand, and the market, on the other, it bears repetition that we will foreground craftspeople of high skills. In many cases these men and women were wealthier than the porters, donkey drivers or barbers that probably made up the majority of guildsmen. But in my view, this price is worth paying, and other scholars doubtless will soon fill the lacunae that the reader will find in the present study.

Autonomy versus central control – with market forces intervening

Against the background of the research discussed here, many historians now are asking themselves whether it is really true that in the Ottoman polity, taxpayers in town and countryside confronted a powerful state apparatus merely as individuals or families, in other words 'on their own'. Scholars have questioned the old claim that in the Ottoman world there were no organizations mediating between families and business enterprises and an overpowering state. As voluntary organizations were remarkably weak during the early history of the Turkish republic, there has been a tendency to project this state of affairs back into the Ottoman period. Furthermore as noted before, our documentation emanates largely from the authorities, and this state of affairs has introduced a notable bias: then as now, officialdom has tended to assume that it can totally control the functioning of society.

Yet the time surely has come to re-examine this issue, and a beginning has been made. Christian and Jewish congregations, organized around churches and synagogues, have attracted special attention in this context. But the craft guilds that existed in many Ottoman towns from the sixteenth century onwards also qualify as non-business organizations at least to a significant extent, and they certainly do not pertain either to the familial or to the state sphere. When celebrating the access of new masters by a picnic out of town, and setting up pious foundations to lend money and support conviviality, the guilds built solidarities that could be mobilized in times of crisis. Craft guilds therefore may be viewed as one of the ways and means for urban society to organize itself on the margins of, though not totally separate from, the framework of the Ottoman state. However, certain scholars see this issue differently and continue to privilege the role of the state.[31]

To sum up the main points: Ottoman guilds were organizations that accepted new members, determined quality standards and in many instances the prices at which artisans could sell their goods. Most importantly for our purposes, these organizations often litigated in court and petitioned the authorities in craft matters; from the 1600s if not earlier they were represented by guild elders and chiefs in whose appointment both artisans and officialdom had a say. With more or less success at different times and in different places, Ottoman artisans also tried to control access to their respective crafts. More often than not the results of their initiatives were communicated to the authorities only *ex post facto*. This situation meant that guilds possessed a degree of autonomy, especially in the provinces: documentation on the craftspeople of Diyarbakır or Sarajevo is so scarce presumably because their everyday problems were solved on the local level, often by the guild elders. Non-guild workmen were doubtless at a disadvantage, but given the hierarchical structure of the polity as a whole, we do not find them complaining very frequently. Perhaps they did not see any realistic chances of making their voices heard.

On the other hand, although the artisans even of the closely controlled capital city of Istanbul showed a considerable talent for improvisation and 'muddling through', the central state and its elites did set parameters that in many cases craftsmen were powerless to change. After all, while it is important to avoid the state-centred bias of the older literature, it would also be a mistake to downplay the role of the constantly expanding Ottoman bureaucracy and its political and cultural projects. Throughout, the guilds undertook major tasks demanded by officialdom, ensuring above all that the army and the court obtained the goods and services they required. Moreover, concerning the 1700s, a time when, as we shall see, the sale of offices was widespread and even guild wardenships were for sale, it would be over-optimistic to assume that craft organizations always were headed by men who had the best interests of their fellow guild members in mind.

Yet in certain contexts the guilds did defend the interests of the masters against even the powerful Ottoman state apparatus. Thus these organizations were Janus-faced, and artisans must have figured out what to do in each individual case on the basis of local knowledge now mostly inaccessible to us.[32] Whether craftsmen opted for conformity or defiance depended on time and place.

Present-day perspectives have had and continue to have an impact on the picture conveyed by twentieth- and twenty-first-century research. Some scholars choose to highlight the defence of artisan interests while others prefer to focus on service to the state. By refusing to limit our attention to one or the other, we have made the tension between centralization and tendencies towards autonomy into a major organizing principle of our study.[33] Given a constant tug-of-war between decentralizing initiatives and coercion in artisan life, we will attempt to give a fair account of both aspects. Admittedly the relatively autonomous activities of Ottoman craftspeople are less well known than the already quite extensively researched measures by which the central state attempted to control them.

But at the same time consumption, market demand and material culture enter the picture as well: it makes little sense to pretend that at least the better-off buyers had no say in what was produced by artisans. Finally, autonomous spheres of action needed to be defended, and the manner in which guildsmen attempted to do this, peaceably or not, forms part of what we might call Ottoman grassroots politics.

Thus it becomes possible to at least partly remedy the 'top–down' perspective of our documentation: the craftsmen's successes as well as their failures tell us a good deal about the interface of Ottoman state and society. Again and again we will deal with the tension between powerful representatives of the state apparatus and the 'poor subjects', as Ottoman sources so graphically put it. In so doing we will summarize what is known today and hopefully provide a starting point for the many exciting studies on the interface between Ottoman state and society that currently are being projected.

CHAPTER I

Writing about Artisans

The state of the art

The historiography of Ottoman artisans may not be very extensive but it is indispensable for any work of synthesis: whether we like it or not, our assumptions here and now are shaped by what has been done or left undone by our predecessors. Moreover to readers who approach our topic from the outside, the full meaning of certain statements will only become clear in the light of previous discussions. The latter will therefore be presented in a short overview, which by the same token will introduce topics to be dealt with in later chapters.

To announce a complete change of paradigm is a great advantage to any author; such a claim brings prestige and helps to sell books. We will certainly move away from certain concepts prevalent in the secondary literature of past decades.[1] But I do not believe that the history of Ottoman artisans at present is undergoing a complete revolutionary turnover. By contrast, incremental changes are numerous, and perhaps these are the harbingers of some future paradigm change – it is too early to tell. Given this situation the present study is intended as a further step on the long road of Ottomanist historiography, both of the older socio-economic variety and of the more recent 'culturalist' one.

Religion and the economic mentality of craftsmen

At the earliest stage of scholarly research on Ottoman guilds, those few historians interested in the topic tended to concentrate on what might be called the 'ideological' aspects of craftsmen activity. A special interest in the spiritual concerns of artisans was perhaps due to the fact that studies of Ottoman guilds were first undertaken by scholars whose major focus was on the religion of Islam, and who usually worked on the period before about 1500 or 1550. After all, the literary texts in the broader sense of that term, which largely constitute the source basis of the medievalist, emphasize morals and ceremonials rather than the mundane problems of artisans' daily lives.

These linkages between religion and guild activities were a major interest of Franz Taeschner (1888–1967), an early student of Ottoman guild life. Through his work on medieval Anatolian hagiographies and their reception in the craft milieu, Taeschner was able to show that certain features of the fourteenth- and early fifteenth-century brotherhoods known as the *ahi*s, widespread in Anatolia during that time, in certain cases continued to be relevant to guild life as late as the 1700s.[2] Although more or less contemporary evidence on the *ahi*s is rather thin on the ground, consisting largely of the names of personages who founded mosques and other charities, the religious aspect of these urban groupings in which some artisans must have taken part, has rendered the latter continuously attractive to conservative historians. Taeschner himself fell into that category. Moreover it was known that, for instance, in the central Anatolian town of Çankırı, twentieth-century artisans perpetuated ceremonies presumed to have been derived from those of the *ahi*s: today this town houses a lodge serving this very purpose. Scholars and politicians celebrating the memory of the *ahi*s probably wished – and wish – to distance 'good' artisan organizations from 'bad', areligious trade unions: an interest in historical instances of male bonding sometimes is thrown in for good measure.

Taeschner's contemporary Abdülbaki Gölpınarlı (1900–82), best known for his many works on the dervish order of the Mevlevis, approached the *ahi*s not as a specialist on Ottoman artisans but as a religious historian. As the treatises known as *fütüvvetname*s, presumably at one time current in the *ahi* milieu, were relevant to his work on dervishes and their beliefs, around 1950 Gölpınarlı published and translated several such texts; his commentaries are the basis of all further work on the subject. These treatises enumerated the qualities expected of a perfect brotherhood member (*fata, fityan, ahi*). The *ahi* was supposed to practise modesty, abnegation and self-control, a complex of virtues known as *fütüvvet*, and the writings in question also described the rituals which the *ahi*s regarded as central to their associational commitments. *Fütüvvetname*s were copied out in artisan circles and thus must have been important long after the *ahi*s as actual organizations had faded away.

As certain narrative texts from the 1500s detail 'disreputable' trades, contempt on the part of certain artisans for others presumably counted for something in everyday social relations during those years.[3] However, we do not know to what extent; and there is no indication that Ottoman government authorities considered these expressions of contempt on the part of some guilds for the members of other craft associations as significant from a policy point of view. Except for tavern keepers and a few others, all artisans officially speaking seem to have been regarded as equal, and inter-guild disputes about ranking only rarely surface in official documentation. If Evliya Çelebi was correct, and there really existed guilds of pickpockets and other marginal folk in mid-seventeenth century Istanbul, these groupings would certainly have been considered disreputable. But at present the existence of such guilds has only exceptionally been confirmed by outside sources, although the work of Eyal Ginio and Marinos Sariyannis recently has unearthed quite a bit of evidence on marginal people.[4]

Moreover certain *fütüvvetname*s have been studied by religious historians of the twentieth century because they demonstrate a widespread popular veneration for the descendants of the Imām ʿAlī, the relative and son-in-law of the Prophet Muhammad. This sentiment was common not only among people with Shiite leanings but also among Sunnis, and it was particularly well attested in certain craft milieus.[5] The *fütüvvetname*s thus form one of the very few available sources on the mental makeup of at least a section of Ottoman artisans, and as these guildsmen, in some aspects of their associational lives, strongly focused upon Islamic values and ceremonials they have remained for quite some time the *chasse gardée* of religious specialists.

On the other hand, the economic historian Sabri Ülgener (1911–83) saw the Ottoman craft guilds in quite a different light. Ülgener was one of the first Turkish scholars to get interested in the German school of economic history and the theories of Max Weber; he had encountered this line of thinking when studying with Fritz Neumark and Alexander Rüstow, who had come to Istanbul as refugees from Nazi persecution.[6] The link between Calvinism and capitalism that Weber assumed to have existed in the early modern period prompted Ülgener to ask himself in what ways the religious views of Ottoman artisans had affected their economic behaviour.[7]

If this concern with Weber tied Ülgener to the social sciences of the early twentieth century, seen from another perspective he was himself a pioneer. For in the Ottoman context, Ülgener's work was one of the first attempts to study a topic that from the 1970s onwards came to be called the 'history of mentalities'. This kind of research had been pioneered by French historians such as Michel Vovelle (b. 1933), and though it was adopted, somewhat belatedly, by a few Ottomanist historians, on the whole the history of mentalities has been relatively neglected by the representatives of our field down to the present day.[8] Following a Weberian trajectory Ülgener arrived at a set of scholarly interests in some ways similar to those developed later by Vovelle: these included a concern with the views of people who wrote little, if at all, and whose manner of thinking must be 'teased out' of sources which refer to these thoughts and feelings only in an indirect fashion.

More specifically, Ülgener asked himself why Ottoman craft producers had failed to make the transition to capitalism. His answer was that because of the shift of international trade routes away from the Mediterranean, beginning in the sixteenth century, the Ottoman economy increasingly found itself in a backwater, with access to international markets severely limited. To this lack of opportunity on the 'macro' level, craftsmen supposedly responded with an ideology that made a virtue out of necessity by emphasizing the values of modesty and also a kind of egalitarianism, all this embedded in a culture of poverty. Or at least, this was the ideology: in real life, this spirit of abnegation was often conspicuous by its absence, and townsmen who could afford it were inclined towards opulence and 'lord-like' consumption.[9]

In spite of his own family background linked to the religious and dervish milieu, Ülgener considered the positive values that might have been inherent in Ottoman artisan ideology less important than the concomitant denigration of worldly activity, ambition and drive, and he was acutely sensitive to the pettifogging jealousies which in the narrow limits of a small-town market all too often flourished behind the façade of otherworldliness. After all, as an economist Ülgener was confronted with the problems of his own time, more specifically the mid-twentieth century, and in his perspective quite a few contemporary economic difficulties could be derived from the fact that Ottoman craftsmen and petty traders had so thoroughly rejected the idea not only of foreign but also of home-grown capitalism. Ülgener did not live long enough to observe the drastic changes of the last few decades.

In discussing the problem why a well-developed market economy such as the Ottoman had not made the transition to commercial and industrial capitalism, Ülgener's emphasis on endogenous factors and 'ideological' considerations limiting economic expansion did not sit well with the concerns of scholarship during the 1960s and 1970s. For at this time some Ottomanist historians became involved with 'world economy' studies in the Wallersteinian manner.[10] According to the latter model, the reasons for Ottoman economic stagnation and even 'de-industrialization' were located squarely in developments taking place outside the confines of the empire, namely in northwestern Europe; these changes in the long run were to result in the economic marginalization of the Mediterranean world.

Exogenous factors thus monopolized attention almost exclusively. Certainly Ülgener also had considered the isolation of Ottoman crafts from the lifelines of international trade as the principal reason for their 'involution'. But this aspect of his work was not, in the 1960s and 1970s, taken into serious consideration by economic historians. To top it all, Ülgener never had analysed the 'hard' data derived from the Ottoman archives, which to the present day form the basis of most work on the pre-nineteenth-century economic history of the sultans' realm. This fact must also have counted against him in those years, when archival work was seen as the *conditio sine qua non* of 'scientific' history. After a long period of relative neglect on the part of Ottomanist historians, it was only around 1980 that a new interest in Ülgener's work became noticeable in Turkey.[11]

That said, it is also important to stress where present research diverges from Ülgener's claims. First of all, we are no longer as convinced of artisan stagnation as he had been, perhaps under the impact of the poverty and isolation so widespread in Turkey during the 1930s and 1940s as a consequence of lengthy wars (1912–23) and the world economic crisis beginning in 1929. After all, during the early years of the republic the ideology of 'bir lokma bir hırka' ([content yourself] with a mouthful [of food] and a dervish cloak) retained wide currency, at least outside of the elite, so much so that studying this attitude became a significant preoccupation of the empirical social science that emerged in Turkey after the Second World War.

Present-day scholars in addition are less convinced that the Ottoman world really turned into a commercial backwater once Europeans began to use the oceanic routes. On the contrary, it has been shown that overland connections or combined land-and-sea routes leading from India to Cairo, Baghdad and even Moscow continued in use until the late 1700s.[12] In other words, today we tend to assume that there was more international trade, and perhaps more outlets for Ottoman artisan production were available than were recorded in European documents. Moreover the sultans' subjects in the main manufactured not for the world market but for domestic use; even so, trade over long distances was often involved, as the empire encompassed three continents. And even when in the mid-nineteenth century Ottoman craftsmen had to confront the full impact of imported factory-made goods, many of them were able to adjust and their enterprises did not wither away, albeit at the price of seriously declining real wages.[13] At least some of these petty entrepreneurs seem to have seized market opportunities whenever they presented themselves, and they were not necessarily inimical to commercial expansion.

Ülgener had assumed a professed – if not necessarily real – lack of interest on the part of Ottoman artisans in worldly success, an attitude often expressed in religious terms. Yet more recent research has shown that while this frame of mind was not unknown, it did not mean that entrepreneurial success was widely disapproved of. In practice many craftsmen were willing to accept the leadership of their economically most successful colleagues.[14] Most importantly Ülgener had regarded Ottoman guilds as static and preventing all changes in production methods, while more recent research has shown that this was not true, or at least not as generally true as he had assumed: a degree of flexibility was possible, at least in certain locations and at certain times.

The state of the art: towards an examination of social structures

Ottoman studies of artisans and guilds took something of a new turn in the early 1960s. Now it was not the connection with religious history but a rather more practical approach that became dominant. This new enterprise involved linking up with a quite different scholarly tradition, namely the historical study of Istanbul's urban administration. Here the pioneer, who had begun his work already during the closing period of the empire, was Osman Nuri, in republican times Osman Nuri Ergin (1883–1961).[15] For it must not be forgotten that in the first half of the twentieth century, Ottoman guilds still belonged to the fairly recent past, and one of the early republican mayors of Istanbul had felt it necessary to obtain extensive information concerning their activities. At least in the port of Istanbul, guilds had been politically potent even in the years preceding the First World War, and in the transport sector some workmen's organizations perhaps became more rather than less cohesive during the struggles of the late nineteenth century.[16]

While in the 1950s craft and service guilds were no longer of much practical concern, emphasis on the 'secular' aspects of artisan activity continued to dominate historical research. Apart from the secularist commitments of many social historians, this tendency may have been due to the fact that new document finds from the Ottoman archives were rarely relevant to the religious aspects of craftsmen's activity. Certainly the sultans' officials always assumed that Muslims were devoted to their religion, and non-Muslims to their own particular *ayin-i batile* (invalid religious rites), but this was not a matter on which the authorities had much to say. Of course there were exceptions. But under 'ordinary' conditions the religious convictions and rituals of artisans were almost never mentioned in official Ottoman sources.

How historians made the state usurp the place of Ottoman craftsmen

Normally the documents from the Turkish state archives, which from the 1940s onwards increasingly came to the attention of Ottomanist historians, dealt with the artisans' place in the urban economy, and more prominently with the services the latter were expected to render to the sultans. A pioneer in archival research was Ahmed Refik (Altınay) (around 1880–1937), who published the first sampling of documents concerning Istanbul life in 1917, continuing this activity until his death.[17] Archive-oriented historians found evidence on the craft rules which shoemakers, weavers or dyers were expected to follow, both in order to protect the public and to keep down competition among masters. Such rules were only written down when a complaint was made to members of the state apparatus, who possessed a literate culture quite different from the largely oral one of the artisans themselves. This discrepancy must have caused distortions which we can guess at but not rectify.

Furthermore when modern historians concerned themselves with the social structures in which craftsmen operated while earning their daily bread, most of the information they found dealt with the exigencies of the Ottoman state. Just like the bureaucrats that had authored their sources, mid-twentieth-century Ottomanists came to view the artisans as the obedient servants of the sultan and his officials. With but a moderate degree of exaggeration we may say that in early republican historiography, state and guild came to be seen as the two sides of the same coin.

If, however, Ottoman history as written between the late 1930s and late 1970s was so strongly informed by the viewpoint of the sultans' officeholders, this was only in part due to the state-centred character of the available documentation. During this period historians of conservative but also, from the later 1960s onwards, left-wing backgrounds saw good reasons for the foregrounding of the Ottoman state. From the second half of the 1930s onwards, the Depression and the state policies devised to relieve it, followed by the military mobilization which Turks were obliged to live through in spite of their country's neutrality during the Second World War, combined to focus attention on the role of the state in economic life. In the perspective of Ömer Lütfi Barkan (1902–79), to whom we owe an important publication of early sixteenth-century lists of administered prices (*narh*), which incidentally throws much light on the activities of artisans, it was the proper role of the Ottoman state to direct craft production towards the needs of its conquering armies. Nor did state control let up in times of relative peace, when efforts were directed towards city building through the medium of officially sponsored pious foundations.[18] From this point of view, strongly informed by republican etatism, Ottoman craftsmen appeared almost as a variety of soldiers. Thus the bias of the sources and that of the historians using them powerfully reinforced one another.

Nor was this way of regarding the condition of artisans limited to the Turkish historical community. In 1970 the Israeli historian Gabriel Baer (1919–82) published several articles in which he tried to prove that Ottoman guilds were not 'guilds' in the sense in which the term is used by Europeanist historians. In other words, these organizations were not meant to defend the interests of the master artisans making up their memberships.[19] Rather they had been established by the state with the intention of remedying the lack of urban institutions; by means of these guilds Ottoman officialdom, which in the sixteenth or seventeenth century formed but a small body of men, attempted to control the inhabitants of towns and cities. Rather similar to the state-organized trade unions which existed in many places during the 1950s and 1960s, Ottoman guilds were supposed to function as 'transmission belts' relaying the demands of the central government to urban craft producers.

Possibly the state-sponsored trade unions of his own time had inspired Baer's thinking. But in addition, a recent study has shown that there was an empirical basis for his assumptions: Egyptian guilds in the mid-1800s were at least temporarily used as tax collectors for the recently established viceroys of that country. Given the paucity of studies at the time of writing, presumably Baer tended to generalize from those examples he knew best. Moreover towards the end of his life, after taking cognizance of the work of his former student Haim Gerber, Baer significantly modified his views.[20]

Stagnation under state protection

A special place must be allotted to the work of Mehmet Genç, fundamental to the study of the eighteenth-century Ottoman economy and the place of artisans in it.[21] The author has studied tax records in depth, especially those pertinent to lifetime tax farms (*malikâne*), and pioneered the use of these documents for the study of industrial and commercial conjunctures. Instituted in 1695 these lifetime tax farms in the author's vision served to protect artisans and others from over-exploitation by tax farmers with short-term contracts, who therefore were inclined to maximize revenues for a year or two, regardless of the consequences in the long run.

In this context Genç has focused on the 'equalizing' policies of the sultans that, given low profit margins enforced by state officials, made it difficult for any artisans to prosper, much less to accumulate the capital necessary for expansion. Genç's work thus revolves around the state–artisan nexus as an impediment to industrial growth and dwells on the difficulty of capital formation that formed the Achilles heel of the Ottoman economy. But as a compensation for meagre economic opportunities, state officials protected artisan livelihoods, at least as long as military defeats and financial stringencies did not tempt the elites into exaggerating their traditional concern with fiscal gains to the point where it resulted in 'predatory taxation' pure and simple. In my view these studies form the most sophisticated version of the 'state-centred' interpretation of the Ottoman craft world that has been developed to date. However, it is debatable whether our vision of these artisans really should be limited to their connection with the state apparatus.

Vox clamantis in deserto[22]

Presumably because of the dominant state-centred perspective, the position of artisans during the 1950s and 1960s was marginalized by most scholars working outside Turkey. After all, being powerless and lacking initiative, artisans seemingly had little to contribute to an understanding of Ottoman society. Officialdom, in other words people with political power, must have seemed more worthwhile subjects of study; after all, these men issued the orders that all craftsmen would have been obliged to follow.

Apart from Taeschner and Baer, only Fahri Dalsar and Robert Mantran (1918–99) seriously were interested in Ottoman craftsmen at that time.[23] Dalsar had been a public administrator who studied the problems of Bursa's flagging silk industry; in 1960 he brought out a book on the history of this craft, which has remained basic because of the extensive use the author made of the Bursa qadi registers. These documents, of major importance to the historian of Ottoman crafts and of which a large selection was quoted verbatim, provided evidence of the close connection between craftwork and trade in this major Anatolian manufacturing centre. Throughout, the author highlighted this link and even dealt with domestic consumption or, as he has put it, the love of Turkish people for silk clothes.[24] Moreover Dalsar touched on issues that only became major scholarly concerns later on, such as the role of women in preparing silk yarns for weaving or methods of non-guild labour recruitment. Unfortunately his work has not received the belated recognition achieved by certain other Turkish historians of the early republican period.

At roughly the same time, Robert Mantran authored a major monograph on late seventeenth-century Istanbul, strongly emphasizing the impact of administrative structures upon urban life. Owing to the condition of the Ottoman archives during the 1950s the author had access to only a few sections of it, and in the field of urban history this difficulty was especially limiting. Thus Mantran was not able to see the 'complaint' registers (Şikayet Defterleri) that began in the 1650s and shed some light on artisans' grievances. Nor were the qadi registers of Istanbul available to researchers at that time. Mantran, however, did make extensive use of the 'Registers of important affairs' (Mühimme Defterleri), of Evliya Çelebi's great work on Istanbul and the numerous foreign travel accounts describing the city. Furthermore he recognized that Istanbul consisted not merely of officeholders and their underlings, but that the majority of townsmen lived by crafts and petty trade. It is this concern with artisans that he and Dalsar had in common, and their studies continue to be important for the history of Ottoman crafts.

A change in the source basis: the triumph of the qadi registers

After about a quarter of a century, historians finally began to follow the path opened up by Dalsar and use the qadi registers and their down-to-earth records of sales, loans and inheritance cases as sources for artisan histories. A key role was played by Haim Gerber's study of seventeenth-century Bursa, published only in 1988 but known through lectures from the late 1970s onwards.[25] On the basis of the qadi registers, Gerber showed that in this city during the 1600s entry into and exit from local guilds was quite easy, as whoever paid his taxes with a given artisan association was considered a member in good standing. This observation implied that the acquisition of a free 'slot' or 'space' (*gedik*) at this time was not always indispensable for an artisan planning to set up shop. Guilds in Bursa were thus far more flexible than had hitherto been assumed; they adjusted to changing demand and, for example, their members ensured the revival of Bursa silk weaving after a serious crisis in the years around 1600. Evidence concerning state involvement was limited as well; as a result the guilds of Bursa appeared as institutions serving their members and not merely the central authorities. In an article published shortly before his death, Baer handsomely acknowledged the contribution of his former student and admitted that his own thinking had changed as a result.[26]

Bursa apart, qadi registers in the 1980s and 1990s first and foremost served as sources for the history of craftsmen active in the Arab provinces. Jerusalem turned out to be an interesting and idiosyncratic case, as in this relatively small town the judges' registers go back to the 1530s and references to artisans abound – court registers in most other towns have far less to offer on this subject. Amnon Cohen therefore was able to show that the local butchers held a special place: prosperous members of the trade might link themselves to families of religious scholars and, if things went well, prepare the ascent of their sons into the Ottoman governing class. Moreover for the 1600s records concerning Jerusalem, artisans became so numerous that the same author was able to write a series of monographs on individual guilds, an enterprise possible for only a handful of Ottoman towns.[27]

For Damascus and Aleppo a similar project was undertaken by Abdul Karem Rafeq, who devoted a lifetime to the history of what is today Syria in the Ottoman period.[28] An early contribution by this author to artisan studies appeared already in the 1970s, at a time when it was still necessary to introduce the qadi registers to the historical community. At a later stage and on the basis of this same source Rafeq analysed the problems of Damascene and Aleppo artisans once guilds had been introduced after the Ottoman conquest. He also discussed the reactions of artisans when confronted with the competition of European goods; moreover he was one of the innovative historians who approached artisan 'mentalities' by examining the complaints about shoddy workmanship that so often found their way into the court records.

A changing paradigm

These works were part of a paradigm change that around 1980 occurred in the historiography of Ottoman artisans and guilds. Political conditions were partly responsible: after the military coup of September 1980, the 'mixed economy' model which had formed the mainstay of Turkish economic policy during the 1960s and 1970s, under pressure from the World Bank and other external powers, was given up in favour of a neo-liberal policy emphasizing exports and the profit motive. In this perspective, at least certain Ottoman artisans came to be viewed as a kind of proto-entrepreneurs. As a result the emphasis was now not so much on the manner in which the guilds hampered competition among masters but on the ways and means by which some craftsmen managed to survive even in notoriously difficult times including the nineteenth century.[29]

In addition the literature on proto-industry in early modern Europe was finding readers among Ottomanists: Gerber's book also focused on non-artisan investment in Bursa's silk production. Responding to this stimulus historians began to search for evidence of practices that could be described as the 'putting out' of raw materials to be made up by rural and urban non-guild producers.[30] Certainly the evidence never was thick enough on the ground to justify the claim that in certain regions of the Ottoman Empire industrial conjunctures replaced good and bad harvests as determinants of demographic behaviour – in any case, owing to the absence of population registration, births, marriages, migrations and deaths are difficult to analyse for the pre-nineteenth-century period. As, however, the very definition of proto-industry postulates a dependence of demographic behaviour on industrial as opposed to agricultural conjunctures, proto-industry studies in the narrow sense of the term never got off the ground.[31] Yet this line of thinking did encourage Ottomanist historians to look at artisan producers in the countryside, where guilds had little or no say.

In this context, we have been reminded that for instance in the villages surrounding Bursa or Ankara, or in certain sections of the Aegean coast of Anatolia, rural industry coordinated by urban merchants was significant even around 1600. This observation was first made by Halil Inalcik, who demonstrated that not all craftworkers necessarily were guild members and thereby disproved a previously widespread view of Ottoman handicrafts, which had insisted that no such activity was possible outside of the guilds.[32] Moreover researchers interested in women's history have shown that while women normally were not members of Ottoman guilds, in some places their contribution to the textile sector was considerable.[33] Thus prosperous artisans or merchants trying to organize production by putting out raw materials such as wool or cotton should have been able to find the workforce they needed.

Yet Ottoman 'putting out' apparently differed from what has been observed with respect to many European regions. Quite a few rural part-time artisans of the Ottoman world seem to have owned their tools and possibly their raw materials as well. Thus their dependence on urban traders was caused not by a lack of the basic means of production but by an intermittent need for loans and most importantly a limited degree of access to the distribution sector. However, these two deficiencies were of major economic and social significance: lack of capital as we have seen was a notorious weakness of the Ottoman economy, and those producers with access to ready money often could count on the subservience of their poorer fellows.

Stratification within the artisan world

Certain rules typical of the artisan milieu implied equality, yet in real life guildsmen were by no means equals.[34] In those craft organizations where crucial raw materials were purchased collectively, artisans certainly were supposed to receive equal quantities of wool, cotton or leather, unless an enterprising guildsman had managed to acquire shares that otherwise would have accrued to his fellows. In her recent work, Eunjeong Yi has stressed that some masters were adept at finding themselves partners belonging to guilds different from their own; and while her observations pertain to Istanbul, records from the eighteenth-century town of Urfa in faraway southeastern Anatolia show that similar practices could be found there as well.[35] Associations between members of different guilds allowed the partners to engage in all the trades represented within the partnership in question; thus these people could pool capital and enlarge the scope of their businesses. Renting premises from members of other guilds, as Yi has shown, could also allow individuals of entrepreneurial talent to be active in more than one trade. Her results are consonant with those obtained for Bursa by Haim Gerber: evidently seventeenth-century guilds in these two cities did not fetter artisan activity as effectively as had been assumed.

However, not many such firms were documented, and even fewer were the cases of artisan enterprises persisting over several generations. [36]A few exceptions proving the rule appeared in the late eighteenth and early nineteenth centuries, when artisan entrepreneurs from the Thessalian village of Ambelakia marketed their wares in distant Austria. Over several generations, the same families were involved in production and distribution, until spinning had been mechanized and the techniques for dyeing red cotton yarn acquired by Austrian entrepreneurs. The foreign market for Ambelakia's products disappeared as a result.[37] Slightly later, in the early and mid-1800s, proto-industrial entrepreneurs in today's Bulgaria secured contracts to supply the Ottoman army and also maintained themselves for several decades.[38]

The emergence of these manufacturers of coarse woollens in a semi-urban context had been preceded by a century of social differentiation in the towns of what later came to be Bulgaria. When we consider the ownership patterns of shops and workshops this process becomes especially obvious: a few people possessed such premises in sizeable numbers, while the majority either owned just the shop that they used themselves or else even rented the necessary locales.[39] Merchants certainly were better placed than artisans when it came to enriching themselves, and in the Bulgarian provinces, too, the production and marketing of woollens sometimes were practised by the same families over several generations. However, in the ordinary course of things, partible inheritance in addition to economic crisis and, at least in eighteenth-century Istanbul, interventions on the part of the central administration prevented most artisan enterprises from flourishing over long periods of time.[40]

Formally recognized inequalities of a different kind have been established in a recent study of seventeenth-century Aleppo.[41] In this city guild headmen were under tight control by officials who bore titles such as 'chief flour manufacturer', in charge of bakers and millers, or 'chief butcher' who controlled butchers and related trades. This arrangement rather resembles that known from seventeenth-century Istanbul, but in Aleppo there was no sultan and no court to be supplied: the officials in question regulated purely local affairs. Quite often members of the same family succeeded one another in office, although these positions were not strictly speaking inheritable. In addition in some guilds there was lively competition for the headman's office, so that there must have been economic and social rewards attached to this position. The Aleppo sources are remarkable for the wealth of detail they provide, and have permitted Charles Wilkins to give quite specific information on the earnings of certain guild headmen. We are left to wonder in how many other cities a similar system with its attendant inequalities was in operation.

Artisans and their customers

Among the purchasers of craft products, down to the 1990s the Ottoman state all but monopolized scholarly attention. As for the broader implications of foreign trade, historians typically neglected the export of Ottoman manufactured goods. When exports were discussed at all, crisis was foregrounded and prosperity discounted. Halil Inalcik, indeed, was exceptional when he pointed out that around 1500 Ottoman Anatolia not only imported raw silk but also exported manufactured goods such as textiles to the lands beyond the Black Sea.[42] He thus was one of the first scholars to point out the importance of consumer demand within the empire and even on its steppe margins.

It is true that very few Ottoman craftspeople mainly worked for export. But when we look at the many rugs and carpets depicted on Flemish, Italian and Dutch paintings between the fifteenth and late seventeenth centuries, we understand that these valuable textiles were exported in considerable numbers.[43] Around 1600, Ankara mohair cloth found customers in Venice and Poland.[44] Iznik pottery occasionally was produced to order for European purchasers; fragments have come to light in southern Italy and the semi-independent principality of Transylvania.[45] At yet a later stage, in the 1700s some cotton fabrics woven and printed in the Aleppo area and which imitated the then highly popular Indian textiles, found purchasers as far off as Marseilles.[46]

Apart from these luxury goods, leather was exported, sometimes clandestinely by smugglers and at other times openly by reputable traders. While in the late sixteenth century many varieties were considered strategic goods whose exportation was forbidden, a Greek scholar has demonstrated that by the 1700s, tanners in the provinces later to become Bulgaria routinely sold their products to Greek exporters for sale in Hungary, by that time part of the Habsburg Empire. These sales apparently were vital for local manufacturers, as certain merchants commented that guildsmen often exerted considerable pressure to ensure purchases.[47] At least for certain limited artisan groups, we therefore must assume that export markets were of some significance, although Ottoman officials certainly had no truck with mercantilism and were in no way interested in promoting exportation.

But in any case, historians of Ottoman crafts have long known the great importance of the domestic market. For the mid-seventeenth century, the extent of inter-regional commerce can be read off from a particularly elaborate Istanbul price register.[48] This document lists numerous speciality items characterized by the names of towns; these goods may have been produced partly in the designated places and partly elsewhere, but *à la façon* of the reputed place of origin. Mübahat Kütükoğlu's commented edition is of special value because the editor has consulted Istanbul artisans still familiar with 'traditional' techniques to provide explanations concerning terminology and workmanship.

Documentation becomes more abundant for the 1700s, or else at that time there really was a major expansion of consumption among well-to-do townspeople – I would opt for a combination of both. Researchers have concluded that the 'consumerism' of the upper and middle levels of society in eighteenth-century France and England had a modest parallel in the Ottoman lands, at least before the political and economic crisis beginning in the 1760s drastically cut into disposable funds.

As yet studies of consumption and local demand for Ottoman craft products are still limited in number and scope.[49] Where the 1700s are concerned we know more about clothing codes that limited the types of garments an individual might wear, to show his place in society if male, and to demonstrate modesty by unobtrusiveness if female. We need, but do not as yet possess, many studies of estate inventories that focus on the material goods owned by people from this period, apparently in growing quantities. Damascus is one of the few localities well studied in this respect, but doubtless much more can be done.[50]

Most consumption studies, however, are oriented towards the 1800s. Not only do we possess an abundance of European sources for this period, usually quite easy to access, but material remains are also much more abundant than for earlier centuries. Thus it becomes possible to match written sources and objects surviving in museums. Moreover, from the mid-nineteenth century onwards, an Ottoman press came into existence which promoted the consumption of manufactured items as diverse as books and fezzes. An expanding group of urbanites sent not only its sons but also its daughters to school, and women were encouraged to judiciously acquire goods and services to enhance the well being of their families as well as their own.[51] As for the pioneering volume of Ottoman consumption studies, Donald Quataert as the editor has made a point of including work on both earlier and later periods.

A sense of place: Cairo as opposed to Istanbul

For Cairo artisans the baseline is still the great work by André Raymond, published over 30 years ago.[52] Artisans here are studied through a combination of Ottoman and European sources: Evliya Çelebi's account of Cairo's guilds around 1670 forms the starting point, and the descriptions authored by Napoleon's savants mark the end of Raymond's story. What happened 'in between' has been read off from estate inventories, which record the possessions left by deceased craftspeople as well as their obligations to merchants and to the military corps of which they had been members. Apart from slow changes in the artisan condition, caused, for instance, by changing trade patterns, Raymond has analysed the drastic deterioration characterizing the later 1700s when the households of Mamluk lords had managed to overpower and 'colonize' the other military corps. Once that process was complete, internecine rivalries broke all bounds, leading to arbitrary taxation and widespread impoverishment, which was exacerbated during the troubles of the following Napoleonic occupation. Raymond has thus shown how political struggles on both the domestic and the international plane could affect the life chances of very modest urbanites.

Outside of Cairo the early modern crafts of Egypt rarely have been investigated. Nicolas Michel has provided a valuable study of the town of Asyut, located in the far south of Egypt; in the seventeenth century this place was a significant producer of cotton textiles.[53] From the craft historian's viewpoint, however, Cairo remains the key site, especially since the city's houses so often were built in stone and therefore examples of the builder's and decorator's art have survived not only from the Ottoman but even from the medieval (Mamluk) period. Some work has been done on the building industry; since the Ottoman dynasty did not sponsor many major construction projects in Egypt, this activity was less regulated by the state than its counterpart in mid-sixteenth-century Istanbul.[54] Some work also has been done on the various and highly skilled crafts that cooperated in the decoration of expensive palatial homes, such as joiners, specialists in mosaics or decorative painters. But since these studies have been undertaken by art historians, typically the focus is on the work itself and not on the workmen.

For icon painting, another activity on the border between arts and crafts, recent studies have highlighted the work of two eighteenth-century figures named Yuḥanna al-Armānī and Ibrāhīm al-Nāsikh.[55] These masters signed and dated some of their works, which is why we know that they were associated by 1745 and worked together until the 1780s. Admittedly painters, makers of boxes with precious inlays and other highly skilled individuals are not representative of ordinary artisans. Yet work on these unusual craftsmen is of great value for the social historian, for, given the scarcity of sources, written records on any kind of craftworkers are a great boon.

Where Istanbul is concerned, comparable studies based on material objects have also been undertaken. But we are confronted with the problem that their makers so often remain unknown, as, unlike their Christian colleagues, Muslim artists/artisans did not often sign or date their works.[56] As a result Ottoman social historians and their colleagues working on the fine arts have often had trouble assimilating one another's results. To complicate matters yet further, art historians working on Christian or Jewish artists/artisans have tended to do so in the context of researches concerning the relevant communities. All too often the Ottoman context is neglected in favour of possible connections to Byzantium or western Europe. We can only hope that this attitude will change in the near future.

On the 'ordinary' labour force of Cairo in the early 1800s, a short but substantial study by Pascale Ghazaleh continues the work of Raymond while challenging some of his conclusions.[57] Ghazaleh particularly criticizes the older scholar's pessimistic assessment of the performance of Cairo artisans in the late 1700s. In this context she suggests that French observers and particularly the savants who accompanied Napoleon may have had their own reasons for downgrading the work of Cairo craftsmen. After all, the claim of the Napoleonic administration to represent progress became more credible once the 'old regime' was discredited as a time of stagnation and decline. It is a great pity that art historians largely have neglected Egyptian artefacts of the Ottoman period: even a recent and beautifully illustrated volume on the Islamic Museum of Cairo mainly showcases objects with an Istanbul provenance.[58] Yet for our present purpose locally produced items are of major importance, as they allow us to judge the performance of Cairo artisans and figure out whether or not there was a decline in craft standards.

Like Ghazaleh's study, most work on the craftspeople of Egypt concentrates on the late eighteenth and especially the nineteenth century. Based on registers kept by local qadis, Judith Tucker's study is a real pioneer, for it is the first book-length treatment of women who lived and worked in an Ottoman province, at least if we regard Egypt when governed by the khedives as still forming part of Ottoman territory. Tucker's work focuses on women who made a living or at least substantially contributed to household income, and this workaday concern has seldom been taken up in later studies concerning the female condition in the sultans' territories. Where urban women are involved Tucker's study covers the ubiquitous textile producers and also yet another category of artisans-cum-artists, namely the singers that performed at weddings and other festivities. These women possessed a skill which was well respected at least until the mid-nineteenth century, when it lost status dramatically.[59] Once again while women feature more or less prominently in a number of recent studies of Istanbul working people, there as yet exists no comparable broadly based study on the female earners of cash in the Ottoman capital.[60]

Most recently John Chalcraft has produced two substantial studies of Cairo craftsmen and service workers, focusing on their organizations, both formal and informal.[61] The cab drivers who in late nineteenth-century Cairo staged a major strike and forced the British colonial government to back down even feature in the title of his book.[62] With regard to our present project, Chalcraft analyses the relationship between working people and the state, first the vice-regal government of the descendants of Mehmed Ali Paşa and, later on, British colonial power. In a chapter famously entitled 'Out of the frying pan, into the fire', Chalcraft has demonstrated that the state of the khedives, with its public works and other self-strengthening projects, undermined the economic status of craftworkers by heavy taxation. As for the guilds, the government eroded their legitimacy by making the headmen into unremunerated tax collectors. For by doing what the khedive's officials ordered them to do, the heads of most guilds lost the members' confidence and as a result the organizations atrophied. When the colonial state came in, the taxes demanded from craftspeople were lightened substantially, but as there was little investment in human capital, in the end artisans and service workers came out even worse than before.

In Istanbul by contrast there was no colonial state, and the empire officially continued to exist until 1922. In consequence, the demand for taxes remained heavy. Furthermore, unlike the Egyptian situation, guilds formally were abolished in the Ottoman realm between 1910 and 1912, and this action may be viewed as one of the many indicators of contemporary state centralization and official involvement with the manufacturing sector. Where the Ottoman centre was concerned, a hands-off attitude with respect to urban crafts never seems to have been an option. Whether this made a substantial difference in the life chances of urban craftspeople, however, remains an open question.

Guilds in the course of time

In contrast with older studies, recent work on Ottoman guilds has become more historical in orientation. Previously historical change or its absence was rarely discussed explicitly, but earlier scholars seem to have assumed that once the guilds had come into being, they continued to operate in the accustomed fashion until their demise in the nineteenth or early twentieth century.

A decisive change in this attitude was first signalled in an article by Engin Akarlı.[63] The author discussed the eighteenth- and nineteenth-century practice of limiting the right to open a shop to those masters who first had acquired an 'opening' or 'slot' (*gedik*). Akarlı pointed out that restrictions of this kind had but rarely been applied before 1750. In his perspective, the *gedik*, or, expressed differently, the right to open a shop in a given place, was invented by Ottoman artisans in order to defend their rights to their workplaces, which at least in Istanbul were often the property of pious foundations. When in the crisis years after about 1760 the state demanded increasingly heavy contributions from these latter establishments, foundation administrators attempted to make up the shortfall by increasing rents. This proceeding, however, placed the artisans, themselves hard hit by the crisis, in an impossible situation. By claiming in self-defence that the right to open a shop formed a special kind of property, only to be transferred among fellow guildsmen, the artisans attempted to limit competition for workspace and the concomitant bidding up of rents. The most salient feature of Akarlı's argument was the claim that guilds of the sixteenth and seventeenth centuries, when *gediks* were relatively rare, differed fundamentally from their late Ottoman successors, where, in contrast, this limitation of artisan initiative was widespread.

A recent spate of studies on urban policing in the late eighteenth century has added another factor that may have been relevant to the process of guild consolidation.[64] Betül Başaran, Nalan Turna and Cengiz Kırlı have all studied the critical years when Selim III occupied the throne (1789–1807). Given massive grain scarcities and negative reactions of the Janissaries against the young ruler's attempts to reform the military, Selim III reacted in what had become a time-honoured fashion: he proclaimed that the city was overcrowded and full of 'undesirable elements'. Stringent controls therefore were ordered to document the inhabitants of the different regions of Istanbul and weed out those that might be considered 'surplus'. The latter included not only people without regular work but also artisans who supposedly were not needed by the local inhabitants. It is quite likely that guilds and particularly their headmen had considerable input when it came to making decisions about who got to stay and who needed to leave; and artisan subservience to guild headmen, and thus enhanced organizational cohesion, may well have been the result.

Other changes concerned the relationship of Muslim and non-Muslim artisans. Seventeenth-century guilds could be organized on a religious or even denominational basis, but in many instances Muslims and non-Muslims shared the same guilds. The warden (*kethüda*) in mixed craft associations was always appointed from among the Muslims, and it might happen that a guild otherwise consisting, as far as can be discerned, entirely of Greeks had a Muslim *kethüda*. However, the latter could not automatically count on the support of the qadi when his fellow guildsmen were dissatisfied with him.[65] Already in Mantran's view, the relative frequency of multi-religious guilds was an argument against the assumption that seventeenth-century Istanbul craft organizations possessed a strongly religious character. After all, if Muslim piety had been intimately bound up with all guild life, the non-Muslims would have had no role to play and probably would have left.[66]

Such a separation did in fact occur, but in the later 1700s and throughout the 1800s rather than in the sixteenth and seventeenth centuries. Given the lack of data, it is hard to make specific claims, but the impression of growing guild segregation remains nonetheless. In the historiography of the last few decades it has often been assumed that this tendency was indirectly due to an increasing European presence in the empire's markets and that non-Muslim craftsmen in general adjusted more easily to the new situation. Moreover wealthy non-Muslims, at least from about 1800 onwards, were less willing to defer to Muslims, and that change in attitudes also exacerbated inter-religious rivalries. However, Onur Yıldırım's recent study has pointed out that even in the eighteenth century, tensions between guild masters expressed in terms of religious antagonism were not unknown, at least not in occupations strongly oriented toward an inter-regional market.[67] On the other hand, the segregation of guildsmen by religion also occurred in crafts which lost ground owing to the technical developments of the nineteenth century, even though they were not directly exposed to the inter-regional or international market. Therefore the increasing prosperity and self-confidence of non-Muslims cannot have been the only factor furthering inter-religious tensions. Segregation by religion apparently occurred at varying times, and from one city or even one craft to the next relations between Muslims and non-Muslims might differ substantially. The problem definitely needs further investigation.

Manufacturing in the 'long' nineteenth century

Beginning with the 1830s, we encounter quite a different setup, for now Ottoman craftspeople were confronted with the competition of European factory-made goods. Given the strong positions of England, France and even the Habsburg Empire, low customs duties were demanded for their imported items, which could be sold cheaply as a result. For an impoverished population, a low price was often the key consideration, as contemporary European observers never tired of repeating.[68] Ottoman manufacturers thus came under considerable pressure. Yet contrary to what had been claimed by historians down to the 1970s and sometimes beyond, artisans both in the Ottoman central provinces and in Egypt managed to remain in business.

In another context we have already encountered John Chalcraft's work on Cairo, with its emphasis on small masters who survived by paying minimal wages ('labour squeezing') and were forced by the competition to charge prices so low as to make productive investment impossible ('self-exploitation'). A couple of years earlier, Donald Quataert had already shown that similar strategies were adopted by manufacturers in Anatolia and the Ottoman Balkans, where women and children also laboured for derisory pay. While in Cairo, workmen employed by petty producers did not rebel against exploitation by their employers, Sherry Vatter has shown that such protests did occur in nineteenth-century Damascus.[69]

Factories, which otherwise had attracted a good deal of attention from economic historians concerned with the nineteenth century, did not much interest Quataert, given limited output and the relatively small number of workers employed.[70] Concentrating on the textile industry in preference to the service sector, Quataert focused on production techniques and economic constraints rather than the socio-political factors highlighted in Chalcraft's book. Artisans using imported yarns occupied centre stage, particularly when they produced cloth that was either cheaper or better adapted to local demand than the imported product. Thus Quataert demonstrated that in nineteenth-century Anatolia, for instance, a great variety of textiles was produced that today survive, if at all, only in local museums.

A recent synthesis and a conclusion of sorts

Given the accumulation of research reflected in these foregoing pages it is not surprising that recently a synthesis has been attempted: it concerns Istanbul between 1453 and approximately 1800, although the title, *Artisans et commerçants du Grand Turc*, recalls André Raymond's great study of eighteenth-century Cairo. By contrast the outline is a close approximation of the structure of Robert Mantran's study dealing with Istanbul between 1650 and 1700, evidently intended as homage to the second French historian of Ottoman artisans.[71] After an introductory chapter on the reconstruction of Istanbul as an Ottoman city by Mehmed the Conqueror, the history of local artisans has been recounted as it might have appeared to a viewer regarding the issue from a great distance, with evidence from the 1500s and the 1700s often introduced in a single breath. After all, the outline chosen does not easily lend itself to a narrative of changes over time. As for Mantran himself, he did not encounter this particular difficulty, as his book dealt only with a relatively short period.

However, into this traditional receptacle Hitzel has poured the new wine of recent research, and his outline has the advantage of encouraging comparison of our recent work with that of Mantran, now over 45 years old. Hitzel thus shows up those sub-fields where recent studies have made a significant contribution – for instance in elucidating the material conditions of artisan life or the craft activities of women. Of course the comparison also shows up where little has been done, as for instance in certain sectors of institutional history.

Artisan production and the closely connected demand generated by 'ordinary' consumers thus have emerged as major research topics. Put differently, Ottoman artisans have been shown to operate within a market. Certainly this market was not autonomous; rather its functioning to a considerable extent was determined by state authorities both central and local. However, the present study argues that while the 'command economy' put in place by these powerholders dominated certain sectors such as the trades supplying the sultan's court and military apparatus, these sections should not be viewed as identical with the Ottoman urban economy as a whole. A divergence between sectors under tight state control and others where artisans possessed more room for manoeuvre is especially apparent when we move away from Istanbul into the manufacturing towns of Anatolia and the Balkans, to say nothing of Syria or Egypt. In all likelihood an exaggerated emphasis on the 'command economy' found in a significant proportion of the literature has to a large extent been caused by the all too narrow focus of our research: the recent accumulation of regional studies should help us overcome this deficiency.

In addition a perusal of the secondary literature shows that there has been a tendency to project backwards into the sixteenth century, for instance, observations that are valid enough for the later 1700s or early 1800s but not satisfactorily attested for earlier periods. In order to disentangle the history of Ottoman artisans during the late 1400s and early 1500s from such perhaps anachronistic assumptions, in the following chapter we will stick closely to the contemporary documentation, while always remaining conscious of the *horror vacui* in our minds which may mislead us into thinking that what is valid at one time and in one place must also be applicable to others.

CHAPTER 2

Before and After 1500: How Artisan Organization May Have Emerged in the Ottoman Lands

Ottoman artisans are known to us mainly by their work: faiences decorated with colourful tulips, carnations, peonies and hyacinths; carpets in vibrant shades of red or blue; or silks and brocades. In addition craftsmen produced a variety of mundane goods: nails and tongs, boxes and earthenware jugs in which to store drinking water. These things have come down to us either because they were carefully preserved through the centuries or through the archaeological digs which during the last few decades have yielded a good deal of information on Ottoman material culture.

But the men – and where the textile crafts are concerned, also the women – who manufactured these items, have remained very much in the shadow. How did they make a living, an undertaking that sometimes meant invoking the protection of the Ottoman state apparatus and in other instances dodging the latter's ubiquitous representatives, namely the market inspectors and tax collectors? Did artisans, in dealing with the problems of workshop and marketplace, rely on family members and neighbours pure and simple, or did they develop specialized organizations to defend their interests? And if the latter was true, what do we know about the emergence of these groupings, which for the sake of convenience we will call guilds?

How these guilds came into being, as well as their early history, is one of the most difficult questions confronting Ottomanists, for sources are at a premium. For readers familiar with the history of artisan and commercial guilds in medieval Europe, this will not come as a surprise. Yet Ottoman guilds emerged within an empire governed by an early modern bureaucracy, whose members produced numerous documents, unlike early feudal society where many important matters never were written down. Even though the world of Ottoman artisans was dominated by the spoken word, sultanic commands survive, as well as registers compiled by Islamic judges beginning in the late 1400s and increasing in number throughout the 1500s. On these early sources we will base our discussions in the following two chapters. Only

Ottoman ornamented jug, late seventeenth to early eighteenth centuries.
(Courtesy of Völkerkundemuseum, Munich)

where no older evidence has been found has some seventeenth-century material been included as well.

In the perspective of the Ottoman ruling group, artisans were known through their products, good or bad as they might be. In addition, officials recorded that these objects were sold at official prices or else were smuggled into town by night. As persons, however, Ottoman working people rarely entered the officials' field of vision.

This leather purse once contained Ottoman letters, one of them by Abdurrahman Paşa, the last Ottoman governor of Buda, addressed to the Margrave Hermann of Baden. The letters were sent in 1685 but lost in the Second World War. The purse is of leather, the embroidery of gilt-silver wire, an elaborate example of the saddler's skill. Less luxurious purses of this type were sometimes brought back from Istanbul by central European visitors as mementoes, but we do not know whether this particular item came from the capital. (In the Badisches Landesmuseum, Schloss Karlsruhe, published in Ernst Petrasch, Reinhard Sänger et al, *Die Karlsruher Türkenbeute, die 'Türckische Kammer' des Markgrafen Ludwig Wilhelm von Baden-Baden, Die 'Türckischen Curiositäeten' der Markgrafen von Baden-Durlach* (Munich: Hirmer Verlag, 1991), pp 345–6, no. 296)

The place of artisans in the social order: pre-Ottoman and early Ottoman environments

For the fourteenth and early fifteenth centuries, there is no evidence for any activity on the part of craft organizations, and apart from Bursa, Edirne and Istanbul this observation is also valid for the later 1400s and even the first half of the sixteenth century. With respect to these periods we do not find any traces of organization in the registers of the qadis' courts, or anywhere else for that matter. Nor do we encounter any craft representatives, appointed, elected or informally self-selected, who negotiated with the officials representing the Ottoman state.

In future discussions, we will consider two activities, namely litigation in court and negotiations with state officials, as being constitutive of Ottoman guilds (see Introduction). We will therefore not assume that the activity of recognized headmen (şeyh, kethüda) was an indispensable criterion without which we cannot assume the existence of a craft organization in a given town, although some scholars in the field have taken the opposite view.[1]

In the perspective of the educated sectors of the Islamic world during the 1400s and 1500s the Ottoman sultans were latecomers who had set up their principality and later their empire on the fringes of the Islamic world. As a result the officials and religious scholars serving the early Ottoman rulers probably reproduced certain institutions and – in consequence – human relationships that already existed in long-established Islamic territories such as Syria, Egypt and Iran. With some variations Ottoman urban society of the fourteenth and fifteenth centuries must have replicated models known from the central Islamic lands.

But some of today's historians assume that in the Middle Ages at least Egypt and Syria did not possess any guilds. After all the well-studied Geniza records of Cairo's Jews provide especially dense documentation for urban life in the Egyptian metropolis during the tenth to thirteenth centuries. Moreover, given the close connections between Jews and Muslims during that period, the Geniza records also document quite a few members of the Muslim majority.[2] Evidence on craftsmen's concerns is relatively abundant in these records, but no guilds ever enter the picture. Yet if such organizations had existed, they surely would have had some input on the ways in which raw materials were acquired from sometimes remote sources or on how the next generation of artisans was trained.[3] Thus it seems as if guilds were indeed a novelty that emerged in the Ottoman heartlands of Anatolia and the eastern Balkans, where Islamization as yet was a relatively recent phenomenon.

Even more closely than to Syrian or Egyptian models, the social organization of the Ottoman subject population must have conformed to the arrangements that had existed in the various minor Anatolian principalities of the 1300s and early 1400s. After all, down to the conquests of Murad I (r. 1362–89) and Yıldırım Bayezid (r. 1389–1402) the Ottoman dynasty ruled just one such principality among many. Within the limited means at their disposal, Anatolian townspeople of the later 1200s, the 1300s or the early 1400s continued arrangements that previously had existed under the Seljuks of Rum; this must have applied especially to the major cities of Konya, Kayseri, Sivas and Erzurum.[4]

Byzantine antecedents could have been of some importance in the western coastal regions of Anatolia and in the Balkans, where the Ottomans conquered lands that for centuries had been in the hands of the 'unbelievers'. But our knowledge about provincial Byzantine urban society is just as limited as the relevant information on the post-Seljuk principalities. In many medieval towns of Byzantine Anatolia there probably were but few artisans; how the latter were organized, if at all, is anybody's guess. Even in the Ottomans' homeland of Bithynia, where a careful investigation has been made both of written sources and archaeological remains, little evidence of artisan activity has come to light, apart from the ubiquitous fortresses and potsherds. A few references to silk weavers serving the Palaeologue court in Nicaea/İznik are the proverbial exceptions confirming the rule.[5] Thus while it is quite possible that certain characteristics of artisan life persisted from the Muslim and non-Muslim past well into the Ottoman period, it is not very helpful to explain one 'unknown' by another.

Information about medieval artisans in southeastern and central Europe is not exactly abundant either. While the Ottomans from the beginning of their history were based in the Balkans (in Ottoman: Rumeli) as much as in Anatolia, to this date no evidence has been found that Ottoman artisan organization owed anything to the traditions of medieval Serbia, Bulgaria or – after the mid-sixteenth century – Hungary. In the latter case it seems that techniques, for instance in leather-working, were learned by Hungarian artisans and later transferred to western Europe.[6] But where social organization was concerned the limited information we possess indicates that, contrary to the central Ottoman lands where guilds containing both Muslims and non-Muslims were not rare, in Hungary between 1526 and 1688 the two groups kept themselves to themselves.

Male sociability in pre-Ottoman Anatolian towns

Some incidental information about the craftsmen of Konya under the rule of the Seljuk sultans can be gleaned from the *Menâkıbü 'l-'ârifîn*, a book of legends surrounding Mevlânâ Celâleddîn Rûmî (1207–73).[7] From this text we learn that the early followers of the Mevlânâ were recruited at least partly among artisans. This scandalized some people, and apparently even the disciples of Rûmî were much annoyed by the fact that at one time, their master chose an illiterate goldsmith's apprentice as his deputy. The latter's authority over the followers of the Mevlânâ probably would have been a more contentious issue had the goldsmith not predeceased his master.[8] But no information has been unearthed concerning the manner in which goldsmiths and other craftsmen of Konya were organized, if there was indeed any kind of organization beyond families and coteries of relatives. After all, the dervish order of the Mevlevîs itself did not as yet exist at this time either, but was only founded in the fourteenth century.[9]

Nor do there survive any Ottoman archival documents from the 1300s and early 1400s relevant to the activities of artisans. We are therefore limited to what a few narrative sources have to say, one of the more informative being the account of the Moroccan world traveller Ibn Baṭṭūṭa. But what did this scholarly judge learn at first hand about Anatolian artisans? Among the latter, knowledge of Arabic must have been rare, and the traveller knew no Turkish; in fact he has left lengthy complaints about the limitations of his translator.¹⁰ We therefore can not guarantee that Ibn Baṭṭūṭa did not overlook or misunderstand some of the phenomena that he saw, especially forms of organization he had not known in his native Morocco.

In the tantalizingly brief accounts of the many Anatolian towns he visited, Ibn Baṭṭūṭa was the honoured guest of groups of people that he called the *ahi*s. In some cases more than one grouping of *ahi*s existed in one and the same place, and there was great rivalry over who would get to show hospitality to the distinguished foreign visitor.¹¹ In all likelihood the rank and file of these urban brotherhoods were craftsmen, but Ibn Baṭṭūṭa was more interested in princes and men of religion than in people of relatively low status. As to the elite figures whose names alone have been recorded, *ahi*s of high station were also active as founders of mosques and other charities: the Arslanhane mosque, built by two *ahi*s in 1290, still exists in the heart of old Ankara. It has even been assumed that when at one point there was no sultan exercising power in central Anatolia, the local *ahi*s governed Ankara and finally offered it to the Ottoman Sultan Murad I, who may himself have become a member of their brotherhood.¹²

Ahi prestige was even more long lasting in nearby Kırşehir, where Ahi Evran, a local saint who, according to his extant legendary vita, had no connection with the tanners, was adopted by this group of craftsmen sometime after his death.¹³ Dervish lodges named after Ahi Evran existed in quite a few Anatolian towns including the caravan crossroads of Tokat, where this sanctuary was documented in the second half of the fifteenth century. As to the heads of the tanners' guilds in other places, they adopted the title of *ahi baba* as well; this was true for instance of the tanners of Manisa in the late sixteenth century, where the head of the guild even claimed descent from the patron saint. In Manisa during the same period, the weavers also called their guild elder their *ahi baba*.¹⁴ The activity of an *ahi baba* as a guild head, in this instance also perhaps without connection to the tanners, is even attested in Jerusalem.¹⁵

Thus it would seem that in the pre-Ottoman period the *ahi*s, or at least those among them about whom we have some information, were urban notables; whether and how they acted as leaders of craftsmen remains unknown. In two fifteenth-century lists of artisans covering the town of Tokat, quite a few men bore the title of *ahi*: in 1455 there were 21 such persons, and in 1485, when the craft population had contracted significantly, perhaps because of continuous warfare, 11 of them remained.¹⁶ In those places where *ahi*s were on record after the mid-fifteenth century, they apparently often had some special connection to the tanners. But as our information about the *ahi*s is scanty in the extreme, it does not seem very helpful to claim that the *ahi*s provided the organizational model that ordinary artisans adopted for themselves — it is possible nonetheless.

On the other hand the ceremonies once devised by the *ahi*s of Anatolian towns may well have provided models for certain practices that in later centuries became characteristic of at least a certain number of Anatolian guildsmen. This hypothesis is based on the observation that some treatises describing the moral and religious attitudes expected of so-called 'young men' (*fata, fityan*, probably to be equated with the *ahi*s) were copied out by guildsmen throughout the Ottoman period, at a time when the *ahi*s themselves probably were a distant memory. These *fütuvvetname*s or books of conduct 'befitting a young man' described a rite of initiation in which the new member was ceremoniously girded and all those present affirmed the importance of self-control in word and deed.[17] The manner of accepting new masters into a variety of guilds is spelled out most clearly in the so-called 'Great Fütuvvetname' of Seyyid Mehmed b Seyyid ʿAlâʾ eddîn, composed in 931/1524.[18] But overall, it is hard to say how intensely the religious aspect of such ceremonies was experienced.

*Fütuvvetname*s also were in use among the artisans of Ottoman Cairo; apparently this novelty had come to Egypt after the Ottoman conquest.[19] The relevant manuscripts were written locally for the most part during the 1600s and early 1700s, but the text they relay with a few variants was probably composed before 1650. Of special interest are the lists of holy patrons (*pir*) protecting the different crafts; in Cairo as elsewhere, these documents connected the artisans in question to personages who once had played a role in the life of the Prophet Muhammad and also to the prophets of the pre-Islamic era. It has been suggested that these manuals were no longer adjusted to changes in artisan life after the early 1600s. Thus while trades connected to coffee were included in the *fütuvvetname*s Cairo style, this was not true of those linked to tobacco, which had entered Egypt rather later. It thus makes sense to conclude that the heyday of *fütuvvetname*s lay in the sixteenth century, and in this respect the situation in Cairo resembled that observed in the Ottoman core lands.

Authors of *fütuvvetname*s were not expected to be original, and translated or adapted sections from medieval Arab and Persian writings were frequently included in the Turkish versions. A remarkable example is the treatise put together by a certain Yahya b Halil, descendant of Çoban and probably nicknamed al-Burgâzî — there are variants of this word in the surviving manuscripts.[20] Yahya b Halil may have had connections to Aleppo and/or Antalya, and his text is one of the oldest examples of Anatolian Turkish to have come down to us. But from our perspective the importance of Yahya's work lies in the fact that it was so often copied in later centuries: there survives a manuscript dated 1517, which thus fits nicely into the formative period of guilds that concerns us here. But there was another copy produced in the early 1600s and at least two further manuscripts from the eighteenth century, to say nothing of even more recent versions. This distribution means that the values detailed in Yahya's text, including honesty, keeping one's promises, hiding the faults and failures of one's fellow men, and the denigration of pride and desire for worldly goods, were still being transmitted throughout the Ottoman period, even though the social and political context had changed dramatically.

*Fütuvvetname*s sometimes also detailed trades of low prestige, whose practitioners could not obtain the honour of membership in the societies of high moral tone envisaged by the authors of these tracts. Among 'non-respectable' trades, Yahya b Halil mentioned attendants in public baths because they served both Muslims and non-Muslims without distinction. Brokers also were not well regarded, as it was claimed that they did not distinguish between friend and foe, presumably because they were only concerned about selling the goods entrusted to them at the maximum price obtainable. Weavers were refused entry because, the author claimed, when they had promised to deliver at a certain date they rarely kept their word. The author does not explain why this argument was not used against other artisans who could well have been accused of the same misdeed. Perhaps there was another reason that remains unspecified for disqualifying the weavers and no one else. Butchers were deemed acceptable if they gave up slaughtering; again we are left to guess whether the other low-prestige trades were considered so demeaning that the relevant artisans were rejected even after they had changed their occupations. Hunters also were considered unsuitable; our text dwells particularly on those who entrapped and ensnared birds whose young were then left to perish.[21] Given the fact that most of these attacks were directed against trades needed for the functioning of an Ottoman town, it is hard to say whether these strictures had more than a purely theoretical significance.

We do not have much evidence on despised trades during the Ottoman period, with the exception of tavern keepers and a few others. The early sixteenth-century prescription that cook-shops in Edirne should not employ non-Muslims may, however, have originated in a milieu in which the strictures propounded in the *fütuvvetname*s were taken seriously.[22] A story relayed by Evliya Çelebi also is relevant in this context. When describing a great parade of artisans and officials ordered by Murad IV (r. 1623–40) he claims that the Istanbul butchers and the traders bringing Egyptian goods to the capital got into a dispute about precedence, in which the traders stressed the purity of their own wares against the dirt, brutality and misery that were the unavoidable accompaniments of slaughterhouses. After a lengthy defence of the butchers the *şeyhülislam* decided that the merchants should march first and the butchers immediately after them. We thus can conclude that the latter were in fact less esteemed than certain other trades, though by no means treated as pariahs.

In a rather different vein we also have testimonies of so-called 'halva conversations' which seem to have taken place among Anatolian artisans mainly in winter. These ceremonies also possessed a strongly religious colouring, as the preparation and consumption of this sweet dish was accompanied by the recitation of texts inculcating devotion to the family of the Prophet Muhammad. This form of piety was popular among Sunnis and thus not necessarily a Shiite characteristic; in varying forms it is attested from the thirteenth through to the twentieth century.[23] But once again it is impossible to say how widespread these halva ceremonies were and whether they were more popular in certain periods than in others; certainly it is prudent not to view them as necessary or universal characteristics of Ottoman artisan life.

Why organize – and how? The 'naming' of artisans by Ottoman officials

Ottoman guilds thus seem to have emerged sometime between the late fifteenth and the late sixteenth centuries. We can assume but not prove that the sultans' governing apparatus furthered this development. This statement is rather vague and not very satisfactory, but simply a way of expressing our very limited understanding of the question. On the other hand, we must distinguish carefully, for any given time-span, between what we know and do not know; for only in this manner can we hope to avoid projecting back in time phenomena of the 1700s and 1800s. Owing to the small number of early sources, this latter method unfortunately has been common in studies of Ottoman artisans.

Apparently in the years around 1500 there existed in Istanbul, Bursa and Edirne groupings of craftsmen whose representatives, known as the *ehl-i hibre*, were capable of appearing in front of the qadis and explaining the customs and standards of their respective crafts.[24] The terminology used for artisans at this time was quite simple; thus the 'law of the market supervisor' (*ihtisab kanunnamesi*) covering Istanbul and dated 1501 in one instance used the term *ehl-i hirfet* for craftsmen in general. *Ehl-i sanʿat* and *ehl-i suk*, terms probably intended as synonyms, also occurred at least once in the instructions issued to the qadi and market supervisor of the Ottoman capital.[25] As to the terms *sanʿat* and *hirfet* taken by themselves, which in later times designated guilds, in the very beginning of the sixteenth century they were used in such a non-specific fashion that they might be translated simply as 'crafts'. Otherwise the activities of artisans such as tailors, shoemakers or tanners were mentioned in the 'law of the market supervisor', but there was little official concern with craft organization. Occasional references to the *ehl-i hibre* apart, no guild officials, to us the most significant indicators of artisan organization, are mentioned in the *kanunname* of 1501.

We can confirm these statements when analysing an analogous set of instructions from the city of Bursa, dated 1502. In the Bursa case the reasons for compiling the text were set out at the beginning: Sultan Bayezid II (r. 1481–1512) had sent an order to enquire about officially recognized prices (*narh*) and also about the application or non-application of the latter in the urban marketplace. For today's historian this introduction is instructive because of the terminology used and also the fact-finding procedures described in it. We learn that the different *hirfet* were summoned separately along with their 'experienced specialists', the *ehl-i hibre*, and questioned about craft standards and officially administered prices. Once again there was no record of other guild officials. Yet in spite of a relatively low degree of organization, the crafts in question were bounded clearly enough for every man to know with which group he was supposed to appear for official questioning.

Quite possibly in the early 1500s the guilds were still in their formative years, and the officials so characteristic of later times were only just beginning to appear on the scene. In 'Ayntâb/Gaziantep during the 1540s the process was more or less complete insofar as the bakers were concerned, for along with their sheikh they appeared before the qadi's scribe and declared that they undertook to provide the townspeople with bread 'in good days and in bad'.[26] A similar text has recently been discovered in the qadi registers of the Thracian town of Tekirdağ (in Ottoman: Rodoscuk); here, however, the initiative was taken by just a single person, with no reference to any guild or guild elders.[27] In Jerusalem as well, individuals operating on their own could undertake to supply the townsmen with bread: in 1534 five millers promised to do so, and to that end engaged 'their responsibility, their trust and their money'.[28]

Thus it would seem that in Rodoscuk/Tekirdağ and Jerusalem, by the mid-1500s there were as yet no guilds of millers and bakers, or if they did exist they did not wield much power.[29] Admittedly with some trepidation, we may conclude that in these towns an intervention on the part of the guild was not yet required when a new baker wished to set up shop. However, in later years, and in 'Ayntâb/Gaziantep already in the 1540s, it was the guilds and not individual entrepreneurs who took responsibility for supplying the townsmen with bread, and the established masters demanded to have a say whenever new people attempted to enter their trades.

At first glance the declarations from the Gaziantep, Tekirdağ and Jerusalem registers may appear as local peculiarities. But the similarity of the formulas applied, in spite of the enormous distances involved, makes it seem likely that such declarations somehow had been imposed by the Ottoman central government, probably through the agency of the qadis. Moreover, even though references to this kind of promise are not very frequent, the lack of documentation may be due to the simple fact that for most Ottoman towns, court registers only survive from the years after 1570, when the consolidation of the bakers' guilds had made such documents obsolete.

A formal promise may have been required from a prospective baker, because in order to supply his fellow townsmen under all circumstances, he needed to lay in a significant stock of grain. This requirement was spelled out in the Istanbul regulations of 1501, where bakers were ordered to hold supplies of flour sufficient for two months. In some cases, this obligation was reduced to a single month, probably due to scarcity. Bakers who did not comply and thus proved incapable of supplying their fellow townsmen were even threatened with execution. In the very same paragraph, however, it was admitted that prices in the grain market would vary in accordance with availability. What bakers were supposed to do when there was no grain to buy, or if the price demanded was beyond their means, was left unmentioned.

These organizational principles were of remarkable permanency, being refined progressively in the course of the centuries. In the case of Istanbul, an intimidating bureaucratic apparatus was put in place to ensure that the bakers did in fact keep their storehouses well filled.[30]

That said, in Jerusalem during the period before 1550 there were also some guilds that already possessed headmen (şeyh) and were cohesive enough to promise that their members would ply their trades in one and the same location. This was true of the goldsmiths and silversmiths, who in the early 1540s were relocating to the former 'sultan's market', now known as the market of the jewellers.[31] There seems to have been strenuous competition between some guild sheikhs and the market supervisor, who occasionally negotiated with individual artisans while bypassing the heads of the guilds.[32] By the later sixteenth century the sheikh of the jewellers' guild seems to have won out: by now finished work could be handed over to the customer only after the sheikh had approved it; the latter also supervised deliveries of silver and gold to the members of his guild, set prices and in general was the final authority in all matters pertaining to his craft. But such sweeping authority was rare and may have been connected to the particular importance of jewellery making in this pilgrimage town with its numerous wealthy visitors.[33]

By the second half of the sixteenth century organization in certain Bursa guilds had also become far more elaborate. Now the silk spinners, divided into several complementary organizations, might appear in front of the qadi stating that they wanted such and such a person to be appointed *ehl-i hibre*; in this context they might also state the abuses that the appointee should repress. Guild wardens (*kethüdas*) took office in a similar fashion: the relevant guild, or at least its representatives, appeared in court and explained why the position was currently vacant, specified the person they wanted and detailed the complaints that he would have to redress in accordance with the sultan's commands.[34] By the latter 1500s at least in Bursa, the guild system was firmly in place.

These observations make us wonder about the reasons for establishing cohesive artisan organizations particularly during the 1500s. Obviously this move was not due to simple administrative fiat: we have no knowledge of a sultanic command establishing guilds in this or that place and even less in the empire as a whole. But as we shall see, the demands of the Ottoman state for artisan dues and services became more insistent after the campaigns of the sixteenth century; after all, the sultans now had a small but active financial bureaucracy in readiness that could enforce such demands. Under these circumstances artisans may have banded together more closely and intensified pre-existing ties in order to ensure an equitable division of the taxes and services demanded. But whether this is the whole story – or even the true story – at present remains unclear.[35]

Local speciality crafts and the organizations of their practitioners

Throughout the fourteenth century and even in the early 1400s Bursa functioned as the Ottoman capital; and even after the seat of government had been moved to Edirne and later to Istanbul, the city remained a centre of manufacturing. Unfortunately no one has yet attempted to write an overall history of Bursa artisans, but the 'law of the market inspector' contains a few lively notes on disputes between the different craftsmen engaged in the manufacture of velvets and other silk fabrics. At issue was the question why recently inferior red dye (*kızıl boya*) had come to be used in place of the more expensive gum lac (*lök*), and all craft representatives were quick to blame the merchants who monopolized the available dyes and increased prices to the point where producing silk cloth according to previous standards became impossible. While once again the regulations of 1502 are not very informative on the internal organization of the artisans involved, it is clear that craftsmen in one and the same field could act as a group defending their own interests while their spokesmen provided information to representatives of the Ottoman government. Thus even in the very beginning of the sixteenth century they fulfilled the conditions that we consider necessary in order to accept a group of artisans as an actual guild.

Given the wide grasslands of Thrace, cattle, sheep and goats were raised in appreciable numbers in the surroundings of Edirne, and the town already in 1501–02 had become a centre of the leather trades. Therefore the relevant 'law of the market inspector' begins with a discussion of tanning, shoemaking and the manufacture of horse gear.[36] In accordance with the priority that the Ottoman administration always accorded to the needs of the local population, butchers had to sell skins and hides to local tanners, who in turn were forbidden to send leather away to other places. Only supplies remaining unsold could be turned over to merchants, and Edirne's shoemakers and saddlers thus enjoyed protected access to leather. Possibly this matter was given special emphasis because Edirne was the staging point for Ottoman campaigns in the Balkans, and accoutrements made of leather were indispensable for warfare. While arrangements of this kind were often observed throughout the Ottoman territories, it is noteworthy that again, the entire paragraph discussing this issue did not once mention guilds or guild officials.

Yet references to craft organizations were not completely absent. Thus the prices for horse gear were determined by an agreement of the saddlers among themselves (*kendülerin ittifakiyle*) and the same thing applied to the owners of cook-shops with respect to their own wares.[37] How such price-fixing worked in practice, whether all the craftsmen came together and deliberated, or whether the 'little men' could only acquiesce in the decisions of their 'betters' remains an open question. But at least the fact that certain artisan groups could make binding decisions about prices had in this case been officially recognized by the Ottoman centre. An even more spectacular piece of information concerns the bakers: in the presence of the qadi or one of his representatives several headmen or wardens (*kethüda*) came together and detailed the manner in which the price of bread had been computed during the last seven years.[38] As we have seen, in most other crafts guild wardens were not as yet in evidence. Thus if the conclusions drawn from the three 'laws of the market inspector' are at all reliable, the bakers of Edirne should have already possessed a more formal organization than most other trades.

Further information on early Ottoman artisan organization comes from Jerusalem, where the qadi registers survive from the 1530s onwards; in other words, they go back to the aftermath of the Ottoman conquest in 1516. However, they do not provide much evidence on the emergence of guilds in a town that until quite recently had formed part of the Mamluk sultanate and where guilds should thus have been unknown. Even so the Jerusalem registers give us valuable information concerning the social hierarchy within certain trades. The craftsmen that killed animals and prepared them for human consumption included 'ordinary' and 'master' butchers. The latter were supposed to stand surety for the former, an arrangement that was to crop up every now and then in Ottoman towns even as late as the eighteenth century.[39] In sixteenth-century Jerusalem as in Istanbul during the 1700s, the 'higher-ranking' artisans or traders thus supervised their more modest fellows.

In addition in Jerusalem there operated lower-level dealers who could be described as 'meat salesmen', for they depended on the fully fledged butchers for supplies. Furthermore two subordinate categories of artisans are documented: these men were not permitted to set up shop on their own but either slaughtered or else supervised the slaughtering process and dressed the carcasses prior to their transferral to the butchers' shops. It is unlikely that such an elaborate arrangement existed in all or even most branches of Jerusalem's craft world. But as it was encountered here and there we can conclude that the town's guilds certainly were not egalitarian.[40] Once again this hierarchical organization may be due to the fact that butchering was a more vital craft in the urban economy of Jerusalem than elsewhere, because of the demand generated by a sizeable pilgrim population.

Market supervision and prices enforced by administrative means

Another precious bit of information gleaned from the Jerusalem registers concerns the market supervisors, about whose professional identity in sixteenth-century Anatolia we have little information. In Jerusalem some of these officials had started their careers as butchers, and thus came from an artisan milieu; this feature is worth noting because it was normally quite difficult for members of the Ottoman subject population to enter the service of the sultans. Even more remarkably, the Jerusalem market supervisors, before their elevation into officialdom, had not even exercised a highly respected trade: for owing to their association with slaughter and killing the reputation of butchers did not stand very high.[41] However, by taking on the office of market supervisor, these former butchers gained social prestige and sometimes even married into families of religious scholars. Only further research will tell us whether this kind of social ascent was limited to Jerusalem or whether it was possible in other towns as well.

As we have seen, the instructions issued to qadis and market inspectors by the central authorities made little reference to the internal organization of craftsmen. Put differently, the surviving documents were compiled for the specific purpose of asserting the control of the Ottoman sultan and his officials; occasionally a 'tightening up' was attempted by sending out an official who was to put the fear of God into errant artisans.[42] That these men may have sometimes overestimated their powers of enforcement is of course an entirely different matter. On the other hand, when artisans needed to solve problems in which the authorities did not see fit to intervene they must have discussed them orally, and for the most part the solutions they found never made it into writing.

According to the 'laws of the market inspector', this official (*muhtesib*) was immediately concerned with the supervision of craftsmen. In medieval Islamic towns his predecessor had been responsible for urban order in a very general sense of the term.[43] Yet by 1500 the *muhtesib*'s responsibilities largely had narrowed down to market affairs, but he was still in charge of punishing people who did not say their prayers, to say nothing of false witnesses and people who made use of fake documents supposedly issued by a qadi (*tezvir hüccet*).[44] However, these delinquents became the responsibility of the *muhtesib* only after their crimes had been demonstrated in the qadi's court.

If we can believe our documents, inspection must have been all but ubiquitous in the marketplaces of major Ottoman towns. The *muhtesib* was supposed to supervise sales, collect market taxes, ensure that vendors did not cheat their customers, and enforce prices that had been decreed by the authorities or else agreed upon by the artisans themselves (*narh*). To do all this he must have had numerous helpers, but the 'laws of the market supervisor' do not tell us very much about them. Apart from a scribe and an aide or representative (*kethüda*) he could count on the services of people who physically patrolled the markets and shop-lined streets; in Bursa these men were accused of taking bribes from the owners of bakeries and turning a blind eye to the sale of inferior bread.[45]

The market supervisor had the right to punish infractions, either by monetary fines or physical punishment. The Istanbul regulations discouraged the imposition of fines. Instead they recommended beatings or else exposing the culprit to the scorn of the populace by passing his head through a plank with a hole in it and parading him through the town: this sign of disgrace was known as a 'wooden collar'. Further evidence for the early 1500s is lacking, but studies dealing with a slightly later period show that public shaming of this kind could have serious consequences: such a person probably had a 'black mark' against his character and, if a Muslim, may well have been regarded as ineligible to be a witness in court.[46]

A major reason for punishing an artisan was shoddy workmanship; but as the qadi and the market inspector could not know what constituted acceptable practice in any particular guild, officials normally asked for the opinion of experienced masters (*ehl-i hibre*) and recorded the statements of the latter as standards by which future performance might be judged. Thus the edicts regulating the activities of the Istanbul, Bursa and Edirne market inspectors of the early sixteenth century specified, for instance, how long a shoe could be expected to last and who, the shoemaker or the tanner, was to be held responsible if the item in question fell apart before the specified time.[47] Durability sometimes was linked to price: thus for every silver coin (in Ottoman: *akçe*) spent, shoes were meant to last for two days; as these items cost 15–20 *akçe*, repairs should have become necessary within a month or two. In addition shopkeepers could be punished for not using the correct weights and measures: thus the sellers of a fine silk cloth used for shirts were told to sell pieces that were five ells (*arşın*) long, and they could be penalized if the lengths of yarn or fabric they marketed turned out to be substandard.[48]

In Bursa and later in a few other places, sellers were obliged to have fabrics stamped by an official who charged a fee for this service. Already in the early 1500s, when tax farming was less widespread than it was to become later on, the person entrusted with the stamps (*damga*) frequently farmed his charge from the Ottoman government; this arrangement seems to have gone back to the times of Mehmed the Conqueror (r. 1451–81).[49] On other occasions a person not necessarily part of the regular administrative apparatus (*emin*) was charged with the collection and paid a rather substantial salary for his trouble; the *emin*'s stamps were kept in safe storage in the Bursa covered market.

When in the 1570s Damascus also became the seat of a stamp-tax office, this caused trouble for merchants who brought what was probably a mixed silk-cotton textile from Syria to the markets of Bursa. While as a matter of principle stamp dues were to be collected only once, traders complained of being made to pay twice over, both at the beginning and at the end of their journeys. In Istanbul by 1564 yet another *damga* had been instituted. This new office was concerned only with silks containing gold thread: evidently it was meant to limit the production of these fabrics and thereby to enhance the rarity of textiles favoured by the Ottoman court, at the same time reducing the use of gold and silver for non-monetary purposes. All these measures resulted in a gradually increasing degree of state control at least over those artisans who served the upper end of the market.

Even more frequent than disputes about substandard quantities and qualities were admonitions to sell only at the officially decreed price (*narh*). However, a *narh* was not promulgated for all craft products; thus while the Istanbul dyers were threatened with punishment in case of work that was technically unsatisfactory, in their case the regulations say nothing about prices.[50] The latter must have been determined by the guildsmen themselves. As to the situation in Bursa the reigning Sultan Bayezid II was determined to find out whether the prices administratively determined at the beginning of his reign were still being adhered to, and if not, why not.[51] The result was not particularly flattering for the administration, for the witnesses questioned were of the opinion that during the past five or six years these prices had mostly fallen into oblivion. Whether it would be possible to return to the administered prices of the 1480s is not expressed very clearly; presumably officials were to proceed pragmatically. For as our text so pithily put it, 'administered prices are [all] about scarcity and abundance'.[52]

Artisans and merchants

Where the 1400s and 1500s are concerned the relationship of artisans to merchants is best documented for Bursa; we will therefore concentrate on this town. Some of the marketing must have been undertaken by traders who had started life as artisans, or who even combined sales on a reasonably large scale with manufacturing. Thus in 1586 a complaint concerning the interruption of silk supplies from Iran was signed by one man owning 40 looms, while another was the – by now seriously worried – possessor of 46 such implements.[53] But much earlier, towards the end of the fifteenth century, there had already been some fairly rich men who had almost their entire recorded estates bound up with the silk trade.[54] People in this line of work must have suffered badly when Selim I (r. 1512–20) as a measure of economic warfare against Shah Ismāʿīl I (r. 1501–24) prohibited the importation of raw silk from Iran, imprisoned importing merchants and confiscated their goods. Probably even worse was the fate of the workers who made a living from weaving silk cloth.[55] Presumably it was not only for reasons of legality and legitimacy that shortly after ascending the throne Süleyman I (r. 1520–66) reversed his father's policy: after all, bankrupt merchants and out-of-work weavers could not be good taxpayers.

Apparently some dealers also took orders from customers who wanted ready-to-wear clothing, passing along the silk fabric chosen by the purchaser to dyers and tailors. Or else the dealers may have been part of the 'material chain' through which silk was transformed into velvets and brocades. As almost all our information is derived from estate inventories, attempts to reconstruct the movement of money and materials on the basis of single 'stills', in other words data compiled shortly after the deaths of the dealers, is bound to remain problematic.

Non-guild workers: apprentices and waged labour

Presumably only recognized masters had a say in guild affairs, and apprentices remained without a voice. We know very little about the recruitment and training of the younger generation, and the scanty evidence we do possess concerns only the final years of the sixteenth century. In the year 1600 the velvet makers of Bursa asserted that 'according to ancient custom', in other words at least during recent decades, in their guild an apprenticeship of four to five years had been customary.[56] There must have been a certain amount of variation from guild to guild. In Bursa, where unlike other places, slaves played a significant role in the textile industry, slavery might also involve an informal apprenticeship: thus at the end of the fifteenth century, when the estate inventory of the recently deceased silk merchant Hacı Hızır b Ahmed was compiled, it turned out that he had promised freedom to nine of his female slaves, who were known as skilled weavers.[57]

Whenever masters claimed that untrained men had opened shops and demanded the elimination of these 'unfair' competitors, they could count on a sympathetic hearing on the part of Ottoman officials. By contrast it was all but unknown for these officials to query whether the years of unpaid labour rendered in the complainant's workshop had not been extended beyond reasonable limits. Some young men might try to evade the controls of their elders by setting up shop on the margins of town; this was, however, feasible only in large centres with vibrant markets such as Bursa.[58] An apprentice was not paid, and a master who asserted that he had hired a given man not as a labourer but as an apprentice received the sanction of the Ankara qadi's court when he refused to pay.[59] At the end of the apprenticeship some masters might present their new colleagues with the tools needed for their trade; this also sometimes happened when slaves who had learned to weave received their manumission documents.

We also lack evidence on disputes between masters and apprentices, or, if the boys in question were still very young, between master artisans and the parents concerned. Yet sometimes a money-hungry master might seriously compromise the child's well being. This becomes evident from a late sixteenth-century Ankara court case initiated by Piri b Abdullah and his wife against Hacı Yahya b Hacı Kasım, to whom they had apprenticed their son. Hacı Yahya had taken the boy on his travels, and when he returned home the apprentice had disappeared. The distraught parents managed to locate the boy in another town, where he had been sold as a slave for the very substantial sum of 18,000 akçe.[60] Evidently if the parents had been less resourceful, the child might have ended his life in servitude.

Waged labour in craftwork is mentioned in archival sources with reasonable frequency: thus in the vicinity of Ankara, peasant women span for local textile manufacturers.⁶¹ As there were no female guilds and the existing organizations were all male, these spinners must have been unorganized wage-workers probably paid by the quantity of yarn produced. Women also were active in the Bursa silk industry: thus a silk dealer who died in the late fifteenth century owed money to two women who may have worked for him.⁶² Evidence becomes more available in the 1500s: in 1530, a certain Hacı Mehmed had entrusted silk belonging to the Ottoman state to a woman silk winder. As the latter had lost the material, she was made to compensate the man who had employed her, who was probably an *emin* or else a tax farmer; indirectly she must have paid the exchequer. A few years later yet another document referred to one woman employing another to wind her silk; given the unpleasant conditions under which this work took place even in the first half of the twentieth century, these female silk winders were probably very poor.⁶³

We can surmise that some of the Orthodox women who embroidered liturgical fabrics also worked for entrepreneurs, some of whom probably were female as well. Thus a surviving piece of fine quality is signed by a certain Theodosia Poulopos and dated to 1599; she may have been the head of a workshop.⁶⁴ The textile artistry of Greek women went back a long way, for Ibn Baṭṭūṭa spoke with admiration of a cloth manufactured in Denizli, also known as Ladik (Ottoman: Lazkiye), whose female inhabitants embroidered a cotton fabric with gold thread; because of the excellence of the materials, this fabric was not only decorative but durable.⁶⁵

Some wage-workers were definitely non-guild; in other cases this is less clear. In late sixteenth-century Ankara, for instance, a shoemaker left an inventory of about 600 pairs of shoes, and a sizeable number of men appeared to claim money from his estate. It is impossible to say whether these men were rural or semi-rural people who earned a bit of extra money in the slack season or whether they were masters who did not possess the wherewithal to open their own shops and thus accepted work put out by this better-capitalized shoe merchant. Whatever the situation, the producers should be regarded as wage labour.

Pious foundations as investors in artisan infrastructure

In Ottoman towns, artisans often kept their homes and shops separate. However, to this rule there must have been exceptions: modest artisans, especially when unmarried, may have spent the night in their shops, and looms sometimes were situated in dwelling places so that women might participate in the production process. While homes and tools were normally owned by the craftspeople themselves, shops and workshops were often the property of pious foundations. As a result, already in late fifteenth-century Istanbul artisans in their everyday lives were obliged to deal with the – sometimes elite – administrators of such institutions.

Among the most valuable commercial real estate were the complexes of mosques, schools and other charities that Ottoman sultans, viziers and princesses built mainly in the successive capitals of Bursa, Edirne and Istanbul, but also in the major provincial cities. Ordinary shops as well as tanneries, dye-houses and saddlers' workshops were rented out to provide these charities with the necessary revenues, although admittedly the really major foundations relied more on rural than on urban sources of income. Even so, the number of shops rented out by charities established by certain members of the Ottoman ruling group was enormous. When, as recorded in a register dated 1546, Mustafa Paşa converted a Byzantine church into today's mosque of Koca Mustafa Paşa, almost 250 shops were assigned to it in Istanbul alone.[66] But, according to the same register, an even more modest founder, namely a trader in or manufacturer of 'pastes' (*ma'cun*) named Kasım b Abdullah, about whom we otherwise know nothing, had supplied his mosque and theological school with 14 shops. In addition this same charity owned a butcher's shop and a workshop for the production of slightly fermented millet beer (*boza*).[67] Rental income was not enormous but still appreciable: if everything developed according to the intentions of the founder, on average these shops should have produced over 50 *akçe* per year in rents.

In most cases we can assume that a shop was tenanted by a single craftsman, but things were quite different in the case of tanneries or dye-houses. Presumably even in such settings, every artisan had a cell (*höcre*) to himself; but vats for dyes, tanning agents and other chemicals were used in common, and thus the artisans needed to agree on their purchase and upkeep. Organization was even more necessary if the tenants of such a building had been accorded monopoly rights to the marketing of a given product: at least in the reign of Mehmed the Conqueror, the tanners of Yedikule and the saddlers of Saraçhane, both situated in Istanbul, seem to have been in this position. In the foundation document concerning the Conqueror's mosque and schools, 110 shops were listed. When all these locales were tenanted, major compounds virtually must have formed town quarters of their own.[68] Such groupings were more likely to give themselves 'strong' organizations than coteries of artisans working individually, but documentation is so scanty that proof is impossible.

Conclusion

Given the present state of our knowledge, what we can say about the emergence of organization among Ottoman artisans is largely hypothetical. But in the interests of future research it must be spelt out: the male associations known as *ahis/fityan* that flourished in the 1200s and 1300s must have contained large numbers of artisans, and the writings produced in these groups continued to be copied throughout the Ottoman centuries. Yet there is no proof that in organizational terms, the *ahi*s were directly connected to the guilds. The social morality enunciated in the *fütuvvetname*s, however, was quite a different matter: from this source an ideology apparently developed that denigrated as worldly vanity qualities such as initiative, competitiveness and the striving for profit.[69] However, as we shall see, in their actual lives by no means all artisans subscribed to this morality – quite the contrary – and neither did the Ottoman state adopt the hierarchy of moral worth proposed by authors such as al-Burgâzî.

It appears that guilds gradually emerged in the later fifteenth and throughout the sixteenth century: by the middle 1500s even intensively monitored trades such as baking did not necessarily possess a guild organization. This statement is tentative because the Ottoman term *hirfet* may refer to the craft in and of itself and not exclusively to formal guild organization. Direct evidence of guilds, such as the activity of *kethüda*s, is often hard to come by. In this early period the qadi and in larger towns the market supervisor dealt with local craftsmen face to face. If the group was small the masters might appear in their entirety; if larger, the authorities relied on the testimonies of experienced masters who might or might not have been formally chosen by the members of the craft in question. *Kethüda*s that in later periods were to play key roles in artisan affairs probably as yet existed only in a few guilds in larger towns. Yet the sheikhs that in the Arab provinces formed the counterpart to the *kethüda*s are documented from the mid-sixteenth century onwards, at least in the case of Jerusalem. Whether this means that formal organizations emerged more rapidly in newly conquered territories is difficult to decide in the face of the scanty evidence we possess.

As the close involvement of qadi and market supervisor shows, Ottoman artisans operated in a setting many of whose salient characteristics were determined by the sultans and their servitors. Customers addressed their recriminations to public officials, at least if direct complaints in the marketplace did not produce positive results. Moreover the administration assumed that goods offered to the customer should have fixed prices. These were to be determined either by the artisans themselves, perhaps with later endorsement by the authorities, or else by the qadi and market supervisor after consultation with the craftsmen and merchants involved. After all, while the possible emergence of a black market is never openly discussed, any experienced administrator must have been aware of such a possibility.

It also is very probable that the Ottoman administration encouraged the formation of guilds; but how exactly this was achieved remains obscure. Certainly so far we have not located any sultanic orders demanding that guilds should be instituted in this or that town. But it is obvious that Ottoman officialdom did have an interest in promoting craft organization. How that concern manifested itself is a question that will occupy us in the next chapter.[70]

CHAPTER 3

Services to the State

From the mid-fifteenth century onwards, if not earlier, preparations for Ottoman wars resulted in an increased demand for finance, cavalry soldiers and above all materiel.[1] The outcome was a growing tax load, payable in money and in labour. From the early 1500s onwards the situation was aggravated when in the Habsburgs and Safavids the sultans encountered rival empires, as opposed to the Venetian colonial outposts and frequently rather petty principalities they had confronted so far. While the medium-sized but decentralized kingdom of Hungary was conquered quite rapidly (1526–47), during the following years expansion became more costly and far less certain.[2] An intensive mobilization of craftsmen was the result. As ever more armies were being raised, an ever increasing quantity of craft services was necessary to make the soldiers functional in battle.

Craftsmen's resources were easily tapped, as they lived in towns where the sultan's administration was also based; thus war-related demands must have affected them more immediately than the inhabitants of outlying, inaccessible areas. In addition artisans inhabiting Ottoman provincial towns frequently suffered from the indirect consequences of war, especially insecurity on the high roads.[3] Unrest and robbery stifled trade and thus closed many of the outlets for craft production. Through levies of money and labour as well as through spoliation by the soldiery and lack of civilian demand for their products, craftspeople thus got to shoulder a significant part of the burdens resulting from early modern state formation, Ottoman style.[4]

The Ottoman Empire has acquired a reputation as a 'perfect war machine'. Certainly it does not seem right to claim that regarding warfare as *the* major activity of any ruler worthy of the name was a peculiarly Ottoman phenomenon. On the contrary, historians of early modern western and central Europe have demonstrated the centrality of warfare to French, Habsburg and other potentates, who also used every trick in the book to gain access to revenues useable for war.[5] But perhaps it is fair to say that in a world in which warfare was viewed as the *raison d'être* of any empire, the Ottomans of the 1400s and 1500s accomplished this aim with greater efficiency than most of their rivals.

In addition to being conquerors, the sultans of the fifteenth and sixteenth centuries were also noted builders. Most obviously they constructed mosques, theological schools, dervish lodges, public soup kitchens and hospitals. Favoured sites were the successive capitals of Bursa, Edirne and Istanbul, but such buildings were also put up in provincial centres such as Manisa or Damascus, to say nothing of the pilgrimage centres of Mecca and Medina. This meant that artisans in the building and decorators' crafts were pressed into service in often remote locations, in addition to those mobilized for campaign duty.[6] In fact working on one of the empire's great construction sites was considered an alternative to following the army; this observation once again confirms the structural parallels between organizing warfare and large-scale building projects.[7] Certainly many such pious foundations, once terminated, made available shops and workshops (see Chapter 2), and thus benefited some artisans. But at times the rents these pious foundations demanded might be higher than impoverished craftsmen and/or traders were able or willing to pay.

Probably towards the late 1500s a realization that victory against European 'infidels' and Iranian 'misbelievers' could no longer be taken for granted began to de-legitimize grand viziers and sultans in the eyes of certain urbanites.[8] To counteract this danger Ottoman officials tried to focus loyalty onto the rulers by means of great public celebrations; in these events craftsmen also had to participate, whether they liked it or not. Artisan mobilization, whether for war, sultanic building projects or court festivities, will therefore form the main focus of the present chapter.

Artisans accompanying the army (*orducus*) and their recruitment

It has sometimes been said that the commissariat was a strong point of Ottoman military organization, and artisans contributed appreciably towards it. Soldiers needed not only bread and vegetables but also arms, tents, boots and clothes in addition to horseshoes and other gear if they happened to be in the cavalry. There was also a lot of repair work to be done, not only to the possessions of the soldiers themselves but also on the carts or Danube boats that carried supplies to the Habsburg battlefront. Moreover Ottoman soldiers were not accompanied to war by their womenfolk, as frequently was the case in seventeenth-century European armies. Therefore the housekeeping services many such women performed either had to be done by the soldiers themselves or else by specialized workmen. In order to maintain discipline, the sultans' commanders tried to keep their soldiers away from the business districts of Ottoman towns located close to army routes. Whether it was always possible to do so is of course a different issue, especially when certain goods and services were lacking in the camp or the soldiers had numerous prisoners to sell as slaves.

Occasionally lists of artisans to be recruited for this or that sultanic campaign have survived in the Ottoman archives.[9] While the earliest documentary evidence is from the mid-sixteenth century, the custom must have been much older, and chroniclers refer to the presence of artisans in the Ottoman army in the late 1300s. Responsibility for recruiting whatever artisans were required by the mid-1500s had been assigned to the qadis, especially those officiating in the three great cities of Bursa, Edirne and Istanbul. And when the sultan moved between his capital and Edirne, as happened rather often in the sixteenth century (*göç-i humayun*), these trips also took the shape of minor campaigns, with a number of artisans drafted expressly for that service.

In certain respects the arrangements concerning the *orducu* resembled those encountered for instance among Balkan nomads (*yürük*) serving in the Ottoman armies.[10] Typically the men in question were organized in units, called *ocak* in the case of the *yürük*, while the guilds must have fulfilled a similar function among craftsmen. Men on active service were rotated with some regularity, while those who did not go on campaign themselves paid for the outfitting of their fellows who did so. But while *yürük* until the later sixteenth century served as soldiers and thus needed arms and tents, artisans by contrast required funding to buy the outfits and materials they would need on campaign, and finding the necessary cash was the responsibility of their stay-at-home colleagues. Smaller guilds sometimes were recorded together with larger ones for the purpose of supplying *orducu*s; this may have helped to limit administrative overhead.

In addition the expansion of the navy in the course of the sixteenth century required large numbers of rowers, further increased because the death rate on war galleys was high. In addition to other sources of manpower the authorities also drafted a certain number of rowers from among the guilds of Istanbul. This obligation fell largely on the boatmen who ferried goods and passengers over the Bosporus and the Golden Horn, but also on the keepers of taverns.[11] Thus at least certain guildsmen were obliged to perform risky and presumably highly unpopular services that were not even compensated for by the possibility of windfall profits, as may have been enjoyed by some artisans who supplied soldiers on campaign.

Jewish manufacturers of woollen cloth in Salonika and elsewhere

As the Ottoman Empire possessed a standing army already in the fifteenth century, when this institution was as yet unknown in western Europe, the need for military supplies was regular and not limited to wartime. A major item was uniforms, also customary at least among certain corps within the Ottoman military establishment long before the same custom took hold in European armies. Ever since the concluding years of the fifteenth century a regular supply of woollen fabrics for the janissaries was secured from Jewish manufacturers who had been driven out of Spain after the fall of Granada in 1492. These people were established partly in Istanbul but mainly in Salonika. In the countryside surrounding Salonika, we find them setting up fullers' mills from where, if pressed for time, the janissaries might pick up their uniform cloth directly. From Salonika the manufacturers had easy access to the raw wool of the Balkans. Though at times honoured mainly in the breach, the official rule was that owners of flocks could only sell their wool to merchants once the Jewish manufacturers of Salonika had supplied themselves. However, the merchants of Dubrovnik and Venice competed for this same supply of not very high-grade wool and could afford to spend more money than manufacturers supplying the state at strictly controlled prices. Moreover the janissary cloth was to be dyed blue with indigo, which did not grow in the area and thus occasioned further expense.[12] These constraints, to say nothing of recurrent plagues, often impaired the timely delivery of uniforms.

During most of the sixteenth century the Ottoman military establishment may have paid very little, but the manufacturers did receive some compensation.[13] The obligation to provide the janissaries with woollen cloth was regarded both by the Ottoman authorities and the Jewish community as a *corvée*, on a par with other obligatory services demanded by the sultans.[14] With the political and military crisis of the later 1500s, the number of janissaries grew, and as a result, the demands for uniform cloth also escalated. While in the early sixteenth century the janissaries had demanded 95,000 ells, by the century's end this delivery had been increased by almost 200 per cent and now amounted to 280,000 ells.[15]

Before the 1580s the manufacturers had financed themselves by selling in the open market; the cloth they produced was of medium quality and thus appealed to an urban clientele of moderate wealth. However, in the crisis-ridden final decades of the sixteenth century, this market contracted and finally collapsed. Given the increase of prices due to the debasement of the Ottoman currency and, where prices expressed in grams of silver were concerned, to precious metal imports from America, Balkan wool supplies tended to get more expensive.[16] In addition English merchants anxious to establish a foothold in the eastern Mediterranean sold their cloth at cut-rate prices. As a result English cloth was relatively cheap and of high quality; and the market for Salonika textiles further contracted.

In addition the Jewish manufacturers of Salonika suffered from the competition of lower-cost textiles which many now impoverished former customers may have come to prefer. Alternatives included lined vests containing a layer of cotton wool or else cloaks made out of rough woollens (*aba*) produced all over Macedonia and also in the region of Filibe/Plovdiv. Around 1600 these latter garments, which were to gain wide currency during the eighteenth and nineteenth centuries, were beginning to enter the market; they could be found in general stores (*bakkal*) and outlying caravan stops (khans), much to the annoyance of specialized artisans.[17] All this meant that by the mid-seventeenth century Salonika woollens ceased to be commercially viable, and manufacturers turned into mere dependants of the state apparatus concerned with the production of military supplies. Their numbers decreased accordingly: by 1645–46 there were apparently 190 looms while in the past there had been 300.[18] Therefore the emergence of workshops where a sizeable number of weavers laboured together, which at first glance might appear as a measure of economic rationalization, did not bring about a positive change in the manufacturers' situation. But because of janissary support, in this non-commercial form the industry survived until the abolition of the corps in 1826.

Certain Salonika weavers responded to these bottlenecks by emigration to other localities where they hoped to produce for the market and be rid of their obligations to the janissaries. Some of them found a new home not far away, in the town of Kara Ferye/Verroia, where they produced woollens probably resembling the Salonika product. Since, however, these moves increased the load of those weavers remaining behind in the city, the latter complained to the authorities in Istanbul and/or to local judges. In the case of Kara Ferye, the result was a long-drawn-out court case. It hinged on the question whether the weavers of the smaller town were emigrants or descended from the latter and thus required to return to Salonika, or whether they had lived in Kara Ferye from 'time immemorial' and thus could remain in place.[19] In the end a compromise was reached which greatly favoured the weavers of Salonika and their patrons, the janissaries: a very few men were recognized as autochthonous, while the remainder were regarded as migrants. But whether the people so classified really returned to their obligations remains unclear. Other refugees from Salonika's malaise appeared in the Aegean coastlands of Anatolia, where in the seventeenth century the port of Izmir was booming.[20] Some manufacturers of woollens settled in Manisa where they produced a cloth known as *velençe/velense*; once again refugees from Salonika were commanded to return and resume their obligation of providing for the janissaries.

In material terms *velençe*, whose name probably derived from the Spanish town of Valencia, was related to those modest woollens known as *aba* which, as we have seen, poorer customers now preferred to Salonika woollens. Protruding threads, woven as loops and then cut, often gave the finished product the appearance of a rustic rug, somewhat similar to today's 'Siirt blankets'. In addition to black and white, *velençe* came mainly in red, yellow and blue. By 1640 customers in Istanbul could choose between *velençe* from Kara Ferye and that produced in Salonika. In fact manufacturing this kind of cheap cloth was one of the ways in which weavers who continued to supply the janissaries tried to make ends meet.[21] As *velençe* was a simple textile for everyday use, few examples have survived. But better-quality items, typically used as blankets, were also available, and some sixteenth- and early seventeenth-century examples survive in the collections of the Topkapı palace.[22]

As the obligation to provide woollen cloth was incumbent on the Jewish community as a whole, the Ottoman records do not refer explicitly to any guild organization. Whether the term 'group (*taife*) of Salonika Jews manufacturing woollen cloth (*çuha*) for the janissaries' that occurs in certain documents indicates craft- as opposed to community-based organization is impossible to tell.[23] Complaints about bottlenecks in the supply of raw wool, or else insufficient labour due to plague epidemics and emigration were submitted by the Jewish community rather than by a – hypothetical – guild of manufacturers. However, in other parts of the Ottoman realm Jewish guildsmen were by no means rare: in sixteenth-century Jerusalem, for example, there probably existed Jewish sections of both the butchers' and the shoemakers' guilds, and Jews were also prominent in the tri-communal guild of jewellers.[24] But where deliveries to the state were concerned, the Jewish community as a whole seems to have been more important than any guild.

Sailcloth and under-garments for army and navy

In addition to woollens, cotton textiles were also demanded by the Ottoman army and navy. The amounts required were substantial: thus in 1628–29, in addition to non-textile items, the administration demanded 2,000 pieces of Menemen (cotton) cloth and 30 *kantar* of cotton yarn.[25] Slightly earlier the provinces of Aydın and Saruhan in western Anatolia had been required to deliver 22,000 bales, equal to 44,000 pieces, of 'lining cloth' for the janissaries.[26] In 1656–57, 40,000 ells of rough cotton fabric to clothe the slaves in the arsenal were acquired from Cyprus: while at first five *akçe* were to be paid for every piece, the person charged with the collection halved the price, and the administration confirmed that 100,000 *akçe* and no more had now been apportioned for this purpose.[27] This was a minimal amount: we only need to compare the 2.5 *akçe* per piece thus expended to the 25 *akçe* per item that the administration was willing to pay at roughly the same time to the manufacturers of the cotton cloth required from the Thessalian town of Yenişehir-i Fener (Larisa). Even if we assume that quality and transport costs in the latter case may have been higher, the difference is still striking.[28] While textile deliveries to army and navy thus were in principle paid for, considerable delays and cutbacks often made life difficult for the producers.

However, at least in part, cottons were collected from the countryside, and thus not necessarily the work of full-time craftsmen. Yet in some instances we observe the intervention of – perhaps informally – organized artisans even in fairly small towns. Thus in Bergama, which in 1573–74 contained about 8,000–9,000 inhabitants, the weavers of cotton cloth appeared before the qadi in 1564–65 and complained about traders buying up cotton yarn from the surrounding region and selling it to the 'unbelievers'.[29] A few years later, the weavers of the small town of Sımav near Kütahya collectively complained about a market tax that had not been demanded previously but now had been included in the recent tax register. The artisans, probably for the most part illiterate, had thus managed to obtain information on the contents of both the old and the new register and get the market tax abolished as an 'evil innovation' (bidʿat).[30] Once again nothing is said about the organization that preceded the craftsmen's move; but obviously communal 'togetherness' was vital for poor weavers to make their voices heard against the powerful Ottoman bureaucracy. However, once again we cannot be sure that in the 1500s or early 1600s guilds were a prerequisite for artisans planning to negotiate with officials at the centre.

Service in the mines

Most information on early Ottoman mining concerns the Balkans, where the Ottomans took over forms of organization that had existed under medieval Serbian and other princes. Regulations concerning the operation of mines in Serbia go back to the thirteenth century, and in Ottoman parlance often were described as Sas (Saxon), for many of the Serbian–Ottoman rules were derived from mining law as first developed in the Harz Mountains in present-day central Germany. Over the centuries these regulations were transferred to many mining regions all over central and southeastern Europe.[31] After his Balkan conquests, Mehmed II (r. 1451–81) set out detailed regulations that were further elaborated under his successor Bayezid II (r. 1481–1512).

While the Ottoman sultan held eminent domain over all the subsoil in his empire and more specifically owned all mines, mining entrepreneurs with extended rights of possession known as *urbar* financed and organized operations.[32] In case of abandonment the sultan took back the mine and, after a delay of several weeks in which the former *varak* was free to return, could assign the enterprise or even a share in it to another operator. In the pre-Ottoman period these *varak* sometimes were the descendants of the immigrant mine operators of the high Middle Ages, who had been assimilated into local urban society. Quite a few *varak* seem to have been monks and priests, while village headmen (*knez*) were also active in this field. Thus many of these entrepreneurs were not personally involved in the day-to-day running of the mine. A *varak* could conclude contracts with third persons to improve the mine of which he was a shareholder; however, he first needed to gain the consent of his fellow possessors. In case of disputes there were several types of officials chosen from among the mining community who might be involved before the matter was brought to the qadi. In our present context the most interesting are the *yarar adamlar* or *mu'temed adamlar* (capable or trustworthy men) who in central European terminology were known by the Latin term of *iurati*. When there were disputes between *varaks* the *yarar adamlar* inspected the site and aided the *urbarar* or chief mine operator in settling them. Whether the parallel to Bursa's or Istanbul's *ehl-i hibre* is meaningful or simply a matter of chance at present remains unresolved.[33]

Around 1500 mine labour apparently was difficult to recruit and to retain: this may have been due to the fact that Mehmed the Conqueror originally had taxed the miners at the same level as the local peasantry. Quite a few of them took flight, and Bayezid II alleviated their taxes in an effort to retain them.[34] By the new dispensation *varak* and their officials as well as mineworkers were classed together as *madenci* who paid a due of one gold coin (*flori*) per household, in addition to a tithe on the minerals they extracted and any grain that they or their families might cultivate. They were, however, exempt from the head tax (*harac*), a privilege rarely granted to the sultans' non-Muslim subjects, and in some cases also from a host of irregular taxes. Thus the Balkan miners were categorized together with pass-guards and others who served the Ottoman administration in return for fiscal advantages. Whether this arrangement involved a guild-like organization has remained unrecorded, as the internal affairs of the mining community were only of limited interest to the sultans' officials.

Several specialities are on record among the miners: some of them stoked fires so that rocks would fissure prior to the opening of new galleries, others baled out water by hand or with pumps, while yet others transported the minerals extracted to the surface, using horse-drawn wagons whenever the galleries were long and wide enough. In addition there were specialized blacksmiths who manufactured the miners' tools.

The *varak* hired mineworkers as needed and were responsible for their wages, which were paid partly in coin and partly in goods. At times the workers received a share of the mineral they had extracted as payment, which they then sold back to the *varak*; this practice must have opened the door to many abuses. In some places workers were paid according to the quantity and quality of the material they had mined. This arrangement would have discouraged them from working seams demanding a great investment of effort, and in fact certain rulings claimed that the workers did not take good care of the mines. As the sultan demanded his dues before the *varak* could collect their shares and the workmen their pay, some miners probably fled their workplaces because they had not been paid for a long time. If the *varak* was insolvent, his workmen had the right to secure their wages by pawning his share in the mine.

The mining regulations of Bayezid II have little to say about auxiliaries, for instance the men who provided the transport animals, timber and foodstuffs without which no mine could have functioned. Some information, however, is available on the nomads of the Balkans, largely de-tribalized by the mid-1500s, whose originally military responsibilities were progressively eroded.[35] These men often were employed in guarding mines and organizing the safe transport of the relevant minerals to public construction sites and army depots. A special organization was not needed, as the nomads already formed *ocak*s; as we have seen, when it came to serving the Ottoman administration there were certain parallels between guilds and *ocak*s.

As to fifteenth- and sixteenth-century Anatolia, our best evidence concerns the copper mines of Küre that were already of some importance before the Ottoman takeover.[36] In Küre the mine operators were known as the *küreci* and we encounter no trace of the non-Ottoman terminology so typical of the Balkan mines. In our sources little is said about the workmen; we are left to guess whether the many slaves employed in the copper mines during the later 1600s were present in earlier periods as well. Some miners and 'servants of the Küre mines' whose responsibilities were not defined very clearly lived in the surrounding villages, and the same thing applied to the people who supplied timber boards and other materials. These people travelled considerable distances to work, and we can assume that the arrangements in the post-1850 Zonguldak mines were inspired by the practices that had been common from at least the sixteenth century.[37]

In the naval arsenal

Mines and shipyards/naval arsenals can be discussed together because of the close interest Ottoman officials took in their finished products. In the shipyards, however, intervention was even more direct, as the naval arsenal was commanded by a high-level officer, while in the mines day-to-day control was in the hands of private contractors. Venetian and Ottoman arsenals resembled each other in terms of technology: for galleys, which down to the mid-1600s were still important in Mediterranean warfare, were relatively standardized. Once discovered, the most efficient ways of producing them spread rapidly from one shipyard to another.

Yet while in the Venetian arsenal of the 1500s assembly-line production was the norm, this technique was not adopted by the Ottomans.[38] When new ships were urgently needed the Istanbul authorities relied on subsidiary arsenals in the provinces to produce the hulls, which were then finished in Istanbul. As a result, from the mid-seventeenth century onwards the Ottoman navy was able to cut costs during years without engagements at sea, for the master shipbuilders were then dismissed; during such slack periods they were free to work for private ship owners.[39] On the other hand the Ottoman authorities did not benefit from the economies of scale that allowed the Venetians to keep up a significant naval strength even in the seventeenth century, when their commercial supremacy was a thing of the past. But with greater supplies of materials and men at their disposal the administrators of the Ottoman arsenal were not under as great a pressure to rationalize as their Venetian competitors.[40]

Some prisoners of war were housed on the arsenal grounds and occasionally employed in shipbuilding, but in Istanbul as in Venice the many specialized artisans working in the naval arsenal were free men. A wage list from 1529–30, when the Ottomans were at war with the Habsburgs and shipyard workers laboured every single day without time off even for the major religious holidays, shows that the four key craft groups consisted of caulkers, carpenters, mast-makers (*barudreşan*) and augerers.[41] Caulkers were the 'labour aristocracy', earning more than three times the wages paid to carpenters and mast-makers; the economic reasoning behind this differential remains unknown. In the early 1500s most workmen in the arsenal were Muslims, but by 1645, when the Ottoman–Venetian war over Crete had just begun, the majority of these craftsmen were Greeks, partly residents of the capital and partly immigrants from the islands including – probably – Venetian possessions. We do not know the reasons for this changeover, but it is conceivable that Cretan workmen, unable to find employment at home because the Venetians had cut back shipbuilding in Candia, offered their services so cheaply that they came to replace the locals.[42]

Which workmen in the imperial arsenal organized themselves in guilds also remains unclear; but when Evliya Çelebi compiled his great inventory of Istanbul guilds, supposedly on the basis of a list dated to 1637, he claimed that the caulkers were a military unit. We do not know whether this had been true in earlier times as well. To their officers Evliya gave the titles of *ağa* and çorbacı, both of which were typical of military affiliation.⁴³ As to the arsenal itself, according to Evliya, for the most part it had been built in the time of Sultan Süleyman, but unfortunately the doubtless difficult task of guarding the galley slaves was of greater interest to the author than the conditions of their employment while on shore.⁴⁴

Providers of war materiel

Recent studies have shown that both in the recruitment and the armaments sector, the Ottoman Empire down to the later seventeenth century performed more or less on a par with its Habsburg enemies, and certainly better than the Serenissima, to the latter's great cost.⁴⁵ While decentralized and therefore not standardized, the production of weaponry was also reasonably efficient. Weapons specialists have investigated the surviving large and small Ottoman arms; however, little is known about the workshops that produced them. We only know that they were numerous and widely distributed; therefore all attempts on the part of the Ottoman central government to prevent members of the subject class from obtaining firearms were spectacularly unsuccessful.⁴⁶

Gunpowder was also up to the standards of early modern battlefields, and the relatively ample supplies of saltpetre on Ottoman territory made it unnecessary to invade the privacy of the subjects to the same degree as was common, for instance, in early modern England. Saltpetre procurement was in the hands of people who by right of descent could have been assigned tax-collection privileges instead of cavalry service (*sipahi, sipahizade*), but who for one reason or another had not received such grants. To retain the advantages of their tax-exempt status, which were considerable, these men had to serve in a 'saltpetre brigade', even though this employment often involved a good deal of travel and expense.⁴⁷

As for the cannon foundry (*tophane*) in Istanbul, Evliya Çelebi has left a description which unfortunately for the labour historian abounds in the formulae so common in Ottoman oral literature. But even so, some concrete features do emerge.⁴⁸ The building was heavily fortified, and there were arrangements for people to circulate on the roof so that they might extinguish any fires caused by the still glowing particles ejected from the chimneys. Evliya also described the manufacture of the forms into which the gun metal was poured as the penultimate major stage of the casting process. These forms were placed under the furnaces, one end was sealed up with clay, and the liquid metal then was allowed to enter them. Earlier on, inside the form determining the outer shape of the cannon the Ottoman gun-makers had secured an iron pole covered with clay that had been mixed with a large number of eggs. When the process was completed the clay-coated pole could be pulled out and a newly cast cannon emerged.

But Evliya was particularly impressed by the preceding process of bronze manufacture. For this purpose there were two domed structures known as the *furun-ı tuc*. Evliya also explained that a certain quantity of used copper was added to the mixture to serve as a starter. After the metals had been allowed to heat up for a day, the workmen dressed themselves in protective caps and gowns of felt, looking rather like figures in a shadow play, and stirred the mixture with wooden poles. It was common practice to invite viziers and religious-legal officials who were expected to accompany the process with their prayers. But apart from the metal workers and their distinguished visitors, no one was permitted to attend certain stages of the job for fear of the evil eye. Accidents apparently were common; on occasion workers and attending viziers had been killed. Even so the presence of the latter dignitaries was deemed necessary, doubtless in part because they were expected to contribute the small quantities of gold and silver added to the bronze during the production process.

Once again Evliya has provided detailed information on a place that few other authors had ever described.[49] Quite apart from the fact that cannonmaking must have been a military secret, the strongly religious colouring of the event and the pervasive fear of the evil eye meant that almost no European traveller would have been able to witness Ottoman gun manufacture. But Evliya's account has little to say on the social organization of the gun-makers: just like the arsenal masters they were soldiers commanded by officers and who received soldiers' pay (*mevacib*). Only when 'luxury' cannons were fileburnished by goldsmiths do we encounter artisans probably organized in guilds (*ehl-i hiref*), and surely such specialized services were not required very often.[50] Until evidence to the contrary is located, we can thus assume that guild organization was of no great significance in those enterprises crucial for state service: in the mines non-guild labourers of rural background were probably in the majority, while in the naval arsenal and the cannon foundry, many artisans, whether guildsmen or not, were essentially soldiers.

Palace artists and artisans

The metalworkers in the cannon foundry were highly skilled, and as viziers and religious functionaries honoured them with their presence their work was visibly valued by officialdom. Present-day historians, however, are more interested in those craftsmen whom we today consider artists, such as miniature painters, designers of colourful faience, brocades and jewellery. Registers of sixteenth-century palace craftworkers did not make this distinction, and the people who specialized in these valuable items were recorded in the same way as the manufacturers of bows, headgear and other items of everyday use; yet of course such modest items also might be produced in luxury versions.⁵¹

Artisans in the service of the palace, and also pages who had trained in one craft or another, were expected to present the ruler with works of their own manufacture on festive occasions. But the court did not necessarily monopolize the services of the best craftsmen of the realm: the latter may have worked for private customers whenever the sultan did not need their services. If this was the general rule, then the pay recorded in the registers should have been a retainer rather than a fully fledged wage. In addition intellectual figures such as the historian and *littérateur* Mustafa ʿÂlî (1541–1600) might be employed for a few months to advise the miniature painters illustrating a work that he had authored.⁵²

The oldest extant register of palace craftsmen dates from 1526, when the memory of the occupation of Tabriz by Sultan Selim I (r. 1512–20) was still vivid. But even earlier, during the reign of Bayezid II, there were painters who had come from this city to Istanbul, probably of their own volition: this may have applied to the artist Hasan b Abdülcelil, whose father was described as a 'master from Persia'.⁵³ In addition prominent figures of the elite might present the sultan with promising young slaves to be trained as palace artisans: again according to the 1526 register a sword-maker named Ahmed had been given to Sultan Bayezid by a certain Üstad Ali; 14 years later this craftsman was still on the list of palace artisans.⁵⁴ A goldsmith had been presented to Bayezid by his son Prince Mahmud, and after Bayezid's death this artisan served Selim I and Süleyman (r. 1520–66) in succession.⁵⁵

From Selim's reign, in 1520 there also remained the painter (*nakkaş*) Şahkulu who had been banished (*sürgün*) to the Ottoman lands; he was originally from Baghdad or at least had spent time in this city. We may assume that he had been taken prisoner during Selim's campaign against Shah Ismâʿîl and while not a slave had been assigned a place of residence that he could not leave, at one point in Amasya, later in Istanbul. At 22 *akçe* a day, his pay even in 1526 was respectable, and it increased during the following years, for Şahkulu's later career was brilliant.⁵⁶ In 1545 he was the chief of the so-called Rumî corps; a non-official source claimed that he had a workshop in the palace grounds where Sultan Süleyman occasionally visited him. When he died in 1556, he was on the point of receiving a gratification of 3,000 *akçe* and a gown.

Quite possibly it was the material rewards of Ottoman service that had attracted those Iranian artists/artisans who had come as voluntary migrants. The opportunity to work without too many distractions was probably a consideration as well: the fall of the Türkmen dynasties of Iran and the state-building efforts of Shah Ismāʿīl caused a good deal of instability and for many years made court patronage in Iran unreliable. Even by mid-century, a group of artisans in the service of Sultan Süleyman was still on record as 'having come from Tabriz'.[57] Among these men we find 16 painters headed by Şah Muhammed; in addition there was a mélange of goldsmiths, scribes/calligraphers, seal cutters, rug-makers and even a lowly cleaner of raw cotton.

The overwhelming majority of the artists/artisans serving the palace in 1526 were Muslims, but in many cases they were converts of more or less recent date, as indicated by their ethnicity. We find Russians, Ukrainians, Croats, Hungarians and even a few people probably from further west known simply as Franks. But at this time conversion was not an absolute prerequisite for entering the sultan's service: thus we encounter the Frank Bastiyan, who had been banished to Istanbul from Egypt (*sürgün*).[58] Bastiyan was a manufacturer of seals; the Ottoman army probably picked him up at the Mamluk court, a desirable addition to the palace staff as he was also skilled in cutting diamonds. Two shield-makers explicitly characterized as Christians (*gebr*) had been assigned residence in Istanbul after the Ottoman army had captured them in Tabriz.[59] As to the manufacture of muskets (*tüfenk*) it was a speciality of mostly unconverted Russians/Ukranians and also of Jewish artisans.[60]

Most of these craftsmen trained apprentices who were sometimes themselves the sons of palace artisans. Thus while in principle people entered the sultan's service because of their special skills, this did not exclude the formation of families supplying the court with a tradition in this or that speciality. Some of these men established themselves and their descendants as members of the elite: thus, for example, Derviş Mehmed Zılli, from the Anatolian town of Kütahya, in the sixteenth century became a goldsmith in the sultan's service and married an Abaza/Abkhasian woman. The latter's relative Melek Ahmed had a brilliant career, ultimately becoming grand vizier, while a son from Derviş Mehmed's marriage entered the palace as a page in the service of Sultan Murad IV (r. 1623–40). This young man went on to become the famous travel writer Evliya Çelebi (1611–after 1683) without whose ten-volume work Ottoman social history would be all but impossible.[61]

In addition to the highly qualified artisans who had arrived as prisoners of war or as voluntary immigrants, there were those who had received their training in the Ottoman palace itself. For while the pages educated in the Topkapı Sarayı were for the most part destined for military and administrative careers, those with artistic talents were encouraged to develop them. A good example is Mehmed Ağa, a former soldier and as a young man an officer in Syria. While in later life he became the architect of the Sultan Ahmed mosque, as a youngster he had trained in marquetry, making boxes and other items of furniture with inlays of ivory, mother-of-pearl and precious woods.[62]

Nakkaş Hasan Paşa was a well-known miniaturist, yet he had a straightforward palace-cum-military career: in the late sixteenth century he filled several offices of trust, including responsibility for the sultan's keys. In 1603, when Ahmed I ascended the throne, he graduated from the palace with the rank of 'senior doorkeeper'. Under the same ruler Nakkaş Hasan was appointed janissary commander and later vizier, preparing a campaign against the rebel mercenaries who at that time laid waste large stretches of Anatolia.[63] How in the course of an active career he made time to illustrate 20 books on historical and literary topics remains unknown. Nor can we tell how he got his training; presumably his talents had been discovered while he was a palace page.

In the sixteenth century the sultans maintained what might be called a design office (*nakkaşhane*). It was located just outside the palace grounds on the upper floor of a disused Byzantine church. The *nakkaşhane* was moved in the early 1600s when the area became the construction site of the Sultan Ahmed mosque.[64] As in this period very similar designs appear on faiences, silk fabrics, copperware and woodwork, it has been concluded that the painters/draftsmen of the *nakkaşhane* produced models that artists and artisans in the luxury crafts were expected to follow.[65] This may have been true in some cases, but as only a skilled weaver can produce brocades that will hang well, arrangements must have been flexible enough to allow textile and other designers the necessary latitude. In some instances motifs may have spread by emulation only and not by some chief designer's fiat.[66]

Imperial architects formed part of a special corps known as the *miʿmârân-ı hassa*; throughout the better part of the sixteenth century, the chief architect was the famous Sinan (d. 1588).[67] Young men who wished to specialize in public construction could serve an apprenticeship and once they had acquired the basic skills might be sent to a provincial town where the sultan or more commonly a vizier wished to put up a mosque complex. In such cases the plan would be the work of the chief architect or his senior aides and the trainees were probably supplied with drawings and perhaps a model on the basis of which they instructed the workmen.[68]

But some of the most brilliant Ottoman architects of the 1500s and early 1600s were trained outside the architects' corps. As we have seen, Mehmed Ağa had received his initial training in design and geometry when learning the art of marquetry; and while at one time he had been a student of Sinan's, we have very little information on that stage of his career. As to Sinan himself, he came from a village near Kayseri and had been drafted through the levy of boys (*devşirme*). Later he entered the janissary corps and learned to construct ships and bridges; during a campaign against Iran he commanded a flotilla he had himself constructed and which was sent out to patrol Lake

Van and reconnoitre Iranian military activity. It was only when Sinan was already an officer of some standing that he left the army, moved to Istanbul and executed a number of private commissions for mosques.[69] The outcome must have impressed Sultan Süleyman enough that he entrusted Sinan with his first major complex, which the ruler wished to dedicate to the memory of his son Prince Mehmed who had died as a youth. Sinan must have received much of his training while on the job, and doubtless there were written texts which he and his colleagues studied. But of these teaching materials no trace has yet been found.

There is no evidence that Sinan ever was a member of the carpenters' guild even though he had trained in this craft. Nor was it necessary to enter the corps of architects as a youngster if aiming for a career as a builder for the sultan. While the palace painters and other craftsmen trained apprentices, we do not hear that the Istanbul guilds were in any way involved in the process. Whether association with the palace removed an artisan from guild purview, or whether this impression is merely due to the brevity of the surviving register entries, remains an open question at least where the 1600s are concerned.[70]

Imperial worksites: building mosques and palaces

The sultanic building site best known to historians is the Süleymaniye complex (1550–57). In addition to day-by-day accounts recording the presence of workmen and the wages they were paid, there survive quite a few individual commands, issued in the sultan's name by his council and concerning the procurement of materials and workmen.[71] These have permitted a detailed reconstruction of the processes involved, including the transportation of materials from distant provinces such as Egypt and Syria.

Moreover, to add some spice, in his old age, long after Süleyman's death, Sinan recounted his own memories of the project. While the official accounts emphasize the order and regularity, which in fact must have been dominant, as otherwise this gigantic project could not have been completed within just eight years, Sinan also remembered some of the more dramatic mishaps. Thus his enemies had accused him of being unable to ensure the solidity of the dome, and for that reason he presumably held back the completion of the building. Thereupon the sultan supposedly got very angry and threatened Sinan with the dire fate that had once befallen an architect predecessor of his, who had had the misfortune of displeasing Mehmed the Conqueror. Perhaps with some relish Sinan narrated that in response he had committed himself to the completion of the mosque in only two months' time and against all odds managed to be as good as his word.[72]

From the organizational point of view these reminiscences are valuable because Sinan claimed that when pressed for time he farmed out all projects that lent themselves to such treatment. This indicates that there were entrepreneurs able and willing to enter contracts for major portions of work to be completed under pressure. Thus at least some people in the Ottoman building trades had not as yet exhausted their resources even after the enormous Süleymaniye project had been going on for about eight years.

But for the most part the building site was controlled by state officials, while the workmen were partly artisans normally employed by private customers and partly, especially in the unskilled sector, by candidate janissaries (*acemi oğlan*). A relatively small number of hours were also put in by prisoners of war. Some of the workmen, especially Istanbul residents and migrant labourers, may have applied for employment of their own free will. But a large number of building craftsmen were draftees, often from remote parts of the Balkans and Anatolia; inhabitants of the Arab provinces were notable by their near absence. Most of the responsibility for finding the appropriate workmen once again lay with the qadis who were also considered responsible if unqualified workers arrived instead of the accomplished masters demanded by the government. To prevent escapes en route the draftees were obliged to stand surety for one another. They were issued small sums of money, not always paid out on time, for their travel expenses.[73] In some cases they seem to have made their own way to the capital, in others they travelled under guard. Once on site, some allowance was made for religious concerns: thus Christians regularly got Sunday off.

In the absence of comparable data for the private sector it is difficult to say whether the pay on the Süleymaniye construction site was more or less competitive, or whether, as often happened when the Ottoman state made its demands, the builders were paid way below market rates. A dispute about pay on a sultanic construction site is on record, but it concerns the crisis-ridden 1580s. After a major devaluation of the currency that the administration preferred to re-define as a 'scarcity' presumably caused by natural factors, the builders had refused to work unless they got a raise. With a palpable bad grace the administration gave in, but those men who might still refuse to work at the increased rate were threatened with dire punishment, so the raise was probably not very generous.[74]

The Süleymaniye documentation shows that certain jobs were undertaken by Muslims and others by Christians. The division of labour, however, was by no means watertight: a minority of Christians was sometimes found in Muslim specialities or the other way around. On the Süleymaniye site many of the highly skilled workmen were Muslims, but surprisingly, according to a document from the 1590s, when a pavilion was under construction in the Topkapı palace grounds, the artisans who manufactured the sophisticated decoration known as *muqarnas*, with its intricate geometry, a hallmark of Ottoman building decoration, were on record as being Christians. We do not know whether the division of labour on the few documented construction sites was idiosyncratic or else followed a pattern of some kind.[75]

Participation in sultanic festivals, and who paid

To what extent craftsmen were involved in the brilliant festivities that Süleyman the Magnificent sponsored especially during his early years remains an open question; artisans must have manufactured many tents, costly textiles and other accoutrements, but evidence is lacking. By the century's end, however, artisan involvement is well documented. For the circumcision of Prince Mehmed (later Mehmed III, r. 1595–1603) in 1582 an illustrated manuscript was prepared that shows the artisans participating in the parades that may have been a relative novelty at the time in question but came to be a noteworthy feature of later celebrations.[76] The miniaturist in question was Nakkaş Osman, who headed a workshop of illustrators, calligraphers and binders, in other words people belonging to the corps of palace artisans. In all likelihood the artists had been witnesses to the procession, and moreover the event had attracted so much attention that it should not have been difficult to collect information on this subject even in 1588, when the painting project was finally completed.

Nakkaş Osman's miniatures depicting artisan parades feature quite a few craftsmen carrying floats that represented their shops and workshops; the 'workmen' were usually young apprentices. Thus we possess illustrations of glass-makers' ovens, looms and bakeries; we are also shown men at work in their characteristic garb.[77] For the pre-photography period, such rare images are extremely precious to the historian. But on the other hand, the floats were 'theatrical decorations' and not real workshops; aesthetic considerations therefore may have been more important than realism. Even so, the images show the existence of luxury trades we might not otherwise know of, such as flower-sellers.[78] Closely associated with the fruit merchants even when Evliya wrote in the mid-seventeenth century, their prominence in the miniatures of 1588 may in part be due to the beauty of their wares, but partly also to a relatively high demand for flowers among well-to-do residents of Istanbul even at this early date.

Elaborate floats were expensive to prepare and moreover, as many tradesmen carried samples of their goods, there must been quite a bit of wastage: torn fabrics, broken faience, fruit and flowers trampled in the mud. In addition the artisans were expected to make gifts to the sultans, just like the palace craftsmen did on a regular basis. The traveller Nicolaus Haunolth, an eyewitness of the 1582 processions, reported that these gifts were graded by the wealth of the donors and that the sultan responded by presenting each of them with a hundred *akçe* or so.[79] But such relatively small sums could have paid only a minor share of the craftsmen's expenditures.

Conclusion

Demands made upon artisans by the sultan and his servitors were thus substantial in war as in peacetime; highly skilled craftspeople were involved, but also modest trades such as boatmen and flower-sellers. However, throughout the sixteenth century, the guilds did not function as significant 'transmission belts' for such demands. Had it been otherwise, we would have expected artisan organizations and/or their headmen to crop up in official documents much more often than was actually the case. Even in instances where the guilds intervened once they had achieved a reasonable degree of cohesion, namely the recruitment of *orducu*s and building workers, the central authority relied on the qadis more than on guild elders. When evidence is sparse, conclusions *ex negativo* must be regarded with great caution. But I would submit that while evidence from the 1400s is so scanty as to make any conclusions impossible, enough material is available from the sixteenth century to warrant our downplaying of guild activity where state demands were concerned.

This conclusion is in line with our earlier observation that in the 1500s many guilds were still in the formative stage. Ottoman craft organizations were not forced on more or less unwilling artisans by a state apparatus searching for guarantees that craftsmen drafted to serve the armies could actually do their job. Nor do the early guilds seem to have recruited artisans for public construction: as we have seen, the relevant orders went to the qadis, and they were never expected to seek the cooperation of local guild leaders. Moreover the presence of artisans working for the palace must have weakened the position at least of the Istanbul guilds, for the documentation concerning these often distinguished masters, while it says a good deal about apprentices, is completely silent on the role of the guilds in supervising the training of the next generation. For public projects of all kinds the sultans relied rather on their 'regular' officials or else on the sub-contractors, military men and tax farmers who have briefly appeared in our account.

However, these observations do not invalidate the conclusion we have arrived at in the preceding chapter, namely that guilds emerged because of the challenges posed by the administration's growing demands on artisan resources. Certainly the government relied on its own bureaucratic apparatus, yet the craftsmen themselves stood to profit if they banded together. When under pressure these people therefore consolidated the perhaps informal groupings that may have existed even in earlier times. It is a major argument of the present study that Ottoman guilds served the interests of their artisan members, but what these interests were in any given situation was determined by outside forces, namely the policies of sultans and viziers.

Viewed from a different angle, the guild pageant of 1582 does leave the impression that around the turn of the century, Istanbul's artisans had achieved a significant degree of internal cohesion, for the participating craftsmen were grouped by trade and not, as might have been a conceivable alternative, as denizens of this or that khan, of covered market or shop-lined street. By the mid-seventeenth century, artisan organizations were cohesive enough to celebrate festivals and have saintly patrons; in other words, they claimed the commitment of their members and even a connection to the realm of the other-worldly. How this came about in the Ottoman capital and also in Cairo will be the subject of the next chapter.

CHAPTER 4

Guildsmen of Istanbul and Cairo

In this chapter we will concentrate on artisans active in the two metropolises of the Ottoman Empire between about 1600 and 1670. Our task is greatly facilitated by several high-quality urban monographs dealing with this period and highlighting the role of craftsmen.[1] These latter studies are largely based on the Islamic court records that begin in the 1500s but for both cities only become abundant during the seventeenth century. In addition we will look at the numerous sultanic commands addressing the administration of the capital city; while precious and much utilized in the Istanbul case, no comparable documentation is available for Cairo. We will also base ourselves on the descriptions of these two cities by Evliya Çelebi, who as a young man had explored the highways and byways of the Ottoman capital and who spent the last decade or so of his life in the Egyptian metropolis.

Metropolitan populations

For both Istanbul and Cairo official population figures are a rarity and estimates are fraught with uncertainty. For Istanbul in the late fifteenth century the sultan's officials counted 16,337 households; this was before Jewish and Muslim refugees from Spain were settled in the Ottoman capital. Estimates of the entire urban population vary widely, as household size remains unknown. For the late 1400s, the minimum suggested is 60,000–70,000 persons and the maximum 167,000–175,000. For the 1600s some estimates go beyond half a million, but more cautious historians have suggested that a figure of about 300,000 is more realistic.[2]

Whichever figures we assume, there was a rapid rise of population from 1453 to the mid-seventeenth century, and this increase must largely have been due to immigration. In the fifteenth century many migrants had not come of their own free will; in other words, people especially but not exclusively from newly conquered provinces had been more or less forcibly settled in the new capital (*sürgün*). But by the late 1500s and early 1600s the situation had profoundly changed, and now many more people were arriving in the Ottoman capital than the administration considered desirable. By this time quite a few provincials arriving in Istanbul were in fact escapees from the disturbances caused by revolting mercenaries all over Anatolia, the plight of the local inhabitants being made worse by a sequence of droughts.[3] With the roads frequently closed and trade at a standstill, many artisans must have hoped that in the capital food might be more plentiful, charities more numerous and the demand for their services greater. We thus hear that Armenians from the eastern Anatolian town of Kemah fled all the way to Istanbul, only to be sent back when Murad IV (r. 1623–40) maintained that robbery had now been repressed and the country was once again safe.[4] The sultans' administration was concerned about a possible over-use of the capital's food and water supplies and also feared the trouble-making potential of immigrant young men without regular jobs and away from the restraining impact of their home communities. Officials therefore tried to counteract immigration by controlling the roads leading into the city and undertaking periodic raids within Istanbul proper. Yet plague, which occurred frequently throughout the region, presumably drove down population far more drastically than any official action.

With respect to the total population of Cairo one of the few available data concerns the very late eighteenth century, when Napoleon's experts came up with the figure of about 263,000 inhabitants. As for the 1670s the data collected by Evliya Çelebi make it appear probable that the economically active population was close to 150,000 including beggars and 'street people', but this figure did not comprise women and children.[5] On the basis of the numerous new buildings of Ottoman times and also the geographical expansion of the built-up area, a connoisseur of Cairo has suggested that contrary to widespread assumptions the city experienced spectacular growth during the Ottoman period: for in 1517 Cairo had been home to 150,000–200,000 people. Thus there was a noticeable recovery after the calamities of the later Mamluk period, even though the city probably lost population once again through the economic and political crises of the late 1700s. Towards the end of the period treated in this section, in the late 1600s and early 1700s Cairo may have had well over 263,000 inhabitants, and this figure would imply a virtual parity with the Ottoman capital at least on a temporary basis.[6] Compared to cities in early modern Europe, both Cairo and Istanbul were enormous conurbations, comparable only to Paris and Naples.[7]

The qadis' courts as centres of Istanbul life

One of our major topics will be the relationship of Istanbul and Cairo artisans to a bevy of local administrators, especially the qadis.[8] Before the mid-1800s, there was no specialized urban administration, although the qadi of *intra muros* Istanbul, along with his colleagues of Galata, Üsküdar and Eyüp, did a good deal of the work that nowadays is the responsibility of town administrations. People turned to the qadis' courts if they wanted to complain about artisans' shoddy work or incorrect weight received in the marketplace. The qadi was also expected to oversee the market inspector and his minions, who – within limits – could punish delinquent craftsmen on the spot. Disputes concerning the location and maintenance of shops and workshops were also decided here; in addition the qadis' scribes acted as notaries who recorded a multitude of contracts often relevant to the marketplace. Moreover guildsmen, by their self-policing, did jobs that today fall to municipalities.

Legal historians have attempted to classify the activities of Ottoman courts within a world-historical context. We may conceive a spectrum, at one end of which we find judges who impose their decisions on plaintiffs and defendants, and, on the other, those who see themselves as mediators or facilitators, encouraging both sides to come to an agreement.[9] On the face of it, Ottoman qadis were well equipped to impose their decisions, based on Islamic religious law and/or the commands of the sultan. This way of approaching matters doubtless was characteristic of the men who under Bayezid II (r. 1481–1512) compiled the code of the Istanbul market inspector (see Chapter 2) and also later collections of market regulations.[10]

But this 'top–down' activity was only one side of the picture and in other situations Ottoman judges might prefer to mediate. Artisans and more generally members of the urban population were not obliged to bring their each and every dispute to the qadi's court, for they could turn to their guild officials and also to influential neighbourhood figures such as the prayer leaders of local mosques. If Christians or Jews, they could apply to the relevant religious court and were in fact pressured to do so by priests and rabbis. If, these possibilities notwithstanding, not only Muslim but also non-Muslim artisans used the Islamic courts with considerable frequency, we can assume that the latter offered the plaintiffs something they could not find elsewhere. In certain instances Islamic religious law might have been more favourable to a non-Muslim plaintiff than that of his/her own religion. But in addition the qadi's role as a mediator invested with considerable authority might also have had something to do with the popularity of the Islamic courts.

Qadi registers from the period before 1670 have survived from a sizeable number of Istanbul courts. In addition to the army judge of Rumeli and the four urban courts covering Istanbul *intra muros*, Üsküdar, Galata and Eyüp (also called Havâss-ı Refia), there were many district-level courts. Records survive of the so-called İstanbul Bab *mahkemesi*, Âhi Çelebi, Balat, Hasköy, Kasımpaşa (a single register), Beşiktaş and Tophane.[11] Only a fraction of these registers have been studied to date, and as yet we know very little about the activities especially of the lower-level courts.

The qadis of Istanbul were of very high rank; in the hierarchy of religious-cum-judicial dignitaries, they were fourth in line after the *şeyhülislâm* and the two army judges of Rumeli and Anatolia. This fact, as well as the sheer size of the city, probably explains why there were so many district-level courts in operation, the latter probably run by substitute judges under the responsibility of the nearest fully fledged qadi. Control by the higher-level judge was facilitated by the geographical proximity of higher and lower courts, and propinquity must also have facilitated the use of the courts by busy artisans unwilling to leave their shops for any length of time.

Apart from documents dealing with governmental demands, the qadi registers are valuable because they record the claims of plaintiffs and defendants who were often involved in craftwork. While the scribes had their own jargon for recording complaints and agreements, occasionally they 'slipped' into everyday speech, giving our texts the appearance of protocols covering real-life sessions.[12] Such appearances could be treacherous, as some officials apparently considered it desirable from a stylistic point of view to contrast rude, everyday speech with their own polished idiom. Some 'quotations' therefore were perhaps at least partly the work of the recording scribes.[13] On the other hand, even such imitations of everyday speech were presumably based on what people really said. In any case, while caution is of the essence, we do not possess any sources that get us closer to the lives of seventeenth-century artisans than the images conveyed by the qadis' scribes of Istanbul and Cairo.

The courts of Cairo

While Istanbul's history as a Muslim city began with the Ottoman conquest of 1453, Cairo during the thirteenth, fourteenth and fifteenth centuries had been the major centre of religious and legal scholarship, where students from the entire Islamic world flocked to hear the most distinguished teachers. Legal expertise was thus widely available. However, our understanding of the functioning of Cairo's courts is limited by the loss of any registers they may have kept before 1517. Yet after the Ottoman conquest, registers had a far better chance of survival: the archives of all 15 courts active in seventeenth-century Cairo still possess at least a few documents from the 1500s, in some cases a fragment or two going back all the way to the 1520s.[14] On the whole the structure of Cairo's court system resembled that of Istanbul. Thus in both cities, a principal court was called the Bāb ('gate') and specialized courts dealt with inheritances. The judge concerned with the estates of members of the subject class was in charge of the *qisma ʿarabiyya*; his counterpart in Istanbul was called the *beledi kassam*. Other courts were named after the urban region in which they were located. But unlike Istanbul, where the area *intra muros*,

Galata, Eyüp and Üsküdar counted as separate cities, in Cairo only the Bāb court boasted a pre-eminent position. This is noteworthy because places such as Old Cairo and Būlāq were located at some distance from the city centre and could have qualified as separate settlements.

Cairo's chief judge was known locally as *qāḍī ʿaskar*, although in the official hierarchy he ranked way below his counterparts in charge of Rumeli and Anatolia. He always came from Istanbul and judged according to Hanefi law, dominant in the centre of the empire. But the number of auxiliary judges (*nā'ibs*) may well have been larger in Cairo than in Istanbul, because all four law schools were represented and people could have their cases adjudicated by a *naib* from whatever school they happened to belong to.[15]

As in the central lands, whenever special knowledge of a given craft was required Cairo judges relied on the testimony of artisan experts called *ahl al-khibra*. In the seventeenth century this was most often the case when disputes concerning buildings needed to be adjudicated, and the *ahl al-khibra* thus occupied a prominent place in this sector. Such experts were also called in when inheritances were to be divided and the judges in the *qisma ʿaskariyya* and *qisma ʿarabiyya* needed to determine the monetary values of the various items contained in the relevant estate inventories.

It is hard to say whether these experts were also often invoked when it came to disputes about pay and complaints of shoddy workmanship.[16] However, we know that a surgeon could be called in as *ahl al-khibra* to determine whether a slave was healthy or not; in this case the expert thus vouched for the reliability of the dealer who had sold the slave. By the mid-seventeenth century complaints about substandard wares also could be investigated by the sheikh and assistant head of the guild concerned. Thus when in 1612 a man who had founded a mosque and had it decorated was dissatisfied with the quality of the painter's work, he applied to the qadi, who sent the sheikh, assistant head and an unspecified number of other painters to investigate. This committee returned a detailed list of the deficiencies they had spotted.[17] Unfortunately it remains unclear whether on a general level, by the 1600s the *ahl al-khibra* were being superseded by the sheikh and his aides.

Particularly when the plaintiff claimed that a customer had not paid for goods delivered, disputes involving craftspeople often wound up in Cairo's courts; the frequency of such situations makes it seem likely that quite a few deals involved credit.[18] When the qadi considered the claim justified, he ordered the debtor to pay; if the latter refused, the judge normally had him jailed.[19] Imprisonment for debt, however, could last only 100 days, and debtors were automatically freed if their creditors failed to come to an agreement with them within the stipulated time. This custom should have accorded a measure of protection to poor people, artisans among them.

When it comes to the relevance of the qadis' courts to the lives of local artisans, what has been said in the Istanbul case about artisan voices and their – imperfect – reflection in the registers is valid for Egypt as well. The legal basis of court activity has been more intensively studied for Cairo than for Istanbul, if only because the coexistence of several schools of law in Egypt has made this issue more obvious than for Istanbul with its entirely Hanefi Muslim population.[20] But at least for a non-reader of Arabic much remains obscure. What were the legal strategies favoured by Egyptian artisans, and were these practices similar to or very different from those observed in contemporary Anatolia?[21] At present we do not know.

Control of the market: soldiers confronting local guildsmen

In addition to their functions as judges and ultimate overseers of market affairs, the qadis were in charge of supplying the necessary labourers to whatever construction projects the sultans might undertake, to say nothing of the demands of army and navy (see Chapter 3). However, officials whose functions were mainly military also had a major role in determining the parameters of artisan life in both metropolises. In Istanbul the most important figure was the grand vizier himself, who in his afternoon meetings with high-level officials (*ikindi divanı*) often discussed matters pertaining to the capital: the all-important bread supply and the conduct of millers and bakers occupied prominent places on the agenda. Inspection tours by the grand vizier were an occasion to punish delinquent artisans on the spot.[22] If, as often happened, the grand vizier was otherwise occupied this duty was performed by his representative, the *kaymakam*. Police powers were exercised by the commander of the janissaries and where the naval arsenal and its many workers were concerned by the chief admiral.[23]

In everyday life, however, quite a few Istanbul artisans were supervised by much less prominent officials, namely men in charge of revenue collection that sometimes also supplied the palace with a given type of commodity. These temporary state employees (*emin*) might farm their charges or else receive salaries: for Istanbul Evliya Çelebi enumerated over 30 offices of this kind, some certainly more influential in the artisan world than others.[24] Thus the *emin* of the public centre of grain distribution in Unkapanı had authority over bakers and also over the porters carrying sacks of grain. Silk merchants and probably also silk weavers needed to remain on good terms with the *emin* of the weighing scales for silk, where dues from this precious raw material were collected. As for the weighing scales for edible fats (*yağ kapanı*) the *emin* in charge could count on the deference of dealers in vegetable oils and clarified butter but also of the artisans operating olive presses. If they wished to continue in business undisturbed, the various silversmiths preparing bullion for use in the mint needed to retain the support of the relevant *emin*. As to the *kassabbaşı*, or chief butcher, he was probably a military man, since in Evliya's time so many Istanbul butchers were janissaries. This person could count on the loyalty not only of the butchers themselves but also on that of the cook-shop owners' guild; the latter boiled/roasted sheep's heads, a cheap variety of meat often consumed by soldiers.[25] Last but not least, all these officials had numerous helpers and thus provided employment to many hundreds of modest Istanbul residents.

Even more central was the role of the *muhtesib*, who by the 1600s typically farmed his position. Evliya's account shows that this office commanded profound respect in the city, but at the same time its holders were much feared owing to the scandal and even violence that they might cause.[26] Evliya expressed the matter in religious terms, claiming that the first *muhtesib* understood very well that his office demanded such encompassing knowledge that only God was qualified to fill it. Yet somebody needed to regulate market affairs with the limited information accessible to a mere mortal. As to shame and violence, the numerous attendants of the *muhtesib* – Evliya claimed there were 300 – could hang camels' bells around the necks of artisans accused of selling underweight goods, to say nothing of the animals' entrails they might wind around the offender's head before parading him through the city streets. As the scales in use at the time were not always exact, and false accusations easily made, the *muhtesib* must have terrified even those artisans who had never knowingly cheated anyone.

In Cairo's streets and markets the Ottoman central administration was not directly visible, but the authority of military men and tax farmers tangible nonetheless. Artisan subordination to state officials was by no means guaranteed, as apparent from a dispute between the painters' guild and their current sheikh (1642). The painters complained that the sheikh 'was responsible for putting them under the authority of al-Amīr Yūsuf Miʿmārbāshā and this move they denounced as contrary to their traditions.[27] Apparently at the first stage of the dispute, the qadi agreed with the plaintiffs and the sheikh lost his position; his successor was proposed by the guild and then appointed by the qadi. Yet the *miʿmārbāshā* still managed to have the last word, for a few days later he came to court in person, with a number of painters in his retinue and armed with two official orders investing him as the superior in all building trades, with the right to examine any complaints about defective work. Thus the newly appointed sheikh of the painters' guild was forced to accept a situation which had cost his predecessor the sympathies of his fellow craftsmen. We do not know whether after this defeat, the new sheikh could remain in office for any length of time.[28]

As to the role of the Cairo *muhtasib*, Evliya has provided some information in connection with one of the numerous pageants for which the city had become famous – the ceremony known as the *ru'ya* (sighting), which was meant to determine whether the new moon marking the inception of the Ramazan fast actually had become visible.[29] In the opinion of the Ottoman traveller, all the artisans of Cairo were subject to the *muhtasib*, but this was especially true of singers and dancers.[30] To mark his power, this official was escorted by a large number of soldiers, both local and Bedouin. A combination of singers and soldiers provided the splendour and also the deafening noise that accompanied the progress of the *muhtasib*. Unflatteringly, Evliya compared this event to the coming of the Antichrist. In the same parade there also marched the police officials, known to our traveller as *subaşı*; by contrast no men of religion participated in this event, which they might only watch from the sidelines. The young sons of the – probably better-off – artisans were, however, much in evidence, sometimes on horseback and dressed up in all their finery. This event clearly demonstrated the Cairo artisans' subordination to the *muhtasib* and also their connection with the military. While this latter process only was to be completed during the eighteenth century, by about 1670 it was well enough advanced to be dramatized in a public procession.[31]

As for the *muhtasib* of Cairo himself, during the seventeenth century he was associated with the regiment of the Čāwīshiyya. This being one of the less powerful units, in the early 1700s the more influential *mustahfizān* regiment took over. Just as in Istanbul the market inspector farmed his charge, but only influential people of the 'correct' regiment could present themselves as candidates, who were then introduced to the governor.[32] Other officers, according to Evliya's report, also headed groups of artisans and must have profited from the relationship: thus the ships' carpenters paraded under the leadership of the *kapudan kethüdası*, in other words a naval officer. The butchers, who slaughtered in the state slaughterhouse outside of the walled city, were subject to janissary officers, who fined them if they took their business elsewhere. On the other hand the furriers benefited from the patronage of the governor's chief furrier; as a result they had become so wealthy that they refused to submit to anyone and therefore marched by themselves.[33]

These details concerning the position of the Cairo *muhtasib* show that the military men of the city were closely involved with branches of civil administration. In fact Ottoman cities of the 1600s saw a general move of soldiers into tax collecting and the public offices that went with it, as the central government now demanded armies far larger than could be financed from its own relatively modest revenues.[34] With soldiers' pay declining as a result of frequent currency debasements, those military men with but few resources took up a trade. Those with money and political clout involved themselves in tax farming, a phenomenon well studied especially for Cairo and Damascus.[35] Many high-ranking officers saw artisans and merchants simply as 'sheep to be shorn'; with the revenue extracted, these commanders financed the competition between military corps and/or militias that dominated the political life of Cairo during the 1600s and 1700s.

Artisan organization

By the mid-1600s artisans in both Istanbul and Cairo were normally organized in guilds. Guild formation involved agreeing on a headman and getting him appointed by the qadi. Called *kethüda/kahya* in Istanbul, in Cairo this person was known as a sheikh. According to the custom of the capital, in large guilds or organizations with both Muslim and non-Muslim members the *kethüda* might be assisted by one or several *yiğitbaşıs*. While the title of *şeyh* was uncommon in Istanbul, the goldsmiths seem to have had one, with a *nakib* as his assistant, but maybe this was simply a more formal manner of referring to *kethüda* and *yiğitbaşıs*.[36] By the seventeenth century the *fütuvvet* ethos that apparently had played an important role in earlier guilds (see Chapter 2) was losing its importance in both cities.[37]

Even so, most artisan organizations recognized holy men from early Islamic history as their saintly patrons. Certain sanctuaries outside Istanbul were often visited by artisans who combined this religious observance with a picnic (*teferrüc*). The dervish lodge located close to the mosque of Piyale Paşa was particularly favoured for this purpose; but Kâğıdhane, known to later Western writers as the Sweet Waters of Europe, occupied an even more prominent place.[38] This was the site of a goldsmiths' festival that Evliya linked to Süleyman the Magnificent who had been trained in this craft when a prince. The author claimed that, as his own father had been a chief goldsmith, he had in person attended three such festivals and kissed the hand of Sultan Murad IV, who with his presence had honoured at least one gathering of this type. As often happened at similar occasions, the goldsmiths' festival was marked by an exchange of gifts: while the sultan distributed money, he received an array of valuable presents when newly promoted master goldsmiths were permitted to kiss the royal hand.

According to the traveller's description once every 40 years (meaning: once in a long while) the goldsmiths and silversmiths, presumably of Istanbul and the surrounding area, feasted for 'twenty days and twenty nights'. The celebration marked the promotion of 'twelve thousand' former journeymen (*halife, kalfa*) to fully fledged masters; this is an early reference to an intermediary stage between masters and apprentices.[39] Supposedly guildsmen from the provinces shared in the expenses. Evliya also provided references to another inter-regional gathering of artisans: supposedly the barbers held yearly assemblies in honour of their patron saint, Selmân-ı Pâk, whose grave was venerated near Baghdad. But to the present day archival confirmation for such inter-urban contacts is lacking, apart from the connections of tanners from all over the empire to the lodge of Ahi Evran in Kırşehir.[40]

As we have seen (Chapter 3) certain of the smaller craft organizations were considered 'helpers' (*yamak*) of the larger ones: when artisans were demanded for army service, the *yamak* supported the main guilds to which they were connected. Thus, for example, the Albanian cheese vendors of Istanbul were *yamak*s to the powerful butchers' organization.[41] However, neither in Cairo nor in Istanbul was there a fixed hierarchy of guilds: as far as we can tell, precedence in parades was negotiated *ad hoc*. Guilds could decide on the competence or otherwise of an apprentice wishing to set up on his own, and in the interests of the established masters most craft organizations formally or informally tried to limit the number of newcomers allowed entry.

One of the major guild activities was the procurement of the raw materials needed by its members. Such purchases were often undertaken in common, and at least in theory every member was to receive his allotted share and nothing more; overseeing this process was the responsibility of the *kethüda*. Depending on the craft in question, these raw materials might be purchased from other guilds or else from tax farmers responsible for the operation of a mine or other source of mineral. Given the far-reaching powers of many such tax farmers, it made sense for modest artisans to negotiate as a group. Whenever it was other craftsmen that had produced the materials required for further processing, inter-guild arrangements served to keep the material needed within the city proper and out of the hands of merchants who might sell it elsewhere. These issues were of special significance in Istanbul, because the often artificially low prices enforced in the capital must have induced many owners of raw materials to send their goods elsewhere. Studies on Cairo guilds do not have much to say on collective purchases, so perhaps the custom was less widespread in Egypt.

Flexibility and the tolerance of inequality

For quite some time historians assumed that Ottoman guilds prevented economic development by the rigid rules they imposed on their members. However, in accordance with the positive re-evaluation of the guilds that has taken place in the historiography of early modern Europe during recent years, this negative view has been challenged for the Ottoman context as well. A study of the artisans of Istanbul during the early 1600s has demonstrated that these men were not nearly as inimical to economic expansion as previously asserted.[42] While an ideology of 'equality in poverty' probably was propounded to craftsmen by their guild elders and others, not everybody seems to have acted according to these teachings. Some artisans found ways to avoid the constraints imposed: thus members of one guild might enter into partnerships with people from other craft organizations and expand the array of articles they could offer to the customer. The same aims could also be achieved by subletting: an artisan who wished to enter a given trade could rent a shop along with the necessary materials and tools and thus engage in a different trade 'on the sly'. If business was brisk enough, the established masters merely might demand that the new shop owners pay taxes like themselves.[43] A similar observation has been made for Bursa: in the seventeenth century, entering or leaving a guild was not especially difficult, and apparently a craftsman who paid his dues along with a given guild was considered a member in good standing.[44] In Bursa, as well as in Istanbul, much depended on agreements within a given craft, and while there were attempts to limit the number of shops in this or that speciality, these were relatively rare, and guild membership was determined by purely economic considerations.[45]

Rich artisans, while certainly not the norm, were not unheard of either. Nor is there much evidence at least for the early seventeenth century that craftsmen who had become too rich were excluded from their guilds. Claims to that effect have been made, but presumably in practical life there was more tolerance than the prescriptive rules of conduct allowed for.[46]

Working for wages on an Istanbul construction site

In many early modern cities building sites are the only enterprises providing some evidence relevant to wages, and Istanbul is no exception to this rule. But as our data come mostly – though not exclusively – from construction projects sponsored by the sultans, there is no guarantee that these figures were also applicable to private undertakings. Yet on the other hand, we are in luck, for a recent study allows us to relate these wage data to the cost of living as based on a standardized 'basket' full of goods. On the basis of the analysis provided by Süleyman Özmucur and Şevket Pamuk, *longue durée* developments emerge, and therefore we will discuss the period between the late fifteenth century and 1670 in its entirety, instead of either focusing on the pre-1600 data (Chapters 2 and 3) or else on the period between 1600 and 1670 (Chapters 4 and 5).[47] By a further piece of good fortune, the base year (1489–90) for the index computed by Özmucur and Pamuk (defined as 1.00) corresponds more or less to the beginning of the present study.

In the late 1400s Istanbul builders' wages were relatively high compared to what their successors would receive in the sixteenth and seventeenth centuries, presumably because at this early date there was as yet no 'reserve army' of masters and labourers seeking employment. Until 1549 the losses in purchasing power of qualified carpenters and other building workers remained within limits (0.92). Unskilled labourers lost more, as their purchasing power declined to 0.86. It remains unclear why there was a drastic drop in 1550–59, when the construction of the Süleymaniye was still continuing. We can only surmise that many workmen had been drafted from all over Ottoman Anatolia and Rumeli, and as a result the accountancy office calculated that the building could be completed on time even if wages were lowered. We are also left to wonder whether the delays that so infuriated Sultan Süleyman (see Chapter 3) were not perhaps due to a decline in the morale of construction workers who saw their purchasing power drastically reduced. While skilled craftsmen continued to be in trouble during the last years of Süleyman the Magnificent, the wages of unskilled labourers picked up again (see Fig. 1).

After 1570 and especially 1580, however, the good times were definitely a thing of the past; in 1580–89 the index for skilled workers was down to 0.53; in other words *ceteris paribus* these men could now afford slightly more than half of the goods that their ancestors could have purchased in the reign of the 'saintly Sultan Bayezid'. The second half of the 1580s was especially appalling, but the years around 1600 which marked the height of the mercenary rebellions in Anatolia were not any better. Possibly the advisors of the young

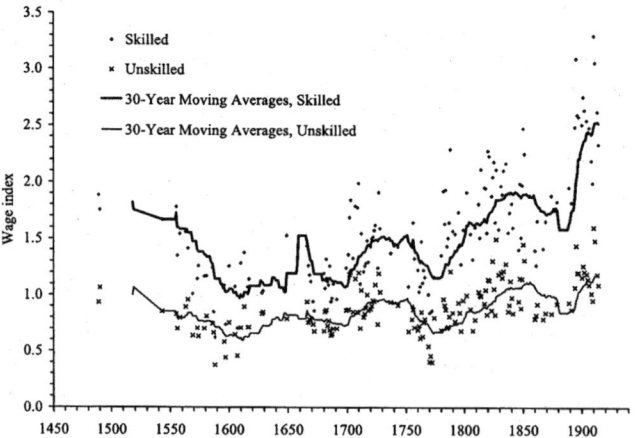

FIGURE 1
REAL DAILY WAGE OF CONSTRUCTION WORKERS: ISTANBUL, 1489–1914
(1489/90 [unskilled] = 1.0)

ruler Ahmed I (r. 1603–17) did not dissuade him from his grand building project in spite of vehement criticism because they knew that wages were at an extremely low level. Thus the construction of the Blue Mosque complex was less costly than it would otherwise have been and moreover offered work to jobless artisans.[48] As to the period following the completion of the Sultan Ahmed mosque (1617), even though great building projects were no longer being undertaken, wages recovered somewhat, with unqualified labourers sometimes doing a bit better than the masters. Although masters always made more than their men, this tendency towards wage equalization continued during the 1700s, and was only reversed in the nineteenth century.

Wage data concerning Istanbul become more meaningful when set against those of other cities; unfortunately a comparison with other Ottoman venues including Cairo is not feasible due to the paucity of data.[49] More fruitful is a comparison with early modern European cities.[50] For the period preceding 1700 we can distinguish London, Antwerp and Amsterdam from all other cities. As these centres consistently gave 'better value for labour', they attracted a substantial number of immigrants. Among the places with lower real wages we find a metropolis such as Paris and medium-sized towns such as Valencia or Leipzig. Istanbul's labourers and masters clearly formed part of this lower tier (see Fig. 2). Before 1550, when the poverty-stricken building workers of Leipzig first enter our records, unqualified helpers on Istanbul construction sites fared worst among their European colleagues. For the next 100 years, the unskilled construction workers of the Ottoman capital ranged just above those of Leipzig; and when around 1650 the latter slightly improved their lot, it was now the labourers of Valencia whose purchasing power was lowest. Put differently the Istanbulis earned little but their Spanish colleagues even less. As to the fully trained masters, from 1550 to about 1620 those working in Istanbul did better than their counterparts of Leipzig or Valencia (see Fig. 3). But by the mid-1600s if not somewhat earlier, the wages of the Leipzig masters had come to buy slightly more goods than those of their Istanbul colleagues. Yet more important than these minor differences is the observation that until about 1750, changes in the purchasing power of Istanbul builders 'fitted in' so well with general European trends.[51]

Producing for the market

Both Cairo and Istanbul were home to a large number of crafts and craftspeople; but while Istanbul's artisans worked largely for the consumption of the Ottoman elite and for their fellow townsmen, some of the goods produced in Cairo also found their way to more distant markets.

On the goods manufactured and marketed in Istanbul, information is

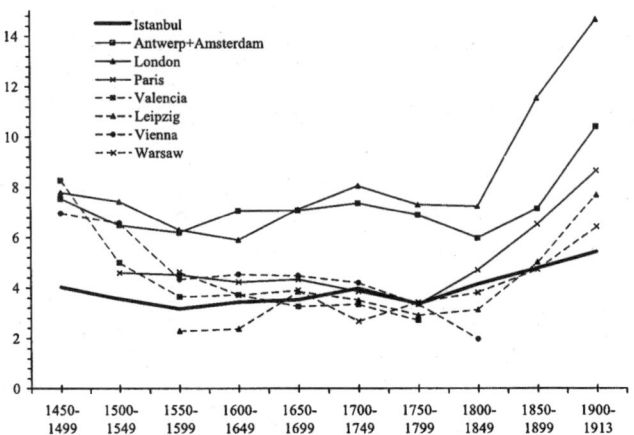

FIGURE 2
REAL WAGE OF UNSKILLED CONSTRUCTION WORKERS IN EUROPEAN CITIES,
1450–1913
(wages [in grams silver] divided by CPI [in grams silver])

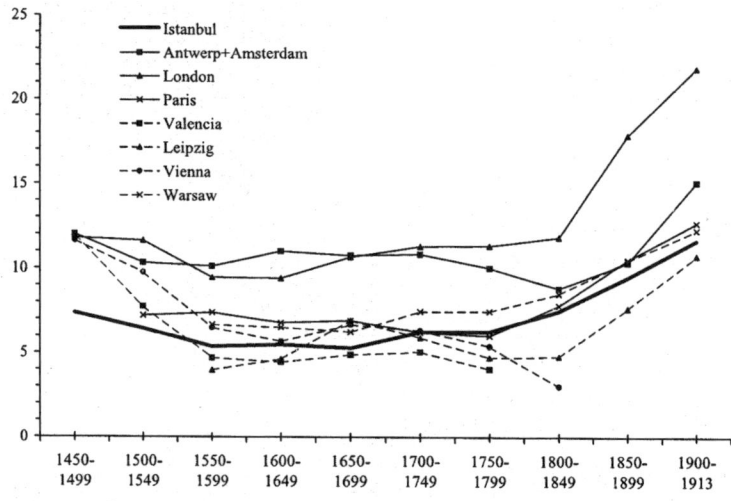

FIGURE 3
REAL WAGE OF SKILLED CONSTRUCTION WORKERS IN EUROPEAN CITIES,
1450–1913
(wages [in grams silver] divided by CPI)

available in an unusually detailed price list from the year 1640. This was prepared because after a re-valuation of the currency the authorities wanted to ensure that the now temporarily enhanced silver content of the *akçe* did in fact translate into lower prices.[52] In the textile sector, local manufactures were much in evidence: a fabric named İstanbul *beledisi*, made of either cotton or linen, was used for embroidery and thus must have been of good quality.[53] A cotton fabric from the same city, dyed black or blue, was competitively priced in a market already filled with cottons from all over the empire. Waistcloths of different styles, made of cottons, silks or various mixed fibres were also manufactured in the Ottoman capital, as were face towels and kerchiefs (*makrama*).[54] A fine linen cloth was on record as possessing silk edgings; these must have formed a decoration when the fabric was made up into shirts, of which there were several ready-to-wear varieties on the market.[55] By 1584 the dealers in yarn boasted a fully fledged guild, complete with *kethüda* and subordinate *yiğitbaşıs* who complained about the short lengths of yarn arriving in the city; presumably these yarn dealers sold most of their goods to the weavers who needed standardized lengths because they wove pieces of predetermined sizes.[56]

In addition, Istanbul was a city of silk weavers; however, the number of looms producing a heavy brocade-like fabric was limited to 100 so as to save precious metal. But the manufacture of expensive cloth tended to increase as soon as the authorities 'looked the other way'. To allow the silk weavers to make a living outside the brocade sector, they were expressly authorized to produce high-grade silks without metal thread. Competing with Florentine and Bursa wares, Istanbul-manufactured silks of good quality were available in several colours, with red apparently a favourite.[57] A more modest type of silk was used for belts, while the makers of turbans (*kavuk*) also employed Istanbul velvets.[58] Moreover, while the production of rugs and carpets is normally associated with western Anatolia, Istanbul rug merchants may have sold local products in their shops as well.[59] Among the non-textile products, the register of 1640 mentions glassware, with particular emphasis on candleholders that from the fifteenth century onwards were being manufactured in Istanbul.[60] Copper pots were also made locally, but they competed against items from the northern Anatolian town of Kastamonu. Realistic or not, the 1640 register gives the impression that apart from things to be consumed fresh, or else cheap and bulky goods such as roof tiles, the artisans of the capital concentrated on textiles.

Where high-quality craftsmanship was at issue the artisans of Cairo mainly responded to the cultural orientation of the local upper classes. Thus in the later Mamluk period wooden ceilings as opposed to stone or brick vaults became fashionable among this clientele and the same tendency continued after the Ottoman conquest. As timber was virtually unavailable in Egypt it had to be imported, mostly from Anatolia. Often smugglers had a field day; in the 1500s but apparently not later, the sultans' administration was also involved in the importation of timber into Cairo.[61] Many ceilings were painted: in the period under discussion, motifs were still mainly derived from models already current in the Mamluk period.

Other highly skilled artisans produced the wooden grilles that covered the windows in well-to-do homes: while simpler items were made of slats, the best examples were manufactured by turners creating sophisticated designs. Another luxury craft was the inlaying of wood with pieces of bone, ivory, ebony or mother-of-pearl, a craft which, as we have seen, was much in vogue in the Ottoman palace as well. On the facades of buildings similar inlays were produced out of multi-coloured marbles. With the exception of boxes or Koran stands, the products of these highly qualified craftsmen were mainly used in buildings and thus non-transportable.

But the 1640 price list shows that, even so, certain Egyptian products did make their way to Istanbul; since, however, both Cairo and Egypt were called Mısır in Ottoman parlance we cannot differentiate between the city and the province. *Alaca* both from Mısır and from Damietta was for sale on the Istanbul market; the term denoted a fabric either of mixed fibres or else ornamented with multi-coloured stripes. In the 1670s Evliya Çelebi also mentioned the activity of Cairo cotton printers, and claimed that the abundance of weavers was peculiar to this city.[62] Textiles from this source could also be purchased after tailoring as women's kaftans, either fully or partly lined; these garments also came in a quilted variety as a protection against the humid cold of the Istanbul winter.[63] Other Egyptian fabrics, probably varieties of cotton or linen, were sold already sewn up into wide pants.[64] Presumably Egyptian/Cairo tailoring was fashionable in seventeenth-century Istanbul, for certain garments were explicitly described as being of Cairo-style cut.[65]

In addition we can piece together some information on carpet-making, a high-prestige industry situated in Cairo, the products of which survive in quite a few samples; but this was not an industry with a major output or employing significant numbers of people.[66] As the conquest of Selim I in 1517 did not result in any dramatic changes in style, it is not always possible to determine which pieces had been manufactured under the Mamluk sultans and which ones should be dated to the Ottoman period.

Court patronage continued to be significant: the enormous dimensions and elaborate designs of the major carpets would have made them inaccessible to buyers of middle income. Cairo carpets were ordered, for instance, when the newly built Süleymaniye was fitted out in the 1550s.[67] In addition we possess the register copy of a famous document, dated 1585, in which a number of Cairo masters known for their skill in carpet manufacture were ordered to relocate to Istanbul.[68] However, carpet-making did not languish in Cairo after this time. By the mid-seventeenth century Cairo or Egyptian-produced mosque carpets with spaces for seven men at prayer were available in Istanbul at 650 *akçe* apiece and apparently Egyptian techniques were copied

Ottoman silk fabrics, sixteenth and seventeenth centuries. (C Abegg-Stiftung, CH-3132 Riggisberg, 2000 (Photograph: Christoph von Virág), inventory nos. 345 and 2200. Courtesy of the Abegg-Stiftung)

in western Anatolia: a reference to a prayer rug from Kula with an Egyptian-style design or embroidery probably described an item of this kind.[69]

Evliya Çelebi in his description of Cairo claimed that the carpet industry employed 300 workmen in 20 shops, so that at least some of these enterprises were of substantial size with upwards of 15 people employed. Certain rugs woven there were made of silk and priced at 2,000–3,000 guruş, princely sums even if the figure is toned down to allow for some exaggeration.[70] Evliya was impressed by the quality of the Cairo carpets and claimed that they were more valuable than those of Anatolia, with only the products of Isfahan a possible competition.[71]

In addition we have the short but instructive description by Jean Thévenot, the contemporary of Evliya whose pertinent remarks have not received the attention they deserve.[72] Thévenot claimed to have visited one of these workshops in person during his 1657 stay in Cairo. A man with a design drawing of the carpet to be produced passed through the workshop and made quick stops at different looms. He instructed workmen, young boys with nimble fingers among them, as to the number of knots of each colour that they were expected to produce. To speed up the work every artisan held several skeins of wool in his left hand and a knife in his right. When the knot was complete, he rapidly cut off the yarn. Although Thévenot did not say so, this practice of dictating the colour and number of knots, if done in a sufficiently loud voice, would have made it possible for different groups of artisans installed at their respective looms to manufacture identical carpets by following the master's instructions. From this description it also becomes clear why the workshops mentioned by Evliya were relatively large. We know nothing about the fates of the carpet-knotting boys: did they stop working in this field once they got older and, if so, what trades did they subsequently enter? Presumably only those with some capital and the necessary connections could hope to head their own workshops one day.

Another luxury textile of Cairo manufacture was the *kisve* or cover of the Ka'ba in Mecca. In Evliya's time the silk was black, as had been the custom ever since Abbasid times. In the 1570s, however, there had been plans to manufacture a white one with black lettering, as the glaring sun of Mecca tended to bleach the textile and make it look unsightly.[73] Designers were also instructed not to place the bands with inscriptions from the Koran on the edges of the cover, as at times of crowding pilgrims were likely to trample on them. But while on later images that have come down to us the inscriptions do in fact appear at a certain height, apparently a white covering was never manufactured. As this cover was renewed every year, and its size impressive, there was a permanent workshop employing – if Evliya's claims can be believed – 300 highly skilled persons.

Foreign craftsmen and their local colleagues

We have seen that in the sixteenth century Iranian masters had a role to play at the Ottoman court, but not much is known about newcomers active in the 1600s. Some such people must have been present in the Ottoman capital, if only because, after the campaigns of Murad IV, some Iranian prisoners of war probably did not return home. But the marked lack of enthusiasm for miniature painting at the Ottoman court during the 1600s must have made Istanbul seem less attractive to artistically trained Iranians than had been true in the times of Selim I and Süleyman.

A bit of evidence, but not more than that, is available on craftsmen from the west. Most of those on record served the foreign community associated with the embassy villas located beyond the Galata walls, in what were still the vineyards of Pera, today's busy Beyoğlu. But just as Bastiyan the Frank in an earlier age, such people might also be called upon to serve the Ottoman court. Thus the Dutch painter Cornelis de Bruyn reported that he once accompanied a friend of his, who was a fountain-maker, into the Ottoman palace; the latter had been commissioned to design fireworks.[74] There has been much discussion about foreigners from western and central Europe who worked in the Istanbul gun foundry, but for our period specific data are not available.[75] Other artisans may have arrived because of the interest in mechanical toys that the Ottoman court shared with its European counterparts. Powered by clockwork, these elaborate timepieces were typically made of silver. Such items were manufactured in Augsburg and Nuremberg and before the outbreak of the Long War in 1593 were often part of the tribute that after 1548 the Habsburgs paid for the strip of Hungary that they had managed to acquire. Servicing these timepieces may have provided an occasional job to the clock-makers and watch-makers of Galata.[76]

Other clocks were presumably intended for the market: Evliya Çelebi reported 45 clock-makers' shops in Istanbul, but claimed that additional artisans worked in their homes. Some of these made hourglasses and sundials; but the Ottoman traveller also mentioned French, German and Spanish timepieces available for sale. As the patron saint of the clock-makers Evliya mentioned Joseph the son of Jacob of Old Testament fame, who supposedly had improvised a sand-glass to determine the hours of prayer when imprisoned by the pharaoh. Presumably these clock-makers, whose sophistication Evliya praised highly, were mostly Muslims or at least subjects of the Ottoman sultans: for our traveller occasionally assigned patron saints even to crafts practised by non-Muslims.[77] However, it is unlikely that immigrant foreigners were considered worthy of being protected by a revered holy man.

On the other hand, the clockwork of the time was notoriously fragile, and therefore experts sometimes were sent to the sultans' court by the foreign rulers who presented these items.[78] In time a number of foreign clock-makers and watch-makers established themselves in the Ottoman capital. Making some money in this fashion and then returning home was a common business strategy among Calvinist watch-makers from Geneva who appeared in Galata on a regular basis.[79] In the contracts signed before a given craftsman set out for the Ottoman Empire, his master promised to pay his travel expenses and sometimes even the ransom should the young man be captured en route.[80] Some timepieces were manufactured in Geneva according to the specifications of Ottoman customers, others were put together in Galata out of imported parts, and there were also items of local manufacture. Some Istanbul buyers may have had cases manufactured by artisans from the capital to protect clocks/watches purchased elsewhere: Evliya reported that a Greek master named Mihayil was famous for his enamelled casings.[81] Clocks that indicated the phases of the moon were especially well liked because of their utility in a timekeeping system based on the lunar calendar.

Business-related structures and the artisan world

While between 1617 and the 1670s the only great mosque completed in Istanbul was the Yeni Cami, the construction of khans tenanted by traders and artisans continued throughout the seventeenth century. Both the queen mother (*valide*) Kösem Sultan (d. 1651) and the grand vizier Köprülüzade Fazıl Ahmed Paşa built major structures of this kind, with two or three adjacent courtyards and a small mosque in the centre of the largest one. In addition the *valide* Turhan Sultan, mother to Sultan Mehmed IV (r. 1648–87), had the building today known as the Mısır Çarşısı constructed as a source of revenue for the Yeni Cami; it consists of two covered shop-lined streets that intersect at a right angle. Unfortunately for the craft historian it is not possible to say whether in the 1600s merchants or craftsmen were the principal tenants of these monumental structures.[82]

In Cairo the seventeenth century was not a period of major mosque construction either, but once again the situation was different where commercial buildings were concerned. This development was linked to the growing role of Cairo as a venue from which Ottoman trade with India largely was conducted. Moreover high-ranking Ottomans often restored and rebuilt older pious foundations and provided them with new sources of revenue, including shops and workshops.[83] Recent detailed studies of the urban tissue, in the business centre known as the Khān al-Khalīlī and the nearby jewellers' quarter, have shown extensive construction undertaken in this locality, particularly during the 1600s.[84] Rich traders such as Ismāʿīl Abū Taqiyya (d.

1624) might construct khans of their own and make them into pious foundations, thus effectively protecting them from confiscation, a strategy that was common enough among Istanbul's ruling group as well but has not so far been observed in the case of merchants. Even if many of these structures served traders rather than craftsmen, their presence transformed the overall character of the town quarters where they were located from residential to commercial, and this fact must have attracted craftsmen into the relevant neighbourhoods. In addition many khans featured adjacent rows of shops that must have been partly tenanted by artisans.[85] It thus seems reasonable to assume that the commercial building boom of Cairo during much of the seventeenth century increased the workspace of artisans as well.

Conclusion

In the seventeenth century the conditions of work on Istanbul construction sites, and perhaps in other less well-documented trades as well, did not as yet differ very much from those that have been observed with respect to Vienna, Valencia or Leipzig. During the later fifteenth century, when the population deficit caused by the great plagues had not yet been filled but construction activity was intense, builders made good wages throughout western and southern Europe. Yet with population growth and the costs of state building by absolute rulers, beginning with the later 1500s, living standards tended to go down.[86] The declining wages of Istanbul builders fit well into this pattern. While monetary crisis was a major factor, this only became significant after about 1575. Therefore the losses in purchasing power observed earlier on must have been due mainly to the abundance of immigrant labour on the Istanbul market, but also to the power of the central state that could put enough pressure on its workers to employ them for a modest wage.

Viewed from a different angle, it does not appear as if the guilds were able to enforce equality among craftsmen, despite occasional efforts in this direction.[87] After all, in both cities, but perhaps more visibly in Cairo, artisans tended to flock into military corps. From this position of strength, some wealthier craftsmen must have been able to defy guild regulations and perhaps the opinions of their non-military fellows as well.[88] We are confronted with a familiar pattern: in most societies, our own included, there is a great gap between the values propounded and real-life conditions. We can surmise that quite a few artisans of seventeenth-century Istanbul and Cairo wished that there were more brotherhood and equality among fellow craftsmen, yet they had to live with the fact that there were rich guilds and poor guilds and, even more galling, wealthy and poor members within a single craft organization.

Where artisan output was concerned both cities possessed strong manufacturing sectors, and, as is typical in a pre-industrial economy, textiles dominated the market. Cairo's craft products, including luxury goods, were traded in Istanbul; the emergence of cotton printers in the Egyptian capital even makes us wonder whether Indian technology perhaps had established a foothold. In Istanbul locally woven silk stuffs were available in considerable variety. Thus, contrary to what was believed about 30 years ago, the numerous difficulties of the period around 1600 did not result in a permanent decline of Ottoman crafts. And while both Indian and European fabrics were certainly gaining favour among up-market buyers, high-quality textiles continued to be produced in both Ottoman metropolises.

In addition there was a group of middle-level customers, consisting of people who, so to speak, could afford a silk shirt for their wife and fine cotton for a turban or two, but who were not otherwise in the market for luxuries. Before the calamities of the later 1700s such people must have provided a considerable number of Istanbul and Cairo artisans with business. It was presumably these people whose consumption patterns were reflected in the 1640 price register; on the other hand, the purchases of the really poor, including those of many artisans, continue to escape us.

A further question concerns the differences between Istanbul and Cairo guilds. Here the political context was important: the central administration was omnipresent in the capital but more remote in Cairo. Presumably in a city where there was no sultanic court to supply and where local rebellions did not immediately endanger sultans and viziers, the market was somewhat less tightly controlled. Theoretically speaking, entrepreneurs thus had an easier time in Cairo; but while we know that local merchants might benefit from a less intrusive administration we do not know how many artisans could raise enough capital to try and emulate them. At the same time, the local soldiery's demands for a share of artisan earnings probably were more of a problem in Cairo, where by the 1600s the governors sent by the Ottoman centre could not control the military and contented themselves with the annual remittal of certain taxes. Be that as it may, the artisans of both Istanbul and Cairo contended with circumstances rather different from those faced by their provincial colleagues. It is to the work of these artisans – and that of their wives and daughters – that we will turn in the next chapter.

CHAPTER 5

Provincial Craftspeople and Merchant Networks

Taxes, trade and provincial craftspeople

Up to this point we have largely been concerned with craftsmen who either served the Ottoman state or supplied the highly protected market of Istanbul. We have also focused on Cairo, but that city was so much a metropolis in its own right that it cannot stand for the generality of Ottoman provincial cities. Even so, because of its eminent role in craft production, Cairo will crop up now and then in the present chapter as well. But principally we will deal with the crafts and craftspeople of important but much smaller centres such as Aleppo, Tunis, Bursa and Ankara. Doubtless it is a major drawback that we have so little information about rural crafts. Moreover what evidence does exist concerns workmen and workwomen in the pay of urban merchants and thus, albeit indirectly, is connected to the markets of the more important cities. But at the present state of our knowledge we cannot go any further.

Merchants will be more prominent in this chapter than elsewhere. They tended to leave more evidence than artisans, but that is only part of the story. A chapter dealing with manufacturers in provincial towns must focus on the links between craftspeople and traders, as so many products are only documented because they were traded on an inter-regional basis. This connection with commerce is even more obvious in the case of rural craftspeople, who themselves were unable to market goods for which there were no customers among their fellow villagers. For all these reasons we will devote special attention to the artisan–merchant nexus. Admittedly in our sources, these two categories are not always easy to distinguish, as successful manufacturers might branch out into trade or moneylending and practise their crafts more or less as a sideline. But the transitions between 'craftsmen' and 'merchants', two categories not invented by modern historians but recognized in contemporary sources, are in themselves of great interest.

Some provincial craft products are known to us mainly because they showed up on Istanbul markets and are thus documented in records of administered prices from the early sixteenth century onwards.¹ A significant share of all taxes collected in the provinces flowed to the Ottoman capital, where it was spent by members of the governing group. As a result these tax revenues increased the sums of money available for discretionary spending on the part of Istanbul's traders and, occasionally, even of artisans. In other words, purchasing power was concentrated in the capital city. On the other hand, as silver mines in the empire were few and, in addition, closely controlled by the state, most provincial taxpayers had no direct access to silver and every year were obliged to earn back the money they would need for the next round of taxes. This purpose could be achieved by delivering goods for sale in the capital, and while the impact of taxation on internal trade has been discussed mainly in the Indian context, it can be discerned in any centralized early modern empire including the Ottoman.² Primary sources bear out this hypothesis: in the late 1500s, the Moroccan ambassador at-Tamghrūtī was greatly impressed by the richness of Istanbul's markets, and the price list of 1640 confirms his views.³

In a different perspective, the link between taxation and the flow of goods to the political centre also signifies that a powerful ruling class living in Istanbul was able to encourage the manufacturers of good-quality craft products even in distant locations. After all, it was not necessary for provincials worried about the cash required for the next round of taxes to sell only to the sultans' court. A trickle-down effect meant that merchants, tax farmers, retired officials and Orthodox churchmen also had money to spend, and might even pay better prices than the sultan and his entourage. The goods destined for these better-off, but not necessarily very rich, inhabitants of the capital will particularly interest us here.

That said, we will also discuss goods manufactured in the provinces and traded on an inter-regional basis, but which did *not* find their way to Istanbul. This category is of interest because it allows us to assess, albeit in qualitative and not in quantitative terms, the 'propensity to consume' of certain Ottoman regions, or, to be more exact, of the upper levels of the provincial societies in question. After all, these potential consumers must have been able to secure trade goods against the powerful attraction exerted by Istanbul. In market terms, these men and women bid successfully against consumers in the capital city. But we must not forget that high-ranking persons close to the government often could satisfy their demands by political means, and thus to secure certain coveted goods, some members of provincial elites must have had sufficient power to deflect these pressures.

As we shall see, recent research on a number of Ottoman provinces has shown that a selection of craft goods manufactured outside Istanbul was remitted not to the capital but to provincial consumers within the empire, and there were some exports as well. Studying these manufactures and the artisans active in their production will help us do away with the by now outdated assumption that all artisan activities, beyond those fulfilling very basic needs, merely existed to serve the sultans, their entourages and the military.

Ankara, Aleppo and Tunis: rural craftspeople and their links to inter-regional trade

It has been suggested that when in the sixteenth century the Anatolian population increased, villagers were not always reduced to cultivating ever more marginal lands, as they seem to have done in many parts of medieval Europe during the population expansion of the 1200s. At least some Anatolian peasants unable to obtain sufficient land found supplementary sources of income in rural crafts: this group may have included for instance the migrant coppersmiths who toured the villages around Ankara repairing and re-fashioning copper pots.[4]

Moreover, already in the mid-1500s the traveller Hans Dernschwam who visited this region in the suite of Ogier Ghiselin de Busbecq, ambassador of the Habsburg ruler Ferdinand I to Süleyman the Magnificent, saw village women spinning yarn for the city's manufacturers.[5] The raw material employed came from the mohair goats that at this time were bred almost exclusively in central Anatolia.

While the weaving and finishing of angora textiles (*sof, muhayyer*) were concentrated in towns, in Tosya but above all in Ankara itself, much of the preparatory work was done by part-time rural artisans. Around 1600 some villages in the Ankara area claimed to live mainly by their craftwork, and asked to be excused certain taxes typically collected from agriculturalists.[6] During the same period, the inhabitants of certain places west of Ankara, which we may describe as large villages or perhaps as micro-towns, stated that they could pay their taxes only because they received cash for their mohair, which middlemen marketed in Venice.[7] Thus in the late sixteenth and early seventeenth centuries the merchants of Ankara had spread their nets over an entire region and, especially through their exports to Venice and Poland, substantially contributed towards the monetization of the rural economy.

An even more elaborate set of connections between town and countryside has been documented in the case of northern Syria, whose centre was the prosperous city of Aleppo. Apart from the long-distance importation of Iranian raw silk, mostly re-exported and therefore marginal to our concerns, Aleppo artisans processed cotton and silk yarns that had at least been partly spun in the surrounding villages. Soap manufacture was also in part a rural craft, and so was the production of olive oil, a major ingredient for the soap industry. Towards the end of the period that concerns us here Evliya Çelebi visited İdlib in the Aleppo province and found it a flourishing place, although admittedly it did not possess a covered market – that emblem of urbanity in the Ottoman lands. Prosperity in this semi-rural settlement again was due to the manufacture of soap traded on an inter-regional basis; certain possessors of large olive groves probably supplied most of the raw material.[8] Another example was the small town of Maʿarat al-Nuʿman, in decline since the Middle Ages: in the later 1600s it was still a centre for trade with the Bedouin, who visited its markets to purchase rough cloth that was dyed locally according to the tastes of the desert dwellers.[9]

Thus a market-oriented division of labour gave rise to a hierarchy of settlements, with a product such as soap, also much used by dyers, passing from villages to small towns and from there to the regional capital. As this urban hierarchy, clearly apparent in the Aleppo region, was embryonic at best in the case of Ankara, we may conclude that trade had a much greater impact on settlement patterns in northern Syria. This development was possible because certain village craftspeople provided the labour needed for market-oriented production.

Tunis and its environs formed another relatively well-documented region where, from the seventeenth century onwards, merchants dominated certain urban, suburban and rural craftspeople. While fez manufacture may have been practised in the area before the arrival of Muslim refugees from Spain in the sixteenth and seventeenth centuries, the latter gave a great boost to the industry. At certain times, the headman of the immigrant community was also the sheikh of the fez manufacturers' guild.[10] Women were responsible for knitting, sewing and finishing the caps. However, they had no voice in the craft organization, dominated by a small group of masters who moved the goods from one locality to another, including the little town of Zaghwān about 40 kilometres to the south of Tunis. As the raw wool from which fezzes were made was always imported from Spain, manufacturers needed to invest a considerable amount of capital, and probably often combined commerce and manufacture. Given the limitations of the local market, most of their customers must also have lived in fairly distant places. However, fezzes seem to have appeared in Istanbul only after the mid-seventeenth century, that is, towards the very end of our period, for the traders dealing in them do not occur in Evliya's enumeration of the capital's guilds nor are fezzes mentioned in the detailed register of Istanbul prices compiled in 1640.[11]

The Ankara mohair industry

In the late 1500s Ankara was one of the larger commercial centres of Anatolia, with about 25,000 inhabitants. Its prosperity was due largely to the mohair industry. Hans Dernschwam saw, and rather amateurishly sketched, the stream passing under Ankara's citadel that was used by members of the mohair-washers' guild. Angora wool was washed only after weaving, and the weavers observed by Dernschwam happened to be Greeks.[12] Otherwise our evidence concerning the process is mostly indirect: some workshops formed part of ordinary houses, presumably so that women and girls could participate in manufacture. Among the nearly 350 dwellings that entered the registers of the Ankara judge around 1600, 8.7 per cent were equipped with a workshop, probably for the most part for the processing of mohair (*sof*). Slightly after the end of our period, in the 1680s and 1690s, this figure had risen to 9.7 per cent.[13] But even when weaving was undertaken in separate shops, apparently it remained a cottage industry, workplaces with more than four looms being all but unknown.

Throughout the seventeenth century, Ankara's mohair industry continued to be important, and the city's artisans apparently recovered the losses sustained during the military (Celali) rebellions of the years around 1600. For this relative success, the artisans' ability to hold on to their raw material base was crucial, given the fact that mohair yarn was also demanded by the expanding woollen industries of Leiden and Amiens.[14] In this undertaking, Ankara manufacturers had help from the tax farmer in charge of the mohair presses used to finish the cloth after weaving: in the mid-1600s the latter procured a sultanic command forbidding the exportation of mohair fibre and thus ensured that the presses would not lie idle. Even better, this prohibition was reasonably well enforced: as late as the eighteenth century, the highest grades of mohair were not accessible to foreign merchants.

Through Dernschwam's interest in technical details we also know how the Ankara artisans operated their presses: 'seventy pieces of mohair cloth were piled one on top of the other in copper kettles, with reeds separating each layer. This latter device ensured that water evenly could penetrate every piece of cloth. Only fabrics of one and the same colour were treated together. ... As the next step, the kettle that previously had been set over a ditch in which a fire could be lighted was filled with water that was then heated. At the end of the day, the fabrics were removed and the reeds pulled out.' Then all 70 pieces together were placed under a press, and the water was allowed to run off. The fabric in question must have been delicate, or else so many layers of textile could never have been treated together. After separation, each individual length of *sof* was folded lengthwise and placed under another press, this time every piece by itself. Dernschwam thought that the presses were not at all well constructed and could have been worked with much less manpower if the technology had been more sophisticated. As it was, seven men were employed in the operation of a single press. This sequence of treatments gave the finished fabrics their silky 'watered' appearance.[15]

Given the scarcity of information on technological processes, we are lucky to possess at least this much information on the treatment of mohair. Washers, weavers, dyers and workers at the presses, who may or may not have formed separate guilds, passed fibre, yarn and cloth to one another, closely cooperating in the manufacture of a valuable product.[16] Unfortunately the relationship between merchants and manufacturers continues to be rather opaque. That Ankara was an important trading centre is apparent from the sizeable number of structures in which business could be conducted (khan), and we have already noted the role of merchants in organizing the spinning of mohair yarn.[17] It would also be of interest to know which Ottoman customers were in the market for fine mohair cloth. At the present stage, we only know that in the mid-1500s this textile was fashionable at the sultan's court because Sultan Süleyman, when he became more pious in old age, preferred this elegant fabric to silk, which Islamic law does not allow males to wear.

As we have seen, there also was a substantial export of mohair cloth to Venice and Poland, with traders from these two places making their way to Ankara in person.[18] Some of these foreigners lived in the city for several years, long enough for local tax farmers to try to collect dues from them as if they were non-Muslim subjects of the sultan.[19] With the help of the ambassador of the Serenissima in Istanbul, however, in 1612 the Venetian merchants were able to avoid payment of these taxes. Another indication of long-term residence dates from the same year, when Venetian merchants were granted permission to live within the citadel walls for greater security; after all, the military rebels who had plundered Ankara just a short while earlier had made off with the trade goods stored outside the citadel walls.[20] But in addition there were Ottoman merchants, Muslims, Jews and Christians who travelled to Venice to market angora fabrics. Members of different religions might associate while on the road: at one point a Muslim Ottoman, probably closely connected to Ankara, needed to provide witnesses to the fact that he had been robbed by pirates in the Adriatic; he gave the names of several Armenians who by the time of writing had already returned to Istanbul.[21] Jewish traders, with one foot in the sultan's capital and the other in Venice, often mediated between Ottomans and Venetians.[22]

On the traders who especially between 1550 and 1650 imported large quantities of Middle Eastern fabrics including mohair cloth into Poland, some information is available in the registers of the Ankara judges, but more is found in Polish sources. Here too, both Ottoman and Polish subjects were involved. Muslims not only provided credit to merchants involved in the trade, but some of them even visited Poland themselves. Frequent references to Ankara traders underline the special role of mohair cloth in the Polish market.[23] Demand came mainly from the male members of the nobility and gentry, for while women dressed in the 'normal' clothes of central Europe, these men asserted what was called a 'Sarmatian' identity, and for this purpose used clothes and arms in the 'Turkish' style. Ottoman currency typically was used in these transactions, but bills of exchange were also current; the latter were cashed not only in trade fairs on Polish territory but also in Istanbul and Edirne. Thus for over a century the Polish demand for mohair cloth contributed towards the prosperity of craft production in Ankara and in a broader perspective to a closer link between the Ottoman and Polish business worlds.

Rural carpet producers and their market connections

Certain villagers of the Uşak region – and more generally of western Anatolia – from the mid-1600s onwards apparently found a commercial outlet knotting carpets for sale; the newly emerging port city of Izmir must have favoured the emergence of this manufacture. No evidence has been found to date on the organization of production, and the form and extent of merchant involvement also remains enigmatic. As far as is currently known, the earliest visitor to Uşak who wrote about his experience was Evliya Çelebi, who arrived in the 1670s when the town was at the height of its fame as a manufacturing centre. This indefatigable traveller informed us that the villagers of Boyalı, not far from the town, harvested a root crop from which the red dye for Uşak carpets was manufactured. He must have been thinking of madder, and the cultivation of this plant evidently was a rural activity in the service of an – at least partly – urban industry. As to the town itself, the traveller found it small but quite lively. Traffic jams were by no means a rarity, owing to the carts that carried in wool and dyestuffs and took out the famed carpets, which were sought after by both Muslims and non-Muslims. Evliya distinguished between carpets for domestic use and others intended for mosques. But when describing the Armenian monastery of Jerusalem, which he visited a few months later, the traveller mentioned the fine Uşak carpet owned by this institution. Thus he knew very well that Christian churches might also possess them.[24]

However, in the inventories of servitors of the sultans who died in Edirne between the mid-sixteenth and the mid-seventeenth centuries, of which almost 100 have been published, Uşak carpets unambiguously were encountered only in a single document. Perhaps these large pieces were too expensive even for better-placed households. Possibly the cost of overland transportation to Edirne played a role as well, for the price regulations of 1640 concerning the capital city do contain prices for a variety of Uşak carpets; but then Istanbul was readily accessible by sea.[25] Moreover numerous Uşak carpets were exported and today are found in European museums; we may conclude that once again a partly rural industry centred upon a small town marketed its products over long distances.

As to the rug dealers themselves, the scanty evidence we possess concerns merchants who brought carpets into the Transylvanian towns of Sibiu/Hermannstadt and Brašov/Kronstadt. The customs registers of these two places go back to the fifteenth century and show that carpets were already being imported into the principality before 1526, when the area was still part of the kingdom of Hungary. Moreover the trade continued in later years, when the two towns were subject to the princes of Transylvania, who in turn were subordinate to the Ottoman sultans. After 1526 these carpet exports thus formed part of the Ottoman Empire's inter-regional trade. In the sixteenth and early seventeenth centuries the rug dealers all came from Sibiu/Hermannstadt and Brašov/Kronstadt, and not at all from the producing regions. Thus they probably did not have much of an impact on the organization of carpet manufacturing in far-off Anatolia. After the country had passed under Habsburg control in 1699, Ottoman trade with Transylvania came to be dominated by a so-called Greek company of merchants which in reality also included Armenians and other non-Muslim subjects of the sultans.[26] In this later case as well, no evidence survives concerning the role of traders in the manufacturing process; we do not know with whom orders were placed or who paid for the raw materials.

Some of the rugs and carpets from Ottoman Anatolia were apparently manufactured in sophisticated urban workshops. But carpet experts assume that many of the smallish pieces imported by the nobles and burghers of Transylvania between the late 1400s and the 1700s and sometimes later given away, mainly to Lutheran churches, were indeed of village manufacture.[27] However, some of them were inspired by the designs of sophisticated Bursa workshops, and most importantly for us some of them bear dedicatory inscriptions containing dates.[28] These inscriptions were always added at a later time; nonetheless some go back to our period, in other words to the pre-1670s. They not only give us a *terminus ante quem* for manufacture but also indicate the owners who dedicated the pieces in question to their local churches. Quite often these donors were corporate bodies, namely guilds of the central European variety, which continued to exist in Transylvanian towns throughout the Ottoman period.

Thus we can assume that the customs regulations of the Thessalian fair of Maşkolur (1569) that mention Anatolian rugs and carpets arriving by the cartloads, or else on the backs of horses and camels, were concerned at least in part with the products of rural craftspeople marketed throughout southeastern Europe, including the towns of distant Transylvania.[29] In addition the regulations also contained a brief reference to carpets from the Balkans (Rumeli). But these latter items were brought to market on the backs of porters and thus the quantities involved must have been smaller. This observation is consonant with the assumption of today's experts that the vast majority of the pieces preserved in Transylvania are of Anatolian manufacture.[30] For the export of carpets yet further afield, we have the evidence of numerous fifteenth-, sixteenth- and seventeenth-century European painters, from Flanders, Italy and later the northern Netherlands, in whose pictures Anatolian carpets feature prominently.[31] But in these cases usually even less is known about the traders that brought the carpets to the lands of Latin Christendom; as for the producers and the organization of their labour, we are completely in the dark.

A very special case: weavers, manufacturers and merchants of Bursa silks

Ankara's and Uşak's textile producers, both men and women, were free subjects of the sultan, and this was the norm throughout the empire. During the later fifteenth and throughout the sixteenth century, the silk-weaving crafts of Bursa, however, were exceptional, for they employed a sizeable number of slaves. At this time, Bursa silks were an object of high luxury mainly used in the Ottoman palace, and the raw silk needed for this manufacture was imported by caravan all the way from Iran.[32]

We may assume that in this courtly manufacture, 'money was no object', and thus at least part of the labour force was recruited in a remarkably cost-intensive manner. Slaves brought in from the war zones, first from the Balkans and later from Hungary and the non-Muslim territories to the north of the Black Sea, were often trained to weave silk cloth. From the manufacturer's viewpoint this arrangement led to considerable waste, for the slave had to be fed, allowed to get over the shock of finding himself/herself in a completely foreign environment and learn enough Turkish to be taught a skilled craft. Many slaves probably failed to acquire the necessary skills, or else they might fall ill and die before they came to be of any use to their masters.

But if a skilled weaver did emerge, many owners after a certain time entered into contracts with such persons, promising that the man or woman in question would receive his/her freedom after weaving a specified amount of cloth.[33] These agreements bound both sides: once the master had committed himself in this fashion, he could not go back unilaterally on his word. On the other hand, sometimes a slave was unable to fulfil his/her side of the bargain and thus sank back into unconditional slavery. As manumission after about ten years was common, the relationships observed in the Bursa silk industry can be classed somewhere between indentured labour and 'ordinary' slavery.[34]

This mode of recruitment was only feasible when slaves were abundant, as was the case during the wars of the sixteenth century. Profit margins also needed to remain high enough to offset the inevitable losses. But it has been demonstrated that by the later 1500s these margins were shrinking because increasing European demand for raw silk drove up prices. At the same time, political pressures exerted by the Ottoman upper class and also the availability of cheaper substitutes for silk made it difficult for manufacturers to increase the prices of their goods in proportion.[35] Difficulties were exacerbated by frequent Ottoman–Iranian wars that took place mainly in western Iran and must have disrupted production, while the mercenary uprisings that plagued Anatolia in the later 1500s and early 1600s impeded the manufacture and distribution of silk cloth. Taken together all these difficulties caused a major industrial crisis.

However, after this serious but temporary downturn, Bursa silks recovered by means of a gradual but thorough reorientation. A careful monograph on Bursa's seventeenth-century industries has shown that in the long run local silk manufactures showed considerable staying power.[36] Recovery was facilitated by the fact that raw silk was now also produced locally and dependency on risky importations lessened. In addition during the seventeenth century the availability of raw silk from Italy, and later from India and China, lowered demand for Iranian silks among European buyers.[37] Bursa producers also targeted a different market, as they partly abandoned the heavy fabrics accessible only to the Ottoman court. At least by the early 1700s this reorientation towards commercial production became apparent from the many silk fabrics now found in the possession of people who were but moderately wealthy, yet the groundwork for this later prosperity already was laid before 1670. Cushion covers were favoured by customers of moderate wealth; they typically were manufactured in pairs, with elaborate designs in cut velvet, usually in red and white. While art historians have tended to look down on these products as inferior in quality, from the economic point of view this changeover was a boon: manufacturers had managed to reorient production and expand their markets, thus preventing the demise of the Bursa industry. (See illustration on p 98.)

Another significant market for Bursa silks was the Orthodox Church. Whether the appearance of bishops and abbots commissioning such textiles really was a novelty in the late 1500s and early 1600s is impossible to say, as older examples simply may have failed to survive. Be that as it may, by about 1600 wealthy people donated fabrics or even ready-made clothing to churches for use as ecclesiastical vestments. Sometimes the date of donation and the name of the donor were embroidered on the textiles in question, giving us a *terminus ante quem* for manufacture. Once again this peculiarity is a great help because the number of precisely dated silk fabrics is otherwise quite limited. Even more interestingly from the years before and after 1600 we also have evidence of direct commissions for ecclesiastical use; these can be distinguished from donations of pre-existing pieces because the designs, for instance Mary and the infant Jesus, were woven into rather than embroidered upon the fabric. Such items might be intended for churches in the Ottoman lands, but also went out as gifts to the tsar, who was honoured by Orthodox churchmen as the one and only independent dynast belonging to their faith.[38] (See illustration on p 99.)

Reorientation towards non-courtly customers was, however, only part of the story. Most importantly, as the Bursa population had greatly increased during the sixteenth century, manufacturers now turned to poor free men and women for their labour force.[39] This move must have saved them a lot of money. For even though the prices of slaves dropped radically after successful Ottoman campaigns, by the time these men and women arrived in Bursa, janissaries and other slave traders had probably increased prices considerably in consideration of travel expenses and upkeep. Furthermore when employing free labourers the costs of raising children until they were ready for the workshop fell on the parents and not on the manufacturers. Last but not least, youngsters who had grown up in the city and continued to be helped by their families must have avoided the disorientation probably not rare among slaves suddenly thrust into a strange environment. In all probability there were thus fewer failures in the training process, and with labour and raw material costs radically diminished, the silk manufacturers and their weavers were able to survive.

İznik and Kütahya faiences: manufacture and distribution

Most visitors to Istanbul remember the great tile panels embellished with calligraphy and floral decoration that ornament certain rooms of the sultans' palace and also some major mosques. Because of their cost, such panels could only be sponsored by members of the ruling group. More affordable were the numerous bowls, plates, small decorative items and even coffee cups made in the western Anatolian towns of İznik and Kütahya; moreover these items came in varying qualities and price ranges. From the 1500s onwards, such

These two cushion covers date from before 1691, when they were first described in the inventory of the 'Türckische Kammer' of the Dukes of Baden. When acquired by non-Ottoman collectors/users, covers of this type were often refashioned; in particular the backings were changed so that only traces of the originals now remain. (In the Badisches Landesmuseum, Schloss Karlsruhe, published in Ernst Petrasch, Reinhard Sänger et al, *Die Karlsruher Türkenbeute, die 'Türckische Kammer' des Markgrafen Ludwig Wilhelm von Baden-Baden, Die 'Türckischen Curiositäeten' der Markgrafen von Baden-Durlach* (Munich: Hirmer Verlag, 1991), pp 328–9, nos. 287, 288)

Cope used by an Orthodox priest, seventeenth century. The silk is Ottoman. (C Abegg-Stiftung, CH-3132 Riggisberg, 2000 (Photograph: Christoph von Virág), inventory no. 57. Courtesy of the Abegg-Stiftung)

pieces were made for private customers as well, and there survives a sultanic command in which the ruler expressed his dissatisfaction that local potters neglected official commissions in favour of – doubtless more remunerative – production for the market.[40] Albeit in broken condition these pieces of faience have quite often survived in the ground, and particularly Hungarian archaeologists have used them in order to gauge the extent to which Ottoman-style luxury products were acquired by the officers and administrators of the border province of Buda.[41]

Ottoman sources do not provide much evidence concerning the manufacture and commerce of İznik and Kütahya faiences. Even Evliya Çelebi has little to say on the issue. Yet his description of the latter town is otherwise quite detailed, as it was his family home and the author himself administered a local mosque once founded by an ancestor. About faiences produced in Kütahya, however, he merely penned some general phrases implying that he knew very little about them. Perhaps this scant regard was due to the fact that Evliya, with his courtly background, held Chinese porcelain in much higher esteem than local faiences.[42] Likewise he devoted only a brief remark to the potteries of İznik. Admittedly by the time of Evliya's visit in the early 1670s, the days in which faience manufacture had flourished in this town had long since receded into the past.[43]

As to the producers, the names of a few master craftsmen, all of them Muslim, survive in official correspondence. As İznik was a small town of 2,000–3,000 inhabitants, we can assume that in the most flourishing period of faience-making during the second half of the sixteenth century, a significant proportion of local residents made their living as manufacturers of fritware. Yet as with the glassblowers of Venetian Murano, the İznik potters did not much profit from the high price and reputation of their product. According to visitors the town apparently was a run-down place. In contrast to the 1300s and 1400s, few sultans or viziers of the sixteenth and seventeenth centuries saw fit to establish pious foundations and thereby improve living conditions for İznik craftsmen.[44]

We do not know for sure whether the potters of İznik ever formed a guild. According to an official Istanbul price register from 1599–1600, the makers/sellers of such goods did possess a guild organization, complete with a *kethüda* who could fix a price for the rarer varieties.[45] However, it remains unknown whether this guild was based at the production site or in the capital itself. It has been assumed that all faiences mentioned in the 1640 price register and for which no origin is specified came from İznik.[46] Yet as the scribes preparing these lists were anything but systematic, we have no way of being sure. We may just as well assume that some of the faiences of unknown origin came from Kütahya instead.

If the reference to the *kethüda* in the Istanbul price list refers to a man positioned in the capital, the manufacture of good-quality items in this locality must have been quite common. Unfortunately no further details are known. Yet by the late 1500s, the manufacturers of faience in İznik did possess an organization of some kind, headed by a 'chief faience provider' (*kâşicibaşı*).[47] As this man was in charge of distributing raw materials to artisans, and this responsibility was typical of guild headmen, it is reasonable to postulate the existence of a guild of faience-makers in İznik. Admittedly it functioned under the supervision of an official in charge of supplying the palace, for that was the role of the *kâşicibaşı*. Yet the subordination of guildsmen to palace officials was not rare, especially if the former supplied goods deemed essential by the Ottoman government (compare Chapter 4). There were also traders bringing İznik wares into Istanbul, and even the palace used their services on occasion.[48] Moreover the wealthiest among the Istanbul faience-sellers may have been wholesale merchants. But once again this is mere guesswork.

Other merchants transported İznik-ware to Ottoman provinces. As we have seen, archaeological investigations in Hungary have turned up a quantity of such potsherds but not as many as one might have hoped for. Probably most of the soldiers were Bosnians and thus unfamiliar with Istanbul-style luxuries, which most of them could not have afforded anyway. Given the fragility of faience, breakage must have been frequent and retail prices in Hungary much higher than in Istanbul. But even so, some examples of İznik-ware reached the royal residences of Buda and Visegrád even before the final Ottoman conquest, especially during the years after 1526, when John Szapolyai was king under Ottoman suzerainty.[49] Some wealthy Ottoman officeholders also bought İznik-ware. This was true, for instance, of a financial official stationed in Buda by the name of Ali Çelebi, who died in 1587; he possessed a large bowl of İznik faience and several smaller pieces as well.[50] But since he also owned a number of cups and bowls of Chinese porcelain, to say nothing of a substantial library, it is probably correct to regard him as somewhat atypical.

It was easier to find İznik-ware in Edirne; after all, the sultans regularly visited their former capital on account of the nearby hunting grounds, so that at least seasonally, sellers of luxury goods must have found customers. Among the close to 100 persons deceased in Edirne before and after 1600 whose estate inventories have been published, 21 possessed 274 dishes. Given the prices on record, İznik-ware certainly was something for the better off, although at ten to 15 times the price of faience, Chinese porcelain was the 'real' luxury.[51] Most of the sultan's servitors who died in Edirne did not own costly dishes of any kind, and those who did normally possessed a few pieces. Probably these items were acquired more for display than for use, like the fancy cups and dishes found in many homes today.

Faiences produced in Kütahya seem to have been less precious than those made in İznik; but perhaps because the industry was less subject to the vagaries of the luxury market, it lasted much longer. Kütahya-ware was renowned mainly in the 1700s, but its existence is documented from the early sixteenth century onwards: there survives a water bottle bearing the date of 1529, with an Armenian inscription to the effect that it was made in Kütahya for a bishop residing in Ankara.[52] Moreover this piece conveniently demonstrates that Kütahya-ware was not a product of merely local fame: for apart from having been ordered by a personage residing over a hundred kilometres away, the bottle, in damaged condition, was found on an excavation site in downtown Istanbul. How it got there and through whose hands it passed on the way remains unknown.

Textile manufacture in Egypt and Syria

Both Egypt and Syria had a long manufacturing tradition, and archaeological sites from the Cairo region have provided us with numerous fragments of medieval textiles. However, while we possess a study concerning the Cairo building industry of the 1500s and early 1600s (see Chapter 4), no comparable work on textiles is available.

However, as so often, Evliya Çelebi gives us a glimpse into the local craft world, in this case the manufacture of silks, cottons and linens. Evliya recorded the names of the principal Cairo guilds, with special reference to the dyers who plied their trade in state-owned dye-houses, and among other things produced the black cover of the Ka'ba that was carried to Mecca every year (see Chapter 4). By contrast members of the guild of cotton-printers worked in their own shops. Apart from the artisans who made/sold cloth (*bezzaz*) our author has mentioned the manufacturers of a fabric called *alaca arab kerekesi*; while *alaca* is a common term for striped cloth or mixtures of silk and cotton, the term *arab* may mean that these goods were favoured by Bedouins. They must have sold quite well, as supposedly there were 1,800 artisans who produced this fabric in 200 shops. As to the weavers/sellers of atlas and velvet, Evliya gave their number as 600.[53]

This same traveller's description of Syria in general and Damascus in particular also has some information, tantalizingly brief though it may be, on the manufacture of textiles. A stay-over in Damascus (1648–49) apparently was so short that Evliya did not have much opportunity to describe the city, but on this occasion he did relay bits of information about the textile crafts of Ḥamā and Ḥımıs (Khums). In both places cotton was woven, and in Ḥamā also some silk.[54] Evliya considered noteworthy certain fabrics in white and black, including bath towels, sheets and aprons. In Ḥamā the women wore white veils, which may have been of local make; male clothing by contrast was described as 'colourful' (*elvan*). Over 20 years later in 1671–72 Evliya was finally able to provide a full description of Damascus, and when discussing the most remarkable products of this city he gave pride of place to silk and cotton fabrics.[55] *Dârâya* (in French, *doréas*) could be of cotton, silk or a mixture of both, *alaca* was also such a mixture or else ornamented with stripes, while *helâlî* was always a mixture of the two fibres, with the cotton underside touching the skin of the wearer.[56] A colourful cloth known as *muhattam* was ornamented with white figures, or else chequered.[57] Horse blankets embroidered with gold thread were a speciality of Damascus; trade was lively and the city full of people ready to spend their money. Unfortunately Evliya had nothing to say on the craftspeople that produced these marvels.

Validity and limits of the 'command economy' model

The present overview has shown that even before certain sections of the Ottoman upper class showed an increasing interest in consumer goods, a phenomenon which recent research has placed in the early eighteenth century, textiles were traded on an inter-regional basis, and the same thing applied to a limited range of other goods as well.[58] To put it differently, not all such items either went to the governing class in Istanbul or else were exported, although the consumption of the Ottoman capital was high. To some extent at least, the small amount of evidence on provincial trade has skewed our perceptions.

While the 'command economy' directed by the Ottoman central government mobilized an impressive amount of resources, artisans also worked for private customers with money to spend. Consumption by subjects of the sultans, moreover, ensured the prosperity of provincial traders. Unfortunately Nelly Hanna's detailed study of an opulent merchant of Cairo active around 1600 is likely to remain unique owing to the gaps in our sources. Yet we have seen that some Transylvanian notables and even craft guilds had enough money to buy Anatolian carpets.[59] The demand of an outlying principality on the margins of the empire induced traders to travel the enormous distance from Sibiu/Hermannstadt and Brašov/Kronstadt to Uşak and other towns of western Anatolia. Another case in point involves the merchant-manufacturers of Tunis, who with imported Spanish wool produced fezzes probably at first for Tripolis (Trablusgarb) and Alexandria and later on for the Ottoman capital as well. We also have evidence for the purchase of Damascus fabrics, whose reputation spread far beyond Syria, by merchants from the Bursa region.[60] As for the Orthodox bishops and congregations of middle-level Anatolian towns, some of them placed orders in Bursa or Istanbul in order to decorate their churches. Therefore the claim that Ottoman artisans all had extremely narrow horizons and cared only about the constraints of the local market must be taken as a rule to which there were quite a few exceptions. As we shall presently see, these exceptions were to become more frequent, or in any case better documented, during the 1700s.

Pulling the threads together: crafts and craftspeople before about 1670

Before embarking on the period after about 1670, it is convenient to sum up the results obtained so far. On the whole, guilds seem to have emerged fairly late: at the earliest stage, which in the largest cities corresponds to the beginning of the 1500s, the only organization on record was a group of senior masters capable of explaining the rules and traditions of their crafts to Ottoman officeholders and at the same time of defending the interests of their fellow artisans in court. Presumably guilds acquired a more formal organization but gradually, in the course of the sixteenth century, and this process was faster in large cities than in smaller places.

Yet this statement is only a plausible hypothesis, and the process by which guilds emerged remains enigmatic. Maybe there were different paths leading to fully fledged guilds: our evidence does not tell us. There must have been connections of one sort or another with the *ahis* of late medieval Anatolia: ceremonies and moral precepts were probably adopted although we cannot tell whether many *ahis* ever got involved with the marketplace. The tanners seem to have been one of few crafts whose links to what remained of the *ahis*, in this case the lodge of Ahi Evren of Kırşehir, continued through the centuries. We are left to wonder whether this connection, which in a different manner also apparently existed in Çankırı, was a relic of networks that had been more widespread in earlier periods, or whether the story of the tanners – and that of a few other crafts – was exceptional from beginning to end.

At least as problematic is the manner in which guild organization spread in the Arab provinces where, so medievalists tell us, they had been unknown under Ayyubid and Mamluk rule. There does not seem to have been any sultanic commandment that ordered the establishment of guilds in the newly conquered territories. But as in Cairo these organizations were flourishing by the 1670s, local artisans must have found it advantageous to cooperate more intensively by forming guilds and by proposing to the authorities the names of people who might act as their sheikhs. We are left to wonder whether this formalization of craft solidarities was a response to the relatively high degree of centralization, early modern style, that characterized the Ottoman regime. In any case, the guilds of Bursa and Istanbul were quite informal: artisans apparently entered and left, and paying one's taxes with a given guild was the principal membership criterion.

Organization, however, was but a means to an end: more important was the struggle for daily subsistence. Most craftspeople had trouble making ends meet, as is evident from the official rule that profit margins should be no more than 10 per cent, and 20 in exceptional cases.[61] Given the taxes owed to the state and, in addition, more or less irregular demands from local officials, such low profit margins must have made it impossible for most of these craftspeople to invest in tools and workshops. Observations of this kind were already made by Halil Inalcik almost 40 years ago when he noted that investment was the weakest element in the Ottoman economic system; and Mehmet Genç has recently made this point with even more emphasis.[62]

To compensate, artisans probably honed their manual skills and employed more manpower than would have been necessary had their tools been better; in this manner they often produced high-quality goods with minimal investment in technology. Bursa apart, our records do not often tell us much about women's work.[63] But at least in the textile crafts, the 'invisible' labour of females must also have contributed quite substantially to the support of their families and thus helped compensate for low profit margins. Dernschwam's anti-Ottoman prejudices are obvious and his entire account accordingly must be read with great caution; yet his remarks about skills and tools fit well enough into a broader pattern and should therefore be taken seriously.[64]

At the same time, building workers in Istanbul were paid a wage in the same order of magnitude as that received by their colleagues in Europe, especially if we disregard the 'high earners' of Amsterdam, Antwerp and London. Admittedly in comparison with even less commercially active European towns, Istanbul wages tended to be 'at the lower margin'. On the other hand our documentation is highly selective, and recorded wages in the Ottoman capital presumably were kept down by political as well as by economic factors. Most of the surviving data come from governmental construction sites, or else concern the mosques and other structures that were part of pious foundations sponsored by sultans and viziers. Such people and institutions benefited from prices significantly lower than those paid in the open market, and thus Istanbul construction workers, when in the pay of 'ordinary' customers, may well have been better situated on the comparative wage scale than appears from the documented figures alone.[65] Depending on the amount of work available on buildings belonging to privately sponsored pious foundations, or, in the case of artisans working in wood, on private housing as well, some construction workers may have earned significantly more than meets the eye. We thus can surmise that in spite of the command economy that dominated a large share of the construction sector, building artisans often earned wages not too much lower than those they might have made on the open market. But to what extent earnings in the building sector are comparable to those made by other craftspeople remains unknown.

Not all artisans were male, town-dwelling guild members who sold directly to their customers. Slave labour in crafts was rare, but in the exceptional case of the Bursa silk industry some slaves were employed until the later 1500s. Especially in the textile sector urban women, but also those living in villages not too remote from the city, were often involved in manufacture, although their share is impossible to quantify. Rural craftspeople in most cases were not organized in guilds, and traders must have arranged for the distribution of raw materials and particularly for the marketing of the finished product. Given the low cost of implements, most urban and rural artisans owned their tools and did not need to rent them from traders.

Little is known about the backgrounds of merchants; in some instances they may originally have been artisans who branched out into trade because they had inherited a sum of money or were able to borrow from friends and relatives. These men organized the rural hinterlands of some of the more important towns, tying the livelihoods of villagers to the markets of Ankara, Tunis, Aleppo or Istanbul. In some cases, their connections might reach all the way to Sibiu/Hermannstadt, Brašov/Kronstadt or even Poland and Venice.

Thus we should rid ourselves of the assumption that only the direct producers in addition to European traders had a role to play in the commercialization of Ottoman manufactured goods. First of all, research undertaken during the last 30 years or so has shown that the Ottoman domestic market, in spite of its limitations, was more receptive to local goods than had previously been believed. Secondly, Ottoman subjects, both Muslim and non-Muslim, played an active role in the exportation of goods to Venice, Amsterdam, Lwiw and other places. Lastly and most importantly, the guilds were less constraining than had previously been assumed, and at least in certain places merchants were able to organize urban–rural production circuits that made available manufactured goods suitable for inter-regional trade.

Pulling the threads together: between guild autonomy and state intervention

Our account so far has moved back and forth: two chapters highlighting artisan organizations as they tried to further the interests of their members (Chapters 2 and 4) alternate with two others discussing the interaction of craftspeople with the outside world. In Chapter 3 we have focused on artisan–state relations, while Chapter 5 has dealt with the distribution of goods manufactured by provincial artisans, in other words with the linkages between merchants and manufacturers. For this specific purpose, studying goods produced in the provinces is more instructive than focusing on Istanbul, because so many goods made in the capital were consumed on the spot: artisans must have had much direct contact with the ultimate consumers, and the mediation of merchants was less necessary than elsewhere.

As to guild autonomy, it has been suggested that, on the one hand, both Cairo and Istanbul artisans ran their everyday affairs without too much government intervention. Yet on the other hand, artisan organizations attempted to manipulate officials to gain advantages for their members.[66] This point has been made with respect to the late 1700s and early 1800s, but *mutatis mutandis* it seems valid for 'our' period as well. Therefore we can conclude that the craftsmen's attitude *vis à vis* the state was necessarily ambiguous. After all, the notion of autonomy involves the creation of a sphere which remained, to a certain extent, closed to the intervention of Ottoman officeholders. But at the same time, the state could only be mobilized and manipulated if qadis and market supervisors got involved in disputes between guilds, and sometimes even intervened when there were tensions between members of one and the same artisan organization. Guild wardens might welcome state intervention at certain times and try to minimize it at others, depending on the interests of their 'constituents', the guild masters. Or else, especially if the situation was somewhat unsettled, these two aims could well be pursued concurrently.

These considerations bring us back to the main point of our study, namely the two facets characteristic of guild life. Ottoman artisans did not often state explicitly that outside interference was to be avoided where possible; but actions sometimes speak louder than words. On the other hand, state intervention particularly by the qadis was considered desirable when problems arose that the guildsmen felt unable to handle on their own.

At the same time, the Ottoman sultans asserted their power not only through judges and market supervisors but also through taxation and their capacity to command novel modes of tax collection. In consequence the balance between artisan autonomy and state intervention was not stable, but subject to frequent changes induced by the overall political situation and the manner in which the governing elite tried to cope with recurrent crises. How this balance was maintained, and how it changed or at times even disappeared will occupy us in the second section of our study.

CHAPTER 6

Changes in Istanbul Guilds

The capital's supply system under strain

Istanbul was a city of several hundred thousand inhabitants, and, like other rulers of the early modern period concerned with populations of this size, Ottoman sultans and viziers did not rely exclusively on the market for the capital's provisioning. After all, scarcities – and the food riots that they might cause – so close to the seat of power endangered the political and also often the physical lives of sultans and viziers. As a result, supplies of wheat, barley, raisins and other foodstuffs, as well as essential raw materials, were brought into the city under state supervision and sold at administratively controlled prices (*narh*). In the Middle Ages quite a few Islamic scholars had proclaimed that prices came about by God's will and human beings should avoid interfering with them. But among members of the Ottoman ruling group this opinion was held only by a small minority. Generally speaking rulers and viziers were considered responsible for setting the prices for necessities and enforcing them to the best of their abilities.[1]

Certain sections of the empire easily accessible from the sea had a special status: in these provinces, whatever agricultural products the local population did not need for sowing or home consumption were earmarked for the capital. Istanbul's wheat supplies mainly came from the eastern Balkans: a sizeable share was grown in the region around Salonika, and the same thing applied to the coastlands of today's Bulgaria and Romania.[2] Some of the large landholdings (*çiftliks*) emerging in this region during the 1700s may also have contributed to Istanbul's food supply. After all, grain export to Europe from the Black Sea region was not feasible before the Treaty of Küçük Kaynarca (1774), yet many local *çiftliks* were far older.[3] Throughout the Balkans people of some wealth were required to bring in sheep, the principal source of meat, and sell them to the butchers of Istanbul at controlled prices.[4] From north of the Black Sea came the hides which Istanbul's tanners used for the manufacture of multi-coloured leather, and which also served as the main raw material for the saddlers.[5] Egypt was also integrated into the supply system of Istanbul: rice, linen, linseed oil, some sugar and the fine mats covering the floors of many mosques all figured among the goods sold to the capital.

For its smooth operation this supply system presupposed central control not only over the provinces concerned but also over the eastern Mediterranean and Black Sea shipping routes. Between the early sixteenth and the late eighteenth century the Black Sea, as an Ottoman lake, was more or less closed to foreign ships, with the exception of occasional Venetians or Genoese granted special permits to purchase sturgeon.[6] As for the eastern Mediterranean, the situation was more complicated. Although this maritime space was bordered exclusively by Ottoman territories, the sea was not usually under the exclusive control of the sultan's navy. Both Christian and Muslim corsairs and pirates operated in the Aegean: the Maltese and North Africans 'specialized' in this business, but 'legitimate' seamen from Venice, England and France might also engage in piracy on occasion.[7] Pirates based in the western coastlands of the Balkans were another source of trouble: these freebooters included the Christian Uskoks, loosely subordinate to the commanders of the Habsburg border defence, as well as their counterparts based in Ottoman territories.[8]

Most of the time the system functioned effectively enough – at least it thus appeared so from the Istanbul perspective. Where the producing regions were concerned, the low prices received for grain and other goods must have caused severe difficulties. Even 'regular' deliveries were not highly remunerated, to say nothing of that share of the harvest that was requisitioned for minute and well-nigh symbolic payments, and intended for the direct use of the state. Moreover collection was often less than orderly, and the men in charge might impose 'loans' at usurious rates of interest on hapless peasants. Throughout, Ottoman policies in favour of the military and bureaucratic apparatus, as well as the Istanbul consumer, must have discouraged agriculturalists from investing in their holdings and increasing production.[9] Structural problems were thus a major long-term cause of scarcities of grain.

Yet the system only broke down completely when military conflict interrupted the flow of deliveries: the last quarter of the eighteenth century and the beginning of the nineteenth were among the worst years for the capital's inhabitants. Most of the disruption was political in origin, although inclement weather had an occasional part to play. Russian occupation of Moldavia and Walachia meant that one of the main sources of grain became unavailable: the first invasion occurred in 1711 and there was a repeat performance in 1736–39. A much longer crisis began with the Russo-Ottoman war of 1768–74, when the Bulgarian countryside close to the Black Sea, an alternative source of supplies, was crossed and re-crossed not only by regular Ottoman armies but also by deserters and bandits. Moreover after the peace, the Ottomans no longer possessed a monopoly of Balkan grain supplies, the tsars had acquired a right to interfere in the affairs of Moldavia and Walachia and, worst of all, from now on wars with Russia became extremely frequent (1787–92, 1806–12, 1828–29, with the Russian occupation continuing until 1834, and once again in 1853–56). In addition Moldavia and Walachia were one of the focuses of the Greek uprising of 1821 and the theatre of an anti-Russian rebellion, suppressed by the Ottomans themselves, in 1848.[10] These two principalities therefore were devastated and/or outside of Ottoman control for considerable periods of time.

Supplies from Egypt also ceased to arrive in certain years: this occurred for the first time when the duumvirs Murād Bey and İbrāhīm Bey stopped paying tribute to Istanbul after 1775. The Ottoman re-occupation by the grand admiral Cezayirli Hasan Paşa (1786) did not remedy the situation for any length of time. From 1798 to 1801 Egypt was occupied by Napoleon's armies and several years passed before Mehmed Ali Paşa re-conquered the country in the name of the Ottomans. Once in power, the new governor certainly fostered the exportation of grain and cotton to finance his ambitious industrialization drives and numerous military campaigns. But by the 1830s, Mehmed Ali Paşa was at war with Mahmud II (r. 1808–39). Thus political conflict prevented the inhabitants of the Ottoman capital from receiving Egyptian grain; furthermore higher prices in European markets probably were more attractive to Mehmed Ali Paşa.

On the other hand, supplies in sufficient quantity could not be obtained from Anatolia before the construction of railways in the last quarter of the nineteenth century. Therefore in war years, supplies for Istanbul, such as they were, came largely from south of the Danube. These sources, however, also were vulnerable when great magnates such as Tepedelenli Ali Paşa (c.1744–1822) were at war with the sultan, and this happened for instance in 1820–22. Furthermore, in wartime, Russian naval activity in the Black Sea must have made it difficult for supply ships to reach the Ottoman capital. It is thus not surprising that scarcities kept recurring during the reigns of Selim III (r. 1789–1807) and Mahmud II.

Supply problems affected the artisans of the capital in a variety of ways. First of all, they suffered directly when grain became scarce. In addition, when wheat was difficult to come by, customers must have spent a larger share of their income on food, so that less was available for the purchase of craft goods. Demand for non-food items therefore should have decreased even though the decline probably was not as dramatic as it would have been had market prices fully prevailed. Last but not least, many artisans depended on raw materials brought into the city from remote provinces. An interruption of supplies to the capital therefore not only meant that artisans went hungry but also that many of them lost their jobs.

Pricing, regulating and policing

Valued goods in short supply are often smuggled and/or adulterated, and the grain destined for Istanbul was no exception to this rule. To prevent smuggling, the Ottoman sultans instituted layers of bureaucracy: a limited number of wholesalers (*kapan tüccarı*) received certificates allowing them to buy specified quantities of grain from officially determined districts. From the mid-eighteenth century onwards many provinces were assigned quotas of grain to deliver. The merchants were responsible for loading wheat and barley onto ships and conveying it to a distribution centre on the Golden Horn known as Unkapanı (weighing scales for flour). As additional safeguards, local qadis needed to confirm that the Istanbul traders had in fact purchased the quantities to which they were entitled and nothing more. In areas located close to the open sea, however, grain smuggling was rife; it most visibly flourished between 1792 and 1815, when the wars following the French Revolution and particularly the Napoleonic conquest of Egypt increased grain prices to astronomical levels.[11]

Once wheat and barley had arrived in Istanbul, the qadi and his aides gathered information from traders and sea captains about harvest sizes in the regions of origin, weather conditions and ships lost at sea. On this basis, they calculated the selling prices of the different qualities of grain.[12] On the whole officially decreed prices probably were not too remote from what the market price would have been, once we take into account the special privileged conditions under which grain was made available in the capital. Had the opposite been true, there should have been many complaints about black marketeers. While, however, there were plenty of recriminations about underweight and poor-quality bread, we do not often hear that grain disappeared from the markets altogether and could only be purchased at prices much higher than the official ones. Thus a good deal of fact-finding and negotiating must have preceded the announcement of official grain prices.

Further regulations covered milling and baking. While in the countryside many people must have baked their own bread, the sultan's administration evidently assumed that in the capital many if not most families bought their bread from bakers. At least this view would explain why, officially speaking, bakeries almost always were attached to mills. Every mill was obliged to deliver flour to the bakery assigned to it, and to sell flour to persons/institutions preparing their own bread was but a secondary concern.[13] Owners of mills that had burned down or otherwise been destroyed needed to restore the facilities or else sell them; only by special permission could they use the land for other purposes.

Bakeries were licensed for specific products only: thus sweet breads (*çörek*), made of dough to which shortening had been added, could only be made by specialist craftsmen, and the same applied to the sesame rings (*simit*) popular in the eighteenth century just as they are today.[14] Attempts to limit the production of fine white bread (*francala*) often recurred, as this procedure involved discarding a significant share of the grain. During scarcities *francala* was prohibited altogether, or else it was the privilege of foreign embassies that often employed their own bakers.[15]

It was a major concern of the sultans' administration to inspect bakeries and ensure that they sold more or less standard-size loaves of standardized quality. These inspections, for which the market supervisor was responsible, were current already in Evliya Çelebi's time.[16] From the year 1720, probably in the context of the reforms following the Peace of Passarowitz (1718), there survives a record of a 'campaign' to eliminate fraud in bakeries.[17] Investigations were conducted on the basis of a comprehensive list of bakers both Muslim and Armenian. For reasons unspecified, the Greeks and Jews were missing; the latter possibly were not recorded because kosher baking increased costs and thus the regime of Jewish bakeries differed from that applying to all others.[18] Loaves were tested and those bakeries selling bread of less than the standard weight and a certain margin of toleration were confiscated and sold to new applicants; the investigation thus should have resulted in some gain to the treasury. In the late 1700s and early 1800s, moreover, the sovereign in person occupied himself with such inspections.[19] In several commands written in his own hand Selim III emphatically expressed his frustration at the poor quality of bread despite personal interventions on his part, and demanded that those responsible be punished forthwith. Such punishments did in fact occur; but as supplies so often were interrupted, presumably bakers had little alternative if they needed to supply a certain quantity of bread.

Immigration into Istanbul during a time of troubles

For the Ottoman administration, the most appropriate response to the capital's supply problems was to limit urban population, but this proved a veritable task of Sisyphus. For during most of its Ottoman history, the city had attracted migrants, sometimes from fairly remote places. Albanians (Arnavut) worked in the gardens just beyond the city walls. Most of them were poor people who never entered the written record, unless they happened to attract the attention of the qadis' scribes if found dead one morning by their neighbours, in which case it was necessary to issue an official protocol concerning the cause of death.[20] Maintaining the pavement of the Istanbul streets was also often an Albanian speciality: in twentieth-century Turkish, cobblestones were still called *arnavut kaldırımı*.[21] Others served as irregulars in the

Ottoman army arriving in Istanbul in the course of their military careers. Service as armed guards in the household of an important person was often undertaken by Albanian migrants as well.

Other immigrants came from beyond the empire's borders; thus jobless Dalmatians periodically left the Venetian domain and found employment as gardeners in and around Istanbul. When in the 1770s the Florentine scholarly traveller Domenico Sestini visited the gardens of Muslim and non-Muslim dignitaries along the Bosporus, he was surprised at being able to converse in – admittedly poor – Italian with some of the people working there.[22] Albanian and Dalmatian migrants often made a living on the fringes of the craft world: paving streets and gardening required artisan-type skills, but many of these migrants doubtless were ordinary casual labourers.

Migration was undertaken in groups, and often the migrants were expected to provide sureties (*kefil*) that would guarantee their appearance in court if demanded; sometimes this guarantee was furnished by their employers. Eventually some migrants formed separate guilds. Possibly some of the older men on retirement called on their sons or nephews to replace them; this arrangement may have prevailed among the general storekeepers doing business in the Eyüp area, many of whom came from a small town in today's central Greece. Such 'serial migrations' could continue over a century and more. Thus on Istanbul construction sites of the late sixteenth century, workmen from Kayseri sub-province (*sancak*) figured prominently, and in the mid-1700s there were still many migrants from this town living in Istanbul.

Given the numerous plague epidemics of the time, immigration into Istanbul mainly filled the gaps caused by recurrent mortalities. Reliable figures do not exist, but in 1778, for example, Istanbul suffered a serious bout of the plague in which 150,000–200,000 people supposedly died, and that in a city that according to the population count of 1844 contained about half a million inhabitants.[23] Even if the number of dead was somewhat exaggerated, and the total population of Istanbul by the mid-nineteenth century somewhat higher than the census indicates, these figures show the order of magnitude that plague-induced losses might reach. The latter were rendered more serious by the frequent recurrence of epidemics: in the 150 years between 1700 and 1850, 94 saw plague epidemics of varying severity. Thus for more than half of the time the inhabitants of Istanbul suffered from the plague, which, however, tended to abate during the winter. Apparently the disease arrived not from the outside but was endemic among the local rat population.[24]

Loss of life apart, business was disrupted when people attended the funerals of their friends and relatives or, even worse, fell ill themselves. Inheritance problems should have complicated matters even further, if a workshop or stock of raw materials fell vacant several times in succession. Deliveries of food and raw materials must often have been interrupted. While Muslims for the most part did not flee when contagion manifested itself, but continued their everyday lives as far as possible, Istanbul, Izmir or Salonika had substantial numbers of non-Muslim inhabitants, who did retreat to the suburbs or surrounding villages if at all possible.[25] Moreover Muslims were not encouraged to enter a region where the plague was raging if they were not already there: presumably certain traders who otherwise would have supplied the city avoided Istanbul as long as the epidemic continued.[26]

In consequence, the plague must have disrupted craft production. However, the sultans' administration was not, as far as we can tell, concerned about the discontinuance of essential services. Apparently the capital's limited food supply and the maintenance of public order were viewed as more immediate issues. Therefore the administration tried to counteract immigration, by increasing levels of control both on the roads and within the city proper. In Istanbul itself, controls were frequent in places where young men, after all the most likely candidates for migration, might find living space, such as communal residences for unmarried men (*bekâr odaları*) and also schools for religious law and theology (*medreses*). After all the living spaces provided for students by their colleges might also be utilized by others, especially when the students went home on leave.[27]

Other controls took place on access routes. Road blocks were often set up at which travellers had to state their business before they could proceed.[28] It even became difficult to exercise the traditional right of Ottoman subjects to present petitions to the sultan's council: at times it was forbidden to send more than one person, and doubtless many petitions did not make it to the capital. Even returning to Istanbul after an absence of a few weeks or months might present problems: people in this situation were sometimes required to present affidavits from their neighbours to the effect that they were bona fide residents of this or that town quarter. These measures were costly, mainly to the subjects themselves but also to the administration that had to pay officials and monitor their work; but limiting immigration into the capital visibly had high priority on the political agenda.

Attempts to police the capital and limit its population reached a high point in the late eighteenth and early nineteenth centuries, during the troubled reigns of Selim III and Mahmud II. From this period there survive accounts of house-to-house and shop-by-shop inspections covering large sections of the city; unfortunately the registers presently known are incomplete. Yet some unexpected and valuable information has emerged: thus around 1800 masters and/or employees commonly saved on housing and lived in their shops, while the older custom had been to keep home and business separate. Some government agents found this behaviour highly suspicious. The registers also show the great popularity of coffee houses that functioned as meeting places for much of the male population. Similarly officials were to determine who had 'responsible' guarantors and an assured clientele; whoever could not satisfy these criteria was to be sent back to his place of origin. Presumably in many cases the heads of guilds provided the necessary data, but little information is available on the negotiations that must have preceded the register entries.[29]

But these measures can only have been of limited effect, otherwise the political elite would soon have complained about labour shortages. Immigrants continued to arrive, and did not always consider it necessary to hide the fact that they had not been born in the Ottoman capital.[30] Apparently the administration de facto tolerated the immigration of organized groups in well-defined lines of work, whose headmen and guarantors were known to the authorities; to stabilize their position immigrants might form a separate guild. On the other hand, provincials 'on their own' who might end up joining the capital's marginal men were to be kept away as far as the practical means of the time permitted.[31]

Istanbul immigrant craftsmen around 1800

A recent study has shown how migrations and the authorities' attempts to channel them translated into 'realities on the ground'.[32] One of the registers prepared by order of Selim III around 1800 lists the business enterprises in two separate sectors of Istanbul, namely the Eyüp and Hasköy regions at the western end of the Golden Horn, in addition to the chain of suburbs and summer residences of the well to do that had formed on the western shore of the Bosporus. Among the 1,859 enterprises listed were 148 gardens and 214 coffee houses; no craft workshop or retailer's shop rivalled the latter in frequency. Masters, apprentices and labourers employed in these locales numbered 4,367, while 1,377 men made their livings as boatmen, water carriers and in similar occupations. Workshops typically were small, employing around 2.5 people per enterprise. Most commonly a shop was run by just one craftsman: the Jews especially often worked alone or with a single apprentice. Larger shops with at least 15 artisans and servants were quite rare and almost always bakeries.

Despite official attempts to prevent immigration, newcomers were numerous.[33] Furthermore this documentation thoroughly demolishes the notion that religious solidarities primarily determined the division of labour in Ottoman cities, an assumption long favoured by Ottomanist economic historians.[34] At the same time, this register shows the importance of local allegiances in determining the craft specialities adopted by immigrants. Certainly in some provincial localities there lived only Muslims or else only non-Muslims, and then we cannot distinguish between religious and local adherence. But often enough a craft recorded in Selim III's registers had both Muslim and non-Muslim practitioners who all came from the very same provincial place. In such instances we can be sure that local ties determined who got to specialize in what line of work. Specialities might be transferred for generations so that no matter where the migrants settled they practised the same craft. But such 'traditions' did not hold sway unchallenged: people from this or that Balkan town who settled in a particular sector of Istanbul might become grocers while their fellow immigrants from the same place established themselves in a different part of the city and became gardeners.[35] Immigrants thus discovered economic niches for themselves and did not rigidly adhere to religiously or locally based solidarities.

Legitimizing sultanic power, grown weaker in the provinces through increasing intervention in Istanbul

In the case of milling and baking, and also where immigrants to the capital were concerned, the sultan's administration of the 1700s and early 1800s never tired of issuing regulations; the cases discussed here could be multiplied almost *ad infinitum*. It is difficult to decide whether control had been just as intensive in the 1500s and 1600s.[36] Surviving documents for the earlier period are few, yet we do get the impression that practices had been more relaxed at that time. Although baking had always been regulated, in the sixteenth century official commands did not go into nearly as much detail as in 1800, and although there certainly were attempts to send 'undesirables' back home, no evidence so far has been located for any systematic investigation of the credentials of sixteenth- or seventeenth-century *medrese* residents. By the 1700s, however, the increased size of the central bureaucracy enabled the government to directly control matters that previously had been left to guilds, neighbours or, if official action was required, to one of the many adjunct qadis on duty in the city.

This increased activity can perhaps be explained by the fact that while losses of Ottoman territory were still limited in the 1700s, the central power exercised much less control over many of its provinces than it had done a century earlier. Lifetime tax farmers turned local magnates had taken over a good deal of provincial administration. Only in northwestern Anatolia, and especially in and around Bursa, were sizeable areas and revenue sources still under the direct control of the central government.

Studies undertaken during the last ten years or so, however, have demonstrated that the consequences of this decentralization of the sultan's standing and power were less dire than had previously been assumed. Most magnates usually professed loyalty to the sultan even if they did not obey his each and every command; for the government was still in a position to mobilize the rivals of any given magnate, who were more than ready to kill him once they had received the sultan's orders.

If powerholders aiming for independence were relatively rare, this was largely due to their investments in lifetime tax farms (*malikâne*) that formed the real basis of their power.[37] Hypothetically speaking, once the Ottoman sultan no longer was recognized, many taxpayers would have seized the opportunity to stop paying. Moreover in a region of some size, typically not one but several families had gained money and status through tax farming. If, also hypothetically, a given magnate had seized power as the new sultan in a seceding province, all others stood to lose their revenue claims once the latter were no longer backed up by the legitimacy that only the dynasty of Osman could confer. Most magnates therefore continued to send substantial revenue to Istanbul; apart from Mehmed Ali Paşa of Egypt (r. 1805–49) and a few others, their activities did not greatly contribute to the break-up of the empire.

At the same time, the central government did not passively watch the growth of magnate power. Substantially revamping the state apparatus after the Peace of Passarowitz in 1718, the sultans expanded their bureaucracy and more particularly increased the central power's correspondence with the provinces. From the mid-1700s onwards, special registers were created, the so-called provincial Ahkâm Defterleri, into which the scribes entered the administration's responses to complaints from members of the subject population as well as of low-level administrators.[38] Compared to the period before about 1750, the volume of sultanic commands increased at an exponential rate. Limitation to a single province also made it possible to follow up a given dispute in the record books, an all but impossible enterprise when dealing with the older registers. In these new record books, Istanbul and its suburbs were treated as a province, although no *vilayet-i* İstanbul was otherwise documented at that time.[39]

Since these sultanic edicts had not been issued spontaneously, but always responded to petitions, many subjects must have felt that their affairs could be expedited by obtaining a sultanic command. From the administration's viewpoint, there was another advantage: through the resulting correspondence officials were able to keep in touch with certain people at grassroots level while bypassing local magnates. Connections to the residents of the capital similarly were developed by responding to their complaints and – at least in some cases – facilitating solutions. Thus officialdom strengthened the sultan's legitimacy and contributed to the relative stability of the empire.

Yet even so, a certain loss of control over outlying provinces was undeniable, and apparently Selim III felt that further compensatory measures were needed. At least in the capital, the ruler had to show that he still could govern. His show of force *vis à vis* recalcitrant bakers, many of whom probably were part-time janissaries, may have been directed at the soldiery in general: disciplining the janissaries and if possible replacing them was a major political project of this sultan. But in addition the protection of the 'poor subjects' in their roles as consumers was a traditional prerogative of the Ottoman ruler, and, by exercising it, he could enhance his legitimacy at the very time when his moves against the janissaries were making him highly unpopular among certain sectors of Istanbul's population.

Interestingly the capital's artisans seem to have responded positively to growing central control. Of course registers containing official responses to complaints are not the best places to find oppositional voices. But as so many edicts were, as we have seen, solicited by the guildsmen themselves, it seems reasonable to assume that official controls usually were quite popular. Presumably Istanbul artisans wished to limit competition in times of economic stringency: following 1760, the relative expansion that had occurred in many Ottoman crafts during the previous 40 years gave way to a profound downturn. This crisis was initiated by the Russo-Ottoman war of 1768–74 and exacerbated by the political instability of the following years.[40] As civilian demand contracted, artisans paid more attention to the shops that their fellow guildsmen were permitted – or not permitted – to open. To be sure, similar petitions had been penned in earlier periods as well.[41] However, the relevant sultanic edicts, and presumably the petitions upon which they had been based, now became much more urgent and specific.

As an example, we will turn to the capital's dealers in fabrics (*bezzaz*), who had the administration confirm their internal ruling that the sale of striped or silk-cotton cloth (*alaca*) was limited to 71 shops, 56 of them in the vicinity of the covered markets and 15 others near a public bath whose location is unknown today.[42] Accordingly two enterprising tailors were forbidden to infringe on the rights of the *bezzaz* by selling Indian fabrics in their shops.

A similar complaint came from the saddlers: they claimed that according to previous sultanic commands their craft could only be exercised in the Saraçhane, a khan that continued to exist into the twentieth century although its tenants were rarely able to enforce their proclaimed monopoly.[43] In this particular case the complaint was directed against a saddler who had served the palace for a long time and, as a reward, had been accorded the right to open a shop in the section of his own house reserved for male visitors (*selamlık*). Incidentally this story is of interest also because it confirms the observation that some Istanbul artisans did not work in the business centre but on the same property on which their dwelling was located. Although the defendant had a document supporting his claim, the surviving edict ordered him to remove his business to the Saraçhane. Unfortunately we do not know anything about the background of the affair. Were there vacancies in the Saraçhane that the established saddlers were trying to fill, were the latter intent on depriving a competitor of a location considered unduly advantageous, or did the dispute concern the jurisdiction of the saddlers' guild, known to have been based in the Saraçhane?[44] As our document covers only a single episode it is anybody's guess whether the saddler with his palace connections perhaps had this decision reversed at a later date. Be that as it may, evidently many Istanbul craftsmen were happy to invoke not only the local qadi but the central administration itself, and constant monitoring and enforcement of 'traditional' rights probably increased the rulers' legitimacy during those troubled years.

The rise of the *gedik*

Presumably neither the tailor selling Indian fabrics nor the saddler who tried to avoid setting up shop in the Saraçhane possessed certain crucial rights: the tailor had not acquired a 'licence' to deal in imported fabrics, and while the saddler possessed a general right to exercise his trade, this activity was not to take place in his private home. Rights of this type were designated by the term *gedik*, which originally meant simply 'gap' or 'slot'. A second meaning denoted a workshop along with its contents, such as tools, instruments, raw materials and perhaps finished goods. Called *kedek* in the Syrian provinces, this right or rather bundle of rights in many cases by the later 1700s was a prerequisite for practising a craft.[45] As, however, this institution is best documented for Istanbul, we will introduce the *gedik* here.

Typically *gedik*s were acquired by inheritance. In some crafts, if the master died leaving a young son, the *gedik* was temporarily turned over to the most senior of the journeymen who had to return it to the master's son as soon as the latter had learned the relevant craft; the new master was expected to pay his temporary stand-in a sum of money for his trouble. Only if there was no competent son at all, not so rare an occurrence given the many epidemics of the time, did the most senior journeyman acquire a full right to the vacant *gedik*. Especially if the master did not have many sons, there was thus a premium attached to staying in the same workshop year after year. Contrary to many of their counterparts in France and central Europe, Istanbul journeymen were thus not encouraged to travel. This arrangement may have been intended to keep skills 'at home', but given the sparseness of our evidence it is hard to be sure.[46]

How this arrangement emerged is only imperfectly known. In the seventeenth century, *gediks* had been exceptional; the relatively free movement into and out of different crafts that has been observed for both Istanbul and Bursa would not have been possible had *gediks* been widespread.[47] One explanation points to the financial difficulties of the central administration in the later 1700s. In response officials began to tax pious foundations more systematically than had been customary earlier on, and the latter tried to compensate for their losses by increasing the rents of the shops they so often owned.[48] Already under strain, the artisans defended themselves by tactics aimed at reducing demand for shops and workshops. They thus invented the *gedik*, in other words, the right to a shop along with the equally important right to pursue a trade on the premises (see Chapter 1). This bundle of rights could be inherited but not freely bought and sold. As a result, all those men, however qualified, who had no right to a *gedik* could not normally become masters, and the number of candidates for mastership was thus drastically curtailed. In this new situation, pious foundations would have had trouble finding tenants and thus be obliged to moderate their demands for rent.

This explanation is attractive because, as we have seen, limiting the number of artisans practising a given craft was a long-term demand of many established masters, rendered more urgent by the difficulties of the period. *Gediks* were thus not a complete novelty, but a line of defence well in accordance with artisan *mentalités*. In addition large-scale workshops grouping numerous artisans became more frequent in the eighteenth century (see Chapter 9).[49] By obliging craftsmen to rent spaces in these complexes, the administrators of certain pious foundations did increase their revenues. But on the other hand, raising money in this manner was not easy, for many artisans held their shops by long-term leases with fixed rents.[50] By contrast, whenever such rent increases were possible, it is doubtful whether the qadis, who had to sanction the institution of *gediks*, would really have done so had they regarded the new practice as detrimental to the finances of pious foundations. After all, qadis and administrators of these foundations belonged to the same milieu. Probably the demands for increased rent were at best a contributing factor in the emergence of the *gedik*.

At least in the view of the present author, economic conjuncture was more important. Whenever the practitioners of a craft/profession feel that they have fewer customers/clients than they would like, they attempt to limit the number of people entering their field. Ottoman guilds were no exception to this rule, and throughout the later 1700s and down to the mid-1800s many Istanbul crafts suffered serious contraction.[51] In this situation artisans probably did not feel that the old *ad hoc* limitations on the entry of newcomers still sufficed, and they demanded stricter regulations. Furthermore *gediks* could be inherited, thus allowing masters' sons privileged access to their fathers' jobs; and while family lines in one and the same craft had been common in earlier periods as well, the institutionalization of this practice made most sense in a period of depression.

In recent historiography the genesis of private property in the late Ottoman Empire has formed a major topic, and in this context the *gedik* has come in for some attention.[52] At least in principle *gedik*s could only be sold to other members of the same guild and thus were not absolute property as we understand it today. However, before the 1700s the selection of items over which Ottoman subjects – if not in the service of the sultans – could command full ownership was limited to movables, cash, gardens and houses; therefore the *gedik*, over which guildsmen had strong ownership rights, has been viewed as one of the 'paths' by which the notion of full property gained further ground within the Ottoman legal system.

Lifetime tax farms (*malikâne*) and the continuing saga of military interference

Making the exercise of many crafts contingent on the ownership of an appropriate position or 'slot' was also consonant with certain crucial changes in eighteenth-century Ottoman financial history. Tax farming had been practised in the empire from the mid-fifteenth century if not earlier, and the practice had gained wider currency since the later 1500s.[53] But owing to the strains of the Ottoman–Habsburg war of 1683–99, the administration wanted to collect large sums of money at short notice, and for this purpose life-term tax farms were sold against payment of substantial amounts of ready cash to be handed over before the holder could enter into possession. As we have seen, this was a crucial basis for the growing importance of provincial powerholders.[54] Unlike the older tax farms, which were normally held for three years but which might be lost at any time if a competitor offered more money, the new-style *malikâne* were secure throughout the holder's lifetime and arrangements could even be made to pass them on to descendants.

Similarly to lifetime tax farming, quite a few positions as guild headmen (*kethüda*) were also offered for sale; this happened in quite a few towns, but in Istanbul probably more often than elsewhere.[55] As candidates consented to considerable financial sacrifices before obtaining their offices, *kethüda*s must have made substantial amounts of money; these dues were known as *kethüdalık avaidi*. Frequently the holder of a military pay ticket, who might or might not be a soldier, turned it over to the treasury in exchange for a position as guild headman. Moreover it was not uncommon for these offices to change hands in quick succession. Normally re-sales of *kethüda*-positions meant that additional pay tickets were handed over to the financial administration. By sanctioning the sale of guild offices the treasury may have recuperated some of the documents that were no longer providing for 'real' soldiers; for by the 1700s janissary pay tickets had become saleable and circulated widely on the market. While most of the relevant pay tickets were military, we occasionally find dervishes and holders of government stipends exchanging their documents for positions as guild headmen.[56] Possibly these people felt that given the notorious emptiness of the treasury, a claim upon artisans and/or their customers offered greater security.

We might think that by this arrangement the guilds became what they had not been earlier on, namely extensions of the sultan's administration; the sale of guild office could well have deprived the craftsmen concerned of all means of making their voices heard. However, in real life the situation was rather different, for qadis usually were not averse to deposing guild headmen against whom the artisans voiced complaints. Presumably the headmen's aides (*yiğitbaşı*), whose offices were rarely put up for sale, were key figures when protests to the qadi's court had to be organized.[57] When this happened, the qadi deposed the headman, but the artisans needed to find a way of indemnifying this former soldier for the pay tickets that he had surrendered. If an alternative candidate presented himself, the latter might promise to make the necessary payments out of his own pocket. Of course we do not know how many headmen who had purchased their offices really fulfilled the duties involved. If they did not, and the guildsmen for one reason or another preferred to not complain, the latter would have to find substitutes, and paying for this service would have been an additional load on artisan backs.[58] But the gist of the matter is that craftsmen kept some control over their organizations even in the face of the *kethüda*s who had farmed their offices; but it was impossible to do so without special efforts and disbursements of funds, which taxed the limited resources of guilds and guildsmen.

In the eyes of ordinary Istanbul artisans, what were guild headmen expected to do? Some indications emerge from the complaints by which craftsmen demanded that their *kethüda*s be fired. Rudeness to members was sometimes mentioned; perhaps soldiers who thought themselves 'above' the craftsmen they were supposed to represent were especially prone to that type of misbehaviour. Punishments of guild members that a significant number of their peers considered excessive might also be cause for complaint.[59] Drunkenness and bribery could lead to deposition as well.[60] Old age was a further source of complaint, and the relative frequency of such complaints may indicate that not all guilds were willing to find substitutes for non-exercising guild wardens.

Purchases of guild offices by military men were only one aspect of the soldiery's involvement in the lives of Istanbul's craftsmen. As in other Ottoman cities, some artisans joined the military corps and some soldiers took up a craft when they could not otherwise make ends meet. But no special study of this phenomenon has been undertaken for the Ottoman capital, and all statements therefore are approximate.[61] Moreover artisans might become victims of marauding soldiers: in the eighteenth century, the sultan's government typically relied on candidates for high-level government offices to provide their own mercenaries. Therefore such people, when lobbying for office in the capital, must have brought along households full of armed men. Presumably the latter quite often took the goods of traders and artisans without pay and were responsible for many of the robberies tersely recorded by the qadi's scribes. All these issues need further study.

Intra-urban linkages

For the most part, the world of Istanbul artisans probably was confined to the capital and its immediate surroundings, unless the people in question were recent immigrants and maintained ties to their places of origin. There were, however, some exceptions: thus, if the surviving inscriptions have been correctly interpreted, the needlewoman Despoineta, active in Istanbul in 1682 and possibly as late as 1715, received commissions from the church of St George in Ankara.[62] Unfortunately we know nothing about the organization of her workshop, nor can we tell who spread Despoineta's reputation to a town located about 450 kilometres away from her place of residence. Moreover it should have been more difficult for women than for men to establish intra-urban contacts, and yet, if our inferences are correct, here we have an example of a female artist/artisan who succeeded in doing so. Therefore we need to tread carefully when making general claims about the limited horizons of each and every craftsperson. Other records documenting the inter-regional contacts of certain masters may still turn up.

However, the artisans whose intra-urban contacts have left most traces in our documentation were undoubtedly the tanners. For mid-seventeenth-century Istanbul, Evliya Çelebi claimed that all tanners were called *ahi* and their patron saint, Ahi Evran, was originally from Kayseri, but later migrated to western Anatolia and ultimately was buried in a large dervish lodge situated in the gardens of Denizli (see Chapter 2).[63] This story may indicate that a strong tanners' organization spread westward, ultimately reaching Istanbul. In the eighteenth century the *ahi baba* resident in Kırsehir was considered an authority by tanners working in often fairly remote localities. As a sign of deference the latter sent messengers in order to take advice from the

Anatolian sheikhs, expressing their recognition by gifts known as *yeşil yaprak* (green leaf). As a result the Kırşehir dervish lodge in which the *ahi babas* resided became quite well to do.[64]

However, by the 1810s the lodge had apparently lost much of its former stature: for when the sheikh of the time petitioned the Ottoman government for aid in the restoration of the by now rather decrepit building, he described a very ordinary dervish residence. A proper assessment of the work to be undertaken (*keşif*), such as Ottoman officials normally required before any building project could begin, was also unavailable.[65] But the damage being considerable, the official who dealt with the petition suggested that intervention was necessary but repairs should be at least partly in wood, thus avoiding the expense of masonry. As the Istanbul tanners apparently did not intervene, we are left to wonder whether the old connection with their guild had not lapsed in the meantime, particularly since the tanners also remained aloof from the acrimonious disputes that plagued the lodge during those years.[66] Once again the links of Istanbul's tanners to the lodge of Ahi Evran remain an intriguing problem requiring further study.

What do we know about artisan culture?

Probably because of the relative neglect of eighteenth-century Ottoman history we cannot as yet answer this question in a satisfying manner. Dervish lodges and saints' mausoleums probably were centres of religious practice and sociability for many artisans: when new masters had been accepted into a guild, it was customary to visit a sanctuary and enjoy a picnic in common. In some guilds at least these outings transcended religious divisions, for both Muslims and non-Muslims were supposed to participate.[67] However, in the case of the eighteenth-century silk manufacturers' guild, we learn that the Christians refused to go along, because they claimed to have been treated badly on earlier outings. What should have been a confirmation of fellowship among guildsmen in the same line of work thus became an object of intercommunal strife. Whether this story was exceptional or not as yet remains unclear.

Some guilds possessed small pious foundations, almost always in the shape of funds instituted to provide loans at moderate interest, while at the same time financing pious activities such as the recitation of poems in praise of the Prophet Muhammad. Among Jewish guilds during the first half of the nineteenth century, charitable collections were common, and both city-wide artisans' guilds and local sub-divisions of these organizations established their own funds so as to dispense alms when needed.[68]

Probably not all guilds owned special meeting places; often people must have come together in the shop of an influential member or in the courtyard of a mosque if the guild was all Muslim. Organizations consisting of Christians exclusively may have congregated in the garden of a church. But some guilds did acquire meeting places of their own, called *lonca*.[69] While these structures are very poorly documented, they must have been more numerous and important than we otherwise might assume, for the older word *hirfet* for guild at some point dropped out of use and *lonca* took its place. It survives in present-day Turkish usage.

Orthodox seamen, organized in guilds like other artisans, have left tokens of their piety and difficult lives in churches, thus documenting affective connections with these places of worship: *ex votos* of ships in ivory or silver gilt survive mainly from the nineteenth century and not necessarily in Istanbul itself. But they were exhibited in earlier times as well: Istanbul and especially Yeniköy, with their large seafaring populations, must once have had many such models of sea-going vessels decorating local churches.[70] These *ex votos* probably documented last-minute rescues from shipwreck. Whether the model of an Ottoman galley that the seventeenth-century traveller Jean Thévenot saw hanging in the Sultan Ahmed mosque had been placed there for similar reasons remains uncertain, but it is probable.[71]

Apart from mosques and churches, coffee shops were places for artisans to congregate; this was especially true of the Ottoman capital that by itself consumed one half of all the coffee drunk in the entire Ottoman Empire. About 600 tons a year were sold in the early eighteenth century and 983 tons a year in 1765; moreover, during the late 1600s and early 1700s, the price of coffee in Istanbul determined prices everywhere else.[72] Coffee shops might be denigrated as places of idle talk, yet the opulence of the coffee dealers documented the success of the Yemenite beverage among artisans, and the urban population as a whole.

Other meeting places for artisans and others were the shops where millet beer (*boza*) was offered for sale. Istanbul contained a large number of *bozahanes*, and different types of *boza* were on offer. As the alcoholic content of some varieties was minimal, it was possible to enjoy this drink without incurring censure. With respect to the mid-seventeenth century, Evliya recounted that the porters of the Unkapanı district in particular spent much time in these places.[73] That porters – and perhaps other service workers as well – awaited customers while sipping their coffee or *boza* is likely but rarely documented for the period in question.

Conclusion

Barring error, between the late 1600s and the mid-nineteenth century artisan

Coffee cup from the Tophane manufacture, nineteenth century. They are inscribed with the names of the owners or makers. The sultan's monogram (*tuğra*) does not belong to any historical ruler, but has a purely decorative function. (Courtesy of Völkerkundemuseum, Munich.) Compare Erdinç Bakla, *Tophane Lüleciliği* (Istanbul: Antik AŞ, 2007)

guilds became more formal, organized and perhaps rigid. Market contraction pushed artisans in this direction: as they sought to defend themselves against competitors, they promoted the *gedik*, which had not been unknown in earlier periods but only became widespread during the economic stringency of the later 1700s. Apart from limiting competition between masters themselves, the *gedik* had the advantage of giving their sons a head start. For journeymen without any claim to such an inheritance, there remained only the rather forlorn hope that the masters' sons might become soldiers, members of a dignitary's household or *medrese* students. We do not know much about the lives and thoughts of such journeymen, stuck in a subordinate position and unlikely to ever acquire a mastership.

From an artisan's viewpoint, controlling membership of his guild through the *gedik* might also be helpful when raw materials were in short supply. When few sheep arrived in Istanbul, tanners, saddlers and shoemakers might wish to 'ration' hides and skins, and that purpose could be easily achieved if nobody but the holders of *gedik*s were accorded a share of the coveted raw materials. Not that these arrangements prevented certain better-off craftsmen from augmenting their stocks, for they could offer suppliers relatively prompt payment and thus demand preferential treatment. Other strategies might involve bribing headmen, and perhaps such acts were behind certain guildsmen's complaints against their wardens. But at the end of the day, a *gedik* should have been quite effective as a rationing device.

The capital was and remained an enormous accumulation of consumers, yet if a provincial artisan wanted to gain access, he was well advised to arrive as part of a coterie of colleagues and, given time, form a guild along with his fellows. For if he did not attach himself to such a recognized group, whose members could stand surety for one another in case of need, he risked eviction as an illegal immigrant – if indeed he even managed to circumvent the roadblocks set up to ward off people like himself. Highly organized guilds thus became a means of self-defence for the capital's craftsmen, and this applied both to those already domiciled in Istanbul and to newcomers who as yet needed to establish themselves.

Dealing with headmen who had purchased their offices also required organization, for if the artisans affected wanted to maintain some control over their guilds, they needed to get together, if necessary transcending rivalries between Muslims and non-Muslims, and convince the qadi that the erring headman must be deposed. Moreover they had to find an alternative candidate willing to commit some funds to buy out his predecessor, and this procedure was easier if the group could pressure one of its better-off members into making a bid for the warden's position.

In the late 1700s and early 1800s artisan guilds were under pressure to form ever more tightly structured organizations. On the one hand, guild masters had to organize in defence against political and economic threats; the latter included increasing demands by the authorities for – poorly paid – goods and services that easily could compromise fragile artisan livelihoods. On the other hand state demands must have favoured tighter organizational structures as well. Only if artisans were closely supervised by their colleagues and headmen could the administration hope to enforce its own rulings. Furthermore sultanic commands obeyed in the Ottoman capital at least to a certain extent legitimized the ruler at a time when his control over the provinces was so often problematic. As a result the aims of Istanbul artisans and those of the central administration were often compatible, at least to a certain degree.

Relative compatibility may well explain why guildsmen so frequently sought official intervention, while from today's perspective it would have made sense for them to keep state officials at arm's length. But probably this latter option did not exist in the Ottoman eighteenth century.

CHAPTER 7

Cairo: From Military Penetration of Artisan Guilds to the State Monopolies of Mehmed Ali Paşa

Crisis, a limited recovery and further troubles

Evliya Çelebi's account of the Ottoman Empire indicates relative prosperity, and Cairo appears as a hive of craft activity. Modern research on the Egyptian metropolis has, to a degree, borne him out: in spite of local ups and downs, between the early 1640s and 1667 no major scarcities of grain occurred in Cairo; however, they did resume that year.[1] After 1667 the situation decidedly changed for the worse: dramatic increases in the price of wheat, sometimes aggravated by currency manipulations, were documented for the late 1670s and again in the late 1680s. As Evliya may have lived in Cairo during this particular period, perhaps, like older people before and after him, he chose to focus on past prosperity. Be that as it may, towards the end of his life there was apparently a brief economic revival that continued until about 1690.[2]

Monetary crises, which hit low-income people including most artisans especially hard, were caused by the circulation of low-denomination coins (*para*) that were either substandard from the beginning or else had been 'rubbed off' by certain people to collect small quantities of silver. As a result prices increased more dramatically when expressed in current coin than would have been true if purely natural causes such as insufficient inundations of the Nile had been at issue. While elite households and pious foundations purchased in bulk and thus were to a degree protected from short-term increases, most artisans bought their supplies on a daily basis and therefore were defenceless against speculative price rises.

From about 1690 onwards and down into the mid-1730s, hard times increasingly became permanent, and the chroniclers mentioned 16 scarcities and 13 monetary crises for a period less than 50 years long.[3] Crises became, more or less, the ordinary state of affairs and a relatively normal grain supply was available only for three to four years at a time. However, between 1736 and 1780 food became more plentiful and the *para* stabilized.[4] Thus there was a time-lag between Egyptian conjuncture and that observed in the central Ottoman lands, where growth had begun rather earlier but where the Russo-Ottoman war of 1768–74 marked the beginning of a lengthy 'time of troubles'.[5] Where Egypt and more particularly Cairo were concerned, it was again a political event, but of a rather different type, that marked the return of hard times: after the death of Muḥammad Abū Dhahab the Mamluk *beys* entered into a spate of fierce internecine strife, and their demand for ever more resources made life very difficult for the working population of Cairo. Almost 20 years of internal warfare throughout Egypt, but concentrated in Cairo, thus preceded the Napoleonic occupation of 1798–1801. This latter event was especially traumatic; however, it has produced a significant number of textual and pictorial sources on local artisans through the activities of the scholars accompanying the French army. Fighting Napoleon, British and Ottoman troops entered the country and must have caused further turmoil.[6]

Through the efforts of Mehmed Ali Paşa, Ottoman governor since 1805, the sultan managed to re-conquer Egypt. But once the pasha had established himself, he founded a regional empire financed to a considerable extent by the control of trade routes and mercantilist state policies.[7] Both the construction of state-owned factories and the monopolization of essential raw materials such as cotton must have placed a severe strain on artisan livelihoods. Moreover in 1840, the British forced Mehmed Ali Paşa to abolish all the monopolies previously instituted, and this turnabout must have forced many artisans to readjust, of course with great difficulty, to the local and/or world market. As a result the present chapter covers two periods of relative prosperity in the late seventeenth and mid-eighteenth centuries, and two rather lengthy 'times of troubles' for Cairo's artisans. Life was probably hardest during the early 1700s and once again from the 1780s to the 1840s.

Continuity and change

At the beginning of our period, in the 1670s, Cairo already possessed a remarkable number of guilds: among the multitude of artisan groups (*taife*) recorded by Evliya Çelebi, 262 units have been identified as associations encompassing the traders and artisans of Cairo proper, excluding those of Būlāq and other satellite towns. As to the data collectors active on behalf of the French occupation authorities, they came up with 195 to 204 groupings; as the criteria that we may use to identify a 'Cairo guild' is somewhat variable, the total result of course varies as well. Eighteenth-century Ottoman-

Egyptian documents and chronicles record a similar figure, namely 196.[8] In all these instances only a minority were manufacturing guilds, while trade and services predominated. But for our purposes, service workers such as barbers and bath attendants also count as artisans.

Probably none of the available lists is complete, partly because guilds and guild membership fluctuated considerably. Craftsmen originally part of a larger guild but working together in a separate location might decide to set up an organization of their own, while the dwindling number of artisans practising a speciality no longer much in demand might attach themselves to an established guild. Yet an outsider to Egyptian urban history may well ask himself whether the substantially greater number of guilds mentioned by Evliya, compared to the late eighteenth-century data, may not reflect a decline in prosperity: before the difficulties beginning in 1690–1700, the city was perhaps more populous and/or more able to consume the wares of numerous artisans than it was to be in later times.

Certain artisan organizations must have disappeared because of changing demand patterns: thus the remarkable decrease in guilds dealing with gold and silver between the 1670s and 1801 may reflect the fact that in the struggles between rival Mamluk *beys* and later against Napoleon, ready cash was preferred to jewellery and tableware of gold and silver. More remarkable is the near disappearance of the artisans who made the luxurious tents for which Ottoman grandees were famous; perhaps this was also a reflection of the fact that by the late 1700s all resources were channelled into warfare pure and simple.[9] In any event the large number of guilds in eighteenth-century Cairo, when compared to other Ottoman cities, does reflect the great economic vitality of the Egyptian metropolis.[10]

The cost of living

Just as in Istanbul, Cairo artisans, even if members of one and the same guild, were by no means equal in material goods and social position.[11] It has long been taken for granted that the headmen (sheikhs) were often not among the wealthiest members of their respective guilds. But this issue recently has re-surfaced in scholarly debate, and it has been re-examined in the early nineteenth-century context.[12] From a sample of artisan estates, we gain the impression that the crisis period of the late 1700s and early 1800s resulted in a concentration of wealth beyond even the substantial inequalities that had existed before: now the top 10 per cent of the sample held about one half of all assets documented.[13]

Unlike Istanbul or Damascus, however, Cairo's guilds remained relatively flexible; local artisans apparently did not need to acquire a free slot (*gedik*) before setting up shop. Entering and leaving guilds seems to have been quite simple: thus the chronicler al-Djabartī reports that when in the early years of Mehmed Ali Paşa's reign the members of certain guilds all too often were summoned to work on state-sponsored construction projects, some of them 'locked up their shops and made their living from another trade'.[14] While villagers often complained of fellow peasants that left and saddled them with an increased tax load, Cairo artisans apparently were quite free to change their guilds; and while the alternative jobs they could find may not have been very remunerative, their right to take them up seemingly was not contested by their fellow craftsmen or the state authorities.

We can try to gauge the well being or misery prevailing among Cairo's artisans whenever modern historians have been able to calculate the real wages earned in the 1700s or early 1800s. Some fleeting impressions can be gained from a comparison between the prices of basic foodstuffs in Istanbul and Cairo between 1660 and 1798.[15] These prices have been calculated in grams of silver; that is, they have been adjusted for the currency fluctuations that caused so much trouble to the poorer urbanites. However, certain consumption historians very much doubt the validity of adjusting prices in this fashion as the latter apparently exaggerate the wealth of the rich and the destitution of the poor.[16] Furthermore the number of measurements documented for Cairo is far smaller than that available for Istanbul.

Until about 1700 food prices seemingly were somewhat lower in Cairo than in the capital, a remarkable phenomenon as Istanbul grain prices were so heavily subsidized by the producing regions (see Chapter 6). After that year, prices in the two cities were about the same and, what is more, they usually moved in tandem: prices in pure silver, though not those in current coin, were relatively stable in both cities until about 1760. There were, however, a few isolated instances of Cairo prices being much higher, presumably due to insufficient Nile floods. Between 1760 and 1780, however, there apparently was a major – but poorly documented – price hike: all we can say is that by about 1785 prices had risen dramatically both in Istanbul and the Egyptian metropolis.

What do these figures tell us about the life circumstances of artisans? It appears that the numerous crises of the late 1600s and early 1700s were relatively short lived. Surely they made for serious difficulties. But the pressures caused by Mamluk infighting after 1780 had disastrous consequences far beyond anything experienced just before and after 1700. During the 1780s and 1790s, in two cases, food prices measured in pure silver almost tripled in Cairo when compared to their level in 1690. In Istanbul the rise was also substantial but not quite so extreme: when prices had reached their highest level, they amounted to twice the quantities of pure silver demanded in 1690.

Presumably the protective measures taken by the central government had some effect in Istanbul, despite their obvious limitations.

The interpenetration of artisans and soldiers

In the course of the eighteenth century the amalgamation of artisans and soldiers that had begun in the later sixteenth century was carried to its conclusion; where the Egyptian metropolis is concerned, this process has been studied with an attention to detail without parallel in any other Ottoman context.[17] By 1730 the only craftsmen not affiliated with one or other of the military corps were the non-Muslims; as Christians and Jews predominated among the goldsmiths, tailors and furriers, these guilds remained 'non-militarized'. From the Istanbul perspective, the military men stationed in Cairo were now a militia and not soldiers on active duty, although a certain number of men did participate in, for instance, Balkan campaigns.

For our purposes, it is more important to see what benefits Cairo artisans hoped for when they consented to significant sacrifices to become soldiers at least in name. For apart from participation in military exercises, membership in one or other military corps meant that the artisans concerned were willing to leave a certain share of their estates to the units with which they had been affiliated during their lifetimes.[18] In the late 1600s payments amounted to about one tenth of the total value of the artisan-soldiers' estates; by the 1700s, when the importance of the janissaries and other paramilitaries had much diminished, this share decreased, and now oscillated between 5 and 7 per cent.[19] Moreover traders and craftsmen paid a due to 'their' corps called *ḥimāya*, protection money. As the term for 'protection' itself was also *ḥimāya*, the close connection between the payment and the social relationship it established is clearly apparent. While in principle to demand protection money was regarded as an abuse, it was an abuse that had gained legitimacy with time; however, it was never quite legitimate enough for the payments in question to become fixed and codified.[20] In a sense the system operating in Cairo was comparable to the 'protection rackets' run by many states of early modern Europe.[21]

On the other hand, membership of a military or paramilitary unit probably involved exemption from some, though certainly not all, dues to which ordinary subjects of the sultans were liable. Membership in the militia also meant that if pressured by other soldiers/paramilitaries, the injured artisans could complain to the leaders of their own corps and hope for some redress. Apparently artisans decided individually whether they wanted to become members of the janissary or other corps; guilds never adhered *en bloc*. Moreover while quite frequently membership in a given corps passed from father to son, this was not an absolute requirement. Thus there must have been some room for negotiating the benefits that a new entrant hoped to gain for himself.[22]

Sometimes the interpenetration of artisan guilds and militias also resulted from the reverse process, i.e. military men themselves might enter the guilds or else encourage their manumitted slaves to do so. When in 1801 the Ottomans re-entered Cairo after the interim of the French occupation, a local chronicler stated that many soldiers immediately began to trade in foodstuffs. In so doing, they eluded the control of the market supervisor, selling their wares at whatever prices took their fancy. However, in more settled times the market supervisor did exercise jurisdiction also over soldiers exercising a craft, and we even hear that a military-man-cum-butcher caught cheating his customers was given a sound beating by this official.[23]

In eighteenth-century Cairo it had become common practice for better-off traders and even artisans to possess military slaves that they ultimately manumitted and who might then follow the trades of their ex-masters. Some Mamluks were able to join the ruling group, a promotion inaccessible to the former owners themselves, as the latter were free-born Muslims and thus could not be enslaved. By acquiring Mamluks, however, prosperous traders and artisans created links to the ruling group, and it was only in the very late 1700s, when Mamluk infighting was at its most savage, that this connection was finally broken.[24]

Unloading the expenses of factional struggles

As to the demands for *ḥimāya* and other payments, they increased so dramatically in part because at the time when ʿAlī Bulut-qapan (the 'cloud-chaser') or the duumvirs İbrāhīm Bey and Murād Bey were struggling for supremacy, it was no longer possible for craftsmen or even merchants to bargain with the Mamluk leaders. Had they been possible, such negotiations would have made the point that extreme over-taxation would lead to the flight and/or death of so many taxpayers that the elite's revenues would be bound to suffer. Beyond such worldly considerations, these discussions would have referred to Islamic law and the 'circle of equity', a set of assumptions to the effect that political power could only maintain itself if people paid their taxes and an army was raised from the proceeds. In turn, the precondition for such a state of affairs was a modicum of justice on the part of the rulers.[25] Successful negotiations between the political elite and the taxpayers therefore presupposed a certain respect for Islamic law and Ottoman statecraft on the part of the ruling group. In earlier times, many military men active in Egypt had been noted for their piety. However, some of the later Mamluk *beys* flaunted their disrespect for Islamic law and defined themselves as 'men of the sword' pure and simple.²⁶

To a considerable extent this breakdown was due to the loss of power the Cairo paramilitaries had suffered in comparison to the Mamluk *beys*, who were now the major power in the land and had marginalized the Ottoman governor himself. In fact by the eighteenth century a great many Mamluks had entered the paramilitary corps, so that these two power centres no longer represented separate social forces.²⁷ Presumably this 'colonization' of the paramilitary corps by the great Mamluk households made the janissaries and others less effective in the defence of artisan interests.²⁸ Firstly, as we have seen, some former military slaves did engage in trade and crafts, but they preferred the former as being more lucrative. Artisans of the 1780s or 1790s thus lacked those contacts to the ruling group that many of them had enjoyed 40 or 50 years earlier. Secondly, the greatest losses certainly were borne by the merchants who were forced to provide loan after loan but had little chance of ever seeing their money again. Yet artisans also suffered, and had fewer reserves to fall back on. Thus when in 1787 Ismāʿīl Bey demanded a tax that mainly hit traders but was likely to be extended to artisans as well, Cairo's guilds reacted so sharply that the grandee preferred to desist.²⁹

Craft specialities

While a good deal of research has been undertaken on artisan organization, much less work has been done on individual crafts, their methods of working and their products. Historians of Egypt – and of other Ottoman provinces that became national states in the twentieth century – have shown relatively little interest in the art history and archaeology of the Ottoman period. Thus we once again find ourselves in the uncomfortable position of knowing least about that aspect of artisan activity that was most time-consuming in real life, namely labour in the shop or on some other worksite.³⁰

In the mid-1700s there was considerable construction activity in Cairo, and many artisans must have found employment. However, no known account books survive that document major building sites. Therefore at least at the present state of our knowledge we cannot compare the wages of Cairo's builders with those of their counterparts working in the Ottoman capital and elsewhere. ʿAbd al-Raḥmān Katkhudā (*c*.1715–76) and other prominent military men commissioned mosques of their own as well as additions to ancient and famous structures such as the college of al-Azhar. In addition, these elite patrons sponsored a peculiarity of Cairo architecture known as the *sabīl-kuttāb*.³¹ This building was two-storeyed, the upper level holding a Koran school, while on the ground floor passers-by could receive a drink of water for free. Nineteenth-century images show that these structures, many of which today have lost a good part of their decoration, were embellished with carvings in stone and wood.[32] On the inside the *sabīl-kuttāb* might be decorated with metal lamps that when lit would cast lace-like shadows on the walls.[33] All this work must have occupied many highly skilled artisans.

In addition to these works destined for the public sphere, fine craftwork is also visible in the great houses that throughout the Ottoman period *beys* and other dignitaries built for themselves; as these structures largely are of stone, brick and plaster, they have survived better than the palatial villas of Istanbul, which were built of wood. Especially the reception rooms (*qāʿa*) were embellished with domes, painted wooden ceilings, carved doorframes and bay windows closed with elaborate *mashrabiyya*s, the latter often veritable masterpieces of the turner's art.[34] Windows were made of coloured glass set in stucco, as was practised also in Istanbul; some fine examples from the seventeenth to eighteenth centuries survive in the Islamic museums of Cairo.[35] Certain well-to-do homes also possessed decorative floors in multicoloured marble, and the laying out and restoration of these was quite labour intensive. On the other hand, the troubles of the period after 1780 probably meant that many potential patrons gave up their projects, and the resulting unemployment must have aggravated the difficulties of Cairo craftsmen.

Most of these artists-cum-artisans remain anonymous to us; one of the few exceptions is the Copt Ibrāhīm al-Nāsikh, who lived in the late eighteenth century.[36] He was an icon painter who also decorated the domes of churches (see Chapter 1). But we find him active in the secular sphere, too, as he supervised the decoration of the house of a wealthy co-religionist. In addition Ibrāhīm worked at the interface between art and scholarship, as a copyist but also as an editor of Coptic liturgical texts. By collating the manuscripts he was able to procure, Ibrāhīm attempted to establish the most authentic versions of the religious works used in his church. Furthermore through his concern with the arts of the book, which included the illumination of manuscripts, Ibrāhīm al-Nāsikh made friends with Muslim copyists, including even the imam of a mosque. Evidently superior skills as an artist-cum-artisan might permit a non-Muslim inhabitant of Cairo during the 1700s to transcend some of the borders that fenced in his co-religionists.

Women at work

While women were not guild members, the nineteenth-century qadis' registers of Cairo and other Egyptian towns provide quite a lot of evidence on urban women who worked for a living.[37] Selling bread, fruit, vegetables and dairy products, female peddlers were not apparently much of a competition to their male colleagues, who instead concentrated on pastries, sherbets and textiles. Better-capitalized women peddlers catered for a well-to-do female clientele, supplying the harem-bound members of the elite who were not permitted to do their own shopping. However, these ladies often controlled appreciable resources and purchased luxury goods; some of the poorer female peddlers were not able to trade in these valuable commodities on their own account but instead acted as intermediaries for male merchants.

A quick glance at these petty traders is apposite because at the modest level at which women so often operated, the dividing line between crafts and trade is not easily drawn. This fact of life is particularly apparent in the textile sector: in addition to putting-out arrangements, where the dominant businessman typically was male, there existed rural Egyptian women who bought flax and cotton and then sold the spun yarn to weavers; just as other artisans, they were therefore independent actors in both manufacture and trade. In Cairo, too, spinning and carding typically were female occupations, yet women apparently were excluded from weaving. But other crafts were accessible: in certain small bakeries, for instance, female bakers prepared the bread that other women might then peddle.[38] This observation demonstrates that baking bread in the Egyptian capital was much less regulated than in Istanbul, where bakers formed a guild and, in addition, had their every move governed by a host of rules and regulations (see Chapter 6).

Some early nineteenth-century craftswomen acted within a familial economy; this might mean working as helpmates of husbands and/or sons. More surprisingly, by the mid-1800s certain women tended to band together with their sisters when it came to major sales and purchases. These associations were probably a form of protection against the vicissitudes of the times: with husbands often absent because they had been drafted into the army or the industrial labour force, sisters were more dependable allies than the relatives of the absent husband, who might easily view the property of a 'stranger', and a female to boot, as fair game.[39] Other women, especially but not exclusively if divorced, appeared as entrepreneurs in their own right. This relative independence was made possible by the rule, enshrined in Islamic law, that married women controlled their own property and were not obliged to surrender it to their husbands. But on the other hand, activity in the marketplace might be a reason to assume that the woman in question would be casual about her domestic responsibilities, and therefore a divorcee that worked risked losing the custody of her children.

Among the most skilled women, often artists rather than artisans, were the singers ('alīma, plural 'awālim) who performed primarily before female audiences at weddings and other celebrations. At such occasions they might be listened to by male visitors as well; however, the latter were unable to see them. An 'alīma needed linguistic and poetical talent, apart from a good voice and instruction in versification, for she was expected to produce verses of her own on the spur of the moment. Story-telling and the playing of a musical instrument figured among the other accomplishments of a successful 'alīma, who was paid handsomely and often ended up as a propertied woman.[40] However, by the mid-1800s the reputation of these performers seems to have suffered and their work increasingly was classed as non-respectable.[41]

Mehmed Ali Paşa's mobilization of resources and the fate of Cairo's craftspeople

In the early 1820s, Mehmed Ali Paşa had organized an army that allowed him to win victories for Mahmud II in the Greek uprising; these successes netted him the governorship of Crete. In the 1830s this army, commanded by his son Ibrahim Paşa, not only added Syria to Mehmed Ali Paşa's regional empire but also defeated his Ottoman overlord and ultimately reached Kütahya, only a short distance from Istanbul.[42]

The military was to be clothed by the products of newly established textile factories. Thus to provide the army with broadcloth for uniforms, a foreign specialist was invited, all the sheep in the country were registered so that the factories could be supplied with wool, and ultimately the wool trade itself became a monopoly of the pasha.[43] While the broadcloth industry suffered from a variety of problems, cotton textiles were in fact produced in Egyptian factories with a good deal of success.[44] To protect these nascent industries, Mehmed Ali Paşa forbade the entry of competing British goods into Egypt; however, he was quite willing to import non-competing items from this same source and succeeded well in exporting his cottons to, among other places, the British Empire itself.[45] Moreover, given the administrative channels by which many factory-made goods were distributed, it is not certain that high tariffs were really needed for the protection of the new industries.[46]

According to one school of thought, all this continued until the 1830s, when the factories first ran into difficulties.[47] Accounting was a major problem: often it remained unclear for considerable periods of time whether a given factory was operating at a loss. Another problem was common to many states-cum-societies that industrialized according to the import substitution model: the machinery used in the Egyptian factories only in part could be made by local artisans. By the mid-1830s, it would have been necessary to renew many machines, and additional imports thus became necessary, for which there was little money. Old and badly kept machines, on the other hand, were inefficient producers. Apart from the army, it was not always easy to find buyers for the factory-made wares, especially when of poor quality; in extreme cases, the goods produced turned out to be quite useless and even the army rejected them.[48] Thus the factories were in difficulty even before the pasha was forced, mainly by Palmerston's intervention, to cut down his army and, as we have seen, abolish all monopolies. As the principal market for Egyptian factory-produced goods contracted with the reduction of the army, these enterprises decayed and ultimately collapsed.

However, quite a different interpretation also has been suggested. Concerning the textile factories, so this argument runs, we have no reliable information about their efficiency or lack of it. If observers close to Mehmed Ali Paşa may have been over-optimistic, the European consuls stationed in Egypt, some of whom very much worried about the potential competition of Egyptian manufactures, may well have exaggerated any difficulties that occurred. Moreover many travellers who observed Mehmed Ali Paşa's factories were no experts, and may well have described temporary work stoppages as final demise. For historians thinking along those lines, it was not the difficulties inherent in the import substitution project per se that caused the decline of the factories, but rather the free-trade policy imposed by Sultan Abdülmecid and ultimately by Palmerston on Mehmed Ali Paşa.[49] For non-specialists it seems prudent to report on the debate without taking sides.

From our perspective the industrial experiment is important because of its impact on Cairo's artisans. Certainly the number of men, women and children who worked in the factories was relatively small, estimated at about 40,000, and the number of fully trained artisans must have been lower still. Therefore it is not a valid argument to say that Egyptian guilds entered a crisis because of the novel predominance of factories. But constraints caused by the monopolization of raw cotton by the state were another matter entirely. Craftsmen who produced cotton textiles should have been in trouble even when they were permitted to do business on their own account, as raw cotton was at a premium. For Mehmed Ali Paşa had this valuable raw material exported, sent to the factories, and, for an albeit limited period of time, even obliged previously independent manufacturers to spin, weave and dye on behalf of his own administration. For when the drive towards a state-run economy was at its height, all purely private trade was forbidden, and artisans were obliged to sell all their products to Mehmed Ali Paşa's officials. After the goods had been stamped, the producers had to buy them back at a higher price before they could offer them for sale in the open market.

Admittedly this stage did not last very long, and direct sale to private customers was allowed long before the industrial experiment itself was abandoned.[50] In addition, some artisans who had worked for the factories probably became independent producers once the latter stopped operation.[51] But all this turmoil must have disrupted production routines, and it has therefore been suggested that while Mehmed Ali Paşa's economic policies were meant to lessen Egypt's dependence on imported goods, the practical effect at least in some sectors was rather the opposite.[52]

Around 1850: guild sheikhs, the significance of 'known faces' and the vexed question of relative guild autonomy

Almost 40 years ago it was suggested that Ottoman guilds in general and those of Cairo in particular were mainly organs of state administration, serving as a means of social control and taxation in an urban environment where other governmental institutions were only weakly represented.[53] A great deal of debate has focused on this claim, and in the present author's view it is not tenable if applied to the Ottoman lands as a whole. Headmen who had purchased their offices at least indirectly from the government might occasionally exercise serious pressure on their subordinates, yet, even so, Istanbul craftsmen retained a degree of control over their organizations.

But for the present we are concerned with a special case, namely Cairo during the 1840s and 1850s.[54] In the debate that pits partisans of relative guild autonomy against those who see these organizations as 'transmission belts' of central control, particular attention has been given to the role of guild sheikhs. Certainly Mehmed Ali Paşa's government used these sheikhs for its own purposes: they were made responsible for supplying workmen and/or finished goods. This pressure was only in part relaxed under the remarkable viceroy's successors, known in Ottoman as the *hıdiv*. Probably some guild sheikhs benefited from this situation, thus accentuating the economic inequalities so characteristic of the Ottoman craft world.

Moreover the Cairo sheikhs were made to ensure that apart from the most menial jobs, nobody could be employed without guarantors to vouch for him/her. It has even been proposed that around 1850 immigrants to the city perforce occupied the lowest rungs of the social ladder because 'known faces' were preferred for almost any task carrying even a modicum of responsibility.[55] Cases in which sheikhs were required to vouch for the members of their guilds also are on record – this practice was perhaps less common in Istanbul.[56] Mutual guarantees among townsmen and peasants were certainly not unknown in the central provinces – quite the contrary. In the capital as well, newcomers often needed someone to vouch for them before they could start work. But had guild *kethüda*s routinely been guarantors for the craftsmen they directed, surely this would have been mentioned in the numerous and often wordy documents by which these elders were deposed or (re)instated. Perhaps surveillance really was stricter in Mehmed Ali Paşa's Cairo.

Recently, however, this emphasis on the semi-official control functions of Cairo's guilds has been called into question, and the 'autonomous' aspects of guild life have re-entered scholarly debate.[57] It is now admitted that there was appreciable change over time: between the mid-1600s and the mid-1700s, many Cairo guild members invested considerable energy in the appointment of their sheikhs. In some instances they even bypassed the qadi and turned to the governor himself. Such procedures would have been unnecessary if the sheikhs had merely been 'transmission belts' in the service of the government. On the other hand, by the early nineteenth century the old-style appointment documents disappeared from the Cairo qadi records. By the 1830s, registers concerning guild affairs emphasized the intention of the state as reorganized by Mehmed Ali Paşa to assert direct control over the craftsmen and their organizations.[58] In this process some guild sheikhs were the government's willing agents. It thus makes sense to assume that in the course of the nineteenth century, many guilds lost their autonomy to the state apparatus, while earlier practices involving a degree of self-government tended to disappear.[59]

Conclusion: craftsmen between Cairo and Istanbul

Where the period after 1670 and particularly the eighteenth century is concerned, a comparison between Istanbul's and Cairo's guildsmen shows significant variety within the dominant 'Ottoman' model. Certainly in both cities, guilds were associations of masters in crafts and commerce, run by headmen, but the duties of the latter seem to have been quite different in Cairo from what they were in Istanbul. Thus the collective purchase of raw materials by guild leaders on behalf on their organizations seems to have been more important in the Ottoman capital than in the Egyptian metropolis.[60] Or at least the topic has attracted more scholarly attention. In the same vein, picnics in the open spaces outside the city, apparently a pleasure as well as a social obligation among Istanbul's guild masters, have not been mentioned in the research on Cairo artisans accessible to me.

Admittedly differences between the two metropolises may have existed in earlier times as well, but only for the period after 1670 are our sources, both primary and secondary, numerous enough for us to focus on inter-urban and inter-regional variation. On the other hand, observing is not always equivalent to explaining: the empire-wide distribution of the *gedik* is a case in point. By 1800 a significant number of Istanbul guilds had adopted this arrangement, but for reasons not as yet clear, in Cairo the *gedik* does not seem to have become popular. Even in the 1840s, when the drive for state control was in full swing, immigrants from the countryside seem to have entered quite a few guilds.[61]

In Damascus, by contrast, an Arabized form of *gedik* called *kedek* ultimately appeared (see Chapter 10). As the Damascenes adopted the Turkish expression instead of coining an Arabic word, we can hypothesize that the institution itself spread to the Syrian provinces from the Turkish-speaking sections of the empire. But why did the *gedik/kedek* become popular in those places and not in Cairo?

Perhaps from this peculiar distribution, we can conclude that in Istanbul and Damascus artisans confronted problems that differed considerably from those experienced by their Cairo colleagues. Although life in the Ottoman capital was difficult enough, there was no parallel to the unbridled rivalries between the households of Mamluk *beys* that plagued the artisans of Cairo during the late 1700s. On the other hand, Istanbul and perhaps even Damascus artisans were called upon to serve their legitimate rulers, in other words the Ottoman sultans, much more often than was true in Cairo before Mehmed Ali Paşa became the de facto ruler and mobilized the local artisans. Possibly the more regulated and legitimized exploitation current in the Ottoman capital gave rise, in self-defence, to a more stringent organization of many artisans through the *gedik*. In the turmoil that characterized late eighteenth-century Cairo, by contrast, tighter forms of organization may not have seemed very helpful: on the contrary, expedients often were necessary, and these could be adopted more efficiently by small groups or even individual masters. Or perhaps in this uncertain environment everyone suspected his neighbour and this impeded the consolidation of guilds. But at the present level of our knowledge such claims are mere speculation.

Obviously this argument only makes sense if we assume that the guilds of Istanbul and Cairo to an appreciable extent served the interests of the masters that were their members, and this assumption does form the basis of the present study. Yet developments in mid-nineteenth-century Cairo show that guild autonomy could be lost, just as the spread of the *gedik* did away with an earlier flexibility with respect to membership (see Chapter 4). What was valid in Istanbul around 1700 need not have applied to Cairo around 1850. In the same vein the 'political' options open to Ottoman craftsmen may also have varied from one period to the next, as we will see in the next chapter.

CHAPTER 8

Political Roles of Craftsmen

In a theoretically absolutist state, where legitimate power was a monopoly of the sultans and their servitors the *askeri*, we must begin by clarifying the term 'politics' when used in connection with members of the subject population (*reaya*). Admittedly by the 1700s the borders between *askeri* and *reaya*, the two major categories in Ottoman politics, were often blurred, if only because artisans and members of a military corps could claim *askeri* status.[1]

In this context we must remember that manual work was never regarded as incompatible with service to the sultan and thus with the status of an *askeri*. In the late sixteenth and early seventeenth centuries, the division between the sultans' servants and the taxpaying population had been taken very seriously indeed.[2] Even so, the estates of people whose only distinction was that they had laboured on behalf of the sultans were the responsibility of the official who dealt with the inheritances of the *askeri* (*askeri kassam*) and, incidentally, ensured that the sultans' treasury received the lion's share. Certain artisans thus could justify their 'political' actions by a – perhaps tenuous – connection to the Ottoman political elite.

Everyday grassroots politics: surveying the field

We will begin by introducing the enterprises that for the purposes of our study will count as 'everyday politics'. On a modest level petitioning the sultan was such a 'political act', and in principle this activity was permitted to all inhabitants of the empire. Craftsmen and their representatives, the guild elders, submitted numerous petitions now mostly lost, yet the surviving official responses form a significant source for many studies of Ottoman craftspeople including the present one.[3] Governors and even their stand-ins (*kaymakams*) could also be approached by artisan petitioners, but since the provincial documentation concerning such cases has survived but rarely we cannot say whether certain types of petition went to the governors and others directly to the Ottoman centre.[4]

Given the element of rivalry and strife, so often the backdrop of craftsmen's petitions, it seems reasonable to define the mobilization of support for the writing and submitting of the relevant documents as political acts, to say nothing of the fund-raising that must have accompanied all such negotiations. For in the absence of a postal service available to ordinary subjects, sending a petition to the capital from a provincial town must have cost an appreciable amount of money. Even when the would-be petitioners lived in the capital, the text needed to be drafted and a clean copy prepared by a competent scribe, employing the proper calligraphy, and presents to doorkeepers and other officials may have helped to speed the document on its way.

Certain activities of artisan groupings in the qadis' courts can also be classified as political. When craftsmen were dissatisfied with the heads of their guilds, had them deposed, found the appropriate successors and at times collected funds to buy out former officeholders, these activities should be classed as small-scale political acts, comparable to the 'office politics' in modern associations or business concerns. Similarly the negotiations that preceded the issuing of the rules governing the exercise of particular crafts, known as *nizam* in eighteenth-century Istanbul and as *uṣūl* in Cairo during the 1840s and 1850s, should also be classed as everyday political acts.[5] Whether a certain kind of dyestuff or the mixing of different types of fibres in the manufacture of a given textile was permitted or forbidden constituted an advantage to certain artisans and a significant loss to others. Generally speaking the rules of the craft must have embodied whatever suited the interests of the most influential guild members.

Catastrophes of one kind or another might also be the starting point for grassroots political activity. When an urban business locale (khan) or collective workshop tenanted by many craftsmen burned down or collapsed, those artisans who had lost their shops at first would scatter all over town. Yet whether they returned after the necessary repairs had been effected might be a contentious issue that required intra-guild politicking and even the qadis' interventions. Masters desiring to evade guild controls might prefer not to return to a common workplace. Therefore considerations from the realm of 'guild politics' might be as important as purely economic issues – for instance, the amount of rent demanded when artisans or craft groups decided whether or not they wanted to return to their former khan.

Certain small-scale political activities became necessary because many artisans worked in structures belonging to pious foundations once instituted by a member of the Ottoman dynasty. In this case, administration devolved upon the Chief Black Eunuch (*kızlar ağası*), a high-level dignitary in the palace hierarchy.[6] In addition even the pious foundations of viziers were often run by people with close contacts to the upper levels of the sultans' administration. Such personages did not concern themselves with mundane issues such as the collection of rent. Yet if the tenants of a given khan or row of shops were dissatisfied with local foundation administrators, they might need to submit the matter to these more highly placed figures in Istanbul. Such cases were especially frequent in eighteenth-century Bursa, where many artisans worked on real estate belonging to pious foundations instituted by the early Ottoman sultans.

Deliberations concerning such issues were considered normal activities for craftsmen and their guild elders. To the present author's knowledge, in the surviving documents we do not find officials of the sultan who proclaimed that artisans should submit to whatever their betters had decided for them. Nor were petitioners enjoined to let elite officials determine the norms of their trade, and when relations between Muslim and non-Muslim artisans were at issue the judges did not tell the disputing parties to avoid getting mixed up in matters beyond their station.

At least as importantly, artisans had to cope with the demands of tax farmers. To what extent the acts of craftspeople resisting these local figures of authority were considered legitimate is, however, much less clear. Certainly upon occasion, we encounter artisans' petitions against the abuses of tax collectors that found a sympathetic hearing among officials in the capital. An example may make this clearer: the farmer of an alum mine had the right to force dyers and tanners to purchase administratively determined quantities of alum at prices that also had been established by administrative fiat. As for the artisans affected by this rule, they might find that the alum in question was of poor quality or in excess of their requirements, if not both things at the same time. Upon their complaint, an order might be issued to the tax farmer in question to abide by customary rules. But if this admonition did not help, artisans might be tempted to smuggle alum, and though the practice was often tolerated it definitely was not considered licit by the government's agents. Yet if we possessed testimonies of the craftsmen who did the smuggling, they might well have responded that they merely defended 'ancient custom' against the evil machinations of local powerholders.

Guarantors of good behaviour

In the Ottoman domain it was common practice to demand guarantors (*kefil*) whenever outsiders arrived in a given locality, often in order to work. The guarantors were to ensure that the person/persons in question showed up in court when called upon (*kefil binnefs*) or else paid his/her debts (*kefil bilmal*). Thus the employers of agricultural labourers in the Bursa region during the late 1500s might be required to furnish guarantees, even if the men in question came from the same area. In Ankara during the early 1600s, when attacks by rebel mercenaries threatened, residents of certain town quarters were required to furnish guarantees that no people of ill repute were living in their midst. Perhaps this measure was designed to weed out people who might open the city gates to the soldiers in revolt. Unfortunately the surviving documents do not tell us very much about the grassroots politics that must have preceded such a furnishing of mutual guarantees in town quarters, markets or perhaps even guilds. People of questionable status must have lobbied for support among their co-residents of good standing, respected artisans included.

In the 1700s a new variant of collective guarantee appeared, known as the *nezir*. In this case the inhabitants of a given village or – much more rarely – town quarter affirmed that if a certain person marked as a rebel/robber appeared in the vicinity they would deliver him to the authorities or else pay over a large sum of money.[7] These documents raise the question whether – and, if so, why – collective guarantees were considered more important in the eighteenth century than they had been in earlier times. The relevance of these issues to the contemporary consolidation of craft guilds also needs to be explored, but that is a subject for future studies.

'Political' roles accepted willy-nilly: artisan participation in the sultans' festivals

As in the late 1500s and early 1600s, Ottoman sultans of the period after 1670 from time to time organized festive processions, and expected craftsmen to participate both physically and financially. Accordingly artisans paraded through the city, produced floats and other decorations and shouldered part of the expense. Guildsmen both in Istanbul and Cairo were important players in the 'theatrical' performances by which the sultans thus asserted their power and piety; especially the Egyptian metropolis was a favoured venue for celebrations, which, among other things, highlighted the outgoing and incoming *hajj* caravans. We will take a closer look at the great festival of 1720, when Ahmed III (r. 1703–30) had his sons circumcised; for the parade of Istanbul's craftsmen, along with their floats, has been immortalized by the poet-cum-painter Levni in a series of miniatures.[8]

Artisans were not the only participants in the numerous parades taking place in September 1720, despite occasional bad weather. Court dignitaries were also involved, but while these men merely showed off their horses, their finery and above all their persons, artisans were expected to be more imaginative. Just like their predecessors in 1582, Istanbul guildsmen had their apprentices act out scenes from life in the shops; these locales were reproduced more or less lavishly according to the means of the guildsmen involved. We do not know who designed these items, or even the gigantic figures and 'ships on wheels' that ornamented the 1720 parade. Architects serving the sultan could have been involved and perhaps also miniature painters including Levni himself.

Design apart, producing these scenes required special skills. A sizeable number of carpenters, experts in stucco decoration, painters and other people must have contributed their labour. At the sultan's court, this fact was well appreciated: at the very beginning of the festivities, the young princes were taken to the workshops so that they could see close up both the skilled labour and the magnificence that was to be deployed in their honour.

Directly or indirectly these extravaganzas were financed by the taxpayers, including craftspeople all over the empire. But the guilds of Istanbul were first in line when it came to contributions. Unfortunately only two documents conveying specific information on this issue have surfaced so far, and they concern traders rather than artisans. But since nothing else is available, these documents provide at least a notion of the order of magnitude concerning the contributions of Istanbul tradesmen. The first document deals with the sellers of fresh fruit, a relatively poor guild whose members did business around the gates of Odun kapısı and Yenikapı on the Marmara coast. These petty salespeople, all Muslims and quite a few of them military men, were the responsibility of a *pazarbaşı*, i.e. an official in charge of purchasing on behalf of the palace (see Chapter 4).[9] This guild was assessed at 800 *guruş*, a substantial sum that in view of the shopkeepers' modest resources may have been about average or perhaps even slightly below the norm. In this particular instance a representative of the *pazarbaşı* had advanced the money and expected later reimbursement from the tradesmen. For this purpose, the wealthier members of the guild were expected to disburse 2.5 *guruş* each and those of middling wealth 1.5 *guruş*. As for the poor, they were not spared either, but got off with just a single *guruş* per person.

In addition to money payments, many guildsmen, whether in the service of the palace or not, were expected to present gifts to the sultans on festive days, and the multiple circumcisions of 1720 were no exception to this rule.[10] Such gifts often must have been resented by the givers, yet the only complaint that I know of concerns the sellers of woollen cloth (*çuha*) in Istanbul, who must have dealt mainly in French and English fabrics.[11] According to these traders' petition, precedent had been violated, for when a great sultanic festival was celebrated in 1675–76, the records of the qadi as well as the special register put together at that time (*defter-i sur-ı humayun*, now both apparently lost) showed that the sellers of woollen cloth were aides (*yamak*) to the great merchants of the Istanbul covered market, and made their gifts together with their richer and more important colleagues.[12] Accordingly the complainants had prepared an appropriate contribution.

After the presents had been made available, however, an official in charge of overall palace purchases (*bazargânbaşı-ı şehriyarî*), probably higher in rank than the *pazarbaşı* who had lent money to the fruit-sellers, claimed the traders in woollen cloth as his own aides. Thus another contribution seemed imminent, but the cloth merchants invoked the practice of 1675 as the norm to be followed, and with the precedent-conscious Ottoman bureaucracy this argument carried considerable weight. Remarkably the traders invoked written evidence and not 'immemorial tradition'; this emphasis may be connected with the growing 'bureaucratization' characterizing the Ottoman eighteenth century. After the official in charge of festival preparations (*sur-ı humayun emini efendi*) had made the appropriate declaration, the merchants received a positive answer to their petition. As in 1675 they were now expected to contribute a jewelled portfolio, a field-flask of chinaware and three pieces of fabric, each suitable for a pair of underpants, or else a set of clothes, depending on the meaning of the word *don* in this context. One of these garments was supposed to be of *hitayi* silk, the second of atlas and the third of woollen cloth; we do not know whether these gifts were in lieu of monetary payments or else supplementary to them.

Our sources do not record what artisans thought of publicly celebrated sultanic feasts. Some may have been pleased at the extra business that such events generated. Being honoured by the presence of princes and court dignitaries, and even of Sultan Ahmed III in person, may have been of significance to others. Especially younger people must have liked the atmosphere of festive exuberance, which allowed some of them to use their theatrical talents and even poke fun at lower-level authorities.[13] But it is also likely that many artisans, especially the householders among them, viewed such events mainly as a source of extra expenditure: if the records of the *sur-ı humayun emini* ever were to surface, it might become possible to gain a better understanding.

Managing religious diversity

Wherever Muslims and non-Muslims worked together – and most large cities of the empire had mixed populations – it was necessary to manage inter-communal relations. While the Ottoman administration considered that Muslims and non-Muslims should inhabit separate town quarters, there was no such official pressure where artisan organization was concerned. On the contrary, mixed guilds were common; however, in the 1800s apparently the number of mono-religious guilds was on the increase. It is early in the day for categorical judgements but it does seem that at this time certain guilds split up along confessional lines.

Documentation on relations between guildsmen of different faiths is not very ample: matters not taken to the qadi or the central administration did not usually make it into written sources. Presumably quite a few disputes were solved in the market, khan or shop-lined street through the mediation of some respected local figure. However, the matter remains opaque as the guilds of non-Muslims, if studied at all, have been discussed in the framework of their respective communities and not in their relationships to Muslim fellow artisans.

However, certain sultanic commands from the later 1700s do shed some light on this question. Thus in the 1760s we encounter a major dispute between the Jewish and Muslim spice-sellers (*attar*), both operating in downtown Istanbul.[14] The Jewish drug-sellers had initiated the complaint, claiming that the Muslims were trying to drive them out of business by mutually agreeing that the drugs imported on European ships would be distributed among themselves only. This arrangement, they claimed, was novel and therefore not permissible. Although the Muslim drug-sellers denied these charges, the administration took the side of the Jews at least in part: they were to once again receive their traditional shares except in the case of coffee and sugar. Both parties were enjoined to avoid further conflict.

If the administration considered that coffee and sugar were to be a Muslim province this concession may have been significant, as these items had become elements of basic consumption, but more importantly the case hinged on economic opportunities and not on socio-political status. If the documents studied so far are any guide, business rivalries were the typical bone of contention when Muslims and non-Muslims were at loggerheads, and the administration, far from assuming that Muslims automatically must be supported against 'unbelievers', emphasized that all recognized artisans and shopkeepers needed to make a living and that keeping the peace was a top priority.

How artisans took on 'political' roles, but guilds did so quite rarely

In addition to these more or less routine conflicts, there were more dramatic events, including protests and even uprisings in Istanbul and Edirne. Certain chroniclers, who probably expressed the views of many members of the Ottoman ruling establishment, deplored urban rebellions as well as the military uprisings with which they were often associated. By themselves, artisans did not rebel very often; rather we find them participating in urban revolts in which the principal actor was some other grouping. When food was at a premium, the *petit peuple* of Damascus might demonstrate against governors and their merchant allies who, as poor people believed with greater or lesser justification, held back grain because they hoped that prices might rise yet further.[15] Undoubtedly many such demonstrators were artisans, but at least according to the available sources, food riots were not organized by guilds.

Given the limited number of rebellions on record with notable artisan participation, we will include one rather remarkable event that occurred shortly *before* 1670. Relatively detailed information can be found in Evliya Çelebi's account covering the protests that cost his relative, the grand vizier Melek Ahmed Paşa, his position. Evliya was an eyewitness to at least some of these events, even being known as one of the pasha's men.[16] As our traveller tells the story, in 1651 the grand vizier needed to send gold coins to the fortress of Azov on the northern shore of the Black Sea to pay the garrison, but the treasury had only silver *guruş* available. Melek Ahmed Paşa decided that the best way to remit the money was to exchange the *guruş* for gold in the bazaar and send the latter, as gold was far easier to transport. However, some of the grand vizier's aides, instead of using the good silver money they had taken from the treasury, distributed clipped coins in the bazaar, in addition to some textiles and alum; these latter goods they assessed at prices way over market value. Indignantly the tradesmen and their allies among the descendants of the Prophet (*seyyid*) complained to Melek Ahmed Paşa, but he flew into a temper and chased them away. While Evliya implied that the vizier had been fooled by his evil advisors, the pasha's angry reaction does make us wonder whether perhaps Melek Ahmed did not know more about the depredations of his underlings than he was willing to admit.

On the following morning, tanners working in the saddlers' compound (Saraçhane) in downtown Istanbul marched to the Topkapı palace carrying flags and drums.[17] Guild elders (*ihtiyarlar*) were much in evidence, and so were the *seyyid*s; they all demanded the execution of a large number of dignitaries. At first it seemed as if the grand vizier was able to win them over, and the crowd dispersed. But according to Evliya the *şeyhülislam* Aziz Efendi, along with one of his predecessors, in other words some high-level *ulema*, instigated the most aggressive elements of the crowd to return to the fray. Ultimately the grand vizier could only save himself by giving up his office and accepting a governor's position in far-away Rusçuk/Ruse.

For our discussion of artisan politics, this story is of great interest, as Evliya reported that 'white-bearded' guild elders took an active role in the events; they did not appear as humble petitioners, but as people sure of their rights and in no mood to accept insults from anyone, including the second-highest dignitary in the empire. In this context Evliya referred especially to the physical toughness of the – often unmarried – tanners whom at one point he called *ahi*s, thus referring to the traditions and solidarity characteristic of this craft. In the traveller's account these artisans played a key role in the disturbance.[18] In addition he had things to say about the devotion of the tanners to their patron saint, Ahi Evran, commenting on the wealth of these artisans and their readiness to come out in defence of their rights. These remarks indicate that at least in this case certain guilds were active participants in an urban uprising.

However, the chronicler Karaçelebizade, who wrote about these events as a former high-level religious dignitary now banished and out of office, highlighted the role of the Istanbul soldiers and courtiers in the uprising, and while mentioning the artisans had relatively little to say about them.

A second rebellion in which guildsmen played a major role occurred in 1688, when defeated and unpaid soldiers from the Hungarian front flooded back to Istanbul. Known as *zorba* (bullies), they robbed artisans and shopkeepers, and, as the administration was not able to either disband or curb them, anarchic conditions resulted. At one point, the current grand vizier Siyavuş Paşa was murdered and the women of his harem sold into slavery. Finally the exasperated artisans rebelled against *zorba* oppression, led once again by a descendant of the Prophet Muhammad (*seyyid*). Seyyid Osman Atpazari was a craftsman himself, but by his leadership acquired so much prestige that he was able to negotiate with the palace on the artisans' behalf. After a new team of high officials had been appointed, which was acceptable to the craftsmen, the *zorba* were dispersed and business resumed. It has been suggested that the close links of many military men and administrative officers to the Istanbul marketplace made them sympathetic to the demand of the artisans that plunder and disorder must finally cease.[19]

In the reports concerning later rebellions, this type of guild involvement did not often recur, and, given the present state of our knowledge, we cannot tell whether eighteenth-century artisans rebelled less often on their own initiative than their seventeenth-century ancestors. Perhaps it had become merely a convention among chroniclers to attribute agency exclusively to soldiers and men of religion.

When military rebellions occurred in the 1700s, artisans were always depicted in a subordinate role, appearing in the streets because they formed part of the relevant militia corps. But in reality, craftsmen probably participated for the most part because they saw their livelihoods threatened. When in the second half of the seventeenth century sultans Mehmed IV (r. 1648–87), Süleyman II (r. 1687–91), Ahmed II (r. 1691–95) and Mustafa II (r. 1695–1703) preferred to reside in Edirne instead of just visiting the local palace for hunting expeditions as had been the custom, seemingly rumours began to spread that the capital was to be moved to this city on a permanent basis. Unrest among Istanbul artisans was the result, as the court was a major buyer of luxury and also of everyday goods. Even if the pay was often low, association with the palace brought prestige and presumably also more tangible rewards. Istanbul craftsmen therefore participated in the 1703 rebellion, and the new sultan Ahmed III (r. 1703–30) was made to promise that he would from now on reside in the capital.[20]

Ahmed III not only gained but also lost his throne at least partly because of artisan discontent: in the 1720s the Ottoman Empire engaged in a series of campaigns designed to benefit from the disintegration of Safavid rule in Iran.[21] For a few years Tabriz was in the sultan's hands, but his armies proved unable to hold the city. A new campaign was planned, and, as usual in such cases, Istanbul artisans were expected to pay the expenses of those among their colleagues who were to follow the soldiers on campaign (see Chapter 3). But in reality the army did not march but waited on the outskirts of the capital, and many taxpayers must have concluded that their sacrifices all had been in vain. In the absence of comments from the craftsmen themselves, it is hard to say to what extent this realization induced them to join the rebellion of the soldiers. Other considerations may have intervened as well: as the war in Iran had been going on for many years, people in Istanbul must have been aware of the hardships of soldiering in the harsh mountain lands of eastern Anatolia, in a campaign directed against fellow Muslims. Quite possibly some artisans were angry at what they may have regarded as the misdirection of the war in general. In addition there were the 'new-fangled luxuries' at court which were unpopular among the poor and for which the grand vizier İbrahim Paşa typically was made responsible.

Once again our sources do not indicate that Istanbul guilds played any visible role in the uprising. Presumably artisans got together within their craft organizations and discussed events, and thus the guilds provided a network of contacts that allowed the dissemination of rumours both with and without foundation. But when people took to the streets, they did so as adherents of military/paramilitary corps, and not as guild members – no banners of Ahi Evran were mentioned anywhere. And when the chief rebels were executed on the orders of the new ruler Mahmud I (r. 1730–54), apparently no guildsmen were among the victims, nor was any blame attached to the city's craft organizations.[22]

Cairo's artisans opposing Mamluk tax demands and, above all, the French occupation

A similar conclusion emerges from the studies of Cairo artisan rebellions of the 1700s and 1800s. These uprisings are better documented than many of the events previously discussed, because the Cairo chronicler al-Djabartī and, for the rebellions of 1798 and 1800, the French occupying authorities have left ample accounts.[23] In Cairo there were 'rebellion-prone' urban quarters such as al-Ḥusayniyya and Rumayla. These were inhabited mainly by poor artisans, with butchers prominent in the vicinity of Cairo's slaughterhouses located in al-Ḥusayniyya. The latter guildsmen, physically strong and accustomed to blood and gore, played an important role in resisting the authorities not merely in Cairo: while avoiding major violent action, their contemporaries and colleagues, the Jewish butchers of Istanbul, were also known for their refusal to 'knuckle under' when it came to the demands of rabbis and community council men.[24]

Close contacts between the young males forming the most active rebels became possible because in al-Ḥusayniyya and Rumayla neighbourly ties were based on membership of the same guild. In some cases, neighbours-cum-fellow-guildsmen also came together in local dervish lodges. In contrast to what happened in Istanbul, where to date evidence about 'rebellion-prone' town quarters has not emerged, a few artisans were so prominent in the Cairo rebellions that their names have come down to us.[25] Possibly some sections of Istanbul were also more active than others when it came to resistance and rebellion, but we do not possess geographically based studies comparable to those dealing with Cairo. A certain obsession of present-day scholars with the doings of the central state perhaps has prevented such 'grassroots' investigations in the Ottoman heartland.[26]

However, rebellions in Cairo were by no means confined to these poor urban quarters. Already in the revolts against the exactions of Mamluk *beys* in the late eighteenth century, participation was much broader. But especially the inhabitants of al-Ḥusayniyya remained on the *qui vive* even after a compromise supposedly had been hammered out with the *beys* and unrest in other urban quarters had died down. As for the two anti-French rebellions, city-wide participation was nearly universal, especially when, towards the end of the Napoleonic occupation, an Ottoman governor and the grand vizier Mustafa Paşa himself were present in the vicinity (1800).[27] But when the military defeat of the insurgents became obvious after the French bombardment of the upper-class residential quarter of Azbakiyya, the 'bourgeoisie' drew back, but not the rebels of the more popular quarters, and this phenomenon prompted al-Djabartī to make some critical remarks about the lack of realism among the common people.[28]

Dervish sheikhs: limited participation in urban politics

Studies of the two Cairo rebellions against the French invasion have emphasized their religious component: the inhabitants took to the streets because they were outraged at the occupation of their city by non-Muslims. Surely before and after prayers in the mosque, there was occasion to discuss the abusive behaviour of the foreign soldiery and other pertinent matters. But in addition many artisans attended religious exercises in dervish lodges, where social contacts must have been even closer than in the relative anonymity of a large mosque. Admittedly the ethos of mystical brotherhoods, a pertinent feature in early Ottoman guild history, may still have survived in some organizations by the late 1700s but was probably almost absent in others; this diversity of orientation applied to Cairo as well as to Istanbul. Yet even so, it was in part through their contacts in dervish lodges that many craftsmen developed the social cohesion necessary for any act of resistance to come about.

Attendance at dervish lodges in Cairo was, as we have seen, largely neighbourhood-based. By contrast members of one and the same guild did not follow mystical exercises in a lodge frequented in common. It has, however, been suggested that intensive contacts in urban quarters, guilds and dervish lodges in combination accounted for the strong *esprit de corps* in a locality such as al-Ḥusayniyya.[29]

As for the central Ottoman provinces, dervishes such as the Melevis, Nakşbendis, Halvetis and Bektaşis have been studied with considerable emphasis on the socio-political roles of their sheikhs, for it is the administrative rather than the religious activity of the latter that is covered by the Ottoman archival documents on which our analysis is so often based.[30] None of the relevant monographs have shown a close involvement of the sheikhs of the major dervish orders in local artisan affairs. When the sheikhs petitioned the authorities, they were normally concerned with the appointment of dervishes to responsible positions within their respective orders, or else they attempted to control the disposal of real estate and movable property belonging to their lodges.

However, our documentation does reflect certain broad political concerns: thus the Halvetis were known as staunch supporters of Sunni right belief and Ottoman rule, to the point that after the latter had ended, most sheikhs left the Balkan countries where they had been born and their lodges had operated for centuries.[31] In the Anatolian towns of Konya and Hacıbektaş, Mevlevi and Bektaşi sheikhs established relatively centralized controls over the lodges affiliated with their orders, although the dervish communities in question sometimes were located in far-away provinces. But these sheikhs do not seem to have participated often in urban and/or guild affairs, and much the same thing applies to the early Nakşbendis. As the one exception to this rule we must mention the *ahi baba*s of the lodge of Ahi Evran in Kırşehir who were in contact with many tanners in Istanbul and elsewhere (Chapters 6 and 7). Unfortunately the activity of the *ahi baba*s as dervish sheikhs leading their followers along the spiritual path remains all but unknown, and we do not know whether these sheikhs ever gave their adherents political advice.

Until sources demonstrating the contrary are found, we therefore can assume that most dervishes and sheikhs did not involve themselves closely in the activities of local guildsmen, although they made broad political commitments to the Ottoman sultanate or, later on, to the emergent republic of Turkey.[32] Nor do we find the names of dervish sheikhs among the 'movers and shakers' of urban socio-political uprisings in which artisans played a part.

Bringing down two sultans: the janissary–*ulema* alliance, with artisans as junior partners

For a brief interlude, we will return to Cairo. Sheikhs in the Azhar, the city's principal centre of religious teaching, sometimes do seem to have played a role in urban rebellions, especially those directed against a non-Muslim occupant. After the murder of Napoleon's general Kléber, some Azhar sheikhs were executed in retaliation; they were accused of having had advance knowledge of the assassination plans that they had failed to report.[33] But most of the time, the men of law and religion (*ulema*), especially those in higher offices, kept out of rebellions and, during the initial stages, waited out developments. Later on, they often attempted to mediate between the political establishment and the rebels; this tendency has been observed both for Istanbul and Cairo during the eighteenth century.[34]

However, to this rule there were exceptions. In the Istanbul uprisings of 1703 and 1730 the rebellious soldiers and craftsmen received the open support of certain *ulema*, usually people in modest positions. Career considerations probably played a role in motivating these scholars. Dealing with the events of 1730, shrewd contemporary chroniclers did in fact comment that Ahmed III had made a grave mistake by keeping the same grand vizier in office for many years. Would-be officeholders, thinking that their turns would never come, were therefore inclined to join the rebels: this consideration should also have applied to religious scholars – after all, potential qadis.[35] At the same time, the insurgents needed the support of at least some specialists in religious law because deposing a sultan and killing high-level officials were serious moves that had to be legitimized in a convincing fashion. Religious-cum-legal opinions (*fetvas*) were required to attest that the rebels had good reasons for their insurgency; and these documents could only be supplied by *ulema*.[36] Quite probably the participation of the latter had a good deal to do with the fact that the 1703 and 1730 movements of the Edirne and Istanbul soldiers, along with their artisan allies, gained empire-wide support: although Mustafa II and Ahmed III both lived on for some years after their respective depositions, we do not hear of any significant movements to reinstate them.

Did religious considerations motivate the rebels at least in part? This question is difficult to answer. Throughout the seventeenth century, movements that decried the inclusiveness of official Islamic practice and demanded a return to the supposedly stricter customs of the early caliphs kept recurring, and especially lower-level *ulema*, including mosque preachers, promulgated this message. In historiography, the adherents of these movements have become known as the people of the Kadızade (Kadızadeliler).[37] While the sources tell us very little about the people who listened to and took up the message of the Kadızade and his followers, we can surmise that many of them were artisans. But adherents were not limited to this milieu: one of the elite representatives of what we might call the Kadızadeli mentality, namely the sheikh Vani Efendi, was preacher to Sultan Mehmed IV in person.[38]

Probably the luxurious lifestyle of the palace was a significant factor leading to the rebellion of 1730.[39] Criticism of luxury could be justified in the religious perspective of the Kadızadeliler; however, on the other side of the balance, there was the 'ancient custom' that demanded that the sultans' court be the scene of stately pomp. Jewelled turbans, horse-gear inlaid with gilt silver and costly brocades had all been part of the trappings of royalty from time immemorial; what is more, the book-loving and parsimonious Ahmed III probably spent less on such luxuries than some of his predecessors had done. On the other hand, these goods were not now confined just to the Topkapı palace, where few artisans ever would have seen them. As the elite more and more used the waterfronts of the Bosporus and Golden Horn as sites of display, certain luxury items were viewed and talked about by many more people.[40] Certainly the supposed 'Westernization' of court culture in the early eighteenth century is now known to have been exaggerated in modern historiography.[41] But it is perhaps irrelevant how many 'foreign luxuries' really did become popular among the courtly elite. For these imports to destabilize the regime, it would have been sufficient if they were seen by a larger number of people than previously and appeared in a context where they were not legitimized by 'ancient custom'.

An interesting aspect, both practical and symbolic, concerns the opening and/or closing of shops during rebellions, well documented for the events of 1730. Closing shops in case of unrest was a means of self-defence, intended to discourage plunderers. But at the same time, such closures showed that the situation was not normal, and officials therefore might put pressure on artisans and merchants to keep their shops open. According to the account of the Habsburg imperial interpreter who reported to Vienna on the rebellion of 1730, the Ottoman chief admiral, also deputy to the grand vizier İbrahim Paşa, admonished shopkeepers to resume business for just this reason.[42]

Furthermore while today it is unfashionable to dwell too much on economic motivations, I think it still likely that Istanbul artisans who themselves produced luxury goods were unhappy to see competing wares make even quite modest inroads into the mansions of the elite.[43] Disappointments on the economic level thus combined with a religiously legitimized 'anti-foreign luxury' stance to bring down the sultan and his grand vizier.[44] Unfortunately our sources do not allow us to determine the relative weight of these different factors.

Deposing a third ruler: military reform as a threat to artisan livelihoods

As the Russo-Ottoman war of 1768–74 had amply demonstrated, a combination of janissaries-turned-militiamen and irregulars was no match for the firepower of the armies of the Tsarina Catherine II. The young Sultan Selim III (r. 1789–1807) soon gave up all hopes of retraining the janissaries, and began supplementing them with a corps that he called the 'New Order' (*nizam-ı cedid*). Ultimately these novel troops were intended to replace the janissaries.[45] To house the 'New Order/New Model' soldiers, gigantic barracks were constructed that still dominate the cityscape between Üsküdar and Kadıköy, and some of the sultan's trusted advisors were sent to European capitals to collect information about a variety of institutions, with military training a major priority.[46] As so many janissaries in reality were artisans, the phasing out of this corps must have been viewed as a threat by many Istanbul guildsmen. For once the professional soldiers of the 'New Order' had come to dominate the scene, janissary privileges were bound to disappear and many artisans may have thought that these losses were impossible to absorb.

To compound the problems facing Istanbul's craftsmen, the late 1700s and early 1800s were a time of economic and financial crisis. Wars were a major cause of the downturn, as the expenses of eighteenth-century military confrontations – which, after all, were high enough to bring down French absolutism in 1789 – were more than the relevant economies could bear. In the Ottoman case there was, moreover, a rather specific problem: as the state apparatus paid for the goods it demanded at prices way below market level, a war-related boom could not develop in the armaments sector, although the slump in the market for civilian goods of course was very noticeable (see Chapter 3).[47]

Therefore wars that demanded great financial efforts and produced no conquests to balance them resulted in major deficits which the administration tried to alleviate by devaluing the currency; the resulting inflation had a negative effect on real wages.[48] After the relative prosperity of the years before 1750, real wages in construction, the only ones that are known to us, declined dramatically, with a 'trough' in the 1770s. In addition, while in the 1600s and early 1700s, untrained labourers on Istanbul's building sites typically did somewhat better than trained craftsmen, this advantage disappeared in the course of the crisis. We may therefore surmise that discontent among ordinary labourers was greatest, and they may well have attributed their losses to the military reforms of Selim III.

Yet again the uprising that brought down the sultan was not a movement of craftsmen and workmen but a military revolt. Supported by certain high-level *ulema*, it succeeded in part because of Sultan Selim's defeatism and partly because the rebels had allies in the ruler's immediate entourage.[49] Only when the soldiers were already on the march do we hear about craftsmen whose actions caught the attention of chroniclers and other observers: some artisans joined in while others merely closed their shops because they were afraid of being robbed. There are also some references to 'the rabble': these men may well have been the common labourers who had lost most heavily in the economic downturn of the years around 1800. As there was no mention of guilds joining in as organizations, in this respect the rebellion of 1807 closely resembled its counterparts of 1703 and 1730.

Conclusion: how a sultan gained – and lost – acceptance in the eyes of his artisan subjects

We can regard the participation of Istanbul craftsmen in rebellions, albeit as 'junior partners' of soldiers and *ulema*, as evidence for the loss in legitimacy suffered by Mustafa II, Ahmed III and Selim III in turn. In the absence of direct testimony any interpretation remains hypothetical. Failures in warfare must have had a role to play: in the reigns of Mustafa II and Selim III, lost battles and humiliating peace treaties upset the course of everyday life in the capital, and this bad news must have discredited the sultans. Ahmed III, on the other hand, himself emphatically a civilian, had presided over a series of Iranian campaigns that, if not disastrous, had not brought any durable gains.[50] As the sultans defined themselves as the ever victorious leaders of Sunni Islam, it makes sense to assume that defeats weakened their positions; but whether artisans reacted more sharply to such misfortunes than other Ottoman subjects remains an open question.

In addition, economic hardship must have been a major factor in destroying the legitimacy of any sultan, who, after all, was expected to provide his 'poor subjects' with the possibility of earning a livelihood. In the long years of the Ottoman–Habsburg war of 1683–99, campaign-related efforts had absolute priority, and if the real wages earned by Istanbul building workers during those years indicate larger trends, the standard of living went down.[51] As the period between 1720 and 1750 was relatively prosperous, a decline in material conditions probably did not play a role in the movement that brought down Ahmed III; however, there were many small complaints resulting in a general dissatisfaction among artisans.[52] Survival problems again became predominant in the late 1700s, when, as we have seen (Chapter 6), interruptions of the grain supply were no rarity. In conjunction with declining real wages these scarcities may well have mobilized the capital's artisans against Selim III.

Well aware of the instability of the situation, sultans and viziers made significant efforts to shore up their legitimacy. Once the Peace of Pasarofça/ Passarowitz had been concluded in 1718, Ahmed III must have had his officials begin preparations for the 1720 festival. Here the labour of artisans was highlighted, although we do not know to what extent the festivities helped legitimize the regime in the eyes of Istanbul craftsmen. Given the great expense involved, in some cases the celebrations may have had the opposite effect. Other measures involved well-publicized concern with the bread supply; we have seen Ahmed III punishing bakers who sold underweight loaves and Selim III inspecting the markets in person and exhorting officials and craftsmen alike to supply good-quality bread (see Chapter 6). Campaigns against luxury, of the kind undertaken by Selim III in times of war, might serve the same legitimizing purpose.[53] Even the particular wrath with which certain eighteenth-century sultans treated 'new-fangled' female fashions may have been intended to re-establish the ruler as the upholder of Islamic values, especially in the eyes of poorer urbanites whose wives could not have afforded the fine light-coloured textiles sported by young ladies of the elite.[54]

Furthermore, from the 1720s onwards, buildings serving pious foundations were constructed in Istanbul in relatively large numbers; through this activity, the administration probably wished to demonstrate that the ruler had the welfare of his subjects at heart. In addition such projects provided work for many artisans and labourers.[55] And in spite of a near-terminal crisis of the Ottoman Empire, Selim III and his successor Mahmud II (r. 1808– 39) did not neglect to build impressive mosque complexes that form part of Istanbul's skyline down to the present day.

Cairo artisans seem to have been more prominent in the grassroots politics that have concerned us in the present chapter. The Istanbul sources do not record any urban wards as 'rebellion-prone' as al-Ḥusayniyya or Rumayla, although this Cairo peculiarity may be well be an artefact of our sources: there was simply no al-Djabartī at work in Istanbul during that time. If, however, our impression is correct at least to some extent, then Cairo's craftsmen may have been especially active because visibly the Ottoman sultan was unable to protect them against the exactions of the Mamluk *beys*. While received with high hopes, the great admiral Hasan Paşa, because of his limited means, had soon been forced to tax merchants and artisans in a manner more or less reminiscent of the *beys* whom he had ousted (see Chapter 7). Moreover Istanbul in this period was spared foreign occupation, but Cairo was not: it was in the two rebellions against the French forces that Cairo's artisans banded together with the city's notables in order to express their indignation with a regime that placed non-Muslims over Muslims and thus disturbed the 'order of the world' to an even greater extent than anything that had occurred in the Ottoman capital.

All these considerations bring us back to the question whether Ottoman artisans were able to act autonomously, and, if so, to what extent. Most of the time, guilds were much less active than militias when it came to articulating discontent; only in the seventeenth century were some artisan organizations prominent in urban rebellions. In other words, after the mid-seventeenth century it was typically membership of a militia that allowed Muslim artisans to rebel, in the hope of setting to rights what they saw as an intolerable disturbance of the world order they knew. At the same time, all militias had started life as military corps. Thus apparently the integration of artisans into the Ottoman state structure – in the wider sense of the term – paradoxically accorded them the means for autonomous actions in times of crisis.

Whatever their political importance, the events in Istanbul and Cairo involved only a minority of all artisans on Ottoman territory. In eighteenth-century Aleppo and Damascus factional struggles were frequent and so too were food riots, but limited space does not permit us to try and disentangle to what extent artisans were involved, both as members of urban militias and as guildsmen.[56] While less active politically than inhabitants of the great cities – or so it seems given the present state of our knowledge – craftspeople in the provinces continued to produce goods and make a living as best as they could. In the next chapter we will discuss these products and activities.

CHAPTER 9

Provincial Craftsmen: How Guilds Adapted to New Circumstances

In the present chapter we will attempt a partial survey of provincial artisans producing for a wider market; the craftspeople of Cairo (see Chapter 7) will be considered metropolitan and therefore excluded. Broadly speaking and with a number of detours our story will move from west to east, from the towns of present-day Bulgaria and Tunis all the way to Damascus and Jerusalem, passing through Bursa on the way. Once again we will take a closer look at the three-cornered relationship which forms the major subject of this study: firstly, the material goods produced plus the consumer demand occasioning them; secondly, the constraints imposed by the Ottoman state and its representatives – the governors or tax farmers; and, thirdly, and for us most significantly, the fates of the producing artisans, both within and outside of the guilds. Consumer demand and artisans' attempts to satisfy it will occupy centre stage, but, as we shall see, quite often the empire's ruling group set the parameters within which both producers and consumers were obliged to operate.

In spite of the crisis of the late 1700s and early 1800s, it is surely outdated to assume an overall decline and ultimate disappearance of Ottoman craftworkers during this period. Even when confronted with factory-made goods in the mid-1850s, certain craftspeople found niches in the domestic market that remained largely inaccessible to importers or else developed new lines of work.[1] If this was true in the age of steamships or mechanized spinning and weaving, surely it must have been even more valid in the 1700s, when involvement with the European world economy was still a localized affair.

Socio-economic differentiation in Balkan towns

Between 1670 and 1850, many Balkan towns came to house a more varied population, although urban development in the region mostly remained modest.[2] At least in certain parts of Greece, social differentiation was quite apparent already in the mid-seventeenth century, but at that time profits from trade and industry did not lead to great wealth and high status. Riches, and the social power accompanying them, were typically connected to tax collection, in which Muslim dignitaries but also Orthodox churchmen might take on a prominent role. These relationships were reflected in the town chronicle that Papa Synadinos, a priest and notable of the Balkan town of Serrai/Serez, wrote in the mid-1600s, shortly before the period covered by the present chapter. The author highlighted the doings of locally respected persons including members of his own family, who were prominent among Serrai's non-Muslims and even wielded a degree of political influence.[3] Circumventing the prohibitions of Islamic law concerning the enlargement and embellishment of churches, these Orthodox notables found ways and means to sponsor quite elaborate ecclesiastical decorations. It is relevant to our story that they thus acted as patrons for artists/artisans. Serrai's craftsmen occasionally entered the chronicle as well, but in a subordinate position. In a similar vein, recent work on Verroia/Kara Ferye in the 1600s has also shown that the elites of this town were not mercantile or industrial, although the town had lively woollen manufactures. On the contrary, the elite of Verroia owed much of its prominence to tax farming and moneylending, the latter providing funds not for investment but rather for consumption and, above all, the payment of taxes.[4]

By the 1700s, however, we do encounter social differentiation based on economic activity. At this time the Ottoman Balkans saw considerable commercial and to a certain extent also industrial development. Demand for Ottoman goods in the economically expanding empire of the Habsburgs encouraged production: not only raw cotton and tobacco, but also semi-finished industrial inputs such as leather and red-dyed yarn were in brisk demand.[5] The Orthodox traders transporting these goods have been well studied: sometimes they bought goods ready-made from local Balkan guildsmen, but in other cases they took the initiative and organized production themselves. However, because of the restrictions placed on the commerce of non-Habsburg subjects in the later eighteenth century, many Orthodox merchants who had been born as subjects of the sultans ultimately settled in Vienna, Trieste or Budapest, and gradually lost their ties to the Ottoman lands.[6]

Merchants trading overseas also formed part of the new non-Muslim 'upper crust', as from the mid-1700s the Greek merchant marine took off. There was probably a connection between the money that shipping brought to the Aegean islands and the growing silk industry of Chios.[7] In part newly enriched traders may have bought these textiles, and so did the sultans' court in Istanbul. In the Greek provinces of the Ottoman Empire a mercantile elite, sometimes with ties to manufacturing, thus emerged in the course of the eighteenth century.

A Bulgarian tanner from Berkovica. Note the aide in the background hanging up the tanned hides to dry. This picture was drawn by F. Kanitz during/after his Balkan travels during the 1860s and 1870s; the author was sympathetic to the Bulgarian national movement and detested Ottoman rule. However, he admired Midhat Paşa as an active and competent administrator. (F. Kanitz, *Donau-Bulgarien und der Balkan, Historisch-geographisch-ethnographische Reisestudien aus den Jahren 1860–1876*, 3 vols.(Leipzig: Hermann Fries, 1875–79), vol. 2, p 352)

Similar commercial-cum-manufacturing expansion has been observed for certain regions that today are part of Bulgaria. Seventeenth-century records apparently reflect a society in which a small number of people, generally affiliated with the provincial administration, were reasonably well off and everyone else was quite poor by comparison. Yet in the 1700s local merchants and sometimes even artisans expanded their businesses, made money, built themselves fancy houses and sponsored schools and churches. Wars such as the Russian–Ottoman conflicts beginning in 1768 disrupted this expansion, as merchants were ruined not only by the fighting and the inevitable war taxes but also by the depredations of unpaid mercenaries and other robber bands. But when the Ottoman central power managed to re-establish itself in the 1820s, commercial and craft development resumed.[8] In fact it has been claimed that during the mid-nineteenth century, the textile crafts of the provinces making up today's Bulgaria were more developed than they were to be in the first years of independent statehood. For when more land became available following the flight of many local Muslims, quite a few peasants, who had worked at part-time manufacturing because they had little land, turned to full-time agriculture.[9] Urban demand by contrast declined. Socio-economic differentiation thus actually seems to have decreased after 1877, as Bulgaria became a more uniformly peasant society; industrial development apparently only began after 1900.[10]

An expanding range of material goods available to better-off urbanites

Concerning England, the Netherlands, northern/central Italy as well as France, many studies have shown that what we might call a consumption culture came into being in the course of the early modern period. In the late fifteenth and early sixteenth centuries, this tendency was visible mostly among the urban elites of Florence and Venice.[11] By the late 1500s and early 1600s the nobles of a medium-sized city like Bologna so often commissioned portraits and devotional pictures that Lavinia Fontana, a woman artist originating from that city, made a reputation and a respectable living besides.[12] In the Netherlands during the 1600s, many families coped with economic difficulties by producing goods for the market 'as a sideline', and in certain Dutch villages women routinely were expected to earn money by petty commodity production or shopkeeping in addition to their household duties.[13] Concerning England, numerous studies have shown how during these years consumer goods previously a privilege of the aristocracy became accessible to better-off town dwellers; and even for villagers, earlier luxuries, such as shirts, became necessities, as peddlers brought them to the doors of even remote cottages.[14] In France the domestic market expanded somewhat more slowly. But by the eighteenth century, textiles appeared in written sources as they never had done before: they were entrusted to washerwomen, sewn up by the nascent fashion industry, stolen from clothes lines and, if officers' uniforms, even sent away for dry-cleaning.[15] With some delay, after 1750 a similar development also occurred in certain German principalities.[16]

Nor was this phenomenon exclusively European: a catalogue of Japanese shop signs shows that in the Tokugawa period (1603–1868) it was common to set up displays of goods and hang up laudatory inscriptions over shop fronts so as to attract prospective customers. The famous Japanese woodcuts of the period advertised both actors and fashions, thus targeting playgoers and purchasers of often elaborate textiles.[17] By the early 1800s, moreover, an extensive travel literature had emerged; by perusing these often lavishly illustrated works, prosperous Japanese townsmen apparently compensated for the limited mobility that so often was their lot in real life.[18]

As yet the study of Ottoman consumption is still in its beginnings, and historians are grappling with the question to what extent parallel developments occurred in the sultans' empire. As yet our knowledge is quite limited. Post-mortem inventories are the most appropriate source for the consumption historian, as they record the possessions that especially the better-off accumulated in the course of their lives. But these documents are beset with numerous pitfalls and therefore understudied.[19]

Apparently there was some increase in the possessions of well-to-do Ottoman urbanites during the relative prosperity of the mid-1700s, and the crafts of this period responded to market stimuli.[20] Conclusions are still tentative, yet it would seem that some luxuries of previous epochs became more widely available at this time. To mention but one example, in the late 1400s even prosperous Bursa women had not owned many clothes that found their way into the inheritance registers.[21] By contrast in the 1730s, some women of the town left respectable stores of textiles, including bedding, curtains and sometimes silk dresses. But in the absence of broadly based statistical studies we still do not know whether this trend was limited to a small group of people in a few large cities or whether before the misfortunes of the later 1700s, textiles, household faience and other prestige goods did become more widely available to a larger number of urban dwellers. A recent study has suggested that most Ottoman homes remained very basic until the post-1850s.[22] But if there was in fact some expansion, the late eighteenth-century crisis resulted in declining urban consumption, and the prevailing lack of enthusiasm for the costly military reforms of Selim III (see Chapter 8) becomes more readily comprehensible.

Making and marketing textiles: conjunctures and crises in Plovdiv and Ankara

To begin with the Balkans, in certain regions of today's Bulgaria rough woollens (*aba*) and the braid that decorated the coats made of this modest fabric (*gaytan*) were manufactured in significant quantities. *Aba* first appeared in archival documents during the late sixteenth and early seventeenth centuries.[23] Already at that time the commercialization of this fabric must have been widespread. From the 1700s onwards, family-based companies operating particularly in Plovdiv/Filibe undertook the marketing of *aba* in Anatolia, where they must have sold their goods so cheaply that peasants were willing to give up wearing homespun.[24]

At first manufacture was concentrated in large villages/small towns, but very soon the peasants of the open countryside were recruited as well, and the manufacture of braid and woollens became both a rural and an urban undertaking. In the towns manufacturers were organized in guilds, and it is noteworthy that successful entrepreneurs did not attempt to dissolve these artisan organizations, as we might expect if we accept the English model of industrialization as a standard. Rather, the most prosperous manufacturers often had themselves appointed to guild office and thus controlled their less well-capitalized colleagues. Manufacturers may have preferred this arrangement, as so often they needed to negotiate with representatives of the Ottoman state whenever, for instance, their demands for wool conflicted with army procurement of mutton, or when the dyers engaged in *aba* manufacture required alum, at least theoretically a state monopoly. In the 1800s such negotiations also occurred when the finished cloth was sold to the armies of Mahmud II. As none of these manufacturers, important though they were on the local level, could hope to confront the Ottoman state single handedly, these men must have seen an advantage in retaining the backing of their guilds.[25]

Guild membership did not exclude putting-out activities: apparently the most prosperous merchants-cum-artisans might own their workshops and also have peasants and peasant women work for them.[26] Moreover, when in the 1800s entrepreneurs like the Gümüşgerdan family founded small textile factories, they only used these establishments for the manufacture of products with a ready market. Other items continued to be made by out-workers, for while it was more difficult to control theft and also the quality of finished goods if the workers were dispersed, fixed costs could be avoided. Factories, in contrast, cost money even if not operating. Thus by the mid-1800s in the textile regions of today's Bulgaria, guild-based production, putting-out and small-scale factories were all present at more or less the same time.

Bulgarian woollens expanded in part because after 1826, when the janissary corps was abolished, the manufacturers obtained contracts to supply the newly formed army corps. Other Ottoman cloth manufacturers, however, may have had trouble finding outlets. To mention but one example, the traders and textile artisans of Ankara must have felt the strain when long-drawn-out warfare over Crete (1645–69) interrupted their exports to Venice. When peace finally came, mohair fabrics apparently had lost their former markets in Italy and beyond the Alps, partly because the Thirty Years' War had ruined the cities of southern Germany.[27]

A workshop in the town of Travna manufacturing braid (*gaytan*) to be sewn on to woollen cloaks. More elaborate types of braid were sewn on to silk fabrics that in turn ornamented luxury horse gear. Kanitz visited a master *gaytancı* producing such ornaments for a pasha, and also a young girl who made very simple versions for ordinary customers, meant to hold up stockings. (F. Kanitz, *Donau-Bulgarien und der Balkan, Historisch-geographisch-ethnographische Reisestudien aus den Jahren 1860–1876*, 3 vols. (Leipzig: Hermann Fries, 1875–79), vol. 2, p 127)

From an Ottoman viewpoint, which emphasized the domestic as opposed to the export market, this development should have been considered advantageous; after all, when foreign demand declined, more angora fabric was available locally. In fact, after a crisis in the early 1600s, the industry did recover, remaining stable for a century and possibly more.[28] But we cannot be sure that all Ankara artisans were happy about the loss of customers for high-quality finished cloth.

Throughout the 1600s and 1700s the best qualities of Ankara raw mohair could not be exported and this gave a competitive advantage to local artisans. Foreign traders apparently did not much try to infringe the relevant ruling, which had been elicited through the combined efforts of local textile artisans and the tax farmers in control of Ankara's mohair presses. Although we have little information on outlets for mohair cloth within the eighteenth-century Ottoman Empire, the domestic market at that time does not seem to have been very lively. Given Dutch and French demand, on the other hand, in the course of our period there well may have been a shift from the manufacture of fabrics to that of yarn.[29] This latter item was used in the French button-making industry and, more importantly, in the cloth manufactures of Leiden and Amiens.[30] For in the manufacture of the Dutch 'woollens' that were markedly successful in the 1600s and early 1700s considerable quantities of mohair were used, sometimes amounting to 50 per cent of the fibre employed. This foreign demand is reflected in the export figures, which remained appreciable until the early nineteenth century.[31]

Making and marketing textiles: Balkan companies in the Habsburg lands

From the last quarter of the seventeenth century onwards, the exportation of mohair and mohair yarn was thus connected to industrial development in the Netherlands and France. As for the Habsburg Empire, certainly it was no pioneer in the realm of manufacturing. Yet in Bohemia and certain sections of Austria, textiles were expanding, and from the mid-eighteenth century onwards, there developed a significant demand for cotton yarn, especially the kind that had been dyed red according to the 'Turkish method', which involved the use of madder (*rubbia tinctorum*).[32] Highly appreciated because of its colour-fastness and brilliance, surviving samples in the Austrian archives show these qualities even today. Given the cheapness and practical advantages of cotton fabrics, the Habsburg authorities apparently assumed that in the long run these textiles would replace the more expensive linens and woollens still being worn by most of their subjects. The government was therefore willing to grant substantial privileges both to locals and to foreigners willing to set up manufactories. Ottoman subjects among the entrepreneurs thus privileged were expected to teach their trade to young locals, a demand that became more pressing once the 'Turkish method' of dyeing red yarn was widely applied in southern France.[33]

However, a sizeable share of the red-dyed yarn used in the Habsburg lands was not manufactured locally, but rather in Thessaly. The village and – for a while – prosperous town of Ambelakia turned into a major centre of the textile trade. Quite often the associations of producers and traders supplying

Austrian and Bohemian markets were formed according to Habsburg law, and their documents survive in the Viennese archives.[34]

Proto-industry in Ambelakia or the Thessalian settlement of Tyrnavos partly took place in workshops where the family head controlled the activities of his relatives, but work was also put out to dyers and spinners.[35] Yet the key figures in the success of these enterprises were the merchants who brought red yarn to Vienna and from there distributed it to semi-rural weavers. Business remained good as long as spinning was not yet mechanized and the production techniques for red yarn were not widely diffused in Austria; but once that happened, the Ambelakia manufacturers were unable to find alternative markets. When the town was plundered by a local strongman, this misfortune was the last straw, and the region figures among the numerous cases in which proto-industry did not lead to industrial development.

Making and marketing textiles: fezzes from Tunis sold in Istanbul

We will now pass from the Balkans to the Ottoman capital and discuss a rather remarkable case of inter-regional trade in manufactured goods. In the early 1900s the fez was considered so quintessentially Ottoman that, after the founding of the Turkish republic, Kemal Atatürk outlawed it.[36] Yet as part of the prescribed clothing of officials and military men, the fez had been introduced by Sultan Mahmud II as late as 1828–29. Previously it had been used merely as a support for the turban; doubtless many sailors and artisans wound very small pieces of cloth around their heads, so that their fezzes remained partly visible. In the mid-seventeenth century fezzes still seem to have been absent from Istanbul markets, at least under that name. But about 100 years later, fashion had changed quite dramatically.[37]

Manufacturing this headgear was a speciality of artisans in Tunis and its immediate surroundings, while competing products from Marseilles or Italy were of interest only to the poorest buyers.[38] Apparently in Tunis the industry was largely in the hands of craftspeople who were descendants of refugees from Spain/al-Andalūs. Manufacture of fezzes passed through rather complicated processes, from the initial knitting to the final packaging; these may have been caused by the fact that originally the production chain had been set up by a coterie of fellow immigrants who retained control of the process. Women spun the yarn and knitted the caps that were then treated so as to produce a dense felt and then dyed red. Elaborate silk tassels were a further hallmark of quality, and as even minor blemishes resulted in a drastic lowering of the sale price, the whole undertaking required a great deal of care. Different sizes were manufactured, as fezzes might be worn by men, women and children. The finished items were shipped to Anatolia and the

Balkans, but our information about distribution is almost totally limited to Istanbul.

In 1729 the sellers of fezzes active in the Ottoman capital received a brevet of appointment, probably intended for the head of their guild. But the situation remains unclear, as the existence of the document is only known from later confirmations. Presumably the fez sellers, who also sold *ihram* cloth needed by Mecca pilgrims, as well as sashes, had been active well before their presence was legally recognized.[39] Fez traders maintained close connections to their hometown, in part because the goods they marketed came from this place; the head of their guild always had to be from the Maghrib. Moreover, given tight control over immigration into eighteenth-century Istanbul, fez sellers contravening the regulations of their guild were threatened with expulsion. This situation should have given the headman considerable authority over the members of 'his' guild.

Yet tight controls did not prevent, or perhaps even exacerbated, disputes among the fez salesmen. At issue was the distribution of the newly imported wares among individual guild members; one of the wardens (*kethüda*) was accused of overcharging his fellow guildsmen and, in addition, appropriating more than his allotted share of the merchandise. Furthermore the 120-odd Tunisian guildsmen active in the capital during the later eighteenth century were no more equal among themselves than the Istanbul artisans whose activities have been discussed in previous chapters.[40] In 1766–67, of the 73 fez-sellers working in Galata, only 34 were shopkeepers, while 39 were described as 'sack-men' who, officially speaking, were subordinate to the shop holders. Presumably the sack-men sold lower-quality items in markets or even peddled them door-to-door. Shopkeepers were probably responsible for getting the sack-men to court whenever there were complaints; presumably they also had apprentices working with them while the sack-men operated on their own. Be that as it may, a substantial number of petty traders were employed in the distribution of Tunisian fezzes in Istanbul alone.

As for the manufacturing, in Tunis during the mid-1700s about 300 people were engaged in this business.[41] By the early 1800s, this figure supposedly had dropped to 166, while by the end of the nineteenth century some 200 men were employed in the industry. Once again some of these masters headed sizeable enterprises while others were petty craftsmen. Given a probably growing demand once the fez had become *de rigueur* for Ottoman officialdom and, at the same time, a smaller number of workshops when compared to the 1750s, in the course of the nineteenth century producers from the Habsburg territories saw a chance of entering the market; and by 1900 a large share of Ottoman fezzes were imports.

Textiles as 'popular luxuries': manufacturing silks in Bulgaria and Bursa

Among increasingly available and yet somewhat luxurious textiles, silks and cotton-silk mixtures (*kutni, alaca*) principally come to mind.[42] That silks were an expanding industry is apparent from the accounts of the Bulgarian trader Hristo Rachkov (mid-1700s–1821), who committed suicide when he feared that his close connections to the Greek uprising of 1821 were about to be discovered.[43] Rachkov exported silk to Russia and Walachia, which he acquired from petty producers either as reels or as home-woven silk cloth. Normally the artisans involved grew/bought their own silk and very simple equipment, but in some cases the raw materials and the basins needed for reeling were supplied by Rachkov himself. For the most part, the producers remained independent decision makers and the only thing they lacked was market access. But in other cases Rachkov had silk reeled by waged labourers; his accounts also reveal that he managed the treatment of silk belonging to a local magnate. While the entrepreneurial skill was his, a substantial share of the capital belonged to the Ottoman dignitary.

Bursa was a much more important silk centre than the Bulgarian provinces, and local silk weavers produced more than just the heavy, expensive velvets and brocades, often lavishly decorated with gold and silver thread, that are on display today. Of the less costly and non-courtly items, museums normally will retain only the sets of cushion covers in cut velvet, with abstract or floral designs mainly in white and red, that formed much of the output of the Bursa silk weavers after 1600. While catalogues typically date them to the seventeenth century, some of these items may well be of more recent vintage; when visiting Bursa in the early 1800s the Austrian scholar and diplomat Joseph von Hammer admired pieces of current manufacture.[44] Hammer claimed that apart from the red variety best known to present-day museum-goers, these covers were available in blue, green, yellow and occasionally in multi-coloured versions as well. The background was always white.

Post-mortem inventories of the 1730s show that well-to-do Bursa families had a variety of silk-based textiles in their houses. Emine bint Mahmud, for example, whose inventory was dated to 1734, left five velvet cushions (worth 450 *akçe* or 3.75 *guruş*) plus a sixth of slightly higher value that probably had been manufactured from the same material.[45] We may assume that these covers were of local make. Emine also owned two gowns (*entari*) of a fine fabric ornamented with metal thread (*telli*) and another of the heavy silk brocade known as *diba*; the latter was valued at 5 *guruş*.[46] A kaftan made of a silk-cotton mixture was priced at 4.25 *guruş*, and among the numerous kerchiefs (*makrama*) that Emine hanım had also owned, one was decorated with metal thread and worth 10.5 *guruş*. The *ocak yaşmağı* in her home, which may have been a screen placed in front of the fireplace, was also quite expensive, valued at 10 *guruş*. If we add Emine hanım's pearl-embroidered sash (11 *guruş*), presumably made of silk, it becomes apparent that this woman, well off but not part of the ruling elite, owned a respectable number of silk and part-silk textiles.

Nor was Emine hanım's case unique: Saliha bint Hacı Mustafa, whose inventory dated from the same year, possessed nine – admittedly cheaper – velvet cushions, valued at slightly less than 3 *guruş* a piece.[47] A large bed cover was of ornamented/embroidered velvet (15 *guruş*), and, above all, her chest contained five silk dresses (*came*): the two most expensive ones were again of brocade (36.5 *guruş* all told), while two others were of *hatayi* (8.3 and 10 *guruş*). As for the cheapest, made of *keremsud* (1 *guruş*), it may have come from Aleppo.[48] *Entari*s, *makarama*s and wrappers, many of them embroidered with metallic threads, rounded off the possessions of Saliha bint Hacı Mustafa, while her fireplace screen was worth over 16 *guruş*. In addition she owned a piece of the fine crepe-like silk known as *bürümcük* that was valued at a modest 2.5 *guruş*.

This latter textile, light and not too expensive, was a mainstay of Bursa's economy. Joseph von Hammer, not much given to flights of fancy, waxed lyrical about a partly translucent and partly transparent cream-coloured fabric that gave the young women wearing it the appearance of 'zebras with gold and silver stripes'.[49] The traveller also was quite impressed with a fabric called *kutni*, which he considered a pure silk textile ornamented either with stripes or else with flowers; it was used for the vests of both men and women. Hammer claimed that more than 100,000 pieces of silk cloth left the city every year, to say nothing of silk tassels. In addition the city also housed a thriving cotton industry which produced good-quality green and blue bath towels – not a bad performance for a time of notorious economic and political strain.

A generation earlier, the Italian traveller Domenico Sestini had also been impressed by Bursa as a textile producer: he visited the local shops and commented on a variety of silk that he called *pescemi*, used for garments and probably also bath towels.[50] *Kutni* attracted Sestini's attention as well, and in addition he noted a kind of flowered velvet made by the local Jews that covered sofa cushions and rather resembled a Venetian import used in Istanbul for the same purpose. Hammer's and Sestini's observations are especially valuable because they both spent years in the Ottoman Empire. More knowledgeable than the ordinary diplomat or traveller, if they spoke of a textile-based prosperity in Bursa, presumably they knew what they were talking about.

What about the workpeople?

As yet there is no monograph on Bursa during the 'long' eighteenth century (from 1700 into the 1840s); as a result it is hard to say what happened to the city's silk workers both within and outside of the guilds. As a first step, we will need to find out whether the craft organizations of Bursa continued to operate in as flexible a manner as they had done earlier. Could new men enter the guilds as readily as they had done during the 1600s, and did partnerships and the subletting of shops once again allow people to undertake jobs for which they had not formally been trained (see Chapter 5)?[51] If Bursa developed in a fashion parallel to Istanbul, we would expect a hardening of guild boundaries in the former city as well, but only a close investigation of Bursa data, which is way beyond the possibilities of the present study, will allow us to be sure.

On the other hand we do know something about a structure that contributed much to solidarity among craftsmen in Bursa and elsewhere, and that was the guild-based pious foundation. This institution had not been common in the sixteenth century. However, by the 1700s pious foundations instituted by guilds were well established in quite a few towns. While in Salonika, for instance, they were not especially numerous, they did appear with some regularity.[52] In Bursa at least, these institutions were required to render accounts every few years.[53] It was a major purpose of such controls to ensure that the money in question was spent according to the stipulations of the founders – and it was indeed a matter of hard cash all around, for in most cases, the guildsmen had supplied their foundations not with gardens, vineyards or other real estate but with money to be lent out at interest.[54] As these pious institutions charged between 10 and 15 per cent, their credit was a bargain compared with the demands of many private lenders.

Both in Salonika and in Bursa, frequently the incomes of guild foundations were to be spent on meals taken in common by the guildsmen – probably the idea was to boost solidarity within the craft – or else members attended the recitation of a poem in praise of the Prophet Muhammad. If practices surrounding this ceremony in the 1700s were not too different from what they are today, these pious gatherings would also have entailed the distribution at least of some sweets. Concern for the poor was much less in evidence: for the most part we find it mentioned explicitly among Christians, who could not establish foundations dedicated to religious purposes and therefore focused on charity. In Bursa, there was a foundation intended to benefit the poor among local Orthodox goldsmiths.

If guild-sponsored pious foundations thus promoted good fellowship among members, their operations also made for wider linkages. For it was in everyone's interest not to keep any money lying in the cash-box unused. Therefore if no reliable members of the relevant guild wanted to borrow, the administrators could lend to artisans from other guilds. These rules applied to the textile workers on whose activities we have focused here, as well as to other craftsmen. Most guild foundations accordingly had debtors from a variety of artisan organizations, and presumably this arrangement encouraged cohesion among the craftsmen of Bursa as a body.

Other arrangements intended to promote social solidarity among guild members have been documented for eighteenth- and early nineteenth-century Sarajevo.[55] For the period between 1726 and 1823, there survive a series of registers of the saddlers' guild that list the men who 'by the grace of the masters' were admitted to the guild in a ceremony held out in the open near a spring or more frequently in the garden of the local Mevlevi dervish lodge. All the men in question were Muslims (I do not know whether there were any Christian saddlers or whether they were excluded from this ceremony). The newly admitted craftsmen, who had been 'girded' according to established tradition, were individually mentioned by name along with their patronyms. Where applicable the registers recorded the military ranks of the new masters as well; clearly the interpenetration of crafts and military corps common in Cairo, Damascus or Istanbul was current in the Bosnian town as well. In addition the registers contained the names of the men to whom the newcomers were 'subject': presumably this latter term referred to the masters who had trained them. By recording this ceremony in writing – the quality of penmanship varied considerably from one register to the next – the masters evidently wished to enhance their prestige by emphasizing both their piety and a degree of access to the world of literacy.

Textiles as 'popular luxuries' on the eastern coast of the Mediterranean

Already in the mid-seventeenth century, the production of raw silk was a going concern in parts of today's Lebanon. As for Damascus, the city had been famous as a producer of silk and silk fabrics already in the 1500s, and its reputation continued over later centuries.[56] Admittedly we do not know whether the *ikat* silks for which Damascus gained recognition in the later nineteenth century were already being produced in the 1700s and early 1800s, but it is very probable. Perhaps the term *mulawwan*, not rare in inventories of the time, refers to cloth of this kind.[57] *Ikat* fabrics were (and still are) produced by tightly tying together bundles of cotton, silk or – today – artificial silk yarn, so that if placed in a dye-bath, the dye would not penetrate the 'bound' sections. The process was repeated so as to obtain colour mixtures; further variations in the woven textile could be obtained by using *ikat*-dyed yarns only for the weft, or else for both warp and weft.

Among the designs, a cypress shape was easily obtained and must have been popular also because of the poetic associations evoked by this tree. At least such romantic connotations were important in the late 1800s and in the 1900s, when *ikat* designs had names like 'brides' hands', 'two green almonds' and 'flowers'. Such fabrics especially were popular for towels used in the public bath (*hamam*).

But even earlier, around 1700, Damascus' reputation as a textile centre was evident from the number of artisans and shopkeepers engaged in the clothing trades. In a recent study, the estate inventories of 277 men from this period have been analysed. In 213 instances, the authors could identify the line of work in which the deceased had been engaged, and among the tradespeople in question 78, or more than a third, were involved in the manufacture and distribution of textiles.[58] Moreover these trades were a highroad to prosperity, as the 78 merchants and artisans in this sector left estates more than five times as large as those of other craftspeople. However, the textile trades also demanded more investment than many other artisan activities: in response, quite a few traders and manufacturers in the clothing sector spent somewhat less on their homes than the 'average' Damascene decedent and probably used the savings in order to augment their commercial/productive capacities.[59]

As usual when dealing with post-mortem inventories, the documents often do not permit us to distinguish between traders and artisans; however, there are a few exceptions. Dyers are easy to make out, and they were mostly quite poor: a few copper basins, a bit of indigo and a pile of firewood might suffice to set oneself up in this business.[60] Dyers who specialized in indigo-based blue normally found their customers among the poor even though the indigo itself was a valuable plant; this contradiction is not easily explained. As for the wealthier dyers, they often combined their work with commerce or even a second craft such as soap manufacture. Working artisans also included the manufacturers of braid that could be sewn onto kaftans, a trade popular in Damascus as well as in the Ottoman Balkans. Braid-makers were mostly as poor as the poorer dyers.[61]

No production without demand, and around 1700 demand apparently was brisk; in addition to the fabrics stocked in local shops, Damascene customers also bought from other sources. Thus while males typically possessed an outer garment of strong woollen cloth (*djūkh*, Turkish *çuha*), this item was rarely stocked by shopkeepers. As woollen fabrics frequently were imported from Europe, quite a few consumers, to say nothing of the tailors, may have bought directly in Sayda or other port towns. Velvet, present in most wealthy households but also not often stocked by shopkeepers, was perhaps bought directly from the inter-regional traders arriving from Bursa or Istanbul.[62]

Embroideries were on record in about 10 per cent of all textiles; we do not know whether they had been produced domestically or else by professionals in shops. As Muslim males are not supposed to wear silk, it is not surprising that most of the silk clothing located in Damascus inventories belonged to women – but interestingly enough, with the exception of the most costly items. In this case, distribution evidently was in the hands of 'regular' textile shopkeepers; it is usually impossible to distinguish between silks made by local craftsmen and pieces brought in from Anatolia or Egypt.

Import substitution: the manufacture of cottons 'Indian style' in Tokat, southeastern Anatolia and northern Syria

Wealthy consumers throughout the Ottoman Empire preferred Indian textiles including fine shawls from Kashmir as well as a large variety of cottons.[63] An impressive number of textile terms of Indian origin entered the Ottoman Turkish language – linguistic testimonies to this lively import trade. These loan words disappeared again once the relevant fabrics had become unavailable.[64]

However, in a history of Ottoman crafts, we are concerned not with the Indian originals but with their local imitations. Trade with India already in the early 1700s was viewed quite critically by the well-known chronicler Mustafa Naima.[65] For Indian traders found few things to purchase on Ottoman territory, and therefore demanded payment in coin; on the other hand, the Ottoman elite, not possessing major sources of silver and gold, constantly worried about losses of bullion. Moreover by this time, the economies of many Ottoman coastal regions had become integrated into European commercial networks, although French or English observers were prone to exaggerate the extent of their commercial domination. Yet even limited integration did cause additional outflows of cash.[66] This latter process being largely outside the control of the Ottoman government, other means of keeping bullion in the country were urgently sought after, and prohibitions of Indian luxuries were part of the late eighteenth-century 'austerity' programme. When Selim III (r. 1789–1807) needed to raise money for his 'New Model' army he not only forbade the importation of Indian fabrics but also tried to promote the use of Ottoman goods among the state elite, presumably with limited success.

In this context we must view the imitation of Indian cottons by subjects of the sultan. In the Anatolian caravan town of Tokat, during the early 1700s if not before, cotton printing had taken hold. Admittedly the official dyehouse, run by a lifetime tax farmer, was in some trouble because of the steep rise of the price of mostly imported indigo.[67] Independent dyers and printers increasingly avoided the Tokat dye-house, using instead the facilities of small towns in the vicinity, where the long arm of the town's tax farmer hopefully would not reach. These semi-rural settlements became sites of dyeing and printing, and local notables 'in on the deal' managed to block many of the tax farmers' attempts to make the dyers return to Tokat.

Yet in the relatively expansive atmosphere of the 1720s and 1730s, this tax farmer still made enough of a profit to build a large dyers' workshop that was to serve as a revenue source for a pious foundation that he instituted in 1740, characteristically not in Tokat but at the seat of power in Istanbul.[68] However, in the long run the increasing price of indigo disadvantaged the dyeing and printing industries; while the tax farmer pressured the artisans to continue using this expensive dye, the latter attempted to find lower-quality substitutes.

This situation gave rise to a three-cornered struggle involving firstly the merchants, secondly the working dyers and printers, and thirdly the tax farmer, who generally could count on the backing of the central administration. Dyers and printers using workshops outside Tokat were chased down by the tax farmer's agents, merchants as well as artisans evaded stamp taxes as far as possible, and by mid-century, rural textiles by far outdistanced those produced in the town. Complaints by artisans who had not been paid for their labour also multiplied – a sign of entrepreneurs in distress. As for the dye-house operated by the tax farmer himself, as we have seen it continued to lose business to small-town competition.[69] By the 1760s when the expansive stage of Ottoman industry was a thing of the past, the market for dyed and printed textiles was supplied from Istanbul or else from southeastern Anatolia. In 1770, the tax farmer of the local dye-house dues actually went bankrupt.[70]

As for the competing cotton printers of what is today southeastern Turkey, they seem to have done better and lasted longer. While Tokat's prints apparently were limited to the Ottoman market, the *indiennes* manufactured between Aleppo and Diyarbakır were sometimes exported; and a few samples survive in French archives.[71] The prosperous period of this manufacture came to an end in the 1760s, a phenomenon well known from other parts of the empire as well.[72] However, even in the crisis period of the early 1800s, the industry was far from dead. When the English traveller James Silk Buckingham was marooned in Urfa (today's Şanlıurfa) because the roads were unsafe, he made the acquaintance of a local textile manufacturer interested in the factory production of cottons as practised in England, on which Buckingham was able to provide detailed information. The Urfa entrepreneur was optimistic enough about the future of his business that he offered the young traveller a job as his technical advisor.⁷³ Evidently this man believed that the local cotton industry would soon recover.

Further south, cotton weaving survived in the Palestinian town of Nablus and at times even prospered.⁷⁴ Textiles had already been manufactured here in the sixteenth century, and cotton weaving was practised in the early 1800s; albeit on a much reduced scale, some production was still carried out 100 years later. In part this long survival was due to the fact that Nabulsis, as well as peasants in the hinterland, wove goods of modest quality for a local market. In an inland town of conservative tastes, European imports were not necessarily competitive and the demand for 'Syrian-made but European-style' novelties was limited even at the end of our period, in the mid-nineteenth century.

Nablus' textile industry was dominated by moneylenders-cum-merchants, who put out cotton and wool for manufacture. While spindles and looms often belonged to the producers, this was of little importance as these implements usually cost very little. What counted was a large supply of raw materials and, above all, enough capital to provide access to the market: as traders could not expect to sell unless they gave credit, direct contacts between artisans and consumers apparently were not common. At least between 1800 and 1850, many workpeople were females paid a mere pittance, and this situation probably explains why, unlike other towns in the region, there were few if any guilds in Nablus. As the qadis' registers do not seem to provide any evidence on craft organization, we may conclude that unlike what has been observed in the provinces making up today's Bulgaria, the merchants of Nablus had no interest in the guilds. After all, local traders dealt not with the powerful Ottoman state, but with dispersed small-scale buyers. Moreover when times really became rough, in the later 1800s, Nabulsi traders shifted their investments to soap and olive oil, and the entire textile sector declined.⁷⁵

Metalwork, its makers and the artisans who – sometimes – commissioned it

Recent studies of Orthodox ecclesiastical silver, extant both in the Benaki Museum in Athens and the Sadberk Hanım Museum in Istanbul, have opened up a new dimension of Ottoman metalwork and artisan activity. For from the eighteenth century onwards, these items survive in reasonable numbers and at times carry inscriptions that tell us something about craft organization within the Greek community. Guilds were known as *esnafia* (from *esnaf*) and *rufetia* (from *hirfet*).⁷⁶ Just like the organizations made up of Muslims, or else of Muslims and non-Muslims combined, guilds that encompassed only Orthodox artisans were in no way egalitarian; rather, the members were ranked according to age and wealth. In addition to trade and craft guilds properly speaking, religious brotherhoods were also active; and while craftsmen probably made up a sizeable part of such organizations, merchants and educated men might become members too. Both guilds and brotherhoods not only donated pieces for liturgical use to the local churches but also engaged in charity, often under the guidance of a bishop or other ecclesiastical figure. In this context we again encounter well-to-do artisans, who were members of the administrative councils that ran Orthodox churches.

Associations of rich tradespeople, such as furriers, might contribute to the maintenance of the Church of the Holy Sepulchre in Jerusalem or, as happened around 1800, donate a gold medallion to the archbishop of İznik/Nicea.[77] But much more modest guilds like gardeners or wood-sellers also commissioned pious gifts including icons; if the donors could afford it, they might have these images decorated with silver covers.

But even those items whose inscriptions do not say anything about the donors may be of value to the craft historian. This applies, for example, to a silver-gilt bottle formerly belonging to the metropolitan church of Trabzon.[78] This piece dates to 1670, and while the overall decorative scheme is inspired by Bursa models, there are also references to European silverwork, especially to designs often seen on watch cases. It has been suggested that the silversmiths of Trabzon encountered these foreign designs when working in Istanbul, as seems to have happened quite frequently. While elements of European ornamentation were still fairly subdued at the beginning of our period, by the 1820s and 1830s, when a good deal of surviving church silver was commissioned from Orthodox silversmiths, these imported motifs had become more prominent. Perhaps the 'classical' taste of European patrons of the period made these models seem especially desirable. Viewed from a different perspective, when Trabzon's Greek – and also Armenian – traders came to play a major role in commercial exchanges with Europe in the early nineteenth century, their interest in the decorative arts of that region may also have increased.

More widespread than silver were pots (*sahan*), carafes and plates (*leğen, ibrik*) made of copper. As attested by numerous estate inventories, every household owned a few pieces, and it was also customary to donate them to pious foundations. Once again a major manufacturing centre was Tokat in north-central Anatolia.[79] Coppersmiths bought the ore after it had emerged from the mines, and then turned it over to refineries in the town. In the eighteenth century, copper refining was mostly controlled by local notables, including a lodge of Mevlevi dervishes, whose sheikh had managed to oust smaller enterprises from this lucrative business. For the craftsmen using copper, the concentration of refining in a few hands was a disadvantage, and they frequently responded by avoiding the refineries in Tokat altogether.

However, this proceeding destabilized the copper mines in Gümüşhane and Keban near Elazığ, financed out of refinery revenues. In 1738 the mines were owed large back payments by the coppersmiths, and their operators claimed to be close to bankruptcy. In response to these complaints, the guild elders of the Tokat coppersmiths were asked to justify their conduct to the central administration.[80] Under serious pressure, the guild headmen promised to pay over a lump sum in short order, and increase their purchases from the two mines. But as some copper was available also from the nearby Kastamonu region, we may wonder for how long these promises were kept.

Refining did not remain the undisputed province of local notables, as already in the 1760s certain magnates with close contacts to the central administration began to take over. This early centralization, which intensified in the 1790s, is remarkable in that it occurred in a period otherwise characterized by tendencies in the opposite direction. Centralization was motivated by military preoccupations, as copper was crucial to the weapons industry. Demands from the state frequently clashed with the interests of coppersmiths, who owned much of the available metal and were not necessarily prepared to part with it at the modest prices typically offered by the government. This whole saga, the ins and outs of which cannot be narrated here, indicates that the coppersmiths of Tokat were well organized and at least some of them possessed financial resources. Taken as a group, these artisans were not necessarily at the mercy of the government.

Decorating the homes of elite figures

Costly textiles as well as high-quality silverware and copperware are situated on the vague and indeterminate border between artwork and craft. With respect to the period between 1670 and 1850, some information, vague and unsatisfactory though it may be, is available about certain manufacturers. However, we are not usually so fortunate when it comes to the painters who from the eighteenth century onwards decorated rooms in Ottoman palaces and soon in wealthy provincial dwellings as well. Muslims, Christians and Jews all conformed to the prevailing fashion. During the period under discussion, Muslims generally avoided images of humans and animals, and instead focused on landscapes, *nature mortes* and city views, particularly of Istanbul.[81] As a result, such decorations were possible even in religious contexts, and the landscapes adorning the mosque of Kara Mustafa Paşa in Merzifon, painted about 1850, are but one example among many.[82] By the late eighteenth century, some of these landscape artists aimed at rendering depth, a concern that had not been prominent in Ottoman miniatures. Perspective apart, the more accomplished painters showed haze on the horizon, and/or used rococo frames to direct the viewer's gaze.[83] Typically these images formed a band located over the windows and underneath the zone that marked the transition from wall to ceiling.

In most cases these paintings were unsigned, and the commissioning process is unclear.[84] We do not know how the owners of wealthy residences chose the images they wanted to see on their walls: in the late 1800s and early 1900s, postcards sometimes were used for this purpose, and in earlier periods, pattern books may have served the same purpose.[85] Only the names of the patrons and most importantly the iconography can be mined for fragments of information; sometimes the year of execution is also suggestive, especially when the (re)building of the residence can be dated.

Whether the pictures were situated in the capital or in even quite remote provincial towns, Istanbul was clearly a favourite subject of depiction. Cityscapes included images of the Bosporus; rowing boats were often depicted without rowers, so as to avoid human figures. Favourite subjects were domed mosques with slender minarets, waterside palaces and, above all, the Kızkulesi/Leander Tower. In the late 1700s and early 1800s this little building seems to have symbolized Istanbul, comparable to today's employment of the Sultan Ahmed mosque as an urban icon. Perhaps provincial dignitaries viewed the liveliness of the capital with some envy and wanted to share in its attractions, at least in the imagination.[86] But at the same time, these pictures probably served to project the Ottoman identity of the owner of the mansion.[87]

Servicing the pilgrims: artisans of Jerusalem

It so happens that the craftsmen of Jerusalem have left a great deal of evidence in the local qadi's records. On 45 guilds enough material is extant to make short individual monographs possible. This abundance is all the more remarkable as the town was quite small, probably with fewer than 10,000 year-round inhabitants. Certain ground rules of artisan life emerge from these records: thus, for example, no one was permitted to belong to two guilds at the same time.[88] In principle if not always in practice, guild members were to be treated equally: when it came to guild-based taxation, for instance, Muslim and non-Muslim artisans paid the same amount in dues.[89] As for the guild sheikhs, they were expected to furnish the artisans they supervised with the necessary raw materials; in other words they were responsible for purchasing *en bloc*, an arrangement common enough in the Ottoman central provinces but much less so in Egypt. Apparently the position of guild sheikhs in Jerusalem was strong even by Istanbul standards: for we encounter the complaint that a guild elder of the coppersmiths had sold the products of his fellows and pocketed the proceeds. This type of misbehaviour presupposed that the sheikh could lay his hands on the product of other craftsmen in his guild, a situation not often recorded in the Ottoman central provinces.[90]

Among the numerous Muslim, Jewish and Christian pilgrims visiting the holy city there must have been men – and more rarely women – of some means; and this fact explains the presence of artisans such as goldsmiths working for a luxury market.[91] For two generations at least, during the late 1600s and early 1700s, a family of Kashmiri immigrants controlled the guilds of bookbinders and booksellers: Muslim pilgrims must have provided many if not most of the customers. Presumably the activities of silk merchants, many of them Jewish, were also made possible by the demand generated by well-to-do pilgrims.[92]

Little documentary information by contrast has become available on one of the most noteworthy items that better-off Christian pilgrims might bring back, namely models of the Church of the Holy Sepulchre in dark wood, often of the olive tree. Like boxes, these models could be opened so as to show the interior of the sanctuary. Typically they were decorated with inlays of mother-of-pearl or costly varieties of wood; these pieces thus represented a material value in addition to being pious mementoes. Models of the Holy Sepulchre are of historical interest because the makers did not routinely copy their predecessors' work, but rather documented current changes to the building structure. Seventeenth-century models, for example, showed the new *aedicula* covering the spot where tradition placed the tomb of Christ, which had been rebuilt in the 1550s.[93] These models survive in quite a few museums, and we may thus assume that the pilgrims who bought them often knew in advance where they would be available and at what price.

Another stone for our mosaic: pious foundations, large workshops and artisan livelihoods

To conclude our set of vignettes depicting artisan life in the 'long' eighteenth century, we must pay some attention to the investment activities of the major pious foundations, especially those established by sultans, princesses and viziers. In the later 1600s the grand vizier Kara Mustafa Paşa built or acquired several khans in Izmir, a city whose commerce was then booming even though the earthquake of 1688 inflicted serious damage.[94] Especially after about 1720, in quite a few provincial cities new pious foundations were constructed, with sometimes elaborate khans and covered shopping streets. In Urfa/Şanlıurfa, for example, a major khan was built to provide income for a local school of law and divinity; and the library that Sultan Ahmed III (r.

Elaborately decorated models of the Church of the Holy Sepulchre survive in museums. This example is from the Bayrisches Nationalmuseum, Munich. Martin Biddle, *The Tomb of Christ* (Phoenix Mill, Gloucestershire: Sutton Publishing, 1999), pp 42–3, has published an example from the Musée de la Société des Antiquaires de l'Ouest in Poitiers, France; another such item is in the British Museum. (Courtesy of the Bayrisches Nationalmuseum, Munich)

1703–30) established in the third court of the Topkapı palace was financed, among other establishments, by a dye-house located in Bursa.[95]

Presumably this spate of investment was due, on the one hand, to canny foundation administrators in a better position than today's historians to observe the – relative –manufacturing prosperity of the mid-1700s. By building khans and workshops and using their often considerable political clout to oblige artisans to move in, pious foundations could profit from the boom. Furthermore if these institutions made money, so did their administrators, as the latter typically received more or less generous salaries out of institutional revenues. In some places there were also political reasons for setting up shops and workshops: a magnate family such as the Karaosmanoğulları of Izmir and Manisa apparently sought to gain legitimacy by sponsoring a multitude of charities: once again a complex of shops/workshops might provide rental income and enhance the appearance of certain towns all at the same time.[96]

However, these collective workshops did not involve major changes in the organization of labour: the production process was not divided up into smaller steps, which would have meant making the finished products into the work of a lengthy chain of increasingly dependent craftsmen. 'Collective workshops' therefore should not be regarded as manufactories that lacked only the application of inanimate power to become factories.[97] On the contrary, these workshop compounds allowed artisans to supervise one another, if anything more closely than had been possible in the streets of the city centre. In large dye-shops, for instance, where there existed a considerable common investment in copper vats and as yet undistributed indigo, disputes over control of the workshop territory apparently were both frequent and acrimonious.[98] Quite possibly in this environment, it was more difficult for artisans with new ideas to escape the censure of their colleagues.

Conclusion

Up to this point we have surveyed a selection of different crafts, in an attempt to show how artisans were affected by the relative prosperity of the mid-eighteenth century and by the crises that followed. As far as the surviving data permit, we have focused on the products manufactured, the consumers and the market demand generated by the latter. In addition we have discussed the constraints imposed by the Ottoman state apparatus and particularly the fates of the manufacturers themselves. Luxury and high-quality items have been allotted rather more than their fair share, if the probable volume of production is accepted as the standard by which manufactures should be judged. But as luxuries and semi-luxuries are better documented than everyday items, more can be said about them. In addition, our emphasis on material things that actually survive today also implies a certain accent on quality goods.

In this context we have discussed the varying fates of seventeenth- and eighteenth-century craft producers. There were those that we might call 'lucky', for instance people who manufactured Bursa silks that were not 'palace quality', but formed the more modest luxuries of the urban well-to-do. Certain cotton weavers and dyers of southeastern Anatolia and northern Syria apparently enjoyed periods of prosperity as well. To a certain extent at least, domestic consumption seems to have fuelled the limited mid-eighteenth-century expansion of the Ottoman manufacturing sector, even if the 'trickle-down effect', in other words the adoption of governing-class luxuries by the merely well-to-do, was less pronounced than perhaps in England or France. Conversely it is quite probable that the declining consumption occasioned by the wars of the period around 1800 fatally weakened the political prestige and legitimacy of Sultan Selim III.

Eighteenth-century manufacturers were more dependent on the world market than their predecessors had been: the Balkan producers of red cotton yarn and leather did well as long as demand in the Habsburg lands remained high; however, they experienced major problems or indeed collapsed when that demand fell away. The moral of this particular story is that by the second half of the eighteenth century and especially after 1815, certain Ottoman craftspeople were already confronted with the full blast of the capitalist world economy. Admittedly Austria and Bohemia, where the manufacturers of Ambelakia yarns were situated, in the terminology of Immanuel Wallerstein, were themselves part not of the 'core area' but of a modernizing 'semi-periphery'.[99] Certain Balkan manufacturers apparently were poised to take the same step in their own regions; to use Wallersteinian terminology once again, the Ottoman Balkans conceivably might have entered the world economy as a semi-periphery, comparable for instance to nineteenth-century Russia. Political conditions were to prevent that from happening.

But decline was by no means the fate of all Ottoman craft producers, not even after 1800. Many more than had been thought possible until about 15 years ago adapted to the demands of the capitalist world economy and thus survived, albeit at the price of low wages and much unpaid family labour.[100] Using imported semi-finished goods, textile producers catering for a provincial market often responded to the demands of their customers much better than outsiders.[101] Moreover in the nineteenth century, population increased in many parts of the empire, and some craftspeople profited from the resulting market expansion.[102] But others were not so lucky and went under.

This is apparently where the Ottoman state came in: in times of crisis, exporting manufacturers got scant support from the empire's ruling group, and this deficiency made it difficult for them to continue.[103] However, if we look at the economic vicissitudes of the period, not from the perspective of Immanuel Wallerstein but from that of Michael Palairet, it would seem that after independence, the newly formed Balkan states for some time largely dropped out of inter-regional and international trade. They thus exchanged the limited 'peripheralization' of their last decades under Ottoman rule for what one might call 'splendid isolation' from the world market.[104] The advantages, however, at best were ambiguous, as this change implied the fading away of some previously promising industries. Certainly Nikolai Todorov has published data showing that Bulgarian industry picked up again around 1900, and grew rapidly in the years immediately preceding the Balkan wars.[105] Even so we can conclude that under certain conditions the demands of the Ottoman state might further rather than hamper the expansion of manufacturing.

Ottoman provincial artisans confronted the constraints imposed by the state when paying their dues, typically collected by lifetime tax farmers and their underlings. Owing to the late eighteenth-century conflicts with Russia and later Napoleonic France, the needs of the exchequer escalated, and for many artisans increasing taxation resulted in a veritable struggle for survival. Fleeing from the town to the countryside might be an option. But presumably quite a few craftspeople went under because of wartime over-taxation. Furthermore the efficient producers were more likely to be victimized by the empire's agents than their less successful colleagues.[106] But the problems of artisans with the governing apparatus did not end there: in many places soldiers penetrated artisan guilds to a greater or lesser degree, causing disruption and financial loss. Given these circumstances it is reasonable to suppose that tensions between craftsmen and representatives of the Ottoman state apparatus were not at all rare, even if under certain conditions, especially in Istanbul, state-imposed regulation may have been welcomed.

What happened to artisan guilds in this situation? In many places, manufacturers doubtless responded as they did in Istanbul, namely by strengthening guild solidarities: the notable presence of pious foundations sponsored by Bursa guilds indicates that such a tightening of bonds did in fact occur. In addition, the greater frequency of large-scale workshops with their multifarious possibilities for mutual control also meant that the flexibility characteristic of many guilds in the early 1600s disappeared in later times. Yet there is no way of knowing whether this hardening of boundaries was indeed the general rule. One thing, however, is relatively certain: although Ottoman guilds were anything but egalitarian, the wealthiest artisans, even if they had strong military connections, did not establish control over collective workshops to the extent that they could make everyone active in the establishment do their bidding. In some places guilds were dominated by the largest manufacturers and in this fashion survived for lengthy periods of time. But as far we know, this type of control was not a result of the masters in question controlling large collective workshops.

We also may surmise that in certain places where proto-industry – in the broader sense of the term – was widespread, guilds lost relevance and disintegrated earlier than elsewhere.[107] While this fading away was by no means universal, there were places where it did happen. To what extent control by putting-out merchants played a role in this demise of guilds during the late 1800s and early 1900s is a problem that will occupy us in the next chapter.

CHAPTER 10

1850 to 1914: A Different State, a Different Economy and the Disappearance of the Guilds

A painful adjustment to the world economy: 'labour-squeezing', self-exploitation and increasing levels of inter-communal strife

Following the progressive opening up of Ottoman and Egyptian archives, interest in the later 1800s and early 1900s currently is booming; valuable new studies appear almost every few months, and our knowledge of no other period in Ottoman history has advanced so much during the last 25 years. As a result, a claim that almost universally had been accepted by researchers until the 1980s has become increasingly dubious: seen as a whole, the Ottoman lands in the nineteenth century apparently were *not* de-industrialized.[1]

Travellers' accounts and consular reports that claim the contrary are being read with much more scepticism than in the past: the primary sources describing handicrafts that declined or collapsed mostly are European, and certain writers may well have seen what they wished to see. Moreover many nineteenth-century French, English and even Ottoman observers thought that handicrafts were 'backward' and doomed to a more or less rapid disappearance.[2] 'Real' manufacturing in the opinion of these authors could only be factory-based, and by that criterion the Ottoman performance was found wanting. Yet while some handicrafts certainly disappeared, others took their places, often using imported semi-finished inputs. Declining industries including certain kinds of cottons were offset by an expansion of rug and carpet manufacture, lace-making and the production of raw silk.[3] Recent accounts thus assume that there was no absolute decline in manufacturing, both in terms of goods produced and of workers employed in this sector.

However, the conditions under which craftspeople laboured, sometimes before 1850 but certainly afterwards, changed significantly as 'incorporation into the European world economy' came to encompass more geographical regions and broader ranges of activity than had been true in the 'long' eighteenth century. Competing with machine-made goods often though not always meant that merchants financing and organizing production took on a greater role, who might distribute imported semi-finished inputs to local craftspeople. Or else they might negotiate contracts with the Ottoman state: thus before the 1870s, entrepreneurs of the Gümüşgerdan family wove uniform cloth in the towns and villages of today's Bulgaria.[4]

In some cases, putting-out merchants did business with fully fledged artisans, but in other instances women and children were employed in greater numbers than had been true in earlier times. At least in theory the earnings of females and juveniles were not supposed to support a family; therefore merchants could easily justify paying them mere pittances. To take one example arbitrarily selected among numerous others: in the Egyptian town of Asyut during the early 1900s, women created shawls out of tulle and metal strips that were sold to tourists and exported. While these items fetched reasonably high prices, the women's pay was minimal.[5] In other cases women and children were not directly employed by the putting-out merchant, but aided their husbands and/or fathers who had contracted for the family's labour; in this case, members of the workmen's families might toil away without any remuneration at all.

Since our sources tell us little about the feelings and reactions of the men and women affected, we can only guess what they may have thought about this avalanche of unpaid family labour. Perhaps women's work in manufacturing was defined as 'recreational' or 'helping out relatives', as observed in low-income neighbourhoods of 1980s Istanbul.[6] Possibly putting young children to work was legitimized by their elders as a manner of keeping them out of mischief. But the boys themselves saw this matter in quite a different light: an Anatolian miner, who began his work in the late 1800s and continued well into the republic, has authored one of the rare workingmen's accounts that we possess and makes the misery of working children abundantly clear.[7]

For these practices the term 'labour-squeezing' has been adopted; of course not only family members but also apprentices and maybe a waged worker or two labouring for a master artisan could be 'squeezed' in this fashion.[8] Once protective legislation was introduced, usually not before the twentieth century, labourers in small workshops were often excluded from its benefits. While as a result these enterprises might remain competitive, they did so at the expense of their workers.

Essentially 'labour-squeezing' corresponds to what in the language of socialist-inspired authors would have been called 'exploitation'. Presumably the new term has been introduced because the petty masters who 'squeezed' their workers did not themselves make any great profits. On the contrary, they engaged in 'self-exploitation', that is, to remain competitive they charged prices making any significant investments impossible. Apart from subsistence, all they could hope to achieve was to keep shop and inventory in working order; business growth, by contrast, was not an option. While artisans in earlier periods also typically had worked with very few tools and relied on their training and dexterity for often superior results, this became more difficult after 1850, when the purchase of somewhat more expensive equipment was frequently necessary to beat the competition.

In addition, the vagaries of the 'European world economy' meant that producers often found themselves in unforeseen situations: difficulties predominated, although occasionally new opportunities might emerge. Thus the American Civil War, which dramatically increased English demand for raw cotton, must have made life difficult for weavers in the Fertile Crescent who previously had relied on Egyptian fibre, which now was costly and mostly reserved for export.[9] On the other hand, Egyptian peasants who had earned money during the wartime boom were now in the market for more garments: this demand must have stimulated the search for alternative sources of raw cotton, and it certainly benefited the textile manufactures of Aleppo.[10]

Artisans of earlier periods also had sometimes been confronted with sagging demand and contracting supply, particularly in wartime but also when disposable incomes were slashed following bad harvests and rising food prices. However, from the perspective of Ottoman craftspeople, it must have been more difficult to cope with demands coming not from the sultans' officeholders but from an unknown world that, where Muslims were concerned, was especially hostile as it was controlled by 'infidels'. Reactions of this kind were widespread in Damascus before the civil war of 1860: Muslim artisans and shopkeepers apparently felt that their Christian rivals were prospering because of their special contacts with European traders, while they themselves were in serious difficulties. In consequence, a significant share of the people who were punished for their participation in the 1860 destruction of the Christian quarters of Damascus were artisans and shopkeepers.[11]

Craftspeople coping with a new-model state

Moreover craftspeople from the mid-nineteenth century onwards were confronted with a state, or more accurately with three different varieties of state, which differed substantially from those to which they had become accustomed. In the mid-1800s the Ottoman central elites embarked on a wholesale restructuring of the governmental apparatus; the project involved centralization, taxation and the draft, all of them highly unpopular innovations. Where the immediate environment was concerned, modernizing the centres of the more important towns was also a high priority for many public officials. It is thus fair to say that Ottoman artisans of this period needed to cope with a novel type of polity. Secondly, in 1841, when Mehmed Ali Paşa had been forced by the Great Powers to evacuate Syria and Anatolia, he had been granted the hereditary vice-royalty of Egypt (Ottoman: hıdiv, English: khedive); from this time onwards if not earlier, it makes sense to regard Egypt as a separate state with its own trajectory despite continuing close contacts between the governing elite in Istanbul and the Cairo upper classes. Viewing Egypt as a separate – and novel – kind of state is justified especially for the period after 1882, when the country became a de facto British colony. In consequence the artisans of Cairo and other Egyptian cities confronted the imperial state of Great Britain directly, and this colonial establishment figures as the third of the three 'new-model' states at issue here. Confrontation of Cairo's working people with the British colonial apparatus was most likely when the police repressed strikes.[12]

Military expenditure was not very important in Egypt once Mehmed Ali Paşa had been forced by the Great Powers to strictly limit the size of his army. But in the 1860s and 1870s the khedives Saʿid and Ismāʿīl embarked on a programme of 'self-strengthening' that included canal projects, modernization of the Alexandria port and railway construction.[13] To satisfy the demands of often dubious European promoters, taxes were increased and artisans and shopkeepers particularly were hard hit. However, revenues did not cover the debts that the khedive had run up, and the British takeover was at least partly aimed at securing the bondholders' interests.[14]

With self-strengthening no longer a priority, the British focused on irrigation, which increased the amount of cotton available for export, and refrained from most other expenditures on infrastructure, including health and education. This set of priorities had the added advantage of conciliating the Egyptian upper class, whose revenues were based on agriculture and whose spokesmen therefore worried that growing employment opportunities in the urban sector might increase the price of farm labour.[15] In addition Egypt was valuable to British manufacturers as a market for exports; and many self-strengthening projects of Ismāʿīl's period were also viewed as potentially interfering with this role.

Well aware that lowering dues helped legitimize foreign rule among ordinary taxpayers and thereby reduced the dangers of urban uprisings, the British thus began by lightening taxes and dismantling part of the dues-collecting bureaucracy whose personal exactions had contributed substantially to the load that artisans were required to carry. In the long run, however, low levels of investment in infrastructure and human capital increased the difficulties of manufacturers struggling for market share and diminished the life chances of their workers.[16]

In the Ottoman central provinces the situation was rather different. The empire remained independent in spite of the bankruptcy of 1875, although its territory was much diminished in the 1877–78 war against Russia and once again in the Balkan war of 1912. In consequence defence was *the* major priority of the Ottoman state, under threat especially in its most productive provinces by a combination of the imperialist designs of the major European states and burgeoning ethnic nationalism.[17] The Ottoman governments of the Tanzimat (1839–76), Hamidian (1876–1908) and Young Turk (1908–18) periods were thus forced into major military expenditures and this investment in turn contributed towards transforming the officers' corps into a body wielding substantial political power. Artisans, particularly those living in the provinces, were most likely to experience this power if their sons were drafted into the army for virtually life-long service.

For apart from taxes, it was mainly recruits that the Ottoman state in its concluding years demanded from its subjects. As the overwhelming majority of the population was still peasant, most soldiers in their civilian lives had been villagers; and for a while the population of Istanbul was exempt. But especially in wartime, artisans and urban labourers were also drafted, sometimes to provide the bread and other essential goods needed by the combatants. Moreover miners were often turned into soldiers and then put to work in the mines under military discipline. But as the First World War wore on, workmen employed in the coal mines near the Black Sea left their jobs in such large numbers as to endanger the manufacture and transportation of military supplies.[18]

Somewhat special was the situation of non-Muslims: in the 1800s they were normally exempt from the draft and paid a tax in lieu of military service, a privilege that often did not endear them to their Muslim neighbours.[19] However, there were significant exceptions, with Christian boys and young men required to serve in state factories from mid-century onwards, where conditions might be extremely unhealthy.[20] Foreign protégés were exempt as well as foreign nationals, both relatively numerous especially in Istanbul and Izmir. After a law had been passed in 1909 that officially extended military service to non-Muslims, Ottoman Christians were frequently drafted into special corps of labourers, where conditions were at least as appalling as in the regular army, and this practice continued on a larger scale during the First World War.[21]

Urban policing

While artisans in the central Ottoman provinces, and also in Syria before the Great War, thus did not encounter any foreign colonial state directly, they shouldered significant burdens connected with state centralization and war. To ensure compliance the administration attempted to control town dwellers much more closely and directly; forestalling riots and domestic rebellions by efficient policing became a priority of both the Hamidian and Young Turk regimes.[22] Until the mid-1800s and sometimes beyond, the market had been policed by the agents of the tax farmers who had acquired rights to the relevant dues. The most important figure was the market supervisor (*muhtesib*) who had been responsible for good order in the marketplace already from the 1500s (see Chapter 2). Quite often the people who owned or had farmed industrial installations such as dye-houses did their own policing. As we have seen (Chapter 9) this situation could be less than idyllic.[23]

However, in the town quarters where artisans lived, much policing was informal: recent studies have shown that inhabitants deemed undesirable could be asked to leave, although it is not so clear whether they complied very readily.[24] Not that these arrangements were always satisfactory when we adopt, for instance, the perspective of women living alone. When facing their male neighbours, females were in a weak position, as it was so easy to cast aspersions on their morality. Informal policing also might give rise to uncontrollable violence: in certain towns and villages of mid-nineteenth-century Lebanon there were groups of young toughs that defended the settlements in which they were based but whose behaviour often involved arbitrary aggression and even murders.[25] But presumably where poor town dwellers were concerned, these varying arrangements – along with their drawbacks – at least had the advantage of familiarity.

Informal 'old-fashioned' self-policing and 'new-style' policing by government-appointed officials can be viewed as extreme points upon a scale; somewhere in between we may place the arrests of guildsmen and other poor people on the basis of denunciations by their community leaders.[26] The Janus-faced character of such policing is especially evident when offending Christians were arrested on the basis of complaints from the relevant patriarchs: presumably when churchmen and other establishment figures complained, it was often the poor and recalcitrant that suffered the consequences.

When complaints reached the state authorities, the institution responsible for the actual arrests was the İhtisab Nezareti, itself a novel institution but which, as its name indicates, took over certain functions from the market inspector or *muhtesib*. Agents of the İhtisab Nezareti arrested people for reasons partly 'traditional' and partly 'modern': guildsmen who sold at prices higher than those administratively imposed always had been punished by the market supervisor. On the other hand, porters who left their loads in public spaces had committed infractions of traffic rules that probably were taken more seriously from the mid-nineteenth century onwards.

Centrally appointed policemen were often unresponsive to the demands of the people they were expected to supervise; and given low salaries and irregular payment, police forces often attracted illiterate and uninformed recruits. Because of their vulnerable position individual policemen were often easily corrupted and this proclivity did not enhance the prestige of the newly established force.[27] As priorities clearly were in favour of what the authorities regarded as the upholding of the social order, crimes that 'merely' threatened the interests and even the survival of individuals may often have escaped prosecution. Much energy was spent in tracking down real and imaginary conspiracies against the regime: this trend was set in the Hamidian era and continued after 1908. Numerous informers were encouraged to send in reports, and the activities of these men, when known or suspected by their neighbours in shops and workshops, must have been a source of dispute and division.

On the other hand, the Hamidian regime especially attempted and often succeeded in fostering allegiance to the sultan in urban streets and markets. The journalist Hagop Mintzuri, in his youth during the 1890s, employed in a baker's shop in Istanbul's populous Beşiktaş quarter, has left a graphic account of local artisans and traders watching the sultan when he emerged from his palace to attend Friday prayers at a nearby mosque.[28] Charities sponsored by the ruler further cemented loyalties, although artisans themselves at most benefited indirectly, for instance when largesse was distributed to the schoolboys of their town quarter.[29]

Survival against all odds: a sample handicraft industry

Raw silk, carpets and laces apart, Ottoman textile manufacturers produced not for export but for the domestic market, thus continuing a pattern set by the state elite's ancient concern about first and foremost providing for local needs.[30] As one example among several, we will here introduce the textile crafts of Aleppo and the towns in present-day Turkey that were its satellites at that time, such as Urfa/Şanlıurfa, Kilis and 'Ayntâb/Gaziantep; ever since the eighteenth century this region had been a prominent producer of cotton fabrics (see Chapter 9).[31]

Apparently the decline of textile manufacturing in Aleppo proper postulated in much of the earlier literature, has been considerably overstated. Some of the data pointing to industrial crisis are unreliable, as certain consular reports claimed 'decline' from an earlier level that the authors had not experienced directly, but of which they only knew from often unreliable hearsay. Another such dubious interpretation involved the expansion of indigo dyeing: this phenomenon was viewed as an indication that only the poorest of the poor still purchased Aleppo cloth. Yet the same phenomenon may also be regarded as a sign that manufacturers who incidentally used both natural and synthetic indigo were quick to respond to changing market demand.[32] It is, however, true that certain fabrics which previously had been made of silk were turned first into silk-cotton mixtures and then into cottons pure and simple, which does point to a poorer clientele. Yet the growth of a 'mass market' might offset losses in the up-market sector.

Be that as it may, before the 1908 revolution and the troubles that followed, the quantity of textiles exported from İskenderun/Alexandretta, apart from a few bad years, regularly increased, from 235 tons, worth £113,000, in 1889, to 649 tons, valued at £285,000, in 1907. Since İskenderun in this period functioned as the port of Aleppo and its hinterland, we can take this increase as an indicator of growing textile production in the metropolis of northern Syria and the surrounding towns. Rather than a decline, we thus find a growth curve interrupted by a number of bad years, and only the upheavals of the early 1900s seriously diminished cloth sales from the Aleppo region in what remained of the empire.

Working Ottoman mines

When it came to the mining sector the Ottoman Empire had no very important role to play on the world market. However, certain of the rarer minerals, such as antimony, boracite and zinc, by the early twentieth century were mined by foreign companies, while the Ottoman state at least nominally kept control over the mining of gold and silver. But it was coal, a novel source of energy, that now took pride of place, and we will focus on this quintessential indicator of modern industrialization.[33]

One-half to three-quarters of all Ottoman coal came from a single sparsely settled area by the Black Sea. As the land on which it was first found belonged to the sultan, Abdülmecid (r. 1839–61) converted the mine territory into a pious foundation serving charities in Mecca. In the long run, the town of Zonguldak emerged at the centre of the 'coal coast'. However, the French-owned mining company established in 1891 called itself after the older port town of Ereğli (Karadeniz Ereğlisi) from which much of the coal was shipped.

By 1829 the Ottoman navy began to change over from sail to steam, and the government wished to develop the Zonguldak mines to prevent a potentially dangerous dependence on imported coal. Until 1882 the administration monopolized all the coal mined, which it purchased at prices set by decree; this policy conforms to Ottoman practice well known from earlier periods. To encourage higher production, after 1882 mine operators were allowed to sell a portion of their product in the open market; but low productivity remained a constant problem.

In spite of the novelty of coal mining, recruitment of the labour force also conformed to patterns established centuries earlier. Before the French Ereğli Company entered the scene in 1891, mine operators were petty entrepreneurs. Such people, who had a proprietor's rights to the mining installations even though the mine itself along with its products belonged to the ruler, had run Ottoman mines already in the sixteenth century.[34] Operators at work in the Zonguldak area – around 1877 there were about 120 of them – possessed little capital; moreover the government often owed them considerable amounts of money. Apart from a few Croats who had pioneered the whole undertaking, these people were Ottoman subjects, both Muslim and non-Muslim.[35]

Workmen in the mining sector were not full-time employees; rather in accordance with patterns once again in place already by the sixteenth century, peasants were drafted to work in the mine for short periods, usually about two to three weeks at a time.[36] This arrangement meant that the workmen frequently had to travel considerable distances, often on foot because of the poor condition of local roads. Yet part-time mining continued to prevail even after the French company had taken over, although the 'improvised' miners probably performed less well than more professional workers would have done. Accidents were frequent and serious, in part because equipment was often substandard; in addition miners apparently resented the loss of autonomy that taking orders 'from above' involved, so that safety precautions were often not seriously enforced.[37]

Presumably the Ottoman government continued to favour the recruitment of temporary workmen because people who retained a peasant holding, and perhaps more importantly a peasant outlook, would be less demanding when it came to wages and working conditions. Officials also assumed that money earned from work in the mines would be welcomed by the poor villagers of the locality, and therefore until 1907 only inhabitants of a specially designated area surrounding the mines were eligible for these jobs. The miners themselves also preferred part-time employment because they did not lose their livelihoods when the company shut down, as it did temporarily in 1901, because of low coal prices.[38] As a result, the demand of the Ereğli Company for specialized full-time labourers generally remained unfulfilled.

Small but significant: factories in 'Ottoman Bulgaria' and Istanbul

Only a tiny share of Ottoman manufacturing took place in factories, and few people actually were employed there. Yet these enterprises have aroused considerable interest among historians.[39] After all, the founders of factories pioneered a form of production that was to gain significance in Turkey and other successor states of the Ottoman Empire after 1923 and especially after the Second World War.

An 'old' branch of manufacturing in which factories were beginning to appear next to small-scale enterprises was the iron industry of Samakov, located in a province ultimately to form part of Bulgaria.[40] Samakov iron already had been used in the construction of the Süleymaniye complex in the mid-sixteenth century, and at that time ironmasters were small entrepreneurs needing credit from the Ottoman state before they could embark upon a project of any size.[41] Ironworks, known locally as *samakova*, are of relevance to us because fairly detailed information is available about their mid-nineteenth-century workmen. In 1848–49 the engineer A. Daux and his companion Frédéric Le Play, a well-known writer and collector of labour-related data, visited the town. They have left a precious account of an ironworks that perhaps qualified as a factory, for it operated on water power. The proprietor was a Muslim by the name of Raşid Bey, who owned several such enterprises; whether he depended on military contracts, and if so to what extent, is not clear.

As water was unavailable during the summer the foundry studied by Daux and Le Play operated for only six months of the year. Like the miners of Zonguldak, the ironworkers therefore were employed part time, and worked the fields during the agricultural season. The authors concluded that in spite of the low wages prevailing in the area, these men enjoyed a relatively high level of social security, in part due to no-interest loans from the factory owner. Apparently these sums of money were meant to increase the attachment of workers to the factory. If the sample budget that Daux and Le Play published reflected reality reasonably well, the 'typical' working family in good years was even able to accumulate some small savings.

In addition to these local enterprises selling to Ottoman customers, there were others whose products were destined largely for export. As an example, we may refer to the machine-reeling and twisting of raw silk in Bursa.[42] By mid-century there occurred a major increase in European and especially French demand for silk, a consequence of the enrichment of the middle classes during the 'Belle Époque' and a contemporary epidemic among silkworms that affected western Europe before spreading to Ottoman territories as well. With raw silk prices on the increase, the Lyons industry was attracted by the raw silk that since the 1600s was being produced in the Bursa region. Local non-Muslims and a minority of Muslim entrepreneurs as well established small factories where girls and young women, mostly Greeks and Armenians, reeled and twisted raw silk. From being a producer of silk cloth, the region was thus reduced to supplying largely semi-finished inputs to French manufacturers until the First World War and its aftermath destroyed most of this trade.

Many nineteenth-century factories, however, served the military: we have already encountered the Gümüşgerdan enterprise, established in the early 1800s and active until 1880 (see Chapter 9). Some archival records document labour conditions in this private factory, which produced woollens and employed 50–80 workers at the machines. In the 1850s these people made 60–80 piastres a month. Most of the workers were townspeople, and therefore used to working within a guild framework; as we have seen, the factory owner himself was a major figure in the local guild (see Chapter 9). Contracts written in Greek specified that the workmen were to be fed at the expense of the mill-owner, and holidays were to be the same for all workers. The owners' concern with the standardization of employment conditions in part was due to governmental pressure in that direction; as the Ottoman state was the principal customer its officials were in a position to determine conditions.[43]

From the owners' viewpoint, however, the factory was only a small part of a vast accumulation of real estate, rural properties and steam-driven flour mills. Unfortunately it is hard to say to what extent the agencies that the Gümüşgerdan established in Istanbul, Vienna and Manchester did business connected with the textile factory and to what extent they sold agricultural products.

At about the same time a competing factory was founded in Sliven, where the manufacture of woollen cloth in small workshops was already well established. The owner, Dobri Zeljazkov, in 1835 came to an agreement with the Ottoman administration concerning the production of good-quality woollens. After having received a positive evaluation from officially appointed experts, Zeljazkov was given credit that allowed him to construct an additional building and buy machinery in England and Austria. Entrepreneurial profits ranged between 20 and 22.5 per cent, which, while probably considered satisfactory, were below returns from commercial investments; for at this time traders profited to the tune of 24 to 30 per cent. The factory did not survive for long.

Contracts once again provide information on labour conditions: the factory employed 400 workpeople who were paid 70–80 piastres/*guruş* a month and, as in the Gümüşgerdan establishment, their work was regulated according to formal contracts specifying, among other things, the length of the working day and the intervals allotted for meals.[44] By the standards of the times, the factory building must have been relatively elaborate; for in winter the work was to be conducted partly under artificial lighting.

In addition the Ottoman state also set up textile factories of its own, one of them located in Sliven as well.[45] Another such establishment, known as the Feshane or 'House of Fezzes', was situated in the capital itself.[46] Established in 1828 in downtown Istanbul this factory was moved to the shores of the Golden Horn a few years later.[47] In addition to the fezzes that were now the obligatory headgear of officers and civilian officials, the enterprise produced at first mainly coarse woollens for the use of common soldiers. If a newspaper report from the late 1800s is at all reliable, after 20 years of operation the factory had branched out into a variety of products: about 300,000 fezzes were now being manufactured, in addition to both coarse and fine woollens.[48] However, the factory never managed to supply the Ottoman market, and around 1900 most consumers wore fezzes imported from Austria. From the period between 1849 and 1854 there survive account books reflecting fez manufacture, including quantities of headgear turned over to the navy and the corps of reservists. Likewise sales were made to the public, certain Istanbul shops being supplied with the products of the Feshane.

An attempt to produce high-quality goods on a factory basis was made in the carpet manufacture in Hereke on the bay of İzmit, worth a special mention because the enterprise functions to the present day.[49] Opened in 1843 as a factory for cotton textiles, it was ceded to the sultan two years later. In 1874 the director had a shop opened in Istanbul's covered market that was to take orders from the public. However, it has been alleged that bureaucratic impediments, possibly due to the reluctance of the palace to share its favoured designs with ordinary consumers, caused the failure of this undertaking within a year. Alternatively it was a fire in the factory that interrupted production and thus made the shop unviable. A second attempt to sell to the public was made in 1888; this latter shop continued operations until 1925, but it is difficult to say whether it prospered at a time of war and foreign occupation.

By the 1890s, after bringing in workers from the Anatolian towns of Sivas and Malatya, the Hereke factory came to specialize in carpets, particularly fine ones made of silk; in 1894 some of its products won prizes at the Exposition Universelle Coloniale in Lyons. This branch of activity ran into trouble when during the First World War silk became unavailable, but the enterprise surmounted this crisis and even the decline of Bursa silk production resulting from the Great War and the Greco-Turkish population exchange of 1923.

As for the labourers employed in Hereke, from surviving photographs it

Ottoman factory in Sliven producing woollens. Kanitz visited this state enterprise and was impressed by the cleanliness and good order. He commented on the Sinti-Roma women working there, in addition to a few very poor Turkish widows. (F. Kanitz, *Donau-Bulgarien und der Balkan, Historisch-geographisch-ethnographische Reisestudien aus den Jahren 1860–1876*, 3 vols.(Leipzig: Hermann Fries, 1875–79), vol. 3, p 22)

emerges that in the factory there worked a large number of young women and girls, probably both Muslim and non-Muslim. At least this conclusion seems likely since on the published photographs some of the women are veiled and others dressed entirely according to European fashions of the years around 1900. While the young women in 'modern' attire are in all probability non-Muslims, we cannot be sure about the others, as at least Jewish women in Salonika were often veiled.[50] Moreover on one of the photographs, the veiled and the non-veiled appear in clearly separate groups. Apparently the photographer had arranged the women not according to their roles in the workplace but by age — the youngest were up front — and, in addition, by religion or community.[51]

Harbingers of the twentieth century: socialism, ethnic nationalism and political activism in Salonika

Apart from Istanbul and the Bulgarian provinces, there was a major centre of manufacturing and communications in Salonika, until 1912 still an Ottoman city. Here, too, most of the work was done in small enterprises including cotton mills, where 15-hour days were commonly required at least in summer. As in Hereke, young non-Muslim women made up a large share of the labour force employed in the mills, to which their families sent them so that they would earn their dowries. While the presence of large numbers of females is often considered to make for a quiescent labour force, the level of social and political agitation in Salonika came to be considerable when police surveillance decreased for a brief period after the Young Turk revolution of 1908.[52] In the early years of the twentieth century, wages were beginning to rise somewhat, as emigration reached levels high enough to begin affecting the labour market. Some successful strikes occurred even before 1908, affecting textile mills, the tobacco industry and the brickyards. As for the summer of 1908, before the Committee of Union and Progress (CUP, Young Turks) in its turn passed anti-labour legislation, there were strikes in many Salonika industries, including once again tobacco processors and brick-makers.

In this context socialism became an issue for the first time; the relevant debates focused on the problem of how socialists should relate to the 'national questions' forming the major item on the agenda of the political classes in the Balkans of the early 1900s. Mostly wishing to uphold Ottoman rule, the Salonika Jews especially participated in this debate: many of them worried that in a Greek national state, anti-Semitism would be much more dangerous than in the multi-ethnic Ottoman Empire. Among local socialists the best-known figure was Avraam Benaroya, whose activities spanned both the new state of Bulgaria and the Ottoman lands: in later life he became a successful labour organizer in Greece.[53] While Benaroya's socialism probably did not endear him to the conservative leadership of the Jewish community, his advocacy of a federation uniting socialist groups of different nationalities was based on the hope of local Jews that Salonika would remain Ottoman. After all, such a federation made sense only if the empire continued to exist. In Benaroya's perspective, changing over from Ottoman to Greek or Bulgarian domination did not bring any great advantages to the labouring poor, and he abhorred the mutual avoidance of 'nations' that studiously kept apart 'as if fearing contagion'.[54]

In 1911 support from Benaroya's Workers' Solidarity Federation for an Ottoman Salonika was still impressive. Although by now the alliance with the Young Turks had broken down completely, when the socialist organization called for two demonstrations to protest against the Italian attack on Tripolitania earlier that year, respectively 6,000 and 10,000 people showed up – truly impressive figures in a city numbering 150,000 inhabitants. But only a year later the Balkan war of 1912 brought the incorporation of Salonika into Greece; and when all is said and done, with the exception of his Jewish adherents in Salonika, Benaroya had been unable to stem the nationalist tide even among his fellow socialists.

Harbingers of the twentieth century: activism among working people in Cairo and Istanbul

Strikes and political demonstrations also occurred in other large cities of the empire, including Cairo and Istanbul.[55] In 1907 Cairo cab-drivers struck against what they considered unfair competition and interference with their ways of making a living. The competition came from a foreign-owned tramline, and the interference was due to the activities of the British-based Society for the Prevention of Cruelty to Animals. Once Egypt had become a British colony, the Society was able to put pressure on Cairo authorities to confiscate sick horses and punish owners who insisted on working them. Fines and also the arrests of many cab-drivers were the result; the men whose animals were impounded complained about arbitrary treatment by the police, and their protest was taken seriously enough for the authorities to significantly modify their stance on animal abuse.[56]

In Istanbul agitation among Jewish artisans was also linked to the stresses of nineteenth- and early twentieth-century modernization, albeit in a totally different manner. To balance the influence of patriarchs and rabbis, the new regulations issued by the Ottoman authorities in the mid-nineteenth century (Tanzimat) gave non-Muslim lay figures significantly more power in community affairs. In this context a major dispute erupted from an attempt to modernize Jewish education, promoted by the banker of Italian origin Abraham Camondo. As for the wealthiest families who made the crucial decisions in these matters, they were unwilling to raise the necessary funds, and ultimately the Camondos gave up and settled in Paris.[57] But for other community issues as well, the leading families were not willing to levy wealth-based dues but rather relied on indirect taxes on basic consumption goods, which as usual fell most heavily on the poor.[58]

In nineteenth-century Istanbul, stamp tax on meat was a major source of the Jewish community's revenue; the stamp was intended to certify that the meat in question was kosher and fit for consumption by Jews. Butchers and their auxiliary guilds were subject to elaborate regulations issued by the rabbinate in order to ensure the quality of the meat, and the artisans handling slaughtered animals were regularly checked to ensure that they knew these rules and abided by them. But the butchers, accustomed to hard work in the often repellent conditions of the slaughterhouse, were not always amenable to the orders of rabbis and other community leaders. 'Non-political' refractoriness included frequent drunkenness on the job.[59] But in the dispute about the stamp tax on kosher meat a more conscious act of rebellion was involved: the butchers sided with their often wretchedly poor customers and sold them meat without the stamp of the rabbinate, even though some of these guildsmen may well have observed all the prescriptions demanded by Jewish law. Guild-based artisans thus struggled against the councils governing the Jewish community and even achieved a degree of success.

Other disputes involved the Istanbul waterfront: in the last quarter of the nineteenth and the beginning of the twentieth century the workmen here were organized in guilds that were still powerful and cohesive.[60] Even when the jobs that the guildsmen undertook were progressively eliminated by technological change, the guild might remain active.[61] When the Jewish boatmen who ferried people across the Golden Horn lost customers because of the new bridges, and their colleagues operating on the Bosporus were ousted by steamboats, the Jewish boatmen's guild became the major channel through which charity was solicited from the more affluent members of the community.

More dramatic were the activities of the porters who loaded and unloaded the increasingly large ships arriving in Galata, Istanbul's overseas port; here, too, the guild had a significant role to play. In line with a tradition established by the eighteenth century, the heads of the guilds of porters purchased their offices (see Chapter 6). But less traditionally, the pay no longer went to the Ottoman financial administration but rather to that novel creation of the mid-nineteenth century, namely the Istanbul municipality.[62] Guild membership also involved dues of one sort or another, this time collected by the head of the guild; a last payment of this type was made when the former porter gave up his position and returned to his home village.[63] Moreover, in a fashion familiar from eighteenth-century documents, the porters complained about their headmen on account of the illicit charges the latter all too often levied upon them.

In this milieu we find a remarkable feature, namely the requirement that guildsmen turn over their earnings to the head of the guild. In turn the latter was responsible for distributing the money on an equal basis among the members working a particular sector of the port or other workplace.[64] In the seventeenth and eighteenth centuries, by contrast, equality in earnings among guild members seems to have been extremely rare.

Many porters came from the Black Sea coast; ethnically they were a mixed group, including Kurds, Laz, Armenians and Pontus Greeks. Following a pattern also observed among Istanbul's gardeners, by this time often Turks of Black Sea origin, these people typically arrived in the capital without their families. They roomed together, sent money home and returned to their regions of origin when they had accumulated some resources.[65] Group cohesion was such that they could reserve their positions for their fellow villagers alone.

Did small-town artisans inhabit a different world?

In recent years scholars and municipalities have published a few samples of the records that late Ottoman city councils were required to prepare. Most of these registers have undoubtedly perished, but the few surviving items permit tantalizing glimpses into the lives of the inhabitants of Anatolian towns, including artisans.[66] In Çankırı (about 16,000 inhabitants) isolated enough to serve as a place of banishment, the municipality went back to 1869 and a register of receipts (1891–92) has been published. Market dues were an important revenue item, particularly from the sheep and cattle fair that formed the high point of town life. A tax paid by users of the slaughterhouse and dues collected from the public weighing scales – both already known from the 1500s – were farmed out to local dignitaries so that no details are available. Fines collected from artisans were a small addition to the town budget; most often bakers got to pay them, because of underweight or poorly baked bread. A snatch of social life is made visible by the licence fees frequently paid by local musicians. These people played especially at pre-wedding celebrations that involved the outfitting of a new bridegroom: even a shoemaker might hire musicians to celebrate the marriage of his son. An intriguing item is the fee paid by a coffee-house owner for a 'conversation party' (*muhabbet cemiyeti*) for which he proposed to invite musicians: perhaps this was one of the brotherhood rituals practised among local inhabitants, on which the town prides itself even today.[67] However, the register does not refer to any guilds.

The document surviving in Alanya by contrast contains decisions of the town administration during the catastrophic war year of 1915. Slightly beyond the time limits of this study, it has been included because the entries greatly resemble those of the qadi registers of old.[68] Because of wartime rationing the prices of barley, petroleum, straw and olive oil were officially determined and announced by the gendarmerie. Under these circumstances the quality of bread must have been problematic in any case; yet occasionally bakers were fined for selling low-quality 'black' bread. There was no butcher in town, and shoemakers bought hides directly from sheep breeders; how they had these items tanned remains unknown. Throughout, Alanya appears more village-like than Çankırı, but this impression may be due to the fact that numerous men had been drafted, leaving the town market all but deserted.

Snatches of information on the artisans of Sivas come from a different source, namely the report of Boğos Natanyan (1877), whose brief it was to report on compliance to the Tanzimat regulations concerning non-Muslim communities. In response Natanyan has produced a monograph on the Armenian churches, monasteries and charities of that town. Not much is said about crafts, but the author has observed an arrangement of which we have almost no records elsewhere.[69] In Sivas the textile artisans of the Armenian community had divided up the surrounding villages, with each craftsman taking over 20 to 30 settlements. According to a custom that supposedly went back to Armenia, in the fall of any given year he was responsible for gratuitously supplying the clothes of the peasant inhabitants; the author does not specify whether only the Armenian villagers were involved in this arrangement. In the following summer the peasants repaid their debts with deliveries of foodstuffs such as sheep, cheese, grain and butter – late nineteenth-century evidence of artisan remuneration in a cash-poor society.

Evidently the information derived from these scattered records is still very limited. However, it is worth introducing because there is an increasing interest in local archives and authors: more material of this type surely will emerge very soon. At present we can only whet the appetite.

How did the competition of imported goods and the actions of the state affect the survival of guilds?

This question has been studied mainly with respect to Egypt: until recently it had been assumed that guilds disappeared because the industries they had controlled vanished when European factory-made goods flooded the colonial market. However, an alternative explanation has recently been suggested.[70] As we have seen, many handicraft industries maintained themselves, or else new ones took over from those displaced. Yet manufacturing now involved children and especially women much more intensively, and these people never had been guild members. In the larger cities, migrant labour from Italy and Greece also appeared in sizeable numbers, and the Egyptian guilds could not prevent this competition.[71] Furthermore some new manufacturing took place in villages where, once again, guilds had no role to play. To top it all off, the demands of the world market as mediated through putting-out merchants now enforced standards with scant resemblance to those previously imposed by guilds. Given this situation Egyptian guilds progressively became irrelevant to artisans, and when in 1890 the colonial authorities stopped even consulting Cairo guild sheikhs when taxing craftsmen, this measure did not spark any protests, although the potential for popular mobilization in this city was otherwise high. On the basis of the information currently available, this explanation of guild decline seems much more convincing than its predecessor.

Political considerations were also involved. In the mid-nineteenth century the khedive Ismāʿīl had used guild headmen to collect revenue from artisans, effectively turning them into non-salaried petty officials. As they spent time on administrative work, losing opportunities for craft-related gains while handling sums of money on a regular basis, many guild heads 'compensated themselves' and in so doing lost the confidence of the people whose affairs they administered.[72] Probably owing to these circumstances an author who recorded the memories of Cairo artisans at the beginning of the twentieth century found quite a few that saw nothing regrettable in guild demise.

Dependence on the state and alienation from the rank and file meant that many guild headmen no longer protected artisan jobs, as they probably had done even in the 1700s. At the same time, guild solidarities dissolved and guilds fragmented. This process has been reconstructed from the numerous petitions surviving from the later nineteenth century: while petitions by groups of craftsmen were common enough, entire guilds never were involved, and groups of people in one and the same guild might petition against one another. Those former guild sheikhs who did retain a role in public life adjusted to the situation by becoming labour contractors.

We do not have any modern studies of Istanbul artisans which focus on guild disappearance. Therefore only informed guesses are possible. In some respects the story of manufacturing in the territories remaining under Ottoman control resembles the Egyptian pattern. Here, too, we find an increasing number of women and children in the labour force, accompanied by a growing prominence of putting-out merchants.[73] Certain textiles were now woven with imported yarn, while spinners' jobs disappeared and certain weavers adapted to new types of cloth.

Rural industries also expanded, although it is less clear whether guilds lost importance in consequence. Let us briefly return to the Gümüşgerdan: their major enterprise was located outside of town in order to benefit from available water power. Yet this family of entrepreneurs did not use their rural worksite as a reason/pretext for leaving their guild.[74] A different development can be observed with respect to Damascus: here masters and journeymen opposed one another, a phenomenon not common in contemporary Cairo.[75] But in spite of such exceptions the 'restructuring' of artisan work after 1850 in the remaining Ottoman provinces apparently took place roughly within the same parameters as in Egypt.

However, the political framework was substantially different because the Ottoman state, in spite of its dependence on foreign support, still exercised a degree of choice way beyond anything the khedives could have attempted after the Egyptian bankruptcy. As we have seen, self-strengthening through railways, quays and state-sponsored schools continued apace. Furthermore even if factories produced only a small share of all manufactured goods, they still needed to be built and their workpeople paid. As distinct from what happened in colonial Cairo, no tax relief for artisans was forthcoming; on the contrary, the load tended to increase. As the money collected was often meant to support institutions in remote provinces or else the *beaux quartiers* of Istanbul, these state demands were unpopular.

Moreover there was the draft, which Ottoman subjects feared, particularly when soldiers were sent to remote places such as Yemen; presumably in this respect, provincial artisans reacted no differently from other potential draftees. Thus the politically determined aspects of the Egyptian model of guild demise are not applicable to Istanbul or Damascus.

Our information about the end of the guilds in the Ottoman context is connected with a special situation, namely the centralization projects of the Young Turks.[76] This policy involved substituting state organs for the locally selected bodies that had played a major role in urban affairs even under Abdülhamid II. In this context the Istanbul guilds were officially abolished in 1910 and the provincial ones in 1912.[77] In their place the government wished to see 'Craftsmen's Associations' established, in which people who had gained the trust of the Young Turks probably were to hold positions of responsibility. Fifty-one of these new organizations had actually been formed by the beginning of the Great War, although it is not clear whether this figure comprised only Istanbul organizations or else those based in Anatolia as well. Even for Istanbul alone, this figure does not seem very high.

From 1913 onwards, refugees from Salonika came to be influential in the Committee for Union and Progress, now based in Istanbul, and quite a few of them were artisans. These men managed to interest powerful figures among the Young Turks in their organizing efforts, including Dr Nazım and Kara Kemal; after 1923 the latter briefly officiated as the mayor of Istanbul until he fell foul of the Ankara government. This group founded a central organization of all artisans in 1915, although we do not know how much influence it could exert under wartime conditions. Thus in the Ottoman central provinces the guilds must progressively have lost relevance in many trades. But their abolition still was a conscious governmental act, part of a state centralization project.

Guilds, labour organizations and the slow emergence of the working classes

In the Egyptian case, it has been argued that continuity between guilds and twentieth-century labour organizations was minimal.[78] When making the case for discontinuity scholars generally have emphasized the changed political context. The earliest Cairo labour organizations emerged in 1908–09 after the strike wave of 1907, and they were at least partially a product of the alliance between, on the one hand, craft and service workers and, on the other, a section of the nationalist middle classes that was being forged at this time.

Where Istanbul is concerned, the break in continuity is even more obvious. In this city and also in pre-1912 Salonika ethnic diversity, or, to be exact, the ethnic nationalism of the times made the emergence of a cohesive working class very difficult. Competition between labourers of different ethnic backgrounds had existed in the Hamidian period and by no means disappeared after 1908, as Avraam Benaroya found out to his intense frustration. Moreover the wars that followed one another almost without a break between 1911 and 1923 resulted in the deaths and emigrations of many workers and also in the destruction of what little machinery there had been. In many branches of manufacturing after 1923 production had to start 'from scratch'.

On the other hand, however, much of the recent scholarly literature has emphasized the continuities between the Young Turk and early Republican periods.[79] When it comes to labour history it has been demonstrated that working conditions in the Zonguldak mines changed relatively little until after 1945. Therefore insistence on a 'clean break' between guilds and modern-style labour organizations seems to run counter to present trends in historiography, where continuity is a favoured feature.

But these matters are more complicated than appears at first glance; continuities can incorporate elements of discontinuity, while the opposite phenomenon can occur just as well. In Egypt colonial or semi-colonial domination continued throughout the First World War and beyond. The political framework was thus an important element of continuity, or of the *longue durée*, to use Braudelian terms. Yet the emergence of a nationalist and anti-colonial movement after 1907, though led by the middle classes, did change the political parameters within which workers operated and thus introduced an element of discontinuity into Egypt's labour history. Protests against the miserable conditions under which working people and particularly artisans were forced to live from now on coalesced with nationalist and anti-colonial movements.

However, there were no trade unions or other organizations that effectively might have protected the interests of Cairo's workpeople. As a result massive population growth and concomitant immigration from the countryside increasingly drove working men and women into the informal sector, where they had few if any guarantees. To use the term coined by John Chalcraft, 'informalism' proved to be a continuous process, another *longue durée* phenomenon.[80]

As for the situation in Istanbul, certainly a trend towards ethnically more or less homogenous polities, authoritarian modernization and growing centralization was characteristic of both the Committee for Union and Progress and the People's Republican Party that governed Turkey before 1950. Where the Young Turks were concerned, after a short honeymoon with striking workers they soon introduced anti-labour laws. In the early republic widespread dislocation due to war, the population exchange of 1923 and, after 1929, worldwide depression made labour activism difficult and sometimes impossible, given a set of repressive laws enacted in the 1930s.[81] In this case we can say that centralization and authoritarian modernization were long-term continuous processes, which in conjunction with 'outside' political events mostly prevented labour activism. It is in this context that we must view the sharp break and long hiatus between the abolition of guilds and the strikes of the early 1900s – the last examples occurred in the 1920s – and the creation of relatively strong labour organizations in Turkey during the 1960s.

Conclusion

All this brings us back to the question of how craftspeople defended their interests *vis à vis* the market and the demands of the state apparatus. In Egypt after the 1850s, artisans certainly did not disappear because of competition from factory-produced goods, but the concomitant 'restructuring' meant that putting-out merchants and non-guild labour gained such ascendancy that in many types of work, guilds simply faded away. Labour organizations were not normally strong enough to take the places of the now defunct guilds; and this development left artisans without significant protection. As for the British colonial state in Egypt, promoting infrastructural investment and thus making local artisans more competitive was certainly not part of its agenda.

Similar developments can be observed in the Ottoman central provinces soon to become the republic of Turkey. Here war, migration and post-war worldwide depression prevented major improvements in the condition of working people between 1911 and the 1950s. Limited market demand for artisan products must have been a significant reason for the poverty of craftspeople especially in Istanbul; for after war and foreign occupation had come to an end, in 1923 the capital was transferred to Ankara and at least a section of the upper class moved along with the government. Thus the loss of markets suffered by Istanbul artisans was politically determined at least in part; and once again this story shows how economic and political factors were closely intertwined. Craftspeople were caught between the state and the market even though no sultan now occupied the Ottoman throne.

CONCLUSION

Characterizing Guilds Through Comparison

This rapid overview of the history of Ottoman workmen and workwomen has left us with some general notions and many open questions. Quite likely the organizations formed by craftspeople resulted from a conjuncture of interests: on the one hand, artisans of the Ottoman world preferred to defend their interests collectively, with the help of trustworthy spokesmen. On the other hand, the sultan's governments sought formal commitments concerning supplies destined for the larger cities, and this could be achieved by making groups of artisans/traders collectively responsible, although the sultan's officials played the dominant role. Thus the interests of craftsmen and state administrators tended to converge on certain points at least, and given this common interest in craft organization it was not necessary for the sultans to issue any commands demanding the institution of guilds, for instance in newly conquered provinces. Apparently artisan organizations sprung up spontaneously in many but not in all towns: given the present state of our knowledge, it seems that in places such as Mosul or Nablus guilds were less vigorous than in Cairo, Damascus, Jerusalem and Istanbul.

A last glance at an old debate: privileging the state vs relative autonomy

These statements fit into the longstanding discussion concerning the relative autonomy of Ottoman artisans versus the domination of the central state over craft affairs. In this discussion consensus has not been reached and I do not believe that it will be achieved any time soon; for general views of what Ottoman history is all about are at issue. There are some scholars who view the sultan's government as the centrepiece of all social organization. If matters went wrong, the sovereigns attempted to set them right. 'Respectable people' conformed to the rules and regulations ordained by the Ottoman government, even if the tendency to view all subjects of the sultan as 'soldiers' has gone out of fashion these days.

Such views do have some basis in the available documentation, especially the demands for ever more regulation reflected in the eighteenth-century series of sultanic commands concerning the city of Istanbul and its artisans. The latter not only refrained from challenging regulations already in place, but actually asked for official intervention where it did not already exist. Artisans who desired less rather than more regulation did not normally put their demands in writing.

But this gap in our sources does not necessarily mean that no opposition to official policy emerged in the artisan milieu. If in the Ottoman Empire, as elsewhere, it was the first concern of the elite to maintain itself in power, the interests of artisans did not necessarily have high priority. Presumably some craftsmen were aware of this, and reacted by organizing to defend their own interests and priorities. In the present study we have attempted to take both state intervention and artisan concerns into account. Such a middle course doubtless is less elegant intellectually than a defence of one or the other extreme position, and to complicate matters yet further we need to take market demand for the goods and services of Ottoman artisans into account. But all over the world, social realities are complexes of divergent as well as converging interests, and Ottoman artisans and their organizations are no exception to the general rule.

A wider world: links between Ottomanist and Europeanist guild historiographies

Before concluding it makes sense to briefly view Ottoman craftspeople from a somewhat wider perspective. In the long run, satisfactorily situating the artisans of Istanbul, Bursa, Cairo and Aleppo will be possible only if we compare them to their counterparts in Safavid Iran or the Manchu Empire, to name but two reasonably well-documented polities where skilled artisans were numerous. However, comparison is only feasible if the historian is somewhat familiar with the work that has been done on both the settings to be compared. As my own reading has concentrated on the artisans of early modern Europe, I will discuss a few similarities and differences between Ottoman craftspeople and their counterparts in Latin Christendom. Obviously this attempt at comparison is a very modest *ad hoc* effort, which hopefully will stimulate more sophisticated discussions in the future.

For a long time most Ottoman historians dealing with guilds and craftspeople either focused on religious practice or else on the Ottoman state and its demands, while the activities of the masters themselves remained in the shadows. While this situation continued, there was little contact between Ottomanist and Europeanist guild historiographies. After all, historians of Europe had for a long time considered the guilds as more or less autonomous artisan organizations. In some settings, guilds might take on political roles, demanding and, under fortunate circumstances even achieving, participation in urban self-government, as happened in certain towns of Flanders and northern or central Italy during the Middle Ages. On the other hand, English craft guilds had lost much of their significance already in the seventeenth century, and England from the 1700s onwards formed the vanguard of the industrialization process.[1] In consequence, it was assumed that the advance of the absolutist state on the one hand, and the spread of capitalism on the other, reduced the guilds to insignificance. In this perspective, the persistence of guilds in central Europe appeared simply as a sign of political and economic backwardness, not worth a detailed investigation.

However, during the last decade or two, perspectives have changed. From the researches of Caterina Lis, Jan Lucassen, Hugo Soly and their colleagues we now know that during the 'golden age' of Holland's expansion in the late 1500s to late 1600s, new guilds were established in large numbers.[2] And while seventeenth-century Flanders was no longer one of the powerhouses of European economic growth, as it had been in the preceding centuries, it was still a wealthy and active region, and yet its guilds were flourishing.[3] Moreover in the absolutist kingdom of France during the mid-eighteenth century, which experienced considerable economic expansion, craft organizations, though gradually losing ground, still were far from being a *quantité négligeable*.[4] In the Austrian regions of the contemporary Habsburg Empire, where economic expansion and political reform were beginning to transform society and economic life, craft organizations also continued to be significant. Ottoman guilds, relatively late to form and flourish, thus appear as a much less 'peculiar' phenomenon to present-day Europeanist historians.

Even more important for Ottomanists is the observation that much work during the past 30 years or so has been done on European towns of the post-medieval period. By this time, city states and largely autonomous towns in most parts of Europe were in full retreat *vis à vis* the expanding absolutist state.[5] Therefore the political function of the guilds, such as it was, now was reduced to low-key performances on the local level. This has long been known. But while in the first half of the twentieth century, the powerlessness of early modern artisan guilds had been one of the reasons for their relative neglect by scholars, the advent of social history as a field in its own right, with a strong emphasis on 'history from below', changed this perspective significantly. After all, even when power in the governmental sphere was lost, social functions did not necessarily disappear. Guilds might provide self-esteem to the masters through the ceremonial functions that these men attended together with their colleagues, and while Reformation and Counter-Reformation authorities alike often regarded popular practices with a jaundiced eye, they still might welcome or at least tolerate guild attendance at religious services. In the northern Netherlands the arrangements for mutual aid instituted by certain craft guilds even developed into outright insurance funds.[6]

Similarities and differences: limiting access to 'mastership'

Not only did European absolutist regimes before about 1750 make no attempts to do away with the guilds, they were quite inclined to use them for the consolidation of their own power. *Ancien régime* France is especially suitable for comparison with the Ottoman world, for, like the sultans, the French kings controlled a relatively large expanse of land, with interior provinces difficult of access before the railways. Moreover in the seventeenth century both powers fielded large armies, while the navies at best played second fiddle. Furthermore, as in the Ottoman Empire, France before 1789 abounded in local rules and regulations: but, for different reasons, the decrees of the central government were typically superimposed on the practices current in individual towns or regions but did not supersede them.

In the eyes of French bureaucrats during the 1600s and 1700s, guilds were useful because they supervised the quality of the goods produced by their members – a major concern given the significance of export industries. In addition, artisan organizations ensured the training of apprentices and aided in the collection of urban taxes. As readers of this book will have noted, some of these concerns were significant to the Ottoman administration as well: the sultans' officials attempted to enforce production standards and used the guilds as intermediaries when extracting dues and services. Only apprenticeship remained marginal to the Ottoman government's concerns – that is why we know so little about the ways in which young boys of the sultans' domains were taught their trades.

Craftsmen in Dijon, a town of eastern France, offer an opportunity for some interesting reflections. Located in Burgundy, during the seventeenth century Dijon was becoming fully absorbed into the centralized kingdom of France under Louis XIV (r. 1643–1715). Local masters were notorious for trying to limit entry into their craft guilds, as far as possible only admitting the sons of masters to 'mastership'. As a result, many journeymen had little or no chance of ever becoming masters, and the latter prospered often at the expense of their workpeople.[7]

However, the city council was dominated by members of the urban aristocracy and not by guild masters; these councilmen, typically holders of royal offices, opposed the tendency of craft organizations towards exclusiveness: when the latter were in a weak position they typically needed to open entry to larger numbers of outsiders. Several considerations came into play. Officeholders were mainly employed in the royal law courts, and the prestige of these governing families was linked to the control they wielded over townsmen in general and artisans in particular. To members of the town oligarchy, established authority seemed to be in serious jeopardy once guildsmen were allowed to regulate access to master status.[8] Moreover the officeholders that made up the town council viewed matters from the consumers' standpoint; most emphatically they were not merchants and in this respect they had something in common with the Ottoman governing class. As for the traders, they typically focused on distant markets, organizing non-guild textile manufacture in the countryside. As the traders were not interested in supplying the town itself, the craft masters in the Dijon arena were confronted with the holders of political power but had no other opponents.

In their lack of interest in expanding turnover and gaining new markets Dijon's guildsmen showed a pre-capitalist mentality, and in this respect they were not too different from the political class that ruled them. However, elite 'consumerism' apart, some economic considerations were taken into account by urban councilmen. Behind the city government's insistence on greater inclusiveness there was the realization that a smaller number of masters made for less competition. When sheltered in this fashion, guild masters would be able to charge higher prices and perhaps offer lower-quality goods as well.[9]

In the Ottoman context official worries about high prices and shoddy goods also recurred frequently. However, we find few cases in which the central government tried to open up the guilds to new members. When the sultans' officials tried to keep the price level down, they had recourse to administrative fiat: commands were sent out from the centre and administratively controlled prices (*narh*) were (re-)imposed. But Istanbul officialdom apparently did not regard a small number of masters as a threat to stability. On the contrary, in the 1500s and 1600s at least, the sultans' administration inclined towards the opposite argument, accepting guildsmen's complaints about insufficiently qualified fellow artisans at face value.[10] It is worth noting that even though Ottoman officials amply shared the consumerist perceptions of their Dijon counterparts, they never claimed that the market was insufficiently supplied because of the restrictive practices of local guildsmen; rather they tended to focus their attentions on merchants as the possible culprits. Moreover when in the late 1700s Selim III was worried about what he regarded as Istanbul's excess population, his servitors were to track down 'undesirables', a category that included craftsmen whose services were not in demand. The latter were to be expelled from the capital. Artisans were thus a source of worry if they were numerous, but not if they were few in number.

In brief, both Ottoman and Dijon administrators were concerned with urban order and the maintenance of hierarchy, viewing artisan affairs from a consumerist perspective. But while Ottoman authorities were not greatly concerned about a possible scarcity of masters and the effects of such a situation on prices and urban order, this concern was rather important to the authorities in Dijon.

Similarities and differences: price controls, inter-guild sales and differentiation within guilds

Early modern town administrations in many parts of continental Europe were closely involved in the fixing of prices: *laissez-faire* attitudes were not much debated before the eighteenth century, and in practice before 1789 price fixing and quality controls were ubiquitous.[11] A study of butchers, tanners and shoemakers in seventeenth-century Bologna has shown how the law courts and also the Cardinal Legate, the highest authority in this papal territory, were regularly called upon to sanction the fixing of prices.[12] In addition the Bologna case is of particular interest to the Ottomanist historian because here we see an arrangement common among Istanbul and Bursa guilds as well: the butchers were supposed to sell all their hides to tanners and the latter to pass on their leathers to the shoemakers. Once again all these transactions were to take place at prices decided by the Cardinal Legate's officials.

All this sounds rather straightforward, but in reality the opposite was often the case. There were frequent recriminations especially against the tanners who tended to substitute locally harvested bark for the gall-nut imported from the Middle East; when challenged the tanners protested that using Italian bark did not really result in any savings, and therefore it was unfair on the government's part to lower leather prices. Tanners were also accused of dealing with customers in the countryside when Bologna guildsmen had a prior claim upon their wares. When butchers and tanners wanted to sell outside of the city, they needed the permission of the artisans possessing officially sanctioned rights of priority; these permissions were hard to obtain, so that smuggling was rather frequent.

Complaints and appeals resulted in a significant amount of paperwork and probably a degree of insecurity and instability as well. Administratively determined prices often needed to be adjusted because the quality of the skins, hides and leathers on offer could not be completely standardized: rebates for poor quality therefore were common. Apparently the butchers of Bologna were adept at intimidating the members of other guilds while the shoemakers were the weakest and most often disadvantaged as a result.

Apart from these conflicts between guilds there were many disputes within the relevant craft organizations themselves, and quite often over the distribution of hides/skins among tanners. The papal government was concerned that all guildsmen should make a living and 'the poor' buy leather goods at affordable prices. Therefore the authorities tried to ensure that every tanner received a minimal allowance of hides that would permit him to maintain his shop and family. But better-capitalized tanners were adept at securing larger shares, and regulations definitely did not secure equality among members of the Bologna tanners' guild.

Inequality within artisan organizations has also been studied for cities other than Bologna. In eighteenth-century Lyons, a major centre of the silk industry, journeymen with little chance of advancement were numerous. On the other hand a small group of masters controlled not only the industry itself but also the socio-religious organizations of its practitioners, including the chapel of the confraternity.[13] A limited coterie of masters also tended to monopolize guild offices, to the great resentment of those excluded; in fact by 1789, guilds in the Lyons silk industry were disintegrating and modern-style classes in the process of emergence.[14]

Arrangements of the type observed in Bologna were common enough in the Ottoman world as well.[15] Ottoman records also demonstrate that butchers and tanners could disregard rulings or intimidate their opponents.[16] However, the correspondence such affairs generated in the lands governed by the sultans was not nearly as voluminous, so that we do not know which aspects of the Bologna distribution problems were most relevant to Bursa or Istanbul. But even as things stand, the situation is immediately recognizable to the Ottomanist historian, and we can ask ourselves whether similar behind-the-scenes bargains sometimes were not struck among Ottoman artisans.

On the other hand, as has long been known, conflicts between journeymen and masters that resulted in disintegrating guilds were comparatively rare in the Ottoman world. While such a situation did exist in Damascus during the late 1800s, normally guilds disintegrated for other reasons, including the growing importance of the 'informal' sector. In addition there were political considerations involved: at least in Egypt certain guilds were appropriated by the khedival and later the colonial state and thus lost the confidence of their members, while outright abolition by the government was a major factor in the Ottoman central provinces.[17] Of course we also find regions of Europe where guilds did not split at the workplace but ultimately disappeared for other reasons, state intervention playing an important part. Yet at the present state of our knowledge it does appear that differentiation within a given guild resulting in its ultimate disintegration was more common in western Europe than in the Ottoman lands.

A major difference: women's roles in shops and workshops

Further differences between workshop life in Latin Christendom and its counterpart in the eastern Mediterranean are apparent when we focus on northwestern Europe. Dutch and Belgian historians have shown that in seventeenth-century Holland, the wives of sailors, villagers but also artisans very often were expected to contribute to the family budget by labour outside the home.[18] In some crafts such as dressmaking, seamstresses organized to defend themselves against their competitors, the all-male tailors, and, albeit with bad grace, in some towns a few women were even accepted as guild members.[19] None of this happened in France; yet a close and detailed study of Paris bakers in the 1600s and 1700s has shown that the wives of these artisans were indispensable to the functioning of these essential enterprises.[20]

In Parisian bakeries, selling the finished product was typically the responsibility of the wife; in large establishments she supervised the salespeople, but in smaller shops this work fell to the woman herself. Bread was often sold on credit, and it was the master's wife, who knew the customers far better than her spouse, who frequently decided on the creditworthiness or otherwise of a given purchaser. Arguing with buyers who failed to pay their debts frequently fell upon bakers' wives as well. Therefore the latter kept records not only by the time-honoured method of notching a stick but also by recording purchases in writing. Bakers' wives also bought wholesale as long as the seller was present in the city, visiting the central markets for this purpose. On an informal basis, in these transactions wives were regarded as the proxies of their husbands.

Throughout, the wives of French artisans were in an ambiguous situation: they could not be masters or in many cases even dispose of their own property, but during the often frequent absences of their husbands they gave orders to apprentices and journeymen. In a patriarchal society where men were valued more highly than women, this de facto authority sometimes gave rise to considerable resentment: young males employed in craft shops might act out their frustration 'by proxy'. On occasion cats were massacred in such a manner that a modern historian has concluded that the violence was symbolically directed against the master's wife and, through her, against the head of the household.[21]

As far as we know, the wives of Ottoman artisans never played such semi-public roles. But it is difficult to tell whether some of them did not take on a role in production behind the scenes. When masters lived in their shops or at least in the same building, as was relatively common in Istanbul around 1800, such informal participation of wives and daughters may have been more frequent than we might expect.[22] We already know that there were Istanbul or Bursa women who sold the products of their cookery in an effort to support their families, or who worked as silk winders.[23] More intensive studies of the qadi registers may yet yield important results with respect to women's roles in craftwork. But at the present state of our knowledge, the activities of artisans' wives, especially as salespeople, do constitute a significant difference between the artisan worlds of the 1600s and 1700s in, for example, Paris and Istanbul.

Guildsmen as social beings

For a long time, Europeanist historians discussed matters of artisan labour quite extensively, but gave short shrift to the social existence of these people outside the workshop. During the last two decades this approach has come in for a good deal of criticism: in the first place a categorical separation of the workplace from the home is something that many people experienced only in the nineteenth century.[24] For the early modern period by contrast, work and family strategies were often intertwined: guild endogamy, for instance, was encountered with relative frequency. We therefore have been warned to mentally keep the history of crafts separate from that of their practitioners.[25] Other historians have pointed out that the market values that we regard as dominant in the workaday world were late to spread among the inhabitants of many towns, especially the smaller ones.[26] Even in eighteenth-century England non-commercial values that have been summarized as 'the moral economy' long were characteristic of many communities.[27] During the last 20 years or so there have been concerted attempts to show how residence patterns or the choice of marriage partners were affected by and in their turn affected relations between people who also came together in shops or workshops. In addition the terminology by which townsmen of the sixteenth or seventeenth century described their world has come in for attention, and it has been pointed out that categories connected with work might be considered important for self-definition in a given city at a given time and much less important in earlier or later periods.

In brief, there was no automatic self-identification of townsmen in terms of their work, and even less did they automatically adhere to this or that guild.[28] Many guilds contained practitioners of more than one craft. Artisans involved in a speciality newly gaining in importance therefore had some choice in associating with one or another of the established groups or founding a new organization altogether.

Merchants might use guild membership for their own and quite distinct purposes. For the city of Turin in northeastern Italy, for example, such an investigation has been undertaken with respect to the tailors' guild, which in the late 1600s and early 1700s was the most prestigious in the city.[29] During this period the guild contained quite a few members for whom tailoring was at best an incidental source of income; basically these men were silk merchants and often quite wealthy. As for the prosperity and later loss of prestige of the tailors' guild, it was closely connected with the very same silk industry: when membership in the guild allowed merchants to circumvent restrictions on the importation of silk cloths, these people eagerly joined the tailors' guild. But after 1730 the silk industry suffered a prolonged crisis, the tailors going down along with their merchant partners.

To the Ottomanist historian these observations provide much food for thought: after all, we are not yet in a position to treat the history of crafts separately from that of their practitioners, and the present book is an example of this 'old-fashioned' methodology. In a different vein, we have not yet made a concerted attempt to find out which artisans/shopkeepers/market stall-holders associated with others in one and the same guild, or else when the representatives of different specialities parted company. Such movements must have happened when new wares such as clocks and watches appeared on the market and the artisans making/repairing them had to find a place in the guild world. Representatives of small and/or decaying crafts may have preferred to join larger organizations and bargained before doing so.

Admittedly studying the social existence of craftsmen is quite difficult in our field because of the limitations of the sources. But as the work of Cengiz Kırlı, Betül Başaran and Nalan Turna has shown, in the late 1700s Selim III's officials did compile registers of all the shops and workshops existing in certain parts of Istanbul. Documentation of this kind has enabled Europeanists to probe more deeply into the lives of 'their' artisans, and something similar surely is feasible in our field as well.[30] Other advances in this direction can be made with the aid of the qadi registers. Thus studies on life in the town quarters of Adana and particularly Aleppo do allow us to reconstruct the circumstances in which artisans lived; and this concern with the social context does connect the most recent work on Ottoman artisans with studies on Turin, Lyons or Dijon.[31]

Guilds and the state

Last but not least, Europeanist historians have studied the role of state formation in the history of crafts and guilds. During the period beginning in the 1500s and down to the French Revolution, princes in many parts of Europe rode roughshod over the privileges of the towns in their realm. This development affected not only guildsmen but merchants as well; in Turin, for instance, it was the traders who lost control over urban affairs when lawyer-bureaucrats in the service of the prince of Savoy took over.[32] But artisans typically were the lowest rung of the ladder: while the central government whittled away at the prerogatives of the town councils, merchants evicted the craft guilds from the few decision-making positions that they might possess.[33] However, even when marginalizing artisans politically, a centralizing state in the making was not of necessity hostile to the guilds.

In fact some absolutist states were willing to support them. In the Spanish and later Austrian Netherlands (today's Belgium) membership of a guild certainly provided but limited access to political power, and that on the strictly local level. But even after 1750 the authorities in Brussels were hesitant to make major changes when it came to the representation of guilds in urban councils; for the provincial authorities assumed that the existing setup was legitimized by tradition and that changes even in minor matters might bring the whole socio-political system tumbling down.[34] Put differently, the representatives of Habsburg power in Brussels thought that there was a tacit contract between rulers and ruled that should not be jeopardized by unpopular innovations. Perhaps this was a special case, but it does show that the hostility against guilds of the French minister Turgot (1721–81) and, after 1789, of the various revolutionary governments in France was not shared by all absolutist bureaucracies.

Yet in early modern state-building projects throughout Europe, guilds rarely were allotted a major role. On the contrary, while continuing to exist and even multiply, in many ways they were marginalized. When it came to the quality controls that from the seventeenth century onwards the kings of France instituted to increase the appeal of French goods to foreign markets, such controls were not the monopoly of guilds. Rather the latter had to share the right of supervision with officeholders chosen by the central power or else with controllers appointed by city administrations. After all, a second and significant reason for instituting such controls was the search for increased revenues. These could be derived from fines but also from the sale of the relevant positions; French towns might put on the market offices whose possessors checked woollens or leathers, or even measured charcoal and counted fish before the goods were sold to customers.[35] Presumably the kings and their administrations had no desire to see the relevant revenues totally pass into the coffers of artisan guilds; after all, the wars of the 1600s and 1700s swallowed up enormous sums of money.

Remarkably enough, views concerning the 'tacit contract' between ruler and subjects on the basis of a social order regarded as traditional were shared by both sultans' officials in Istanbul and the Habsburg administration in Brussels. The Ottoman dynasty had remained in power over the centuries because the sultans were able to convince their subjects that they were concerned with their well being: subsistence in this world and, if at all possible, salvation in the next. As for officialdom in Brussels, as we have seen, its members feared that tampering with their own version of the social order, guild privileges included, might open the door to unrest and rebellion.

On a more mundane level, farming out offices in charge of market control such as the *muhtesib* certainly was common enough in the Ottoman context, and so was the appointing of former soldiers as guild officials if they gave up their pay tickets – for this practice may be regarded as a variety of office sale. Appointing officials against payment was thus a widespread mode of 'revenue collection-cum-administration' in both France and the Ottoman Empire. However, the militarization of the artisan world that has been observed in Istanbul, Damascus, Cairo and other places had no parallel in French, Bolognese or Turin society. Nowhere do we see artisans joining the armies – if anything, most craftsmen avoided contact with the military if they could. Moreover the controls instituted by French administrations often were part of an attempt to increase exports and, for example, make French woollens competitive with their Dutch or English counterparts, a concern that the sultans' administration certainly did not share. Of course later research may prove us wrong, but at present, militarization of the craft world, a greater 'invisibility' of women's work and an official lack of interest in promoting exports seem to be peculiarly characteristic of the Ottoman setting.

Conclusion

It would be of great interest to further explore similarities and differences between Ottoman artisans and those of Catholic and Protestant Europe. Yet even these brief remarks show that such explorations are useful in two respects. On the one hand, Ottoman urban societies had quite a few features in common with their counterparts in early modern Europe: when investing time and energy in comparative endeavours, we can be sure at least that we are not comparing chalk with cheese. We can postulate an overarching category of craft organization of which the Ottoman and the western and central European varieties form sub-types. Moreover it has already been said, but bears repeating nevertheless, that similar comparisons with Iran or China are high on the list of historians' desiderata.

On the other hand, studying the work that has been done in other historical fields broadens the researcher's imagination, and this is also true when dealing with craftspeople and guilds. After considering the research projects of historians dealing with France, the Low Countries and Italy, the Ottomanist will frequently ask himself/herself whether something analogous can be undertaken with respect to Istanbul, Bursa or Cairo. To take a few examples: after seeing the guild houses that still adorn Belgian towns, the historian will want to find out more about the meeting places of certain Istanbul guilds, the *lonca* that have not survived as buildings but must at one point have been popular enough that artisan organizations were named after them and older designations such as *hirfet* were forgotten. Or, in a different vein, can we learn more about the difficulties that arose when one guild depended on raw materials furnished by another? Or is it possible, at least in certain places, to find out something about the residential and marriage patterns of Ottoman craftspeople?

Certainly in the long run, Ottomanist historians will begin producing some of their own paradigms and cease depending completely on those 'imported' from other fields, European, Indian or whatever the source may be. But even when we get to that stage, and I hope that in the near future we will, 'cross-fertilization' is a source of historical productivity wherever we go. Hopefully ever more scholars will feel intrigued and stimulated by these possibilities.

Notes

Abbreviations

AKS = Ankara Kadi Sicilleri
BOA = Başbakanlık Arşivi-Osmanlı Arşivi (Istanbul archives)
MAD = Maliye Ahkâm Defterleri (Istanbul archives)
MD = Mühimme Defterleri (Istanbul archives)
ŞD = Şikayet Defterleri (Istanbul archives)
TK = Tapu ve Kadastro Arşivi, Kuyudu kadime, Ankara

Introduction

1. See Itzkowitz (1962); Majer (1978) and many others on Ottoman officials. See Schmitt (2005) and Smyrnelis (2005) on foreigners resident in the empire.
2. The most distinguished example is Raymond (1973–74).
3. Dernschwam (reprint 1986), p 186; Tucker (1985).
4. Sahillioğlu (1985); Faroqhi (1984), p 180.
5. Lis, Lucassen and Soly (2006a), p 1.
6. Keyvani (1982), p 38.
7. Lis, Lucassen and Soly (2006b), pp 114–15.
8. Findley (1980), pp 91–100.
9. Inalcik (1969); Genç (1986); Kütükoğlu (1986); Genç (1994).
10. The formula was invented by Mehmet Genç: Genç (1994).
11. Nalan Turna's as yet unpublished dissertation deals with the role of everyday interaction between officials and guildsmen as a factor in nineteenth-century centralization projects.
12. Ersanlı (2002).
13. Uzunçarşılı (1943–44); (1945); (1948); (1965).
14. As a pioneering work see Abou-El-Haj (1991).
15. A rare example has been translated and commented on in Quataert and Duman (eds) (2001).
16. Consult Kal'a et al (eds) (1997–98), especially vols. I and VII.
17. Düzdağ (ed) (1972); Özcan (1983).
18. Özcan (1983).
19. Rozen (2000), p 85.
20. Ergene (2003).
21. Though made in quite another context, I have found the reflections of Roger Chartier germane to our problem: Chartier (1991).

22. Lapidus (1984).
23. Evliya Çelebi (1314/1896–97 to 1938), vol. 10, on Egypt; Evliya Çelebi (1995).
24. Genç (1975).
25. Quataert (2006); Chalcraft (2005); Doğanalp-Votzi (1997).
26. A recent and distinguished example is Yi (2004).
27. Khoury (1997).
28. I do not read Arabic, and, as scholars writing in Turkish rarely concern themselves with the Arab provinces, I have to make do with secondary literature in Western languages.
29. The word 'apparently' has been added because of a small doubt that these women may have commissioned rather than manufactured these textiles; but this is for specialists to decide.
30. Billington (2001), p 18.
31. Kuran (2000), especially pp 51–2.
32. Kütükoğlu (1986).
33. Genç (1986).

Chapter 1: Writing about Artisans

1. In some respects this discussion is an expansion of Quataert's introduction to the group of Ottomanist writings published in *International Labor and Working Class History*: Quataert (2001). However, I read Quataert's article only after the present text was virtually complete.
2. Taeschner (1979), pp 550–7.
3. See, for example, Gölpınarlı (1949–50), pp 1–354. For the commented German translations of some texts of this kind see Taeschner (1979).
4. Evliya Çelebi (1995), pp 222–3; see Rafeq (1991), p 508, for a reference to a guild of thieves, complete with female members in a court protocol; Ginio (2003) and Sariyannis (2006).
5. Mélikoff (1964), pp 180–91.
6. Compare the various necrologies by Ahmet Yörük, Ömer Celal Sarç and Ahmet Güner Sayar in *İstanbul Üniversitesi İktisat Fakültesi Mecmuası* 43, 1–4 (1984–85), *Prof. Dr. Sabri Ülgener'e Armağan*, 1–12, 27–37.
7. In 1981, shortly before his death, Ülgener was able to issue new versions of his two major works, both first published in the 1950s: Ülgener (1981a); (1981b).
8. Vovelle (1982). Recent contributions from Ottomanists include Singer (2002) and Peirce (2003).
9. I thank Yavuz Köse for discussing Ülgener's views with me; see also his as yet unpublished dissertation: Köse (2007).
10. Wallerstein, Decdeli and Kasaba (1987).
11. Kafadar (1989).
12. Dale (1994).
13. Quataert (1993).
14. Todorov (1967–68).
15. Ergin (1914–22), vol. 1.
16. Quataert (1983b), pp 99–109.

17. Altınay (reprint 1988a and 1988b).
18. Barkan (1942); (1963); (1972–79). The last-named study, in spite of its late publication date, was actually written before 1963.
19. For example, Baer (1970a and 1970b).
20. Chalcraft (2004), p 71; Baer (1980); Gerber (1988).
21. Genç (1986); (1987); (1994); in addition a lecture given at Bilgi University in May 2008.
22. 'The voice of [the man] crying in the wilderness'.
23. Dalsar (1960); Mantran (1962).
24. Dalsar (1960), p 27.
25. Gerber (1988).
26. Baer (1980).
27. Cohen (1989); (1990); (2001).
28. Rafeq (1976); (1991).
29. On business history see Çizakça (1996); Gedikli (1998). On the survival strategies of Ottoman craftsmen compare Quataert (1993).
30. Inalcik (1969), p 118; Faroqhi (1995a).
31. Mendels (1972).
32. Inalcik (1969); Ergenç (1975); Gerber (1988).
33. Dalsar (1960); Zarinebaf-Shahr (2001).
34. Yi (forthcoming a).
35. Yi (2004); Faroqhi (1996).
36. Kuran (2000), p 54.
37. Katsiardi-Hering (forthcoming).
38. Todorov (1967–68).
39. Todorov (reprint 1977), no. VII.
40. Genç (1995).
41. Wilkins (2005).
42. Inalcik (1960), p 139.
43. Ydema (reprint 1991); Mack (2002); Carboni (ed) (2007).
44. Ergenç (1975).
45. Atasoy and Raby (1989); Gerelyes (ed) (2005); on the Italian finds, oral information from Joanita Vroom, to whom I am profoundly grateful.
46. Fukasawa (1987).
47. Arıkan (1991); Papakostantinou (forthcoming).
48. Kütükoğlu (ed) (1983).
49. Quataert (ed) (2000); but see also Quataert (1997); Zilfi (2004).
50. Establet and Pasqual (1994); (1998); (2005).
51. Köse (2007).
52. Raymond (1973–74).
53. Michel (2005).
54. Hanna (1984); Maury, Raymond, Revault, Zakarya (1983).
55. Guirgis (2004); Tribe (2004). I am grateful to Febe Armanios, Siegfried Richter and Nelly Hanna for directing me to these articles.
56. See Atasoy and Raby (1989), with a good deal of information on faience-makers.

57. Ghazaleh (1999).
58. Abou-Khatwa (2006).
59. Tucker (1985); Toledano (1990), p 237.
60. Zarinebaf-Shahr (2001) is an article, while Karakışla (2005) focuses on attempts to find work for Muslim women during the First World War.
61. Chalcraft (2004); (2005).
62. *The Striking Cabbies of Cairo and Other Stories.*
63. Akarlı (1985–86); (2004), pp 166–200.
64. Başaran (2006); Turna (2006); Kırlı (2001); also relevant is Kütükoğlu (2000).
65. Inalcik (1986a); Faroqhi (2002a), pp 235–44.
66. Mantran (1962), p 362.
67. Yıldırım (2002).
68. For an anthology of such statements along with a critical discussion see Köse (2007).
69. Vatter (1995); (2006).
70. For one example among many see Küçükerman (1987).
71. Raymond (1973–74); Mantran (1962); Hitzel (2007).

Chapter 2: Before and After 1500

1. Şahin and Emecen (1988), pp 291–2.
2. Goitein (1988), pp 256–7 and *passim*.
3. Lapidus (1984), pp 96–101.
4. Cahen (1988), pp 315–20. Unfortunately evidence is extremely sparse.
5. Geyer and Lefort (eds) (2003); Jacoby (2004), p 135.
6. Fekete (1976), p 50.
7. Ahmet Eflâkî (1973).
8. Gölpınarlı (1959), pp 106–12; Helmuth Ritter, 'Djalāl al-Dīn Rūmī', in *Encyclopedia of Islam*, 2nd ed, vol. 2, pp 393–6.
9. Gölpınarlı (1953), p 29.
10. Ibn Battuta (1854), vol. 2, pp 327, 335.
11. *Ibid.*, p 274.
12. Taeschner (1979), pp 284–5.
13. Cahen (1988), p 319.
14. Şahin and Emecen (1988), pp 290–1.
15. Cohen (1990).
16. Şahin and Emecen (1988), p 291.
17. See Taeschner (1979), pp 468–88, for a German translation with comments.
18. For a listing of manuscripts see Taeschner (1979), p 633; see also Gölpınarlı (1949–50) for a general discussion.
19. Raymond (1973–74), vol. 2, pp 529–38.
20. Gölpınarlı (1953–54), pp 76–7.
21. *Ibid.*, pp 86, 122.
22. Barkan (1942), part 3, p 170.
23. Mélikoff (1964).

24. Barkan (1942), part 1, p 337.
25. *Ibid.*, pp 338–9.
26. Peirce (2001), p 46.
27. This text was found by Özlem Sert, and her article on this issue will soon be published. I thank the author for allowing me to see her manuscript.
28. Cohen (1989), p 100.
29. *Ibid.*
30. Barkan (1942), part 1, p 336; Aynural (2001), p 140.
31. Cohen (1984), p 164.
32. *Ibid.*, p 166.
33. *Ibid.*, pp 163, 253.
34. Dalsar (1960), p 307, documents dated 1567 and 1565.
35. I thank Marcel van der Linden for his comments on this matter.
36. Barkan (1942), part 3, p 168. For some incisive comments on these three *muhtesib* regulations see Rogers (1986), p 137.
37. Barkan (1942), part 3, p 170.
38. *Ibid.*
39. Cohen (1989), p 19; Faroqhi (2002c), pp 256–60.
40. Yi (2004).
41. Cohen (1989), pp 16–19.
42. Peirce (2001), p 38.
43. Robert Mantran, 'Ḥisba', in *Encyclopedia of Islam*, 2nd ed, Ottoman section; Kazıcı (1987).
44. Barkan (1942), part 1, pp 339–40.
45. *Ibid.*, part 2, pp 16, 18.
46. Peirce (2003), p 180. For non-Muslims this question may not have been quite as significant because in any event they could not testify against Muslims.
47. Barkan (1942), part 1, pp 332, 334.
48. *Ibid.*, p 337; Dalsar (1960), p 346.
49. Dalsar (1960), pp 118–19, 344–6.
50. Barkan (1942), part 1, p 337.
51. *Ibid.*, part 2, p 15.
52. *Ibid.*, part 2, p 17.
53. Faroqhi (1995c), pp 204–12; Dalsar (1960), p 335.
54. Faroqhi (1995c), pp 210–11.
55. Dalsar (1960), pp 132–6.
56. *Ibid.*, p 338.
57. Faroqhi (1995c), p 207.
58. Inalcik (1969), p 117.
59. Ankara Kadı Sicilleri (AKS) 7, no. 714 (1008/1599–1600), p 93.
60. AKS 5, no. 140 (1002/1593–94), pp 31–2.
61. Dernschwam (reprint 1986), p 186.
62. Faroqhi (1995c), p 211.
63. Dalsar (1960), pp 377–83, 396.
64. Fotopoulos and Delivorrias (1997), p 298.

65. Ibn Battuta (1854), vol. 2, p 271. In the 1970s a machine-embroidered cotton cloth in varying shades of yellow and gold was still on the market for use as tablecloths.
66. Barkan and Ayverdi (1970), pp 366–7.
67. Ibid., p 365.
68. Anonymous (ed) (1938), p 209.
69. Inalcik (1969), pp 104–6; Ülgener (1981a), pp 56–8 and elsewhere.
70. Veinstein (1988), pp 300–1.

Chapter 3: Services to the State

1. Lowry (1986), p 23.
2. Finkel (1988), vol. 1, pp 7–20.
3. Cezar (1965), p 213.
4. Andreasyan (1976).
5. Tilly (1985).
6. Barkan (1972–79), vol. 1.
7. Veinstein (1988), pp 304–6.
8. Kafadar (1991).
9. Veinstein (1988), pp 301–2.
10. Gökbilgin (1957), p 30.
11. Bostan (1992), p 199.
12. MD 79, no. 1026 (1019/1610–11), pp 409–10.
13. Braude (1979).
14. Gara (2005), p 124.
15. Tezcan (1992), p 227.
16. Pamuk (2000b), pp 125–30.
17. Başbakanlık Arşivi Şikâyet Defterleri (ŞD) 2 (1063/1652–53), p 204; ŞD 3 (1065/1654–55), p 150.
18. MAD 7527, p 21. Because of damage to the paper, the interpretation of the text is conjectural.
19. Gara (2005), p 131.
20. Goffman (1990), pp 82–3; Emecen (1997), pp 35–7.
21. Tezcan (1992), pp 224–5.
22. Ibid., pp 229–30.
23. ŞD 4 (1075/1664–65), p 4.
24. Cohen (1989), p 161.
25. MAD 3457, pp 37, 79. If measured in Istanbul *kantars*, according to Hinz (1955), p 27, the yarn demanded should have amounted to 1,692kg.
26. MAD 3457 (1037–38/1627–28), pp 31, 70.
27. MAD 9840, p 26.
28. MAD 4397 (1055/1645–46), p 158; the delivery of 37,775 pieces was demanded.
29. TK 75, fol. 276b; MD 6, no. 395, p 84.
30. MD 21, no 675 (980/1572–73), p 285.
31. Beldiceanu (1964), pp 85–126.
32. Ibid., p 97.

33. *Ibid.*, pp 104–13.
34. *Ibid.*, pp 119–22.
35. Gökbilgin (1957), p 52.
36. Faroqhi (1984), pp 172–80.
37. Quataert (2006), p 55.
38. Davis (1993); Özveren and Yıldırım (unpublished). I thank the authors for permission to use their study.
39. Bostan (1992), p 66: a detailed discussion of the different artisans working for the naval arsenal.
40. Özveren and Yıldırım (unpublished).
41. Çizakça (1981), vol. 2, pp 776–7.
42. Dursteler (2006), pp 67–8, 80–1.
43. Mantran (1962), p 352; Evliya Çelebi (1995), p 184.
44. Evliya Çelebi (1995), p 177; Müller-Wiener (1986–87).
45. Murphey (1999); Ágoston (2005).
46. Inalcik (1975).
47. Ágoston (2005), pp 114–17; Gökçen (1946a and b).
48. Evliya Çelebi (1995), p 186; Bacqué-Grammont (1999); Hitzel (2007), p 175. On the cannons produced see Ágoston (2005), pp 61–81; Müller-Wiener (1986–87).
49. Müller-Wiener (1986–87).
50. Evliya Çelebi (1995), p 187.
51. Uzunçarşılı (1981–86); Necipoğlu (2005), pp 153–61.
52. Fleischer (1986), p 110.
53. Uzunçarşılı (1981–86), p 26.
54. *Ibid.*, p 41.
55. *Ibid.*, p 31.
56. Mahir (1986), pp 113–17.
57. Uzunçarşılı (1981–86), p 24; Atıl (1987), pp 66–77.
58. Uzunçarşılı (1981–86), p 35.
59. *Ibid.*, p 44.
60. *Ibid.*, p 51.
61. Dankoff (2004), pp 32–82.
62. Caʿfer Efendi (1987), pp 36–8.
63. Artan (2006), p 412.
64. *Ibid.*, p 416.
65. Çağman (1984).
66. Rogers (1986).
67. Turan (1963); Kuran (1987); Necipoğlu (2005).
68. Necipoğlu-Kafadar (1986).
69. Saatçi (ed) (1990), pp 67–9.
70. According to MAD 8590, p 26, in the 1720s a master working for the master of the sultan's stables was exempt from guild regulations.
71. Barkan (1972–79).
72. Saatçi (1990), pp 83–5; Crane, Akın and Necipoğlu (2006), pp 124–5, 150–1.
73. Barkan (1972–79), vol. 1, p 97, n. 7.

74. Pamuk (2000a), p 69; Barkan (1972–79), vol. 2, p 292.
75. Faroqhi (2002d), pp 283–5.
76. Proházka-Eisl (ed) (1995); Atasoy (1997), pp 15–17.
77. Atasoy (1997), pp 38, 50, 60.
78. *Ibid.*, p 40.
79. Stout (1966), p 250, where the relevant text is given in English.

Chapter 4: Guildsmen of Istanbul and Cairo

1. On Cairo see Raymond (1973–74); Hanna (1984); on Istanbul see Mantran (1962); Yi (2004); for a recent synthesis compare Hitzel (2007).
2. Halil Inalcik, 'Istanbul', in *Encyclopedia of Islam*, 2nd ed, vol. 4, pp 239–40; see also Yérasimos (1995), p 106.
3. Akdağ (1963); Faroqhi (1984), pp 272–5; Kuniholm (1990).
4. Andreasyan (1976).
5. Raymond (1973–74), vol. 1, p 204.
6. Raymond (1993), p 226.
7. Braudel (1979), vol. 1, p 463: Paris may have had 180,000 inhabitants in the late sixteenth century, but by the 1640s had doubled to about 360,000. Naples had 300,000 inhabitants towards the late 1500s.
8. Mantran (1962), pp 123–77.
9. Ergene (2003), pp 190–202.
10. For a French translation of a parallel text from 1680 see Mantran (1962), pp 330–47.
11. Akgündüz (ed) (1988–89), vol. 1, pp 85–166.
12. Peirce (2003), pp 100–6.
13. Veinstein (1996).
14. El-Nahal (1979), p 74.
15. *Ibid.*, pp 12–17.
16. At least this is suggested by the fact that El-Nahal (1979), pp 22–3, has nothing to say on this account.
17. Hanna (1984), p 58.
18. El-Nahal (1979), pp 36–7.
19. *Ibid.*, p 41.
20. Most recently Michel (2005).
21. Ergene (2003); Peirce (2003).
22. Mantran (1962), pp 123–6.
23. Uzunçarşılı (1948), p 415.
24. Evliya Çelebi (1995), pp 255–61.
25. *Ibid.*, pp 245–7.
26. *Ibid.*, pp 259–60.
27. Hanna (1984), p 59.
28. *Ibid.*, pp 60–1.
29. Evliya Çelebi (1314/1896–97 to 1938), vol. 10, p 358.
30. According to Raymond (1973–74), vol. 2, pp 577–98, the *muḥtasib* was responsible only for certain trades, especially those linked to alimentation, while the

miʿmārbāšā was in charge of the building crafts.
31. Raymond (1973–74), vol. 2, pp 659–87.
32. Ibid., p 589.
33. Evliya Çelebi (1314/1896–97 to 1938), vol. 10, pp 358–72.
34. Wilkins (2005) has discussed the effects of these demands on the artisans of Aleppo.
35. Raymond (1973–74), vol. 2, pp 587–820; Nagata et al (2006).
36. Evliya Çelebi (1995), p 272.
37. Mantran (1962), pp 365–6; Raymond (1973–74), vol. 2, pp 437–40.
38. Evliya Çelebi (1995), pp 179, 207.
39. Ibid., p 207.
40. Evliya Çelebi (1314/1896–97 to 1938), vol. 10, p 375.
41. Evliya Çelebi (1995), p 243.
42. Yi (2004), pp 58–63.
43. Ibid., p 53.
44. Gerber (1988), pp 36–8.
45. Ibid., p 38.
46. Inalcik (1969), p 105; Yi (forthcoming a).
47. Özmucur and Pamuk (2002).
48. On the debates surrounding this project see Artan (2006), pp 439–41.
49. Pamuk (2000a), p 82; Özmucur and Pamuk (2002).
50. Pamuk (2000a), pp 89–95; Özmucur and Pamuk (2002).
51. Pamuk (2000a), p 95; Özmucur and Pamuk (2002), p 316.
52. Kütükoğlu (ed) (1983).
53. Ibid., pp 258–9.
54. Ibid., pp 129–30, 162, 164.
55. Ibid., p 157.
56. MD 52, no. 921, p 345.
57. Kütükoğlu (ed) (1983), pp 62, 115.
58. Ibid., pp 155–6, 145–6.
59. ŞD 3 (1064/1653–54), p 53.
60. Kütükoğlu (ed) (1983), p 73.
61. Hanna (1984), p 34; Maury, Raymond, Revault and Zakarya (1983), pp 348–65.
62. Evliya Çelebi (1314/1896–97 to 1938), vol. 10, p 372.
63. Kütükoğlu (ed) (1983), pp 54–5, 135.
64. Ibid., p 158.
65. Ibid., pp 66, 123.
66. Irwin (1986) is mainly concerned with the Mamluk period, but compare p 81.
67. Rogers (1982).
68. MD 60, no. 113, p 46, published by Altınay (reprint 1988a), p 133.
69. Kütükoğlu (ed) (1983), pp 177–8. On the basis of visual evidence, Franses (2007), p 86, also speaks of a congruence between Cairene and west Anatolian rugs.
70. Evliya Çelebi (1314/1896–97 to 1938), vol. 10, p 373.
71. Ibid., p 383.
72. Thévenot (1980), p 232.

73. MD 16, no. 407 (979/1569–70), p 211; Evliya Çelebi (1314/1896–97 to 1938), vol. 10, p 372.
74. De Bruyn (1698), pp 150–1.
75. Ágoston (2005), pp 42–8.
76. On an English organ-maker see MacLean (2004), pp 3–48.
77. Evliya Çelebi (1995), pp 271, 275.
78. Mraz (1980), p 44; while his information concerns the later 1500s, clockwork must have been just as fragile in the early seventeenth century.
79. Kurz (1975), p 49.
80. *Ibid.*, pp 54–60.
81. Evliya Çelebi (1995), p 275.
82. Nayır (1975), pp 161–2, 231–4.
83. Behrens-Abouseif (1994), pp 145–77.
84. Tuchscherer (1990); (1999a); (1999b).
85. Hanna (1998), pp 125–33.
86. Braudel (1966), vol. 1, pp 476–7.
87. Wilkins (2005).
88. Yi (2004), p 65.

Chapter 5: Provincial Craftspeople and Merchant Networks

1. Barkan (1942).
2. Bayly (1983), p 63.
3. At-Tamgrouti (1929), p 49; Kütükoğlu (ed) (1983).
4. İslamoğlu-İnan (1994), pp 157–65; AKS 5 (1002/1593–94), pp 100, 310.
5. Dernschwam (reprint 1986), p 186.
6. Ergenç (1975).
7. MD 24, no. 614 (982/1574–75), p 231.
8. Evliya Çelebi (2005), p 193.
9. Abdel Nour (1982), p 291.
10. André Raymond, unpublished lecture on fez manufacture, 8 November 2006.
11. Kütükoğlu (ed) (1983).
12. Dernschwam (reprint 1986), pp 186–92.
13. Faroqhi (1982–83).
14. Israel (1989), pp 262–3.
15. This English summary of Dernschwam's account in early modern German has been taken from my unpublished article, Faroqhi (unpublished a), 'Ottoman textiles in European markets'; see Dernschwam (reprint 1986), pp 186–7.
16. Dernschwam (reprint 1986), pp 183–7.
17. Ergenç (1975), p 154.
18. *Ibid.*, pp 157–9.
19. BOA Düvel-i ecnebiye Defterleri 13/1, no. 436 (Safer 1021/April–May 1612), p 88.
20. BOA, Düvel-i ecnebiye Defterleri 13/1, no. 481 (Ramazan 1021/October–November 1612), p 97.
21. Archivio di Stato, Venice, Documenti Turchi, no. 960.

22. MD 24, no. 614 (982/1574–75), p 231.
23. Dziubiński (1999), pp 40–1.
24. Evliya Çelebi (2005), p 248; compare also Inalcik (1986b), p 55.
25. Inalcik (1986b), pp 56–9; Kütükoğlu (ed) (1983), pp 71, 72, 178.
26. Seirinidou (forthcoming).
27. Ionescu (2005), pp 41–6; Wild (2007).
28. Boralevi (2007).
29. TK no. 60, fol. 212b ff (977/1569).
30. Ionescu (2006), p 63.
31. Mack (2002), pp 73–93.
32. Inalcik (1960); Dalsar (1960), pp 131–45.
33. Sahillioğlu (1985).
34. *Ibid.*, pp 56–8.
35. Çizakça (1985).
36. Gerber (1988), pp 27, 88.
37. Çizakça (1985).
38. Fotopoulos and Delivorrias (1997), pp 308–11.
39. Gerber (1988), pp 11, 27.
40. Atasoy and Raby (1989), p 246.
41. Tóth (2003).
42. Atasoy and Raby (1989), p 18.
43. Evliya Çelebi (2005), p 17.
44. Atasoy and Raby (1989), p 21.
45. *Ibid.*, pp 24–5.
46. Kütükoğlu (ed) (1978).
47. Altınay (reprint 1988b), p 33.
48. Atasoy and Raby (1989), p 287.
49. Kovásc (2005).
50. Fekete (1960), pp 18, 25.
51. Atasoy and Raby (1989), p 26.
52. *Ibid.*, p 74.
53. Evliya Çelebi (1314/1896–97 to 1938), vol. 10, pp 372–3.
54. Evliya Çelebi (1999), pp 40–3.
55. Evliya Çelebi (2005), p 280.
56. Establet and Pascual (2005), pp 312–27.
57. *Ibid.*, pp 337.
58. Zilfi (2000), pp 299–305.
59. Hanna (1998).
60. MD 34, no. 595 (986/1578–79), p 286.
61. Inalcik (1969), pp 106, 139.
62. Inalcik (1969), pp 136–40; Genç, lecture at Bilgi University, Istanbul, May 2008.
63. Gerber (1980).
64. Braudel (1979), vol. 2, p 264; with respect to seventeenth-century Bursa see Gerber (1988), p 73.

65. Özmucur and Pamuk (2002); Pamuk (2000a), p 91.
66. Ghazaleh (1999), p 1; Kütükoğlu (1986).

Chapter 6: Changes in Istanbul Guilds

1. Mübahat S. Kütükoğlu, 'Narkh', in *Encyclopedia of Islam*, 2nd ed.
2. Güçer (1949–50); Alexandrescu-Dersca-Bulgaru (reprint 2006).
3. McGowan (1981), pp 75–7.
4. Cvetkova (1970).
5. Uluçay (1951–52).
6. Faroqhi (reprint 1987); Dursteler (2006), p 53.
7. Fabris (1990).
8. Bracewell (1992), pp 12–15; Stoianovich (1960), p 274.
9. Aynural (2001), pp 11–12; see also pp 5–18 for a detailed discussion of eighteenth-century grain trade regulations.
10. Jelavich (1983).
11. Beaufort (1821), p 83.
12. Güçer (1951–52).
13. Aynural (2005).
14. Aynural (2001), pp 126–8.
15. *Ibid.*, p 123.
16. Evliya Çelebi (2006), p 296.
17. Istanbul Bab mahkemesi (major judge's court), vol. 124, fols. 151b, 152a, 162a, 198a (1133/1720–21). While the originals are presently inaccessible, copies can be consulted at the İSAM library in Üsküdar, Istanbul.
18. Oral information from Minna Rozen, to whom I am most grateful.
19. Aynural (2001), pp 132–5.
20. Faroqhi (1998b).
21. Orhonlu (reprint 1984), p 34.
22. Sestini (1786), p 29.
23. Panzac (1985), pp 58–62, 275–6.
24. *Ibid.*, p 117.
25. *Ibid.*, pp 300–10.
26. *Ibid.*, p 292.
27. Kütükoğlu (2000), p 25.
28. Aktepe (1958b).
29. Kırlı (2001); Başaran (2006); Turna (2006).
30. Faroqhi (1998b).
31. Sariyannis (2006).
32. Kırlı (2001).
33. Başaran (2006).
34. Kırlı (2001), pp 126, 138.
35. *Ibid.*, p 136.
36. Non-Muslim immigrants to Galata working as porters, boatmen and general-store keepers needed to provide guarantors: MD 74, no. 359, p 128 (1004–05/1595–

97).
37. Salzmann (1993); Khoury (1997); Salzmann (2004), p 101.
38. Collective work (1992), pp 24–32.
39. See Introduction; for a ten-volume selection of texts from these registers see Kal'a et al (eds) (1997–98).
40. Genç (1995).
41. Inalcik (1969).
42. Kal'a et al (eds) (1997–98), vol. VIII, 69–70 (1178/1764–65).
43. Kal'a et al (eds) (1997–98), vol. VIII, 63–4 (1178/1764–65).
44. Uluçay (1951–52); Faroqhi (2002a).
45. Akarlı (2004).
46. I owe this reflection to Giorgio Riello.
47. Yi (2004), pp 113–24; Gerber (1988), pp 31–8; Yıldırım (2008).
48. Akarlı (1985–86).
49. Genç (1994).
50. Kreiser (1986).
51. Genç (1995).
52. İslamoğlu (2004); Turna (2006).
53. Darling (1996), pp 119–60.
54. Genç (1975).
55. Genç (1994), p 62; see also Faroqhi (2007).
56. MAD 9908 (Cemaziyelâhir 1133/March–April 1721), p 306.
57. In some cases, however, the office of *yiğitbaşı* might pass from father to son: MAD 9996 (Rebiülevvel 1180/August–September 1766), p 56.
58. Oral discussion with Mehmet Genç; many thanks for his comments.
59. MAD 9908 (Rebiülâhır 1133/January–February 1721), pp 155–6. Many examples can be found in the unpublished MA thesis of Markus Koller (1998). I thank the author for making his work available.
60. MAD 8590 (Cemaziyelevvel 1140/December 1727–January 1728), pp 178–9.
61. On similar developments in Aleppo see Wilkins (2005).
62. Fotopoulos and Delivorrias (1997), pp 307–15.
63. Evliya Çelebi (2006), pp 322–3; for a clever summary of the documented roles of *ahi babas* in various cities of the empire see Wilkins (2005).
64. Şahin (1984–85); Taeschner (1979), pp 550–6.
65. BOA, Cevdet Evkaf, 5132.
66. BOA, Cevdet Evkaf, 12143 and others.
67. Yıldırım (2002).
68. Rozen (2000).
69. Faroqhi (forthcoming b).
70. Fotopoulos and Delivorrias (1997), p 431; Delivorrias (2000), pp 162–6.
71. Thévenot (1980), pp 6–9.
72. Genç (2001), pp 165–6.
73. Evliya Çelebi (2006), p 354.

Chapter 7: Cairo

1. Raymond (1973–74), vol. 1, p 84.
2. *Ibid.*, vol. 2, p 706.
3. *Ibid.*, vol. 1, p 86.
4. *Ibid.*, vol. 1, pp 98–9.
5. Genç (1995).
6. Raymond (1998).
7. Marsot (1984), p 177; Fahmy (1997), pp 294–5.
8. Raymond (1973–74), vol. 2, p 508.
9. *Ibid.*, vol. 2, pp 512–13.
10. *Ibid.*, vol. 2, p 511.
11. Ghazaleh (1999), pp 76–81.
12. Raymond (1973–74), vol. 2, p 556, contradicted by Hanna (1991), p 17.
13. Ghazaleh (1999), pp 79–86.
14. *Ibid.*, p 105.
15. Pamuk (2000a), p 55; Özmucur and Pamuk (2002).
16. I thank Giorgio Riello for this warning.
17. Raymond (1973–74), vol. 2, pp 659–726.
18. *Ibid.*, vol. 2, p 693. These 10 per cent were based on the value of the estate before dues and expenses had been deducted.
19. *Ibid.*, vol. 2, p 701.
20. *Ibid.*, vol. 2, p 691.
21. Tilly (1985).
22. Raymond (1973–74), vol. 2, pp 666–7.
23. *Ibid.*, vol. 2, pp 673–5.
24. *Ibid.*, vol. 2, pp 673–88, 785.
25. Fleischer (1986), p 262; Linda Darling is preparing a study on the circle of equity in the Ottoman world.
26. Raymond (1973–74), vol. 2, p 795.
27. Hathaway (1997), pp 169–73.
28. Raymond (1998), pp 12–25; Raymond (reprint 2002c), p 231.
29. Raymond (1973–74), vol. 2, pp 802–3.
30. *Ibid.*, vol. 1, pp 209–25; his negative views are today often considered too pessimistic: see Ghazaleh (1999), p 12. Michel (2005) is a monograph on textile crafts in the town of Asyut in southern Egypt.
31. Behrens-Abouseif (1992).
32. For an example see Raymond (1995), pp 40–1; Bates (1991).
33. See Abou-Kahtwa (2006), p 206, for an example from the 1500s to 1600s. Most of the Ottoman-period pieces shown in this volume are from the central lands and not from Egypt itself.
34. Maury, Raymond, Revault, Zakarya (1983), pp 354–9.
35. Abou-Khatwa (2006), p 205.
36. Guirguis (2004). I am much obliged to Professor Siegfried Richter for providing me with a copy of this article. On the art historical aspects of Ibrāhīm's activity,

there is now Tribe (2004); heartfelt thanks to Febe Aramanios for making this article available to me.
37. Tucker (1985), pp 81–93.
38. Ibid., p 85.
39. Ibid., p 98.
40. Ibid., pp 91–2.
41. Toledano (1990), p 237.
42. On the decisive Battle of Konya see Fahmy (1997), pp 160–6.
43. Fahmy (1997), p 186.
44. Owen (1981), pp 70–1.
45. Fahmy (1997), p 294.
46. Owen (1981), p 75.
47. Ibid., p 72.
48. Fahmy (1997), p 187.
49. Marsot (1984), pp 177–95.
50. Owen (1981), pp 69–75.
51. Toledano (1990), p 226.
52. Owen (1981), p 76; Toledano (1990), pp 226–7.
53. Baer (1970a and b). According to Ghazaleh (1999), p 22, this opinion is also current among Egyptian scholars writing in Arabic.
54. Toledano (1990), p 226.
55. Ibid., pp 200–5.
56. Ibid., pp 227–8.
57. Ghazaleh (1999), pp 22–6.
58. Ibid., pp 30–1.
59. Ibid., pp 58–60.
60. For one example among many see Kal'a et al (eds) (1997–98), vol. VIII, p 239.
61. Ghazaleh (1999), p 97.

Chapter 8: Political Roles of Craftsmen

1. Barkan (1966).
2. Fleischer (1986), pp 5–7.
3. For a published selection see Kal'a et al (eds) (1997–98).
4. Ursinus (ed) (2005), p 29. The text translated and commented on here is a great exception: it concerns complaints that reached the substitute governor of Rumeli in 1781–83. Unfortunately there were few artisans among the petitioners.
5. See Kal'a et al (eds) (1997–98), vol. VII; Toledano (1990), p 229.
6. Hathaway (2006).
7. MD 23, p 58, no. 122 (981/1573–74); Ergenç (1995), p 221, note 144; Tamdoğan (2007).
8. Atıl (1999); İrepoğlu (1999).
9. İstanbul Bab mahkemesi, no. 124, fol. 112b. The originals in the İstanbul Müftülüğü are not currently available to researchers, but the relevant microfilms can be consulted at the İSAM library at Bağlarbaşı, Üsküdar.
10. Uzunçarşılı (1981–86), pp 23–76.

11. İstanbul Bab mahkemesi, no. 124, fol. 204a (26 Şevval 1132/August–September 1720).
12. Nutku (1972). These registers probably contained information on the deliveries expected from most Edirne and Istanbul guilds.
13. Terzioğlu (1995).
14. Kal'a et al (eds) (1997–98), vol. VIII, part 2, pp 124–5; the dispute was resolved in 1767.
15. Abdel Nour (1982), pp 239–53.
16. Evliya Çelebi (2006), vol. 1, p 132; vol. 3 (1999), pp 163–5; for a commented translation see Dankoff (1991), pp 77–83. No archival records of this affair have been unearthed to date.
17. On guildsmen's banners see Nutku (1997).
18. Evliya Çelebi (1999), vol. 3, p 164.
19. Evliya Çelebi (2006), vol. 1, p 192; Evliya Çelebi (1999), vol. 3, p 164; on Karaçelebizade see Baer (2008), pp 48–50; on the 1688 rebellion see Eunjeong Yi's as yet unpublished article (Yi, forthcoming b), 'Artisans' Networks and Revolt in Late Seventeenth-Century Istanbul'. I am very grateful to the author for making her work available to me.
20. Abou-El-Haj (1984).
21. Aktepe (1958a), pp 73–102.
22. *Ibid.*, pp 178–80.
23. Raymond (1998), pp 131–41, 184–205; Raymond (reprint 2002a and b).
24. Rozen (2005).
25. Raymond (1998), pp 190–2.
26. Behar (2003) deals with an Istanbul quarter that seems to have been quite apolitical.
27. Raymond (1998), pp 178–82.
28. *Ibid.*, p 330.
29. Raymond (reprint 2002a).
30. Gölpınarlı (1953); Le Gall (2004); Clayer (1994); Küçük (2002).
31. Clayer (1994), pp 275–87.
32. Küçük (2002), pp 125–218.
33. Raymond (1998), pp 215–19.
34. Zilfi (1988), pp 111–12; Raymond (1998), pp 126–7.
35. Abdi (1943), p 42; compare also Aktepe (1958a), p 156; Şem'dânî-zâde (1976–78), vol. 1, pp 11–13, 44.
36. Vatin and Veinstein (2003), p 65.
37. Zilfi (1986); Baer (2008), pp 75–6.
38. Gölpınarlı (1953), pp 165–8; Baer (2008), pp 105–20.
39. Aktepe (1958a), pp 41–70.
40. Artan (1993).
41. Artan (2006), pp 465–78.
42. Caspar Momartz (undated), p 3. Momartz was a translator to the Habsburg embassy. Originally written in Italian, his text in a German translation was published as a pamphlet in Ratisbon. I am grateful to Albrecht Berger of the

Byzantine Studies Institute of Munich University, who kindly provided me with a copy.
43. Göçek (1996), pp 99–107.
44. Aktepe (1958a), pp 68–70.
45. Shaw (1971), pp 127–37.
46. Findley (1995).
47. Genç (1995).
48. Pamuk (2000a), p 68; Özmucur and Pamuk (2002).
49. Shaw (1971), pp 378–83.
50. Abou-El-Haj (1974); Aktepe (1958a), pp 98ff.
51. Pamuk (2000a), p 68; Özmucur and Pamuk (2002).
52. Aktepe (1958a), pp 18–40.
53. Shaw (1971), pp 76–7.
54. Zilfi (2004).
55. Artan (2006), pp 475–6.
56. Abdel Nour (1982).

Chapter 9: Provincial Craftsmen

1. Quataert (1993).
2. Todorov (reprint 1977), no. VII; Ivanova (2003).
3. Papa Synadinos (1996); Strauss (2002).
4. Gara (1999).
5. Stoianovich (1960), pp 256–8; Katsiardi-Hering (forthcoming).
6. Seirinidou (forthcoming).
7. Stoianovich (1960), p 256.
8. Palairet (1997), pp 41–57.
9. Palairet (1997), p 171; Todorov (reprint 1998), no. II, p 392.
10. Todorov (reprint 1998), no. I.
11. On Italy see Kemp (1997), pp 187–200, concerning the worldly possessions of the Medici; see also Mack (2002) and Welch (2005) on the culture of shopping in the 1400s and 1500s.
12. Murphy (2003).
13. van Deursen (1998), pp 119–30.
14. Spufford (1984).
15. Roche (1989).
16. North (2003).
17. Levy, Sneider, Gibney (n.d.).
18. Narazaki (1982), pp 7–21.
19. Göçek (1996), pp 97–107; Neumann (2004).
20. Quataert (2000), p 10.
21. Faroqhi (2004).
22. Hanioğlu (2008), pp 30–3.
23. ŞD 2 (1063/1652–53), p 204.
24. Todorov (1967–68).

25. Todorov (reprint 1977), no. X.
26. *Ibid.*
27. Sella (1968).
28. Çizakça (1985); Faroqhi (1987), pp 209–11.
29. Frangakis-Syrett (1992), p 221.
30. Israel (1989), pp 262–3.
31. Frangakis-Syrett (1992), pp 222–3; Quataert (1993), pp 92–3. In England, raw mohair was demanded from about 1820 onwards.
32. Katsiardi-Hering (forthcoming).
33. *Ibid.*
34. *Ibid.*
35. Petmezas (1990).
36. Lewis (1968), pp 101–3.
37. Kütükoğlu (ed) (1983).
38. Valensi (1969); Maitte (2004).
39. Faroqhi (forthcoming b).
40. Yi (2004), pp 61–5.
41. Valensi (1969), pp 381–5.
42. Esiner Özen (1980–81), pp 324, 300. According to this author, *alaca* is ornamented with stripes and made either of silk or cotton. But *alaca* is also used for cotton-silk mixtures; textile terminology often fluctuates.
43. Ianeva (2006), pp 81–3.
44. Hammer (1818), pp 69–70.
45. Bursa *kadı* register B160, fol. 45b. I have taken the *guruş* as equivalent to 120 *akçe*.
46. Esiner Özen (1980–81), pp 311, 336.
47. Bursa *kadı* register B160, fol. 69b.
48. Esiner Özen (1980–81), pp 316, 321.
49. Hammer (1818), pp 69–70.
50. Sestini (1789), pp 193–7; for an English translation see Lowry (2003), pp 56–61.
51. Gerber (1988), pp 36–8.
52. Ginio (2003), pp 168–9.
53. Faroqhi (1995a).
54. See Barkan and Ayverdi (1970), pp xxx–xxxii, for a general discussion of money-lending *vakıfs*. For Bursa see Çizakça (1995).
55. Hajdarević (1998). I thank Cemal Kafadar who has made this publication available to me.
56. Faroqhi (1980).
57. Chevallier (1982), pp 89–120.
58. Establet and Pasqual (2005), p 15.
59. *Ibid.*, pp 26–7.
60. *Ibid.*, pp 84–90.
61. *Ibid.*, pp 67–8.
62. *Ibid.*, pp 251–8.
63. Eldem (2006), p 309.

64. İnalcık (1979–80).
65. Inalcik (1970).
66. Eldem (2006), pp 321–5; Frangakis-Syrett (2006).
67. Duman (1998), pp 115–73.
68. Ibid., pp 124–5.
69. Ibid., pp 128–31.
70. Ibid., pp 137–44.
71. Fukasawa (1987), title page and pp 15–69.
72. Genç (1995). The Turkish original of this article was published in 1984.
73. Buckingham (1827), pp 51–129.
74. Doumani (1995), pp 118–30.
75. Ibid., p 128.
76. Pitarakis and Merantzas (2006), pp 85–92, 126–9.
77. On furriers compare Tezcan (2004).
78. Ballian (1991).
79. Duman (1998), pp 174–251.
80. Ibid., pp 178–80.
81. Renda (1989).
82. Arık (1976), p 65.
83. Renda (1989), pp 73–4.
84. The Cincinnati Art Museum possesses a Damascus room dated 1711–12, whose makers do give their names (see the museum website).
85. On Damascus, where this fashion only became widespread after 1850, see Weber (2002).
86. Renda (1989), p 77.
87. Weber (2002), pp 160–4.
88. Cohen (2001), p 116.
89. Ibid., p 150.
90. Ibid., p 117.
91. Ibid., p 109.
92. Ibid., pp 177, 144–6.
93. Biddle (1999), pp 41–3.
94. Aktepe (1971), pp 129–30.
95. Faroqhi (2002b).
96. Aktepe (1971), pp 130–2; Kuyulu (1992).
97. Genç (1994).
98. Faroqhi (2002a).
99. Wallerstein (1974), pp 349–50.
100. Quataert (1993), p 175.
101. For a late nineteenth to mid-twentieth example see Chevallier (1982), pp 89–120.
102. Owen (1981), p 94.
103. Stoianovich (1960), pp 277–9; Katsiardi-Hering (forthcoming).
104. Palairet (1997), pp 361–70.
105. Todorov (reprint 1998), no. I, p 157.
106. Genç (1995).

107. Chalcraft (2005).

Chapter 10: 1850 to 1914

1. Owen (1981), p 10; Quataert (1993); Chalcraft (2004), pp 30–5 and elsewhere – against Baer (1969), pp 153–4. Baer postulated that Egyptian guilds disappeared because they lost their functions as Europeans more and more invaded the Egyptian economy, and the British colonial state also lost interest in craft organizations. This latter observation is important in Chalcraft's argumentation as well.
2. Quataert (1993), pp 12–13.
3. Ibid., pp 16–17.
4. Todorov (reprint 1998), no. II, p 388.
5. Chalcraft (2004), p 111.
6. White (1994), p 130 and elsewhere.
7. Quataert (2006), p 122; for an Egyptian testimony compare Chalcraft (2004), pp 53–4.
8. Chalcraft (2004), p 10.
9. According to Owen (1981), p 138, cotton prices increased nearly fourfold between 1861 and 1865.
10. Quataert (1993), p 74.
11. Fawaz (1994), pp 140–1.
12. Chalcraft (2004), pp 172–5.
13. Owen (1981), pp 122–9.
14. Chalcraft (2004), p 31.
15. See Chalcraft (2004), pp 119–20, for the translation of a relevant newspaper quote.
16. Chalcraft (2004), p 151.
17. Jelavich (1983), pp 171–93.
18. Quataert (2006), pp 130–47.
19. Fawaz (1994), pp 22ff.
20. Kabadayı (2005).
21. Gülsoy (2000), p 169.
22. Ergut (2004), p 143.
23. On guns as status markers in mid-nineteenth-century Egypt see Toledano (1990), pp 163–6.
24. Tamdoğan-Abel (1998); Behar (2003), pp 122–3.
25. Fawaz (1994), p 35.
26. Kabadayı (2005).
27. Ergut (2004), pp 145–8.
28. Mintzuri (1993), pp 14–16.
29. Özbek (2003).
30. See Genç (1994) on Ottoman 'provisionism'.
31. Quataert (1993), pp 71–9.
32. Ibid., p 78.
33. Quataert (1983a), pp 39–69; Quataert (2006).

34. Beldiceanu (1964).
35. Quataert (1983a), p 45.
36. Quataert (2006), pp 95–103; Faroqhi (1984), pp 172–6.
37. Quataert (2006), pp 200–1.
38. Quataert (1983a), pp 62–3.
39. Todorov (reprint 1998), nos. I and II; Küçükerman (1987) and (1988).
40. Todorov (reprint 1998), nos. I and II, pp 391–2.
41. Barkan (1972–79), vol. 1, pp 363–4.
42. Quataert (1983a), pp 494–9.
43. Todorov (reprint 1998), no. I, p 148; Todorov (reprint 1998), no. II, pp 389–90; Ersoy-Hacısalihoğlu (2008).
44. Todorov (reprint 1998), no. I, pp 148–9.
45. Kanitz (1875–79), vol. 3, pp 22–3.
46. Güler (1999).
47. Müller-Wiener (1986–87), p 273.
48. Küçükerman (1988), p 167. Mustafa Erdem Kabadayı has completed a doctoral thesis on this topic, and I thank him for sharing his information with me.
49. Küçükerman (1987), pp 49ff. I have not seen the unpublished dissertation of Abdükadir Buluş on this factory, but a summary is available in the also unpublished dissertation of Yavuz Köse (2007). I am grateful to Dr Köse for showing me his work.
50. Mazower (2004), p 388.
51. Küçükerman (1987), figs. 37–45, pp 88–93; see particularly fig. 37.
52. Mazower (2004), pp 286–90.
53. Dumont (1980).
54. The translation is by Mazower (2004), p 290.
55. Quataert (1983a), p 113; Chalcraft (2004), pp 145–90.
56. Chalcraft (2004), pp 166–87.
57. Şeni (1994).
58. Rozen (2005).
59. See Rozen (2005), pp 213–15, for a list of punishments.
60. Quataert (1983a), pp 95–120.
61. Rozen (2000).
62. On the Istanbul municipality see Ortaylı (1985), pp 111–205; Çelik (1986), pp 45–8; Neumann (2006).
63. Quataert (1983a), p 101.
64. Quataert (1983a), p 100; Chalcraft (2004), pp 98–9.
65. On the gardeners see Nesin (1977), pp 53–5.
66. Türkoğlu (ed) (2005); Karasu (ed) (2003). Türkoğlu's introduction is of great interest.
67. Türkoğlu (ed) (2005), p 103.
68. Karasu (ed) (2003) has provided summaries of all the entries.
69. Natanyan (2008), p 300.
70. Chalcraft (2005).
71. Chalcraft (2004), pp 194–5.

72. *Ibid.*, p 154.
73. *Ibid.*, p 10.
74. Todorov (reprint 1998), no. II, p 390.
75. Vatter (1995); (2006).
76. Ergut (2004), p 170.
77. Baer (1969), p 158.
78. Chalcraft (2004), p 195.
79. Zürcher (1993), pp 147–58.
80. Chalcraft (2004), p 154.
81. I thank Cem Emrence for discussing these problems with me.

Conclusion

1. On the continued relevance of guilds in the City of London during the 1600s see Ward (1997) and Berlin (1997).
2. Lis, Lucassen and Soly (eds) (1994a).
3. Lis and Soly (eds) (1994a and b).
4. Epstein et al (eds) (1998).
5. Cowan (1998), pp 36–50.
6. Bos (2006).
7. Farr (1988), p 145 and elsewhere.
8. *Ibid.*, p 44.
9. *Ibid.*, pp 44–59.
10. Inalcik (1969), p 117.
11. Masson (1911), p 489, links the decline of Carcassonne woollens to a reduction of official supervision.
12. Poni (1991).
13. Garden (1975), pp 312–14.
14. *Ibid.*, pp 341–54.
15. Gerber (1988), p 55.
16. Rozen (2005); Evliya Çelebi (2006), p 322.
17. Vatter (1995 and 2006); Chalcraft (2004 and 2005); Baer (1969), p 158.
18. Schama (1987), pp 525–35.
19. Deceulaer and Panhuyzen (2006).
20. Kaplan (1996), pp 345–52.
21. Darnton (1985), pp 94–9.
22. Kırlı (2001).
23. Faroqhi (2002e); Gerber (1980), p 237.
24. Poni (1982).
25. Cerutti (1990), p 15.
26. Reddy (1984), pp 4–15.
27. Thompson (1971).
28. Cerutti (1990), pp 14–16.
29. Cerutti (1991).
30. Kırlı (2001); Başaran (2006); Turna (2006).

31. Marcus (1989); Tamdoğan-Abel (1998); Wilkins (2005).
32. Cerruti (1991), p 106.
33. Cowan (1998), pp 22–3, 37–42.
34. Honacker (1994), pp 210–11.
35. Mousnier (1971), p 331.

Bibliography

At times it is difficult to decide whether a certain publication is an edition with an extensive commentary and/or introduction, or else a secondary source. When in doubt, I have opted for the second alternative.

Reference works

Akgündüz, Ahmet et al (eds) (1988–89). *Şeriye Sicilleri*, 2 vols. (Istanbul: Türk Dünyası Araştırmaları Vakfı)
Collective work (1992). *Başbakanlık Osmanlı Arşivi Rehberi* (Ankara: Başbakanlık, Devlet Arşivleri Genel Müdürlüğü)
Collective work (2000). *Başbakanlık Osmanlı Arşivi Rehberi*, 2nd ed (Istanbul: T.C. Başbakanlık Arşivleri Genel Müdürlüğü)
The Encyclopedia of Islam (1960–2004), ed H.A.R. Gibb et al, 2nd ed (Leiden: E.J. Brill) (*EI*)
İslâm Ansiklopedisi, İslâm Âlemi Tarih, Coğrafya, Etnografya ve Biyografya Lugati (1st ed, completed 1988), ed Adnan Adıvar et al (Istanbul: Milli Eğitim Bakanlığı)
Türkiye Diyanet Vakfı İslam Ansiklopedisi (1988–) (Istanbul: Türkiye Diyanet Vakfı)
Yurt Ansiklopedisi, Türkiye İl İl: Dünü, Bugünü, Yarını (1981–84) (Istanbul: Anadolu Yayıncılık AŞ)

Primary sources

Abdi (1943). *1730 Patrona Halil İhtilâli hakkında bir Eser, Abdi Tarihi*, ed Faik Reşat Unat (Ankara: Türk Tarih Kurumu)
Ahmet Eflâkî (1973). *Âriflerin Menkıbeleri (Manakib al-Ârifin)*, trans Tahsin Yazıcı, 2 vols. (Istanbul: Hürriyet Yayınları)
Aigen, Wolffgang (1980). *Sieben Jahre in Aleppo (1656–1663), Ein Abschnitt aus den 'Reiß-Beschreibungen' des Wolffgang Aigen*, ed Andreas Tietze (Vienna: Verlag der wissenschaftlichen Gesellschaften Österreichs)
Akgündüz, Ahmet (ed) (1988–89). *Şer'iye Sicilleri, Mahiyeti, Toplu Kataloğu ve Seçme Hükümler*, 2 vols. (Istanbul: Türk Dünyası Araştırmaları Vakfı)
Altınay, Ahmed Refik (ed) (reprint 1988a). *Onuncu Asr-ı Hicrîde İstanbul Hayatı (1495–1591)* (Istanbul: Enderun Kitabevi)
Altınay, Ahmed Refik (ed) (reprint 1988b). *Onbirinci Asr-ı Hicrîde İstanbul Hayatı (1592–1688)* (Istanbul: Enderun Kitabevi)
Andreasyan, Hrand (trans) (1976). 'Celâlilerden Kaçan Anadolu Halkının Geri Gönderilmesi', in *İsmail Hakkı Uzunçarşılı'ya Armağan* (Ankara: Türk Tarih Kurumu), pp 45–54
Anonymous (ed) (1938). *Fatih Mehmet II Vakfiyeleri* (Ankara: Vakıflar Umum Müdürlüğü)

[Ayvansarayî, Hafız Hüseyin] (2000). *The Garden of the Mosques, Hafız Hüseyin al-Ayvansarayî's Guide to the Muslim Monuments of Ottoman Istanbul*, translated and annotated by Howard Crane (Leiden, Boston, Cologne: E.J. Brill)

Barkan, Ömer Lütfi (1942). 'Bazı Büyük Şehirlerde Eşya ve Yiyecek Fiyatlarının Tesbit ve Teftişi Hususlarını Tanzim Eden Kanunlar', *Tarih Vesikaları* I, 5, pp 326–40; II, 7, pp 15–40; II, 9, pp 168–77

Barkan, Ömer Lütfi and Ekrem Ayverdi (1970). *İstanbul Vakıfları Tahrîr Defteri, 953 (1546) tarîhli* (Istanbul: İstanbul Fetih Cemiyeti)

Beaufort, Francis (1821). *Karamanien oder Beschreibung der Südküste von Kleinasien*, trans F.A. Ukert (Weimar: Landes-Industrie-Comptoir)

Bruyn, Cornelis de (1698). *Reizen door de vermaardste delen van Kleinasia, de Eylanden, Scio, Rhodus, Cyprus ... en Palestina ...* (Delft: Henrik van Krooneveld)

Buckingham, James Silk (1827). *Travels to Mesopotamia, including a Journey to Aleppo* (London: Henry Colburn)

[Ca'fer Efendi] (1987). *Risāle-i mi'māriyye: An early-seventeenth-century Ottoman treatise on architecture*, trans Howard Crane (Leiden: E.J. Brill)

Crane, Howard, Esra Akın, Gülru Necipoğlu (eds) (2006). *Sinan's Autobiographies: Five Sixteenth-Century Texts* (Leiden, Boston: E.J. Brill)

[Dernschwam, Hans] (reprint 1986). *Hans Dernschwams Tagebuch einer Reise nach Konstantinopel und Kleinasien, nach der Urschrift im Fugger-Archiv*, ed Franz Babinger, postface by Roman Schnur (Berlin: Duncker & Humblot)

Düzdağ, M. Ertuğrul (ed) (1972). *Şeyhülislâm Ebussuûd Efendi Fetvaları Işığında 16. Asır Türk Hayatı* (Istanbul: Enderun)

Evliya Çelebi (1314/1896–97 to 1938). *Seyahatnamesi*, 10 vols. (Istanbul, Ankara: İkdam and others)

Evliya Çelebi b Derviş Mehemmed Zıllı (1995). *Evliya Çelebi Seyahatnâmesi, Topkapı Sarayı Bağdat 304 Yazmasının Transkripsyonu –Dizini*, vol. 1, ed Orhan Şaik Gökyay and Yücel Dağlı (Istanbul: Yapı Kredi Yayınları)

Evliya Çelebi b Derviş Mehemmed Zilli (1999). *Evliya Çelebi Seyahatnâmesi, Topkapı Sarayı Bağdat 305 Yazmasının Transkripsyonu –Dizini*, vol. 3, ed Yücel Dağlı and Seyit Ali Kahraman (Istanbul: Yapı Kredi Yayınları)

Evliya Çelebi b Derviş Mehemmed Zıllı (2005). *Evliya Çelebi Seyahatnâmesi, Topkapı Sarayı Kütüphanesi Bağdat 306, Süleymaniye Kütüphanesi Pertev Paşa 462, Süleymaniye Kütüphanesi Hacı Beşir Ağa 452 Numaralı Yazmaların Mukayeseli Transkripsyonu –Dizini*, vol. 9, ed Yücel Dağlı, Seyit Ali Kahraman and Robert Dankoff (Istanbul: Yapı Kredi Yayınları)

Evliya Çelebi b Derviş Mehemmed Zıllı (2006). *Evliya Çelebi Seyahatnâmesi, Topkapı Sarayı Bağdat 304 Yazmasının Transkripsyonu –Dizini*, vol. 1, ed Robert Dankoff, Seyit Ali Kahraman and Yücel Dağlı (Istanbul: Yapı Kredi Yayınları)

Hajdarević, Rašid (1998). *Defteri Sarajevskog Saračkog esnafa 1726–1823* (Sarajevo: Istorijski Arhiv Sarajevo)

Hammer, Joseph von (1818). *Umblick auf einer Reise von Constantinopel nach Brussa ...* (Pest: Adolf Hartleben)

Ibn Battuta (1854). *Voyages d'Ibn Batoutah, texte arabe, accompagné d'une traduction*, vol. 2, ed and trans C. Defrémery and B.R. Sanguinetti (Paris: Imprimerie Impériale)

Kal'a, Ahmet et al (eds) (1997–98). *İstanbul Külliyatı: İstanbul Ahkâm Defterleri*, 10 vols. (Istanbul: İstanbul Araştırmaları Merkezi)

Kanitz, F. (1875–79). *Donau-Bulgarien und der Balkan, Historisch-geographisch-ethnographische Reisestudien aus den Jahren 1860–1876*, 3 vols. (Leipzig: Hermann Fries)

Kara Çelebi-zâde Abdülaziz Efendi (2003). *Ravzatü'l-Ebrâr Zeyli (Tahlîl ve Metin)* …, ed and commentary Nevzat Kaya (Ankara: Türk Tarih Kurumu)

Karasu, Tufan (ed) (2003). *Alanya Belediyesi Encümen Kararları Defteri* (Alanya: DAKTAV)

Kütükoğlu, Mübahat (ed) (1978). '1009 (1600) Tarihli Narh Defterine göre İstanbul'da çeşidli Eşya ve Hizmet Fiatları', *Tarih Enstitüsü Dergisi* 9, pp 1–86

Kütükoğlu, Mübahat (ed) (1983). *Osmanlılarda Narh Müessesesi ve 1640 Tarihli Narh Defteri* (Istanbul: Enderun Kitabevi)

Mintzuri, Hagop (1993). *İstanbul Anıları 1897–1940* (Istanbul: Tarih Vakfı)

Momartz, Caspar (undated). *Umständlicher Bericht Alles desjenigen, Was sich bey vorgewestem Tumult in Constantinopel wider das Ministerium und den Sultan selbsten Merckwürdiges zugetragen* (Regenspurg: Christian Gottlieb Seiffart)

Nagata, Yuzo, Toru Miura and Yasuhisa Shimizu (eds) (2006). *Tax Farm Register of Damascus Province in the Seventeenth Century: Archival and Historical Studies* (Tokyo: The Toyo Bunko)

Natanyan, Boğos (2008). *Sivas 1877*, trans Sirvart Malhasyan, ed Arsen Yarman (Istanbul: Birzamanlar Yayıncılık)

Nesin, Aziz (1977). *Istanbul Boy, Böyle Gelmiş Böyle Gitmez (That is how it was but not how it is going to be)*, trans Joseph Jacobson (Austin: Center for Middle Eastern Studies)

Prohazka-Eisl, Gisela (ed) (1995). *Das Sûrnâme-i Hümayun, Die Wiener Handschrift in Transkription, mit Kommentar und Indices versehen* (Istanbul: The Isis Press)

Saatçi, Suphi (ed) (1990). 'Tezkiret-ül Bünyan'ın Topkapı Sarayı Revan Kitaplığındaki Yazma Nüshası', *Topkapı Sarayı Müzesi Yıllık* 4, pp 55–102

Sestini, Domenico (1786). *Domenico Sestinis Beschreibung des Kanals von Konstantinopel des dasigen Wein-, Acker- und Garten-Baus und der Jagd der Türken*, trans C.J. Jagemann, in *Neue Sammlung von Reisebeschreibungen*, vol. 8 (Hamburg: Carl Ernst Bohn)

Sestini, Domenico (1789). *Voyage dans la Grèce asiatique, à la péninsule de Cyzique, à Brousse et à Nicée, Avec les détails de l'Historie Naturelle de ces contrées* (London, Paris: Leroy)

Papa Synadinos of Serres (1996). *Conseils et mémoires de Synadinos prêtre de Serrès en Macédoine (XVIIe siècle)*, ed and trans Paolo Odorico, with S. Asdrachas, T. Karanastassis, K. Kostis and S. Petmézas (Paris: Association 'Pierre Belon')

Şem'dânî-zâde Fındıklılı Süleyman Efendi (1976–78). *Şem'dânî-zâde Fındıklılı Süleyman Efendi Târihi Mür'i't-tevârih*, ed Münir Aktepe, 2 vols. (Istanbul: İstanbul Üniversitesi Edebiyat Fakültesi)

At-Tamgrouti, Abou-l-Hasan Ali ben Mohammed [Al-Tamghrūtī] (1929). *En-nafhat el-miskiya fi-s-sifarat et-Tourkiya, Relation d'une ambassade marocaine en Turquie 1589–1591*, trans and notes by Henry de Castries (Paris: Paul Geuthner)

Thévenot, Jean (abridged edition, 1980). *Voyage du Levant*, ed and introduced by Stéphane Yérasimos (Paris: Maspéro)

Türkoğlu, Ömer (ed) (2005). *Çankırı 1891–1892, Kengırı Belediye Kalemine Mahsus Yevmiye Defteri 1307* (Çankırı: Çankırı Belediyesi)

Ursinus, Michael (ed) (2005). *Grievance Administration (Şikayet) in an Ottoman Province: The Kaymakam of Rumelia's 'Record Book of Complaints' of 1781–1783* (London, New York: Routledge Curzon)

Secondary sources

Publications directly relevant to Ottoman crafts and guilds have been marked with an asterisk.

*Abdel Nour, Antoine (1982). *Introduction à l'histoire urbaine de la Syrie ottomane (XVe–XVIIIe siècle)* (Beirut: Université Libanaise)

Abou-El-Haj, Rifa'at A. (1974). 'Ottoman Attitudes toward Peace-making: The Karlowitz Case', *Der Islam*, pp 131–7

Abou-El-Haj, Rifa'at A. (1984). *The 1703 Rebellion and the Structure of Ottoman Politics* (Istanbul, Leiden: Nederlands Historisch-Archeologisch Instituut)

Abou-El-Haj, Rifa'at A. (1991). *Formation of the Ottoman State: The Ottoman Empire Sixteenth to Eighteenth Centuries* (Albany, NY: SUNY Press)

*Abou-Khatwa, Noha (2006). 'Ottoman Art (1517–19th Century)', in *The Treasures of Islamic Art in the Museums of Cairo*, ed Bernard O'Kane (Cairo, New York: The University of Cairo Press), pp 187–262

*Ágoston, Gábor (2005). *Guns for the Sultan: Military Power and the Weapons Industry in the Ottoman Empire* (Cambridge: Cambridge University Press)

*Akarlı, Engin (1985–86). 'Gedik: Implements, Mastership, Shop Usufruct and Monopoly among Istanbul Artisans, 1750–1850', *Wissenschaftskolleg-Jahrbuch*, pp 223–32

*Akarlı, Engin (2004). 'Gedik: A Bundle of Rights and Obligations for Istanbul Artisans and Traders, 1750–1840', in *Law, Anthropology and the Constitution of the Social: Making Persons and Things*, ed Alain Pottage and Martha Mundy (Cambridge: Cambridge University Press), pp 166–200

Akdağ, Mustafa (1963). *Celâlî İsyanları 1550–1603* (Ankara: A.Ü. Dil ve Tarih-Coğrafya Fakültesi)

*Aktepe, Münir (1958a). *Patrona İsyanı* (Istanbul: İstanbul Üniversitesi Edebiyat Fakültesi)

Aktepe, Münir (1958b). 'XVIII. Asrın İlk Yarısında İstanbul'un Nüfus Mes'elesine Dâir Bâzı Vesikalar', *Tarih Dergisi* IX, 13, pp 1–30

Aktepe, Münir (1971). 'İzmir Hanları ve Çarşıları hakkında Ön Bilgi', *Tarih Dergisi* 25, pp 105–54

Alexandrescu-Dersca-Bulgaru, Marie Mathilde (reprint 2006). 'Contribution à l'étude de l'approvisionnement en blé de Constantinople au XVIIIe siècle', in *Seldjoukides, Ottomans et l'espace roumain*, ed Cristina Feneşan (Istanbul: The Isis Press), pp 569–600

*Anastassiadou, Meropi (1992). 'Artisans juifs à Salonique au début des Tanzimat', *Revue du Monde musulman et de la Méditerranée* 66, pp 65–72

Anonymous (ed). *Prof. Dr. Sabri Ülgener'e Armagan*, in *İstanbul Üniversitesi İktisat Fakültesi Mecmuası* 43, 1–4 (1984–85)

Arık, Rüçhan (1976). *Batılılaşma Dönemi Anadolu Tasvir Sanatı* (Ankara: Türkiye İş Bankası)

Arıkan, Zeki (1991). 'Osmanlı İmparatorluğunda İhracı Yasak Mallar (Memnu Meta) in *Professor Dr. Bekir Kütükoğlu'na Armağan* (Istanbul: İstanbul Üniversitesi Edebiyat Fakültesi), pp 279–307

Artan, Tülay (1993). 'Noble Women who Changed the Face of the Bosphorus and …

the Palaces of the Sultanas', *Istanbul, Biannual, 1992 selections*, pp 87–97
*Artan, Tülay (2006). 'Arts and Architecture', in *The Cambridge History of Turkey*, ed Suraiya Faroqhi (Cambridge: Cambridge University Press), pp 408–80
*Atasoy, Nurhan (1997). *1582 Surname-i hümayun: An Imperial Celebration* (Istanbul: Koçbank)
*Atasoy, Nurhan and Julian Raby (1989). *Iznik: The Pottery of Ottoman Turkey* (Istanbul, London: Türkiye Ekonomi Bankası and Alexandria Press)
*Atasoy, Nurhan, Walter Denny, Louise W. Mackee, Hülya Tezcan (2001), *İpek. Osmanlı Dokuma Sanatı* (London, Istanbul: TEB İletişim & Yayıncılık and Azimuth Editions)
*Atıl, Esin (1987). *The Age of Sultan Süleyman the Magnificent* (Washington, New York: National Gallery of Art, Harry N. Abrams)
*Atıl, Esin (1999). *Levni and the Surnâme: The Story of an Eighteenth-Century Ottoman Festival* (Istanbul: Koçbank)
*Aynural, Salih (2001). *İstanbul Değirmenleri ve Fırınları: Zahire Ticareti* (Istanbul: Tarih Vakfı Yurt Yayınları)
*Aynural, Salih (2005). 'The Millers and Bakers of Istanbul', in *Crafts and Craftsmen of the Middle East: Fashioning the Individual in the Muslim Mediterranean*, ed Suraiya Faroqhi and Randi Deguilhem (London: I.B.Tauris), pp 153–94
*Bacqué-Grammont, Jean Louis (1999). 'La fonderie de canons d'Istanbul et le quartier de Tophane. Textes et images commentés', *Anatolia Moderna* VIII (Paris and Istanbul: IFEA, 1999), pp 1–219
*Baer, Gabriel (1969). 'The Decline and Disappearance of the Guilds', in *Studies in the Social History of Modern Egypt* (Chicago: University of Chicago Press, 1969), pp 149–60
*Baer, Gabriel (1970a). 'The Administrative, Economic and Social Functions of Turkish Guilds', *International Journal of Middle East Studies* 1, pp 28–50
*Baer, Gabriel (1970b). 'Guilds in Middle Eastern history', in *Studies in the Economic History of the Middle East, from the Rise of Islam to the Present Day*, ed Michael A. Cook (Oxford: Oxford University Press)
*Baer, Gabriel (1980). 'Ottoman Guilds: A Reassessment', in *Türkiye'nin Sosyal ve Ekonomik Tarihi (1071–1920), Social and Economic History of Turkey (1071–1920)*, ed Halil Inalcik and Osman Okyar (Ankara: Meteksan), pp 95–102
Baer, Marc David (2008). *Honored by the Glory of Islam: Conversion and Conquest in Ottoman Europe* (Oxford: Oxford University Press)
*Bakla, Erdinç (2007). *Tophane Lüleciliği. Osmanlı'nın Tasarımındaki Yaratıcılığı ve Yaşam Keyfi* (Istanbul: Antik A.Ş.)
*Ballian, Anna (1991). 'Christian Silverwork from Ottoman Trebizond', in *Cultural and Commercial Exchanges between the Orient and the Greek World, Athens, Greece, 25–28 October 1990*, ed Maria Christina Chatziioannou (Athens: Centre for Neohellenic Research/NHRF), pp 123–38
Barkan, Ömer Lütfi (1963). 'Şehirlerin Teşekkül ve İnkişafı Tarihi Bakımından: Osmanlı İmparatorluğunda İmaret Sitelerinin Kuruluş ve İşleyiş Tarzına ait Araştırmalar', *İstanbul Üniversitesi İktisat Fakültesi Mecmuası* 23, 1–2, pp 239–96
*Barkan, Ömer Lütfi (1966). 'Edirne Askeri Kassam'ına ait Tereke Defterleri (1545–1659)', *Belgeler* III, 5–6, pp 1–479
*Barkan, Ömer Lütfi (1972–79). *Süleymaniye Cami ve Imareti Inşaatı*, 2 vols. (Ankara:

Türk Tarih Kurumu)
*Başaran, Betül (2006). 'Remaking the Gate of Felicity: Policing, Social Control and Migration in Istanbul at the End of the Eighteenth Century 1789–1793', 2 vols., unpublished PhD dissertation, University of Chicago
Bates, Ülkü (1991). 'Façades in Ottoman Cairo', in *The Ottoman City and Its Parts. Urban Structure and Social Order*, ed Irene A. Bierman, Rifa'at A. Abou-el-Haj, Donald Preziosi (New Rochelle: Aristide Caratzas), pp 129–72
*Behar, Cem (2003). *A Neighborhood in Ottoman Istanbul: Fruit Vendors and Civil Servants in the Kasap İlyas Mahalle* (Albany, NY: SUNY Press)
Behrens-Abouseif, Doris (1992). 'The ʿAbd al-Rahmān Katkhudā Style in 18th Century Cairo', *Annales Islamologiques* 26, pp 117–26
Behrens-Abouseif, Doris (1994). *Egypt's Adjustment to Ottoman Rule: Institutions, waqf and Architecture in Cairo* (Leiden: E.J. Brill)
*Beldiceanu, Nicoară (1964). *Les actes des premiers sultans conservés dans les manuscrits turcs de la Bibliothèque Nationale à Paris*, vol. II, *Règlements miniers 1390–1512* (Paris, The Hague: Mouton)
*Berchtold, Thomas (2001). 'Organisation und sozialökonomische Strategien von Handwerkern im späten Osmanischen Reich', unpublished MA thesis, Freie Universität Berlin
Biddle, Martin (1999). *The Tomb of Christ* (Phoenix Mill, Gloucestershire: Sutton Publishing)
Billington, James H. (2001). 'The Projection and Celebration of Power', in *Gifts to the Tsars, 1500–1700: Treasures from the Kremlin*, ed Barry Shifman and Guy Walton (New York: Harry N. Abrams Inc.), pp 11–20
Boralevi, Alberto (2007). 'Western Anatolian Village Rugs and Ottoman Silk Textiles', in *In Praise of God: Anatolian Rugs in Transylvanian Churches 1500–1750*, ed Nazan Ölçer et al (Istanbul: Sakıp Sabancı Museum), pp 103–11
*Bostan, İdris (1992). *Osmanlı Bahriye Teşkilâtı: XVII. Yüzyılda Tersane-i amire* (Ankara: Türk Tarih Kurumu)
Bracewell, Catherine Wendy (1992). *The Uskoks of Senj: Piracy, Banditry and Holy War in the Sixteenth-Century Adriatic* (Ithaca, London: Cornell University Press)
*Braude, Benjamin (1979). 'International Competition and Domestic Cloth in the Ottoman Empire: A Study in Undevelopment', *Review* II, 3, pp 437–54
Braudel, Fernand (1966). *La Méditerranée et le monde méditerranéen à l'époque de Philippe II*, 2nd ed, 2 vols. (Paris: Armand Colin)
Braudel, Fernand (1979). *Civilisation matérielle, économie et capitalisme*, 3 vols. (Paris: Armand Colin)
*Çağman, Filiz (1984). 'Serzergerân Mehmet Usta ve Eserleri', in *Kemal Çığ'a Armağan* (Istanbul: Topkapı Sarayı Müzesi Müdürlüğü)
Cahen, Claude (1988). *La Turquie pré-ottomane* (Istanbul: Institut Français d'Études Anatoliennes)
Carboni, Stefano (ed) (2007). *Venice and the Islamic World, 828–1797* (New York: Metropolitan Museum of Art)
Çelik, Zeynep (1986). *The Remaking of Istanbul: Portrait of an Ottoman City in the Nineteenth Century* (Seattle, London: University of Washington Press)
Cezar, Mustafa (1965). *Osmanlı Tarihinde Levendler* (Istanbul: Güzel Sanatlar Akademisi)

*Chalcraft, John (2004). *The Striking Cabbies of Cairo and Other Stories: Crafts and Guilds in Egypt 1863–1914* (Albany, NY: SUNY Press)

*Chalcraft, John (2005). 'The End of Guilds in Egypt: Restructuring Textiles in the Long Nineteenth Century', in *Crafts and Craftsmen of the Middle East: Fashioning the Individual in the Muslim Mediterranean*, ed Suraiya Faroqhi and Randi Deguilhem (London: I.B.Tauris), pp 338–67

*Chevallier, Dominique (1982). *Villes et travail en Syrie du XIXe au XXe siècle* (Paris: Maisonneuve & Larose)

*Çizakça, Murat (1981). 'Ottomans and the Mediterranean: An Analysis of the Ottoman Shipbuilding Industry as Reflected in the Arsenal Registers of Istanbul 1529–1650', in *Le gente del mare Mediterraneo*, ed Rosalba Ragosta, preface by Luigi de Rosa, 2 vols. (Naples: Pironti), vol. 2, pp 773–87

Çizakça, Murat (1985). 'Incorporation of the Middle East into the European World Economy', *Review* VIII, 3, pp 353–78

*Çizakça, Murat (reprint 1987). 'Price History and the Bursa Silk Industry: A Study in Ottoman Industrial Decline, 1550–1650', in *The Ottoman Empire and the World Economy*, ed Huri Islamoğlu-Inan (Cambridge, Paris: Cambridge University Press and Maison des Sciences de l'Homme), pp 247–61

Çizakça, Murat (1995). 'Cash Waqfs of Bursa, 1555–1823', *Journal of the Economic and Social History of the Orient* 38, 2, pp 313–54

Çizakça, Murat (1996). *A Comparative Evolution of Business Partnerships: The Islamic World and Europe, with Specific Reference to the Ottoman Archives* (Leiden, New York: E.J. Brill)

Clayer, Nathalie (1994). *Mystiques, état et société, Les Halvetis dans l'aire balkanique de la fin du XVe siècle à nos jours* (Leiden: E.J. Brill)

Cohen, Amnon (1984) *Jewish Life under Islam: Jerusalem in the Sixteenth Century* (Cambridge, MA: Harvard University Press)

*Cohen, Amnon (1989). *Economic Life in Ottoman Jerusalem* (Cambridge: Cambridge University Press)

*Cohen, Amnon (1990). 'Gold and Silver Crafting in Ottoman Jerusalem: The Role Played by the Guild', *Tārīkh* 1, pp 55–67

*Cohen, Amnon (2001). *The Guilds of Ottoman Jerusalem* (Leiden: E.J. Brill)

Cvetkova, Bistra (1970). 'Les celep et leur rôle dans la vie économique des Balkans à l'époque ottomane (XVe–XVIIIe s.)', in *Studies in the Economic History of the Middle East*, ed Michael A. Cook (Oxford: Oxford University Press), pp 172–92

*Dalsar, Fahri (1960). *Türk Sanayi ve Ticaret Tarihinde Bursa'da İpekçilik* (Istanbul: İstanbul Üniversitesi İktisat Fakültesi)

Dankoff, Robert (1991). *The Intimate Life of an Ottoman Statesman: Melek Ahmed Pasha (1588–1662) as Portrayed in Evliya Çelebi's* Book of Travels, introduction by Rhoads Murphey (Albany, NY: SUNY Press)

Dankoff, Robert (2004). *An Ottoman Mentality: The World of Evliya Çelebi* (Leiden: E.J. Brill)

Darling, Linda (1996). *Revenue-Raising and Legitimacy: Tax Collection and Finance Administration in the Ottoman Empire 1560–1660* (Leiden: E.J. Brill)

*Deguilhem, Randi (2005). 'Shared Space or Contested Space: Religious Mixity, Infrastructural Hierarchy and the Builders' Guild in Mid-Nineteenth-Century Damascus', in *Crafts and Craftsmen of the Middle East: Fashioning the Individual in the Muslim*

Mediterranean, ed Suraiya Faroqhi and Randi Deguilhem (London: I.B.Tauris), pp 261–82
*Delivorrias, Angelos (2000). *A Guide to the Benaki Museum* (Athens: Benaki Museum)
*Doğanalp-Votzi, Heidemarie (1997). *Der Gerber, der Kulturbringer, Politik, Ökonomie, Zivilisation im osmanischen Vorderasien* (Frankfurt: Peter Lang)
*Doumani, Beshara (1995). *Rediscovering Palestine: Merchants and Peasants in Jabal Nablus, 1700–1900* (Berkeley, Los Angeles, London: University of California Press)
*Duman, Yüksel (1998). 'Notables, Textiles and Copper in Ottoman Tokat 1750–1840', unpublished PhD thesis, University of Binghamton/SUNY
Dumont, Paul (1980). 'Sources inédites pour l'histoire du movement ouvrier et des courants socialistes dans l'Empire ottoman au début du XXe siècle', in *Türkiye'nin Sosyal ve Ekonomik Tarihi (1071–1920): Social and Economic History of Turkey (1071–1920)*, ed Halil Inalcik and Osman Okyar (Ankara: Meteksan), pp 383–96
*Dumont, Paul and Rémy Hildebrand (eds) (2005). *L'horloger du Sérail, aux sources du fantasme oriental chez Jean-Jacques Rousseau* (Istanbul, Paris: IFEA and Maisonneuve & Larose)
Dunn, Ross E. (1986). *The Adventures of Ibn Battuta, A Muslim Traveler of the 14th Century* (Berkeley, Los Angeles: University of California Press)
Dursteler, Eric (2006). *Venetians in Constantinople: Nation, Identity and Coexistence in the Early Modern Mediterranean* (Baltimore, Maryland: Johns Hopkins University Press)
Dziubiński, Andrzej (1999). 'Polish–Turkish Trade in the 16th to 18th Centuries', in *War and Peace: Ottoman–Polish Relations in 15th–19th Centuries*, ed Selmin Kangal (Istanbul: Museum of Turkish and Islamic Arts), pp 38–45
El-Nahal, Galal (1979). *The Judicial Administration of Ottoman Egypt in the Seventeenth Century* (Minneapolis, Chicago: Bibliotheca Islamica)
Eldem, Edhem (2006). 'Capitulations and Western Trade', in *The Cambridge History of Turkey*, vol. 3, *The Later Ottoman Empire*, ed Suraiya Faroqhi (Cambridge: Cambridge University Press), pp 283–385
*Ellis, Charles Grant (1988). *Oriental Carpets in the Philadelphia Museum of Art* (Philadelphia: Philadelphia Museum of Art)
Emecen, Feridun M. (1997). *Unutulmuş bir Cemaat, Manisa Yahudileri* (Istanbul: Eren)
*Ergenç, Özer (1975). '1600–1615 Yılları Arasında Ankara İktisadi Tarihine Ait Araştırmalar', in *Türkiye İktisat Tarihi Semineri, Metinler-Tartışmalar ...*, ed Osman Okyar and Ünal Nalbantoğlu (Ankara: Hacettepe Üniversitesi), pp 145–68
Ergenç, Özer (1980a). 'XVII. Yüzyıl başlarında Ankara'nın Yerleşim Durumu üzerine bazı Bilgiler', *Osmanlı Araştırmaları* 1, pp 85–108
*Ergenç, Özer (1980b). 'Osmanlı Şehrinde Esnaf Örgütlerinin Fizik Yapıya Etkileri', in *Türkiye'nin Sosyal ve Ekonomik Tarihi (1071–1920): Social and Economic History of Turkey (1071–1920)*, ed Halil Inalcik and Osman Okyar (Ankara: Meteksan), pp 103–9
Ergenç, Özer (2006). *XVI. Yüzyılın Sonlarında Bursa* (Ankara: Türk Tarih Kurumu)
Ergene, Boğaç (2003). *Local Court, Provincial Society and Justice in the Ottoman Empire: Legal Practice and Dispute Resolution in Çankırı and Kastamonu (1652–1744)* (Leiden: E.J. Brill)

Ergin, Osman Nuri (1914–22). *Mecelle-i Umur-ı Belediye*, 5 vols. (Istanbul), especially vol. 1

Ergut, Ferdan (2004). *Modern Devlet ve Polis, Osmanlı'dan Cumhuriyet'e Toplumsal Denetimin Diyalektiği* (Istanbul: İletişim)

Ersanlı, Büşra (2002). 'The Ottoman Empire in the Historiography of the Kemalist Republic: A Theory of Fatal Decline', in *Ottoman Historiography: Turkey and Southeastern Europe*, ed Fikret Adanır and Suraiya Faroqhi (Leiden: E.J. Brill), pp 115–54

*Ersoy-Hacısalihoğlu, Neriman (2008). 'Textile Trade in Bulgaria in the Mid-19th Century and the Gümüşgerdan Family', in *Living in the Ottoman Ecumenical Community. Essays in Honour of Suraiya Faroqhi* (Leiden: E.J. Brill), pp 181–200

*Esiner Özen, Mine (1980–81). 'Türkçede Kumaş Adları', *Tarih Dergisi* 33, pp 291–340

Establet, Colette and Jean-Paul Pasqual (1994). *Familles et Fortunes à Damas: 450 foyers damascains en 1700* (Damascus, Syria: Institut Français d'Études Arabes de Damas)

Establet, Colette and Jean-Paul Pasqual (1998). *Ultime voyage pour la Mècque: les inventaires après décès de pèlerins morts à Damas vers 1700* (Damascus, Syria: Institut Français d'Études Arabes de Damas)

*Establet, Colette and Jean-Paul Pasqual (2005). *Des tissus et des hommes, Damas vers 1700* (Damascus, Syria: Institut Français d'Études Arabes de Damas)

Fabris, Antonio (1990). 'Un caso di pirateria veneziana: la cattura della galea del bey di Gerba (21 ottobre 1584)', *Quaderni di Studi Arabi* 8, pp 92–111

Fahmy, Khaled (1997). *All the Pasha's Men: Mehmed Ali, His Army and the Making of Modern Egypt* (Cambridge: Cambridge University Press)

*Faroqhi, Suraiya (1979). 'Alum Production and Alum Trade in the Ottoman Empire (about 1560–1830)', *Wiener Zeitschrift für die Kunde des Morgenlandes* 71, pp 153–75

*Faroqhi, Suraiya (1980). 'Textile Production in Rumeli and the Arab Provinces: Geographical Distribution and Internal Trade (1560–1650)', *Osmanlı Araştırmaları: The Journal of Ottoman Studies* I, pp 61–83

*Faroqhi, Suraiya (1982–83). 'Mohair Manufacture and Mohair Workshops in Seventeenth Century Ankara', *İstanbul Üniversitesi İktisat Fakültesi Mecmuası* 41, 1–4, pp 211–36. Turkish version: 'Onyedinci Yüzyıl Ankara'sında Sof İmalatı ve Sof Atölyeleri', loc. cit., pp 237–59

*Faroqhi, Suraiya (1984). *Towns and Townsmen of Ottoman Anatolia: Trade, Crafts and Food Production in an Urban Setting* (Cambridge: Cambridge University Press)

*Faroqhi, Suraiya (1986). 'Long-term Change and the Ottoman Construction Site: A Study of Builders' Wages and Iron Prices (with special reference to seventeenth-century Foça and Sayda)', in *Raiyyet Rüsumu: Journal of Turkish Studies*: 10, *Essays presented to Halil Inalcik* (Cambridge, MA), pp 111–26

Faroqhi, Suraiya (1987). 'The Venetian Presence in the Ottoman Empire', in *The Ottoman Empire and the World Economy*, ed Huri İslamoğlu İnan (Cambridge: Cambridge University Press, 1987), pp 311–44

*Faroqhi, Suraiya (1991). 'The Fieldglass and the Magnifying Lens: Ottoman Studies of Crafts and Craftsmen', *The Journal of European Economic History* 20, 1, pp 29–57

*Faroqhi, Suraiya (1994). 'Labor Recruitment and Control in the Ottoman Empire (sixteenth and seventeenth centuries)', in *Manufacturing in the Ottoman Empire and*

Turkey, 1500–1950, ed Donald Quataert (Albany, NY: SUNY Press), pp 13–58
*Faroqhi, Suraiya (1995a). 'Ottoman Guilds in the Late Eighteenth Century: The Bursa Case', in Suraiya Faroqhi, Making a Living in the Ottoman Lands 1480–1820 (Istanbul: The Isis Press), pp 93–112
*Faroqhi, Suraiya (1995b). 'Merchant Networks and Ottoman Craft Production (16–17th Centuries)', reprinted in Suraiya Faroqhi, Making a Living in the Ottoman Lands 1480–1820 (Istanbul: The Isis Press), pp 175–98
Faroqhi, Suraiya (1995c). 'The Business of Trade: Bursa Merchants of the 1480s', in Suraiya Faroqhi, Making a Living in the Ottoman Lands 1480–1820 (Istanbul: The Isis Press), pp 193–216
*Faroqhi, Suraiya (1996). '18. Yüzyılın Ortalarında Urfa'nın Merkezi', trans Nur Deriş Ottoman, in Tarihten Günümüze Anadolu'da Konut ve Yerleşme, ed Yıldız Sey (Istanbul: Tarih Vakfı), pp 278–83
*Faroqhi, Suraiya (1998a). 'Between Conflict and Accommodation: Guildsmen in Bursa and Istanbul during the 18th Century', in Guilds, Economy and Society: Proceedings of the Twelfth International Economic History Congress, B1, ed Stephen Epstein, Clara Eugenia Nuñez, et al (Sevilla: Fundacion Fomento de la Historia Economica), pp 143–52
*Faroqhi, Suraiya (1998b). 'Migration into Eighteenth-Century "Greater Istanbul" as Reflected in the Kadi Registers of Eyüp', Turcica 30, pp 163–83
*Faroqhi, Suraiya (2002a). 'Urban Space as Disputed Grounds: Territorial Aspects to Artisan Conflict in Sixteenth to Eighteenth-Century Istanbul', in Stories of Ottoman Men and Women: Establishing Status, Establishing Control (Istanbul: Eren), pp 219–34
*Faroqhi, Suraiya (2002b). 'Between Collective Workshops and Private Homes: Places of Work in Eighteenth-century Bursa', in Stories of Ottoman Men and Women: Establishing Status, Establishing Control (Istanbul: Eren), pp 235–44
Faroqhi, Suraiya (2002c). 'Quis custodiet custodes? Controlling Slave Identities and Slave Traders in Seventeenth- and Eighteenth-Century Istanbul', in Stories of Ottoman Men and Women: Establishing Status, Establishing Control (Istanbul: Eren), pp 245–63
*Faroqhi, Suraiya (2002d). 'Under State Control: Sixteenth- and Seventeenth-century Ottoman Craftsmen on their Way to Istanbul', in Stories of Ottoman Men and Women: Establishing Status, Establishing Control (Istanbul: Eren), pp 267–88
*Faroqhi, Suraiya (2002e). 'Women's work, poverty and the privileges of guildsmen', in Stories of Ottoman Men and Women: Establishing Status, Establishing Control (Istanbul: Eren), pp 167–78
*Faroqhi, Suraiya (2003). 'How to Live and Die Rich in Eighteenth-century Bursa: The Fortune of Hacı Ibrahim, Tanner', in Pauvreté et richesse dans le monde musulman et méditerranéen, ed Jean-Paul Pascual (Paris: Maisonneuve and Larose), pp 99–118
Faroqhi, Suraiya (2004). 'Female Costumes in late fifteenth century Bursa', in Ottoman Costumes: From Textile to Identity, ed Suraiya Faroqhi and Christoph Neumann (Istanbul: Eren, 2004), pp 81–91
*Faroqhi, Suraiya (2005a). 'Eighteenth Century Ottoman Craftsmen: Problématiques and Sources', in Crafts and Craftsmen of the Middle East: Fashioning the Individual in the Muslim Mediterranean, ed Suraiya Faroqhi and Randi Deguilhem (London: I.B.Tauris), pp 84–118

*Faroqhi, Suraiya (2005b). 'Ottoman Craftsmen Complaining to the Sultan' in *Legitimizing the Order: The Ottoman Rhetoric of State Power*, ed Hakan Karateke and Maurus Reinkowski (Leiden: E.J. Brill), pp 177–93

*Faroqhi, Suraiya (2007). 'Purchasing Guild- and Craft-based Offices in the Ottoman Central Lands', *Turcica* 39, pp 123–46

*Faroqhi, Suraiya (forthcoming a). 'Ottoman Textiles in Early Modern Europe', to be published in *Cultural Encounters: Europe, the Ottomans, and the Mediterranean World*, ed Claire Norton with A. Chong and Anna Contadini (Pittsburgh, PA: Periscope, 2009)

*Faroqhi, Suraiya (forthcoming b). 'Immigrant Tradesmen as Guild Members, or the adventures of Tunisian fez-sellers in eighteenth-century Istanbul', in *The Arab Lands in the Ottoman Era (1600–1900): In Honor of Caesar Farah*, ed Jane Hathaway (in preparation)

Fawaz, Leila Tarazi (1994). *An Occasion for War: Civil Conflict in Lebanon and Damascus in 1860* (Berkeley, Los Angeles: University of California Press)

Fekete, Lajos (1960). 'Das Heim eines türkischen Herrn in der Provinz im XVI. Jahrhundert', *Studia Historica Academiae Scientiarum Hungaricae* 29 (Budapest: Akadémiai Kiadó), pp 3–30

*Fekete, Lajos (1976). *Buda and Pest under Turkish Rule* (Budapest: Loránd Eötvös University)

Findley, Carter (1980). *Bureaucratic Reform in the Ottoman Empire: The Sublime Porte 1789–1922* (Princeton: Princeton University Press)

Findley, Carter (1995). 'Ebu Bekir Ratib's Vienna Embassy Narrative: Discovering Austria or Propagandizing Reform in Istanbul?', *Wiener Zeitschrift für die Kunde des Morgenlandes* LXXXV, pp 41–80

Finkel, Caroline (1988). *The Administration of Warfare: The Ottoman Military Campaigns in Hungary, 1593–1606*, 2 vols. (Vienna: VWGÖ)

Fleischer, Cornell H. (1986). *Bureaucrat and Intellectual in the Ottoman Empire: The Historian Mustafâ Âli (1541–1600)* (Princeton: Princeton University Press)

*Fotopoulos, Dionissis and Angelos Delivorrias (1997). *Greece at the Benaki Museum* (Athens: Benaki Museum)

Frangakis-Syrett, Elena (1992). *The Commerce of Smyrna in the Eighteenth Century (1700–1820)* (Athens: Centre for Asia Minor Studies)

Frangakis-Syrett, Elena (2006). 'Market Networks and Ottoman–European Commerce, c.1700–1825', in *The Ottomans and Trade*, ed Ebru Boyar and Kate Fleet (Naples and Cambridge: Istituto per l'Oriente C. A. Nallino, The Skilliter Centre for Ottoman Studies), pp 109–28, also in *Oriente Moderno*, n.s., XXV

Franses, Michael (2007). 'Ottoman Rugs in the Churches of Transylvania: Tracing the Origins of the Designs', in *In Praise of God: Anatolian Rugs in Transylvanian Churches 1500–1750*, ed Nazan Ölçer et al (Istanbul: Sakip Sabancı Museum), pp 51–101

*Fukasawa, Katsumi (1987). *Toilerie et commerce du Levant, d'Alep à Marseille* (Paris: Editions du CNRS)

Gara, Eleni (1999). 'Lending and Borrowing Money in an Ottoman Province Town', *Acta Viennensia Ottomanica, Akten des 13. CIEPO-Symposiums*, ed Markus Köhbach, Gisela Proházka-Eisl and Claudia Roemer (Vienna: Institut für Orientalistik), pp 113–19

*Gara, Eleni (2005). 'Çuha for the Janissaries – Velençe for the Poor: Competition for Raw Material and Workforce between Salonica and Veria, 1600–1650', in *Crafts and Craftsmen of the Middle East: Fashioning the Individual in the Muslim Mediterranean*, ed Suraiya Faroqhi and Randi Deguilhem (London: I.B.Tauris), pp 121–52

Gedikli, Fethi (1998). *Osmanlı Şirket Kültürü. XVI.–XVII. Yüzyıllarda Mudârebe Uygulaması* (Istanbul: İz Yayıncılık)

Genç, Mehmet (1975). 'Osmanlı Maliyesinde Malikâne Sistemi', in *Türkiye İktisat Tarihi Semineri, Metinler – Tartışmalar ...*, ed Osman Okyar and Ünal Nabantoğlu (Ankara: Hacettepe Üniversitesi), pp 231–96

*Genç, Mehmet (1986). 'Osmanlı Esnafı ve Devletle İlişkileri', in *Ahilik ve Esnaf, Konferanslar ve Seminer, Metinler, Tartışmalar* (Istanbul), pp 113–30

*Genç, Mehmet (1987). '17–19. Yüzyıllarda Sanayi ve Ticaret Merkezi Olarak Tokat', in *Türk Tarihinde ve Kültüründe Tokat Sempozyumu, 2–6 Temmuz 1986* (Tokat: Tokat Valiliği Şeyhülislâm İbn Kemal Araştırma Merkezi), pp 145–69

*Genç, Mehmet (1994). 'Ottoman Industry in the Eighteenth Century: General Framework, Characteristics and Main Trends', in *Manufacturing in the Ottoman Empire and Turkey 1500–1950*, ed Donald Quataert (Albany: SUNY Press), pp 59–86

*Genç, Mehmet (1995). 'L'Économie ottomane et la guerre au XVIIIe siècle', *Turcica* XXVII, pp 177–96

Genç, Mehmet (2001). 'Contrôle et taxation du commerce du café dans l'Empire ottoman', in *Le commerce du café avant l'ère des plantations coloniales* (Cairo: IFAO), pp 161–80

*Gerber, Haim (1980). 'Social and Economic Position of Women in an Ottoman City: Bursa 1600–1700', *International Journal of Middle East Studies* 12, pp 231–44

*Gerber, Haim (1988). *Economy and Society in an Ottoman City: Bursa, 1600–1700* (Jerusalem: The Hebrew University)

*Gerelyes, Ipolya (ed) (2005). *Turkish Flowers: Studies on Ottoman Art in Hungary* (Budapest: Hungarian National Museum)

Geyer, Bernard and Jacques Lefort (eds) (2003). *La Bithynie au Moyen Âge* (Paris: P. Lethielleux)

*Ghazaleh, Pascale (1999). *Masters of the Trade: Crafts and Craftspeople in Cairo 1750–1850* (Cairo Papers in Social Science 22/3) (Cairo: The American University in Cairo Press)

*Ghazaleh, Pascale (2005). 'Organizing Labour: Professional Classifications in late Eighteenth to early Nineteenth Century Cairo', in *Crafts and Craftsmen of the Middle East: Fashioning the Individual in the Muslim Mediterranean*, ed Suraiya Faroqhi and Randi Deguilhem (London: I.B.Tauris), pp 235–60

Ginio, Eyal (2003). 'Living on the Margins of Charity: Coping with Poverty in an Ottoman Provincial City', in *Poverty and Charity in Middle Eastern Contexts*, ed Michael Bonner, Mine Ener and Amy Singer (Albany, NY: SUNY Press), pp 165–84

Glassie, Henry (1993). *Turkish Traditional Art Today* (Bloomington: Indiana University Press)

Göçek, Fatma Müge (1996). *Rise of the Bourgeoisie, Demise of Empire: Ottoman Westernization and Social Change* (Oxford: Oxford University Press)

*Göçek, Fatma Müge (1999). 'Osmanlı Ermenilerinin Gündelik Hayatlarına bir Bakış: XVIII. Yüzyıl İstanbulu'nda Ermeni Esnafları,' in *Osmanlı* 5, ed Güler Eren, Kemal Çiçek and Cem Oğuz (Ankara: Yeni Türkiye Yayınevi), pp 555–62

Goffman, Daniel (1990). *Izmir and the Levantine World, 1550–1650* (Seattle: University of Washington Press)

Gökbilgin, M. Tayyib (1957). *Rumeli'de Yürükler, Tatarlar ve Evlâd-ı Fâtihân* (Istanbul: İstanbul Üniversitesi)

Gökçen, İbrahim (1946a). *Manisa Tarihinde Vakıflar ve Hayırlar (Hicrî 954–1060)*, vol. 1 (Manisa: CHP)

Gökçen, İbrahim (1946b). *Sicillere göre XVI. ve XVII. Asırlarda Saruhan Zaviye ve Yatırları* (Istanbul: CHP)

*Gölpınarlı, Abdülbaki (1949–50). 'Burgâzî ve Fütüvvet-Nâmesi', *İstanbul Üniversitesi İktisat Fakültesi Mecmuası* 11, 1–4, pp 3–354

Gölpınarlı, Abdülbaki (1953). *Mevlânâ'dan sonra Mevlevîlik* (Istanbul: İnkilap Kitabevi)

*Gölpınarlı, Abdülbaki (1953–54). 'İslâm ve Türk İllerinde Fütüvvet Teşkilâtı ve Kaynakları', *İstanbul Üniversitesi İktisat Fakültesi Mecmuası* 15, 1–4, pp 76–153

Gölpınarlı, Abdülbaki (1959). *Mevlânâ Celâleddin, Hayatı, Felsefesi, Eserleri, Eserlerinden Seçmeler* (Istanbul: İnkilap)

Güçer, Lütfi (1949–50). 'XVIII. Yüzyıl Ortalarında İstanbul'un İaşesi için Lüzumlu Hububatın Temini Meselesi', *İstanbul Üniversitesi İktisat Fakültesi Mecmuası* 11, 1–4, pp 397–416

Güçer, Lütfi (1951–52). 'Osmanlı İmparatorluğu dahilinde Hububat Ticaretinin Tabi Olduğu Kayıtlar', *İstanbul Üniversitesi İktisat Fakültesi Mecmuası* 13, 1–4, pp 79–98

*Guirguis, Magdi (2004). 'Ibrāhīm al-Nāsih et la culture copte au XVIIIe siècle', in *Coptic Studies on the Threshold of a New Millennium II: Proceedings of the Seventh International Congress of Coptic Studies, Leiden, 27 August–2 September 2000*, ed Mat Immerzeel, Jacques van der Vliet et al (Leiden, Paris, Dudley MA: Uitgeverij Peeters and Departement Oosterse Studies), pp 938–52

*Güler, A. Sinan (1999). 'Sanayi Devrimi, Osmanlı Sanayi Mimarisi ve Feshane Üzerine bir Ön Değerlendirme', in *Aptullah Kuran için Yazılar: Essays in Honour of Aptullah Kuran*, ed Çiğdem Kafescioğlu and Lucienne Thys-Şenocak with Günhan Danışman (Istanbul: YKY), pp 387–99

Gülsoy, Ufuk (2000). *Osmanlı Gayrımüslimlerinin Askerlik Serüveni* (Istanbul: Simurg)

Halaçoğlu, Ahmet (2002). *Teke Mütesellimi Hacı Mehmed Ağa ve Faaliyetleri* (Isparta: Fakülte Kitabevi)

Hanioğlu, M. Şükrü (2008). *A Brief History of the Late Ottoman Empire* (Princeton: Princeton University Press)

*Hanna, Nelly (1984). *Construction Work in Ottoman Cairo (1517–1798)* (Cairo: Institut Français d'Archéologie Orientale)

*Hanna, Nelly (1991). *La maison moyenne et ses habitants aux XVIIe et XVIIIe siècles* (Cairo: IFAO)

Hanna, Nelly (1998). *Making Big Money in 1600: The Life and Times of Isma'il Abu Taqiyya, Egyptian Merchant* (Syracuse: Syracuse University Press)

Hathaway, Jane (1997). *The Politics of Households in Ottoman Egypt* (Cambridge: Cambridge University Press)

Hathaway, Jane (2006). *Beshir Agha, Chief Eunuch of the Ottoman Imperial Harem* (Oxford: Oneworld)

Hinz, Walter (1955). *Islamische Maße und Gewichte, umgerechnet ins metrische System* (Leiden: E.J. Brill)

Hitzel, Frédéric (2007). *Artisans et commerçants du Grand Turc* (Paris: Les Belles Lettres)

*Ianeva, Svetla (2006). 'The Commercial Practices and Protoindustrial Activities of Haci Hristo Rachkov, a Bulgarian trader at the end of the eighteenth to the beginning of the nineteenth century', *Oriente Moderno* XXV, n.s.; also in *The Ottomans and Trade*, ed Kate Fleet, pp 93–107

Inalcik, Halil (1960). 'Bursa and the Commerce of the Levant', *Journal of the Economic and Social History of the Orient* 3, pp 131–47

*Inalcik, Halil (1969). 'Capital Formation in the Ottoman Empire', *The Journal of Economic History* XXIX, 1, pp 97–140

Inalcik, Halil (1970). 'The Ottoman Economic Mind and Aspects of the Ottoman Economy', in *Studies in the Economic History of the Middle East, From the Rise of Islam to the Present Day*, ed M.A. Cook (London: Oxford University Press), pp 207–18

Inalcik, Halil (1975). 'The Socio-Political Effects of the Diffusion of Firearms in the Middle East', in *War, Technology and Society in the Middle East*, ed M.E. Yapp (London, Oxford: Oxford University Press), pp 195–297

*İnalcık, Halil (1979–80). 'Osmanlı Pamuklu Pazarı, Hindistan ve İngiltere: Pazar Rekabetinde Emek Maliyetinin Rolü', *Gelişme Dergisi*, special issue, *Türkiye İktisat Tarihi Üzerine Araştırmalar*, pp 1–65

*Inalcik, Halil (1986a). 'The Appointment Procedure of a Guild Warden (Kethudâ)', in *Festschrift für Andreas Tietze, Wiener Zeitschrift für die Kunde des Morgenlandes* 76, pp 135–42

*Inalcik, Halil (1986b). 'The Yürüks: Their Origins, Expansion and Economic Role', in *Oriental Carpet & Textile Studies II: Carpets of the Mediterranean Countries 1400–1600 (based upon the Special Sessions of the 4th International Conference on Oriental Carpets, London 1987)*, ed Robert Pinner and Walter B. Denny (London: Hali OCTS Ltd), pp 39–66

*Ionescu, Stefano (ed) (2005). *Die osmanischen Teppiche in Siebenbürgen* (Rome: Verduci Editore)

İrepoğlu, Gül (1999). *Levnî. Nakış, Şiir, Renk* (Istanbul: Koçbank)

*Irwin, Robert (1986). 'Egypt, Syria and their Trading Partners, 1450–1550', in *Oriental Carpet & Textile Studies II, Carpets of the Mediterranean Countries 1400–1600 (based upon the Special Sessions of the 4th International Conference on Oriental Carpets, London 1987)*, ed Robert Pinner and Walter B. Denny (London: Hali OCTS Ltd), pp 73–82

İslamoğlu-İnan, Huri (1994). *State and Peasant in the Ottoman Empire: Agrarian Power Relations and Regional Economic Development in Ottoman Anatolia during the Sixteenth Century* (Leiden: E.J. Brill)

İslamoğlu-İnan, Huri (2004). 'Politics of Administering Property: Law and Statistics in the Nineteenth-century Ottoman Empire', in *Constituting Modernity: Private Property in the East and West*, ed Huri İslamoğlu-İnan (London: I.B.Tauris), pp 276–320

Itzkowitz, Norman (1962). 'Eighteenth-Century Ottoman Realities', *Studia Islamica* XVI, pp 73–94

Ivanova, Svetlana (2003). 'The Empire's "own" Foreigners: Armenians and acem tüccar in Rumeli in the seventeenth and eighteenth centuries', in *The Ottoman Capitulations: Text and Context*, ed Maurits H. van den Boogert and Kate Fleet (Naples and Cambridge: Istituto per l'Oriente C.A. Nallino, The Skilliter Centre for Ottoman

Studies), pp 681–703; also in *Oriente Moderno*, n.s., XXII
Jelavich, Barbara (1983). *History of the Balkans*, vol. 1, *Eighteenth and Nineteenth Centuries* (Cambridge: Cambridge University Press)
*Kabadayı, M. Erdem (2005). 'Nascent Factories, Labour Recruitment and Ottoman Industrial Policy in the Wake of Tanzimat', in *IXth International Congress of Economic and Social History of Turkey Dubrovnik – Croatia, 20–23 August, 2002* (Ankara: Türk Tarih Kurumu), pp 263–72
Kafadar, Cemal (1989). 'Self and Others: The Diary of a Dervish in Seventeenth-Century Istanbul and First-Person Narratives in Ottoman Literature', *Studia Islamica* LXIX, pp 121–50
Kafadar, Cemal (1991). 'Les troubles monétaires de la fin du XVIe siècle et la conscience ottomane du déclin', *Annales ESC* 43, pp 381–400
*Kal'a, Ahmet (2006). 'Der Einfluss Istanbuler Zünfte auf die Ausbildung des osmanischen Zunftsystems', in *Istanbul: vom imperialen Herrschersitz zur Megapolis, Historiographische Betrachtungen zu Gesellschaft, Institutionen und Räumen*, ed Yavuz Köse (Munich: Martin Meidenbauer), pp 215–42
*Karakışla, Yavuz Selim (2005). *Women, War and Work in the Ottoman Empire: Society for the Employment of Ottoman Muslim Women 1916–1923* (Istanbul: Ottoman Bank Archives and Research Centre)
*Katsiardi-Hering, Olga (forthcoming). 'Associations of Greek Artisans and Merchants between the Ottoman and Habsburg Empires: the case of red cotton yarn (late 18th – early 19th centuries)'
*Kazıcı, Ziya (1987). *Osmanlılarda İhtisâb Müessesesi Osmanlılarda Ekonomik, Dini ve Sosyal Hayat* (Istanbul: Kültür Basın Yayın Birliği)
Khoury, Dina (1997). *State and Provincial Society in the Ottoman Empire Mosul 1540–1834* (Cambridge: Cambridge University Press)
*Kırlı, Cengiz (2001). 'A Profile of the Labor Force in Early Nineteenth-Century Istanbul', *International Labor and Working Class History* 60, pp 125–40
*Koller, Markus (1998). 'Handwerk und Handwerker in Istanbul im 18. Jahrhundert. Beitrag zur Geschichte der omanischen Zünfte', unpublished MA thesis, Department of the History of Southeastern Europe, Ludwig Maximilians-Universität, Munich, Germany
*Koller, Markus (1999–2000). 'Das Pelzhandwerk im Valide Hanı (Istanbul): Anmerkungen zum Verhältnis esnaf und vaqf im 18. Jahrhundert', *Prilozi za orijentalnu filologiju* 49, pp 177–88
Köse, Yavuz (2007). 'Westliche Unternehmen und ihre Marketingaktivitäten im Osmanischen Reich (1870–1927)', unpublished PhD thesis, Ludwig Maximilians-Universität, Munich
*Kovásc, Gyöngyi (2005). 'Iznik Potters in Hungarian Archaeological Research', in *Turkish Flowers: Studies on Ottoman Art in Hungary*, ed Ipolya Gerelyes (Budapest: Hungarian National Museum), pp 69–86
Kreiser, Klaus (1986). 'Icareteyn: Zur "Doppelten Miete" im Osmanischen Stiftungswesen', *Journal of Turkish Studies*, 10, *Raiyyet Rüsûmu: Essays Presented to Halil Inalcik on His Seventieth Birthday by his Colleagues and Students*, pp 219–26
Küçük, Hülya (2002). *The Role of the Bektāshīs in Turkey's National Struggle* (Leiden: E.J. Brill)
*Küçükerman, Önder (1987). *Anadolu'nun Geleneksel Halı Dokuma Sanatı İçinde Hereke*

Fabrıkası ' … *Saray'dan Hereke'ye giden yol* …' (Ankara: Sümerbank)
Küçükerman, Önder (1988). Türk Giyim Sanayii Tarihinde Ünlü Feshane Defterdar Fabrikası (Ankara: Sümerbank)
Kuniholm, Peter I. (1990). 'Archaeological Evidence and Non-evidence for Climatic Change', *Philosophical Transactions of the Royal Society*, A330, pp 645–55
Kuran, Aptullah (1987). *Sinan: The Grand Old Master of Ottoman Architecture* (Washington, Istanbul: Institute of Turkish Studies and Ada Press)
*Kuran, Timur (2000). 'Islamic Influences on the Ottoman Guilds', in *The Great Ottoman–Turkish Civilization*, ed Kemal Çiçek, 4 vols. (Ankara: Yeni Türkiye), vol. 2, *Economy and Society*, pp 43–59
Kurz, Otto (1975). *European Clocks and Watches in the Near East* (London and Leiden: The Warburg Institute and E.J. Brill)
*Kütükoğlu, Mübahat (1986). 'Osmanlı Esnafında Oto-Kontrol Müessesesi', in *Ahilik ve Esnaf, Konferanslar ve Seminer, Metinler, Tartışmalar* (Istanbul), pp 55–85
Kütükoğlu, Mübahat (2000). *XX. Asra Erişen İstanbul Medreseleri* (Istanbul: TÜSOKTAR)
Kuyulu, İnci (1992). *Kara Osman-oğlu Ailesine Ait Mimari Eserler* (Ankara: Kültür Bakanlığı)
Le Gall, Dina (2004). *A Culture of Sufism: Naqshbandīs in the Ottoman World 1450–1700* (Albany, NY: SUNY Press)
Lewis, Bernard (1968). *The Emergence of Modern Turkey*, 2nd ed (Oxford: Oxford University Press)
Lowry, Heath (1986). 'Changes in Fifteenth-Century Ottoman Peasant Taxation: The Case Study of Radilofo', in *Continuity and Change in Late Byzantine and Early Ottoman Society*, ed Anthony Bryer and Heath Lowry (Birmingham and Washington DC: The University of Birmingham and Dumbarton Oaks), pp 23–37
*Lowry, Heath W. (2003). *Ottoman Bursa in Travel Accounts* (Bloomington: Indiana University, Ottoman and Modern Turkish Studies Publications)
McGowan, Bruce (1981). *Economic Life in Ottoman Europe: Taxation, Trade and the Struggle for Land, 1600–1800* (Cambridge, Paris: Cambridge University Press and Maison des Sciences de l'Homme)
*Mack, Rosamond (2002). *Bazaar to Piazza: Islamic Trade and Italian Art, 1300–1600* (Los Angeles, Berkeley, London: University of California Press)
MacLean, Gerald M. (2004). *The Rise of Oriental Travel: English Visitors to the Ottoman Empire, 1580–1720* (Houndmills, Basingstoke: Palgrave Macmillan)
*Mahir, Bânu (1986). 'Saray Nakkaşhanesinin Ünlü Ressamı Şah Kulu ve Eserleri', *Topkapı Sarayı Yıllığı* 1, pp 113–30
*Maitte, Corinne (2004). 'Adapter les produits, jouer sur les marchés. La fabrication des chéchias, XVIIIe–XXe siècles', in Giovanni Luigi Fontana and Gérard Gayot (eds), *Wool, Products and Markets (13th–20th century)* (Padua: CLEUP scarl – 'Coop Libreria Editrice Università di Padova'), pp 1115–42
Majer, Hans Georg (1978). *Vorstudien zur Geschichte der Ilmiye im Osmanischen Reich, 1. Zu Uşakîzade, seiner Familie und seinem Zeyl-i Şakayık* (Munich: Dr. Rudolf Trofenik)
*Mantran, Robert (1962). *Istanbul dans la seconde moitié du dix-septième siècle, Essai d'histoire institutionelle, économique et sociale* (Istanbul, Paris: Institut Français d'Archéologie d'Istanbul und Adrien Maisonneuve)
Marcus, Abraham (1989).*The Middle East on the Eve of Modernity: Aleppo in the*

Eighteenth Century (New York: Columbia University Press)

Marsot, Afaf Lutfi al-Sayyid (1984). *Egypt in the Reign of Muhammad Ali* (Cambridge: Cambridge University Press)

*Martal, Abdullah (1999). *Değişim Süresince İzmir'de Sanayileşme* (Izmir: Dokuz Eylül Yayınları)

*Maury, Bernard, André Raymond, Jacques Revault, Mona Zakarya (1983). *Palais et maisons du Caire*, vol. 2 (Paris: Éditions du CNRS)

Mazower, Mark (2004). *Salonica: City of Ghosts, Christians, Muslims and Jews, 1430– 1950* (London: HarperCollins)

*Mélikoff, Irène (1964). 'Le rituel du helva, recherches sur une coutume des corporations de métiers dans la Turquie médiévale', *Der Islam* 39, pp 180–91

Mert, Özcan (1980). *XVIII. ve XIX. Yüzyıllarda Çapanoğulları* (Ankara: Kültür Bakanlığı)

*Michel, Nicolas (2005). 'Les artisans dans la ville: Ateliers de tissage et tisserands d'Asyût à la fin du XVIIe siècle, d'après les registres du tribunal du qâdî', in *Society and Economy in Egypt and the Eastern Mediterranean 1600–1900: Essays in Honor of André Raymond*, ed Nelly Hanna and Raouf Abbas (Cairo: The American University in Cairo Press)

Mraz, Gottfried (1980). 'Die Rolle der Uhrwerke in der kaiserlichen Türkenverehrung im 16. Jahrhundert', in *Die Welt als Uhr, deutsche Uhren und Automaten 1550–1650*, ed Klaus Maurice and Otto Mayr (Munich: Deutscher Kunstverlag), pp 39–54

*Müller-Wiener, Wolfgang (1986–87). 'Manufakturen und Fabriken in Istanbul vom 15.–19. Jahrhundert', *Mitteilungen der Fränkischen Geographischen Gesellschaft* 33–4, pp 257–320

Murphey, Rhoads (1999). *Ottoman Warfare, 1500–1700*, (London: LCR Press)

Nagata, Yuzo (1997). *Tarihte Ayânlar, Karaosmanoğulları üzerinde bir İnceleme* (Ankara: Türk Tarih Kurumu)

*Nayır, Zeynep (1975). *Osmanlı Mimarlığında Sultan Ahmet Külliyesi ve Sonrası (1609– 1690)* (Istanbul: İTÜ Mimarlık Fakültesi)

*Necipoğlu-Kafadar, Gülru (1986). 'Plans and Models in 15th and 16th Century Ottoman Architectural Practice', *Journal of the Society of Architectural Historians* XLX, 3, pp 224–43

*Necipoğlu, Gülru (2005). *The Age of Sinan: Architectural Culture in the Ottoman Empire* (London: Reaktion Books)

Neumann, Christoph (2004). 'How did a Vizier Dress in the Eighteenth Century?', in *Ottoman Costumes: From Textile to Identity*, ed Suraiya Faroqhi and Christoph Neumann (Istanbul: Eren), pp 181–218

Neumann, Christoph (2006). 'Modernitäten im Konflikt, Der Sechste Munizipal-Bezirk von Istanbul, 1857–1912', in *Istanbul: vom imperialen Herrschersitz zur Megapolis, Historiographische Betrachtungen zu Gesellschaft, Institutionen und Räumen*, ed Yavuz Köse (Munich: Martin Meidenbauer), pp 351–76

Nutku, Özdemir (1972). *IV. Mehmed'in Edirne Şenliği* (Ankara: Türk Tarih Kurumu)

Nutku, Özdemir (1997). 'Esnaf Loncaları ve XVI. Yüzyıl Esnaf Flamaları', *TOMBAK* 13, pp 48–56

*Olson, Robert (reprint 1996a). 'The Esnaf and the Patrona Halil Rebellion of 1730: A Realignment in Ottoman Politics?', in *Imperial Meanderings and Republican By-ways: Essays on Eighteenth Century Ottoman and Twentieth Century History of*

Turkey (Istanbul: The Isis Press), pp 1–12

*Olson, Robert (reprint 1996b). 'Jews, Janissaries, Esnaf and the Revolt of 1740 in Istanbul: Social Upheaval and Political Realignment in the Ottoman Empire', in *Imperial Meanderings and Republican By-ways: Essays on Eighteenth Century Ottoman and Twentieth Century History of Turkey* (Istanbul: The Isis Press), pp 13–32

*Orhonlu, Cengiz (reprint 1984). *Osmanlı İmparatorluğunda Şehircilik ve Ulaşım üzerine Araştırmalar*, ed Salih Özbaran (Izmir: Ege Üniversitesi Edebiyat Fakültesi)

Ortaylı, İlber (1985). *Tanzimatdan Cumhuriyete Yerel Yönetim Geleneği* (Istanbul: Hil Yayınları)

*Owen, Roger (1981). *The Middle East in the World Economy 1800–1914* (London, New York: Methuen)

Özbek, Nadir (2003). 'Imperial Gifts and Sultanic Legitimation during the Late Ottoman Empire, 1876–1909', in *Poverty and Charity in Middle Eastern Contexts*, ed Michael Bonner, Mine Ener and Amy Singer (Albany, NY: SUNY Press), pp 203–22

*Özcan, Tahsin (1983). *Fetvalar Işığında Osmanlı Esnafı* (Istanbul: Kitabevi)

*Özdemir, Rifat (1988). 'Tokat Esnaf Teşkilâtı (1771–1840)', in *Birinci Tarih boyunca Karadeniz Kongresi Bildirileri, 13–17 Ekim 1986*, ed Mehmet Sağlam et al (Samsun: Ondokuzmayis Üniversitesi), pp 397–423

*Özmucur, Süleyman and Şevket Pamuk (2002). 'Real Wages and Standards of Living in the Ottoman Empire, 1489–1914', *The Journal of Economic History* 62, 2, pp 293–321

*Özveren Eyüp and Onur Yıldırım (unpublished). 'Ottoman and Venetian Shipbuilding in the Early Modern Mediterranean'

*Palairet, Michael (1997). *The Balkan Economies: Evolution without Development* (Cambridge: Cambridge University Press)

*Pamuk, Şevket (2000a). *İstanbul ve diger Kentlerde 500 Yıllık Fiyatlar ve Ücretler* (Ankara: Başbakanlık Devlet İstatistik Enstitüsü)

Pamuk, Şevket (2000b). *A Monetary History of the Ottoman Empire* (Cambridge: Cambridge University Press)

Panzac, Daniel (1985). *La peste dans l'Empire ottoman, 1700–1850* (Louvain: Éditions Peeters)

Papakostantinou, Katerina (forthcoming). 'The Pondikas Merchant Family from Thessaloniki, ca. 1750–1800'

Peirce, Leslie (2001). 'Localizing Legitimation: Bargaining through the Law in a Provincial Court', *New Perspectives on Turkey* 24, pp 17–50

Peirce, Leslie (2003). *Morality Tales: Law and Gender in the Ottoman Court of Aintab* (Berkeley, Los Angeles: University of California Press)

*Petmezas, Socrates D. (1990). 'Patterns of Protoindustrialization in the Ottoman Empire. The Case of Eastern Thessaly (ca. 1750–1860)', *The Journal of European Economic History* 19/3, pp 575–603

Petrasch, Ernst, Reinhard Sänger et al (1991). *Die Karlsruher Türkenbeute, die 'Türckische Kammer' des Markgrafen Ludwig Wilhelm von Baden-Baden, Die 'Türckischen Curiositäeten' der Markgrafen von Baden-Durlach* (Munich: Hirmer Verlag)

*Pitarakis, Brigitte and Christos Merantzas (2006). *A Treasured Memory: Ecclesiastical Silver from Late Ottoman Istanbul in the Sevgi Gönül Collection* (Istanbul: Sadberk Hanım Müzesi)

*Planhol, Xavier de (1975-77). 'Rayonnement urbain et sélection animale: une solution nouvelle du problème de la chèvre d'Angora', *Sécretariat d'État aux Universités, Comité des travaux historiques et scientifiques, Bulletin de la section de géographie* LXXX, II, pp 79-196

*Quataert, Donald (1983a). *Social Disintegration and Popular Resistance in the Ottoman Empire, 1881-1908* (New York: New York University Press)

*Quataert, Donald (1983b). 'The Silk Industry of Bursa, 1880-1914', in *Contributions à l'histoire économique et sociale de l'Empire ottoman*, ed Jean Louis Bacqué-Grammont and Paul Dumont (Louvain: Éditions Peeters), pp 481-503

*Quataert, Donald (1993). *Ottoman Manufacturing in the Age of the Industrial Revolution* (Cambridge: Cambridge University Press)

Quataert, Donald (1997). 'Clothing Laws, State and Society in the Ottoman Empire, 1720-1829', *International Journal of Middle East Studies* XXIX, 3, pp 403-25

Quataert, Donald (2000). 'Introduction', in *Consumption Studies and the History of the Ottoman Empire, 1550-1922: An Introduction*, ed Donald Quataert (Albany, NY: SUNY Press), pp 1-14

*Quataert, Donald (2001). 'Labor History and the Ottoman Empire, c. 1700-1922', *International Labor and Working Class History* 60, pp 93-109

*Quataert, Donald (2006). *Miners and the State in the Ottoman Empire: The Zonguldak Coalfield 1822-1920* (New York, Oxford: Berghahn Books)

*Quataert, Donald and Yüksel Duman (eds) (2001). 'A Coal Miner's Life during the Late Ottoman Empire', *International Labor and Working Class History* 60, pp 153-79

*Rafeq, Abdul Karim (1976). 'The Law Court Registers of Damascus, with Special Reference to Craft Corporations during the First Half of the Eighteenth Century', in *Les Arabes par leurs archives*, ed Jacques Berque and Dominique Chevallier (Paris: Éditions du CNRS), pp 141-59

*Rafeq, Abdul Karim (1991). 'Craft Organization, Work Ethics and the Strains of Change in Ottoman Syria', *Journal of the American Oriental Society* 111, 3, pp 495-511

*Raymond, André (1973-74). *Artisans et commerçants au Caire, au XVIIIe siècle*, 2 vols. (Damascus: Institut Français de Damas)

Raymond, André (1984). *The Great Arab Cities in the 16th-18th Centuries: An Introduction* (New York, London: New York University Press)

Raymond, André (1993). *Le Caire* (Paris: Fayard)

Raymond, André (1995). *Le Caire des janissaires: L'apogée de la ville sous ʿAbd al-Rahmân Kathudâ* (Paris: CNRS Éditions)

Raymond, André (1998). *Égyptiens et Français au Caire 1798-1801* (Cairo: IFAO)

*Raymond, André (reprint 2002a). 'Urban Networks and Popular Movements in Cairo and Aleppo (End of the 18th-Beginning of the 19th Century)', in *Arab Cities in the Ottoman Period* (Aldershot: Ashgate Variorum), no. v

*Raymond, André (reprint 2002b). 'Quartiers et mouvements populaires au Caire au XVIIIème siècle', in *Arab Cities in the Ottoman Period* (Aldershot: Ashgate Variorum), no. xiii

*Raymond, André (reprint 2002c). 'Soldiers in Trade: The Case of Ottoman Cairo', in *Arab Cities in the Ottoman Period* (Aldershot: Ashgate Variorum), no. xiv

Renda, Günsel (1989). 'Die traditionelle türkische Malerei und das Einsetzen der westlichen Einflüsse', in *Geschichte der türkischen Malerei* (Istanbul: Palasar SA), pp 15-86

*Rogers, John Michael (1982). 'The State and the Arts in Ottoman Turkey', *International Journal of Middle East Studies* 14, pp 71–86, 283–313

*Rogers, John Michael (1986). 'Ottoman Luxury Trades and Their Regulation', in *Osmanische Studien zur Wirtschafts- und Sozialgeschichte. In Memoriam Vančo Boškov*, ed Hans Georg Majer (Wiesbaden, 1986), pp 135–55

*Rozen, Minna (2000). 'Boatmen's and Fishermen's Guilds in Nineteenth-Century Istanbul', *Mediterranean Historical Review* 15, 1: *Seafaring and the Jews*, pp 72–93

*Rozen, Minna (2005). 'A Pound of Flesh: The Meat Trade and Social Struggle in Jewish Istanbul, 1700–1923', in *Crafts and Craftsmen of the Middle East: Fashioning the Individual in the Muslim Mediterranean*, ed Suraiya Faroqhi and Randi Deguilhem (London: I.B.Tauris), pp 195–234

*Sahillioğlu, Halil (1985). 'Slaves in the Social and Economic Life of Bursa in the late 15th and early 16th Centuries', *Turcica* XVII, pp 43–112

*Şahin, İlhan (1984–85). 'Ahi Evran Vakfiyyesi ve Vakıflarına Dâir', *Türklük Araştırmaları Dergisi* 1, pp 325–41

*Şahin, İlhan and Feridun Emecen (1988). 'XV. Asrın İkinci Yarısında Tokat Esnafı', *Osmanlı Araştırmaları* VII–VIII, pp 287–308

Salzmann, Ariel (1993). 'An Ancien Régime Revisited: "Privatization" and Political Economy in the Eighteenth-century Ottoman Empire', *Politics and Society* XXI, 4, pp 393–423

Salzmann, Ariel (2004). *Toqueville in the Ottoman Empire: Rival Paths to the Modern State* (Leiden: E.J. Brill)

Sariyannis, Marinos (2006). '"Neglected Trades": Glimpses into the 17th Century Istanbul Underworld', *Turcica* 38, pp 155–79

Schmitt, Oliver Jens (2005). *Levantiner: Lebenswelten und Identitäten einer ethnokonfessionellen Gruppe im osmanischen Reich im langen 19. Jahrhundert* (Munich: Oldenbourg)

Seirinidou, Vassilike (forthcoming). 'Grocers and Wholesalers: Ottomans and Habsburgs, Foreigners and "Our Own": The Greek trade diasporas in Central Europe, seventeenth to nineteenth Centuries'

Şeni, Nora (1994). 'The Camondos and their Imprint on 19th Century Istanbul', *International Journal of Middle East Studies* 26, pp 663–75

*Sert, Özlem (unpublished manuscript). 'Becoming a Baker in Rodosçuk (1546–1552): A Textual Analysis of "Records of Designation"'

Shaw, Stanford J. (1962). *The Financial and Administrative Development of Ottoman Egypt 1517–1798* (Princeton: Princeton University Press)

Shaw, Stanford J. (1971). *Between Old and New: The Ottoman Empire under Sultan Selim III 1780–1807* (Cambridge, MA: Harvard University Press)

*Shkodra, Zija (1973). 'Résumé: Les corporations albanaises', in *Esnafet Shqiptare (Shekujt XV–XX)* (Tirana: Akademia Eshkencavee R. P. Të Shqipërisë)

*Shkodra, Zija (1975). 'Les esnaf ou corporations dans la vie balkanique des XVII–XVIIIe siècles', *Studia Albanica* XII, 2, pp 47–76

Singer, Amy (2002). *Constructing Ottoman Beneficence: An Imperial Soup Kitchen in Jerusalem* (Albany, NY: SUNY Press)

Smyrnelis, Marie Carmen (2005). *Une société hors de soi: Identités et relations sociales, Smyrne aux XVIIIe et XIXe siècles* (Louvain: Éditions Peeters)

Stoianovich, Traian (1960). 'The Conquering Balkan Orthodox Merchant', *The Journal of*

Economic History XX, pp 234–313

Stout, Robert (1966). 'The Sûr-i-hümâyun of Murad III: A Study of Ottoman Pageantry and Entertainment', unpublished PhD thesis, Ohio State University (Ann Arbor, MI: University Microfilms)

Strauss, Johann (2002). 'Ottoman Rule Experienced and Remembered: Remarks on some Local Greek Chronicles of the Tourkokratia', in *Ottoman Historiography: Turkey and Southeastern Europe*, ed Fikret Adanır and Suraiya Faroqhi (Leiden: E.J. Brill), pp 193–221

*Szakály, Ferenc (1971). 'Zur Kontinuitätsfrage der Wirtschaftsstruktur in den ungarischen Marktflecken unter der Türkenherrschaft', in *Die wirtschaftlichen Auswirkungen der Türkenkriege, Die Vorträge des 1. Internationalen Grazer Symposions zur Wirtschafts- und Sozialgeschichte Südosteuropas (5.–10. Oktober 1970)*, ed Otmar Pickl (Graz: Lehrkanzel für Wirtschafts- und Sozialgeschichte der Universität Graz), pp 235–72

*Taeschner, Franz (1979). *Zünfte und Bruderschaften im Islam: Studien zur Geschichte der Futuwwa* (Munich, Zurich: Artemis Winkler)

Tamdoğan-Abel, Işık (1998). 'Les modalités de l'urbanité dans une ville ottomane: Les habitants d'Adana au XVIIIème siècle d'après les registres des cadis', unpublished PhD thesis, ÉHÉSS, Paris

Tamdoğan, Işık (2005). 'Le nezir ou les relations des bandits et des nomades avec l'Etat dans la Çukurova du XVIIIème siècle', in *Sociétés rurales ottomanes*, ed Muhammad Afifi, Rashida Chih, Brigitte Marino, Nicolas Michel and Işık Tamdogan (Cairo: IFAO), pp 259–69

Terzioğlu, Derin (1995). 'The Imperial Circumcision Festival of 1582: An Interpretation', *Muqarnas* 12, pp 84–100

*Tezcan, Hülya (1992). 'Topkapı Sarayı'ndaki Velense ve Benzeri Dokumalar', *Topkapı Sarayı Müzesi, Yıllık* 5, pp 223–40

*Tezcan, Hülya (2004). 'Furs and Skins Owned by the Sultans', in *Ottoman Costumes: From Textile to Identity*, ed Suraiya Faroqhi and Christoph Neumann (Istanbul: Eren), pp 63–79

Tilly, Charles (1985). 'War Making and State Making as Organized Crime', in *Bringing the State Back In*, eds Peter B. Evans, Dietrich Rueschemeyer and Theda Skocpol (Cambridge: Cambridge University Press), pp 169–91

*Todorov, Nikolai (1967–68). '19.cu Yüzyılın İlk Yarısında Bulgaristan Esnaf Teşkilatında Bazı Karakter Değişmeleri', *İstanbul Üniversitesi İktisat Fakültesi Mecmuası* XXVII, 1–2, pp 1–36

*Todorov, Nicolai (reprint 1977a). 'La différentiation de la population urbaine au XVIIIe siècle d'après les registres de cadis de Vidin, Sofia et Ruse', in *La ville balkanique sous les Ottomans (XV–XIXe s.)* (London: Variorum), no. vii

*Todorov, Nicolai (reprint 1977b). 'La genèse du capitalisme dans les provinces bulgares de l'Empire ottoman au cours de la première moitié du XIXe s.', in *La ville balkanique sous les Ottomans (XV–XIXe s.)* (London: Variorum), no. x

*Todorov, Nikolai (reprint 1998a). 'La revolution industrielle en Europe occidentale et les provinces balkaniques de l'Empire ottoman: le cas bulgare', in *Society, the City and Industry in the Balkans, 15th to 19th Centuries* (Aldershot: Variorum, 1998), no. i

*Todorov, Nikolai (reprint 1998b). 'Les tentatives d'industrialisation précoce dans les

provinces balkaniques de l'Empire ottoman', in *Society, the City and Industry in the Balkans, 15th to 19th Centuries* (Aldershot: Variorum, 1998), no. ii

*Toledano, Ehud (1990). *State and Society in Mid-nineteenth-century Egypt* (Cambridge: Cambridge University Press)

Tóth, Anikó (2003). 'An Ottoman-era Cellar from the Foreground of Buda's Royal Castle', in *Archaeology of the Ottoman Period in Hungary*, ed Eva Garam et al (Budapest: The Hungarian National Museum), pp 273–80

Tribe, Tania C. (2004). 'Icon and Narration in Eighteenth-century Christian Egypt: The Works of Yuḥanna al-Armānī al-Qudsī and Ibrāhīm al-Nāsikh', *Art History* 27, 1, pp 62–94

Tuchscherer, Michel (1990). 'Évolution toponomique et topographique de la sāga du Caire à l'époque ottomane', *Annales Islamologiques* 25, pp 321–41

Tuchscherer, Michel (1999a). 'Toponymie et perception de l'espace dans les quartiers commerciaux à l'époque ottomane', in *Le Khan al-Khalili et ses environs, Un centre commercial et artisanal au Caire du XIIIe au XXe siècle*, ed Sylvie Denoix, Jean-Charles Depaule et Michel Tuchscherer (Cairo: IFAO), pp 51–64

Tuchscherer, Michel (1999b). 'Évolution du bâti et des fonctions à l'époque ottomane', in *Le Khan al-Khalili et ses environs, Un centre commercial et artisanal au Caire du XIIIe au XXe siècle*, ed Sylvie Denoix, Jean-Charles Depaule et Michel Tuchscherer (Cairo: IFAO), pp 67–96

*Tucker, Judith (1985). *Women in Nineteenth-century Egypt* (Cambridge: Cambridge University Press)

*Turan, Şerafettin (1963). 'Osmanlı Teşkilatında Hassa Mimarları', *Tarih Araştırmaları Dergisi* 1, 1, pp 157–202

*Turna, Nalan (2006). 'The Everyday Life of Istanbul and its Artisans, 1808–1839', unpublished PhD thesis, Binghamton University/SUNY

*Ülgener, Sabri (1981a). *İktisadi Çözülmenin Ahlak ve Zihniyet Dünyası* (Istanbul: DER Yayınları)

*Ülgener, Sabri (1981b). *Dünü ve Bugünü ile Zihniyet ve Din, İslâm, Tasavvuf ve Çözülme Devrinin İktisat Ahlâkı* (Istanbul: DER Yayınları)

*Uluçay, Çağatay (1951–52). 'İstanbul Saraçhanesi ve Saraçlarına Dair bir Araştırma', *Tarih Dergisi* III, 5–6, pp 147–64

Uzunçarşılı, İsmail Hakkı (1943–44). *Osmanlı Devleti Teşkilâtından Kapukulu Ocakları*, 2 vols. (Ankara: Türk Tarih Kurumu)

Uzunçarşılı, İsmail Hakkı (1945). *Osmanlı Devletinin Saray Teşkilâtı* (Ankara: Türk Tarih Kurumu)

Uzunçarşılı, İsmail Hakkı (1948). *Osmanlı Devletinin Merkez ve Bahriye Teşkilâtı* (Ankara: Türk Tarih Kurumu)

Uzunçarşılı, İsmail Hakkı (1965). *Osmanlı Devletinin İlmiye Teşkilâtı* (Ankara: Türk Tarih Kurumu)

*Uzunçarşılı, İsmail Hakkı (1981–86). 'Osmanlı Sarayında Ehl-i Hiref (Sanatkârlar) Defteri', *Belgeler* 11, pp 23–76

*Valensi, Lucette (1969). 'Islam et capitalisme: Production et commerce des chéchias en Tunisie et en France aux XVIIIe et XIXe siècles', *Revue d'histoire moderne et contemporaine* XVI, pp 376–400

Vatin, Nicolas and Gilles Veinstein (2003). *Le sérail ébranlé* (Paris: Fayard)

*Vatter, Sherry (1995). 'Militant Textile Weavers in Damascus: Waged Artisans and

the Ottoman Labor Movements 1850–1914', in *Workers and the Working Class in the Ottoman Empire and Turkey 1839–1950*, ed Donald Quataert and Erik Jan Zürcher (London: I.B.Tauris), pp 35–57

*Vatter, Sherry (2006). 'Journeymen Textile Weavers in Nineteenth-Century Damascus: A Collective Biography', in *Struggle and Survival in the Modern Middle East*, ed Edmund Burke III and David N. Yaghubian (Berkeley, Los Angeles: University of California Press), pp 64–79

Veinstein, Gilles (1975). 'Ayân de la région d'Izmir et le commerce du Levant (deuxième moitié du XVIIIe siècle)', *Revue de l'Occident musulman et de la Méditerranée* XX, pp 131–46

*Veinstein, Gilles (1988). 'Du marché urbain au marché du camp: l'institution ottomane des *orducu*', in *Mélanges Professeur Robert Mantran*, ed Abdeljelil Temimi (Zaghouan: CEROMDI), pp 299–327

Veinstein, Gilles (1996). 'L'Oralité dans les documents d'archives ottomans: paroles rapportés ou imaginées?', *Oral et écrit dans le monde turco-ottoman*, special issue of *Revue du monde musulman et de la Méditerranée* (Aix-en-Provence: Edisud), 75–6, pp 133–42

*Vroom, Joanita (2003). *After Antiquity: ceramics and society in the Aegean from the 7th to the 20th century A.C. A case study from Boeotia, Central Greece* (Leiden: Faculty of Archaeology)

Wallerstein, Immanuel (1974). *The Modern World-System: Capitalist Agriculture and the Origins of the European World Economy in the Sixteenth Century* (New York, San Francisco, London: Academic Press)

Wallerstein, Immanuel, Hale Decdeli and Reşat Kasaba (1987). 'The Incorporation of the Ottoman Empire into the World Economy', in *The Ottoman Empire and the World Economy*, ed Huri Islamoğlu-Inan (Cambridge and Paris: Cambridge University Press and Maison des Sciences de l'Homme), pp 88–100

*Weber, Stefan (2002). 'Images of Imagined Worlds', in *The Empire in the City: Arab Provincial Capitals in the Late Ottoman Empire*, ed Jens Hanssen, Thomas Philipp and Stefan Weber (Würzburg/Germany: Ergon Verlag), pp 145–71

White, Jenny (1994). *Money Makes Us Relatives: Women's Labor in Urban Turkey* (Austin: The University of Texas Press)

Wild, Beate (2007). 'Transylvania: A Land of Diversity between Worlds', in *In Praise of God: Anatolian Rugs in Transylvanian Churches 1500–1750*, ed Nazan Ölçer et al (Istanbul: Sakip Sabancı Museum), pp 15–23

Wilkins, Charles (2005). 'Households, Guilds and Neighborhoods: Social Solidarities in Ottoman Aleppo, 1640–1700', unpublished PhD thesis, Harvard University

*Ydema, Onno (1990, reprint 1991). *Carpets and Their Datings in Netherlandisch Paintings 1540–1700* (Wappingers Falls, NY: Antique Collectors Club)

Yérasimos, Stéphane (1995). 'La communauté juive d'Istanbul à la fin du XVIe siècle', *Turcica* XXVII, pp 101–33

*Yi, Eunjeong (2004). *Guild Dynamics in Seventeenth-century Istanbul: Fluidity and Leverage* (Leiden: E.J. Brill)

*Yi, Eunjeong (forthcoming a). 'The Supposed Egalitarianism among the Guildsmen: Rethinking the "Ottoman Economic Mind"'

Yi, Eunjeong (forthcoming b). 'An Examination of Istanbul Artisans' Rebellion in 1688'

*Yıldırım, Onur (2002). 'Ottoman Guilds as a Setting for Ethno-Religious Conflict: The Case of the Silk-thread Spinners' Guild in Istanbul', *International Review of Social History* 47/3 (December), pp 407–19

*Yıldırım, Onur (2008). 'Kurumsal Bir Yenilik Olarak Gedik: İstanbul'da İbrişim Bükücü Esnafı Örneği', in *Osmanlı'nın Peşinde bir Yasam. Suraiya Faroqhi'ye Armağan*, ed Onur Yıldırım (Ankara: İmge Kitabevi Yayınları), pp 373–89

*Zarinebaf-Shahr, Fariba (2001). 'The Role of Women in the Urban Economy of Istanbul, 1700–1850', *International Labor and Working Class History* 60, pp 141–52

Zilfi, Madeline (1986). 'Discordant Revivalism in Seventeenth-Century Istanbul', *The Journal of Near Eastern Studies* 45, 4, pp 251–69

Zilfi, Madeline (1988). *The Politics of Piety: The Ottoman Ulema in the Postclassical Age (1600–1800)* (Minneapolis: Bibliotheca Islamica)

*Zilfi, Madeline (2000). 'Goods in the *mahalle*: Distributional Encounters in Eighteenth-Century Istanbul', in *Consumption Studies and the History of the Ottoman Empire, 1550–1922: An Introduction*, ed Donald Quataert (Albany, NY: SUNY Press), pp 289–312

Zilfi, Madeline (2004). 'Whose Laws? Gendering the Ottoman Sumptuary Regime', in *Ottoman Costumes: From Textile to Identity*, ed Suraiya Faroqhi and Christoph Neumann (Istanbul: Eren), pp 125–41

Zürcher, Erik Jan (1993). *Turkey: A Modern History* (London, New York: I.B.Tauris)

Non-Ottoman artisans, artists and merchants; social history of western Europe

Bayly, Christopher A. (1983). *Rulers, Townsmen and Bazaars: North Indian Society in the Age of British Expansion, 1770–1870* (Cambridge: Cambridge University Press, 1983)

Berlin, Michael (1997). '"Broken all in pieces": Artisans and the Regulation of Workmanship in Early Modern London', in *The Artisan and the European Town 1500–1900*, ed Geoffrey Crossick (Aldershot: Ashgate Publishing), pp 75–91

Bos, Sandra (2006). 'A Tradition of Giving and Receiving: Mutual Aid within the Guild System', in *Craft Guilds in the Early Modern Low Countries: Work, Power and Representation*, ed Maarten Prak, Catharina Lis, Jan Lucassen and Hugo Soly (Aldershot, Burlington: Ashgate), pp 174–93

Cerruti, Simona (1990). *La ville et les métiers: Naissance d'un langage corporatif (Turin, 17e–18e siècle)* (Paris: Éditions de l'École des Hautes Études en Sciences Sociales)

Cerruti, Simona (1991). 'Group strategies and trade strategies: the Turin tailors' guild in the late seventeenth and early eighteenth centuries', in *Domestic Strategies: Work and Family in France and Italy 1600–1800*, ed Stuart Woolf (Cambridge, Paris: Cambridge University Press and Maison des Sciences de l'Homme), pp 102–47

Chartier, Roger (1991). *Les orgines culturelles de la Révolution française* (Paris: Seuil)

Cowan, Alexander (1998). *Urban Europe 1500–1700* (London, New York: Arnold and Oxford University Press)

Dale, Stephen Frederic (1994). *Indian Merchants and Eurasian Trade, 1600–1750* (Cambridge: Cambridge University Press)

Darnton, Robert (1985). *The Great Cat Massacre and Other Episodes in French Cultural History* (New York: Random House)

Davis, Robert C. (1993). 'Arsenal and Arsenalotti: Workplace and Community in

Seventeenth-Century Venice', in *The Workplace before the Factory: Artisans and Proletarians 1500–1800*, ed Thomas Max Safley and Leonard N. Rosenband (Ithaca, London: Cornell University Press), pp 190–203

Deceulaer, Harald and Bibi Panhuyzen (2006). 'Dressed to Work: A Gendered Comparison of the Tailoring Trades in the Southern and Northern Netherlands, 1500–1800', in *Craft Guilds in the Early Modern Low Countries: Work, Power and Representation*, ed Maarten Prak, Catharina Lis, Jan Lucassen and Hugo Soly (Aldershot, Burlington: Ashgate), pp 133–56

Deursen, A. Th. van (1998). *Een dorp in de polder: Graft in de seventiende eeuw* (Amsterdam: Uitgeverij Gert Bakker)

Epstein, Stephen, Clara Eugenia Nuñez et al (eds) (1998). *Guilds, Economy and Society: Proceedings of the Twelfth International Economic History Congress, B1* (Sevilla: Fundacion Fomento de la Historia Economica)

Farr, James R. (1988). *Hands of Honor: Artisans and Their World in Dijon, 1550–1650* (Ithaca and London: Cornell University Press)

Floor, Willem (1999). *The Persian Textile Industry in Historical Perspective, 1500–1925* (Paris: L'Harmattan and Société d'Histoire de l'Orient)

Garden, Maurice (1975). *Lyon et les Lyonnais au XVIIIe siècle* (Paris: Flammarion)

Goitein, Samuel Dov (1988). *A Mediterranean Society: The Jewish Communities of the Arab World as Portrayed in the Documents of the Cairo Geniza, vol. V. The Individual: Portrait of a Mediterranean Personality of the High Middle Ages as Reflected in the Cairo Geniza* (Berkeley, Los Angeles, London: University of California Press)

Hafter, Daryl (1995). 'Women who Wove in the Eighteenth-century Silk Industry of Lyon', in *European Women and the Preindustrial Crafts*, ed Daryl Hafter (Bloomington and Indianapolis: Indiana University Press), pp 42–64

Honacker, Karin van (1994). 'De politieke cultuur van de Brusselse ambachten in de achttiende eeuw: conservatisme, corporatisme of opportunisme?', in *Werken volgens de regels, Ambachten in Brabant en Vlaanderen*, ed Catharina Lis and Hugo Soly (Brussels: VUB Press)

Israel, Jonathan (1989). *Dutch Primacy in World Trade, 1585–1740* (Oxford: Clarendon Press)

Jacoby, David (2004). 'The Silk Trade of Late Byzantine Constantinople', in *İstanbul Üniversitesi, 550. Yıl Uluslararası Bizans ve Osmanlı Sempozyumu 30–31 Mayıs 2003*, ed Sümer Atasoy (Istanbul: İstanbul Üniversitesi), pp 129–44

Kaplan, Steven (1996). *Le meilleur pain du monde, Les boulangers de Paris au XVIIIe siècle* (Paris: Fayard)

Kemp, Martin (1997). *Der Blick hinter die Bilder, Text und Kunst in der italienischen Renaissance*, trans Alexander Sahm (Cologne: Dumont Buchverlag)

Keyvani, Mehdi (1982). *Artisans and Guild Life in the Later Safavid Period: Contributions to the Social-Economic History of Persia* (Berlin: Klaus Schwarz Verlag)

Lapidus, Ira M. (1984). *Muslim Cities in the Later Middle Ages* (Cambridge: Cambridge University Press)

Levy, Dana, Lea Sneider, Frank B. Gibney (n.d., probably 1984). *Kanban: Shop Signs of Japan* (New York and Tokyo: John Weatherhill Inc.)

Lis, Catharina, Jan Lucassen and Hugo Soly (eds) (1994a). *Before the Unions: Wage Earners and Collective Action in Europe 1300–1850* (Cambridge: Cambridge University Press)

Lis, Catharina and Hugo Soly (eds) (1994b). *Werken volgens de regels, Ambachten in Brabant en Vlaanderen* (Brussels: VUB Press)

Lis, Catharina, Jan Lucassen and Hugo Soly (2006a). 'Craft Guilds in Comparative Perspective: The Northern and Southern Netherlands: A Survey', in *Craft Guilds in the Early Modern Low Countries: Work, Power and Representation*, ed Maarten Prak, Catharina Lis, Jan Lucassen and Hugo Soly (Aldershot, Burlington: Ashgate), pp 1–31

Lis, Catharina, Jan Lucassen and Hugo Soly (2006b). 'Export Industries, Craft Guilds and Capitalist Trajectories, 13th to 18th Centuries', in *Craft Guilds in the Early Modern Low Countries: Work, Power and Representation*, ed Maarten Prak, Catharina Lis, Jan Lucassen and Hugo Soly (Aldershot, Burlington: Ashgate), pp 107–32

Lucassen, Jan and Maarten Prak (2006). 'Conclusion', in *Craft Guilds in the Early Modern Low Countries: Work, Power and Representation*, ed Maarten Prak, Catharina Lis, Jan Lucassen and Hugo Soly (Aldershot, Burlington: Ashgate), pp 224–31

Masson, Paul (1911). *Histoire du commerce français dans le Levant au XVIIIe siècle* (Paris: Hachette)

Mendels, Franklin (1972). 'Proto-industrialization: The First Phase of the Industrialization Process', *The Journal of Economic History* 32, pp 241–61

Mousnier, Roland (1971). *La vénalité des offices sous Henri IV et Louis XIII*, 2nd ed (Paris: Presses Universitaires de France)

Murphy, Caroline P. (2003). *Lavinia Fontana: A painter and her patrons in sixteenth-century Bologna* (New Haven, London: Yale University Press)

Narazaki, Muneshige (1982). *Hiroshige: The 53 Stations of the Tokaido*, English adaptation by Gordon Sager (Tokyo, New York, San Francisco: Kodansha)

North, Michael (2003). *Genuss und Glück des Lebens, Kulturkonsum im Zeitalter der Aufklärung* (Cologne, Weimar, Vienna: Böhlau Verlag)

Poni, Carlo (1982). 'Maß gegen Maß: Wie der Seidenfaden lang und dünn wurde', in Robert Berdahl, Alf Lüdtke et al, *Klassen und Kultur, Sozialanthropologische Perspektiven in der Geschichtsschreibung* (Frankfurt/Main: Syndikat), pp 21–53

Poni, Carlo (1991). 'Local market rules and practices. Three guilds in the same line of production in early modern Bologna', in *Domestic Strategies: Work and Family in France and Italy 1600–1800*, ed Stuart Woolf (Cambridge, Paris: Cambridge University Press and Maison des Sciences de l'Homme), pp 69–101

Prak, Maarten (2006). 'Corporate Politics in the Low Countries: Guilds as Institutions', in *Craft Guilds in the Early Modern Low Countries: Work, Power and Representation*, ed Maarten Prak, Catharina Lis, Jan Lucassen and Hugo Soly (Aldershot, Burlington: Ashgate), pp 74–106

Reddy, William M. (1984). *The Rise of Market Culture: The Textile Trade and French Society, 1750–1900* (Cambridge: Cambridge University Press)

Roche, Daniel (1989). *La culture des apparences: Une histoire du vêtement, XVIIe–XVIIIe siècle* (Paris: Fayard)

Schama, Simon (1987). *The Embarrassment of Riches: An Interpretation of Dutch Culture in the Golden Age* (London: Collins)

Sella, Domenico (1968). 'Crisis and Transformation in Venetian Trade', in *Crisis and Change in the Venetian Economy in the Sixteenth and Seventeenth Centuries*, ed Brian Pullan (London: Methuen & Co Ltd), pp 88–105

Spufford, Margaret (1984). *The Great Reclothing of Rural England: Petty Chapmen and their Wares in the Seventeenth Century* (London: Hambledon Press)

Thompson, E.P. (1971). 'The Moral Economy of the English Crowd in the Eighteenth Century', *Past and Present* 50, pp 76–136

Vovelle, Michel (1982). *Idéologies et mentalités* (Paris: François Maspéro)

Ward, Joseph P. (1997). *Metropolitan Communities: Trade Guilds, Identity and Change in Early Modern London* (Stanford: Stanford University Press)

Welch, Evelyn (2005). *Shopping in the Renaissance: Consumer Cultures in Italy 1400–1600* (New Haven, London: Yale University Press)

The following works appeared after the present study was completed:

Dağtaş, Lütfü (2007). *Anadolu'da Dericilik* (Istanbul: İDESBAŞ and Dönence)

Inalcık, Halil (2008). *Türkiye Tekstil Tarihi üzerine Araştırmalar* (Istanbul: Türkiye İş Bankası Kültür Yayınları)

Lowry, Heath (2008). *The Shaping of the Ottoman Balkans 1350–1500: The Conquest, Settlement and Infrastructural Development of Northern Greece* (Istanbul: Bahçeşehir University), pp 179–207

Yaman, Bahattin (2008). *Osmanlı Saray Sanatkârları. 18. Yüzyılda Ehl-i Hiref* (Istanbul: Tarih Vakfı Yurt Yayınları)

Index

aba see raw wool
Abdülhamid II 205
Abdülmecid, Sultan 138, 193
Adana 217
administrative prices 7, 88, 213; *see also narh*; price fixing
ahi baba 28, 123, 153, 233
Ahi Evran 28, 123–4, 149, 151, 153; lodge of (Kırşehir) 74
Ahi Evren 104; *see also* Ahi Evran
*ahi*s 2, 28–9, 43, 104, 123, 149
Ahkâm Defterleri 117
ahl al-khibra 69
Ahmed I 59, 77
Ahmed III 145, 147, 151, 154–5, 157–8, 181
Ahmed Paşa, Melek 58, 149
Ahmed Refik (Altınay) 6
Akarlı, Engin 18–19
alaca (textile) 80, 102, 118
alaca arab kerekesi 102
Alanya 202
al-Armānī, Yuḥanna 16
Albania(n) 74, 112–13
al-Djabartī 131, 151–2, 158
Aleppo, Aleppine xiv, 10, 13–14, 29, 87, 89–90, 106, 159, 171, 188, 192–3, 209, 217
Alexandria 103, 189
al-Ḥusayniyya 151–3, 158
'ālima 137; *see also* singers
alliances, between janissaries and ulema 154
al-Nāsikh, Ibrāhīm 16, 135
'Abd al-Rahmān Katkhudā 134
alum 144
Ambelakia xiv, 13, 167–8, 184
Amsterdam xvi, 77, 105
Anatolia(n) xx, xxiii, 2, 9, 11–12, 14, 20–2, 26–9, 31, 50, 61, 68, 76, 79, 89, 95, 96–7, 103–4, 116, 124, 151, 153, 165, 168, 175–6, 178, 183, 187, 189, 205
ancient custom (*adet-i kadime*) xviii
angora 89, 91–2, 166; *see also* mohair
Ankara xv, 11, 14, 28, 40–1, 87, 89, 91–3, 101, 106, 123, 165–7, 207
apprentices 40, 62, 74, 115, 187, 211
architects 145
Armenians 66, 93–4, 101, 112, 178, 196, 201–3
arsenals 54, 70
askeri, askeri kassam 142

Asyut 16, 187, 234
autonomy, of guilds xxv–xxvii, 106–7, 139, 140, 159
Aydın 50
Azhar sheikhs 154
Aziz Efendi 149

Baer, Gabriel 7–10
Baghdad 5, 74
bakers, bakeries, baking 13, 32–3, 35, 37, 43, 62, 70, 111–12, 115–16, 118, 136, 158, 202, 215
Balkan(s) xxiii–xxiv, 22, 27, 35, 48, 51, 61, 95, 108–9, 116, 132, 160–1, 167, 184, 190, 199
Barkan, Ömer Lütfi 7
Başaran, Betül 19, 217
Bastiyan 'the Frank', seal-maker and diamond-cutter 58, 83
Bayezid II, 32, 38, 51–3, 57, 67, 76
bazargânbaşı-ı şehriyarî 147
bekâr odaları 114
Bektaşi 153
beledi kassam 68
Benaroya, Avraam 199, 206
bezzaz 102, 118
Bilād al-Shām *see* Syria(n)
Black Sea 14, 108–10, 149, 190, 193, 201
boatmen 47, 63
Bologna, Bolognese xvi, 163, 213–14, 219
bookbinders 181
booksellers 181
Bosnia(n) 101, 173
boza 125
braid *see gaytan*
Brašov/Kronstadt 94, 103, 106
Braudel, Fernand 206
bread 158, 202, 215
brokers 30
Brussels 218
Bruyn, Cornelis de, Dutch painter 83
Buckingham, James Silk 176
Buda, Budapest 101, 161
Būlāq 129
Bulgaria(n) xiv, 13–14, 27, 108, 160, 162–3, 165, 170, 177, 187, 195, 198–9
Bursa xiv–xvi, xviii, xxi, xxiv, 9–11, 31–2, 34, 37–42, 46–7, 52, 75, 79, 87, 95–6, 103–4, 116, 120, 144, 160, 164, 170–3, 182–3,

271

185, 195, 209, 214–15, 219
Busbecq, Ogier Ghiselin de 89
butchers 13, 30–1, 35–6, 42, 50, 71–2, 108, 133, 152, 200, 213–14

cab drivers 17, 200
Cairo xiv, xviii, xxii, xxiv, 5, 15–17, 20, 26, 29, 64–6, 68–70, 72–4, 77, 79–80, 82, 84–7, 102, 104, 106, 128–31, 133–6, 138–41, 143, 145, 151–3, 159–60, 173, 189, 200, 204–5, 208–9, 219
Camondo, Abraham 200
Çankırı 2, 104, 202
capital formation, difficulty of 8, 12
carpenters 146
carpets 79, 80, 186, 192, 197; of Anatolia 103; of Cairo 80, 82; of Uşak 93–4
Celâleddîn Rûmî, Mevlânâ 27
centralization, early modern xvii, xxvii, 18
Chalcraft, John xxiii, 17, 18, 20, 206
Chief Black Eunuch 143
Chios 161
Christians xxvi, 16, 58, 61–2, 67, 92–3, 109, 124–5, 132, 172–3, 179, 181, 188, 190–1
Church of the Holy Sepulchre, Jerusalem 181–2
çiftlik 108
clock-makers 83
coal 193–4; mines 190
coffee 125, 148; houses 115, 202; shops 125
Cohen, Amnon 10
command economy 103, 105
Committee for Union and Progress (İttihat ve Terakki Cemiyeti) 207
construction 15, 46
consumption, consumers xv, xviii, xxvii, 88, 103, 160–1, 163–4, 200, 212
cook-shops 30, 35
copper xv, 91, 174, 178–9; mines 53; pots 79, 89; vats 183
coppersmiths 178–9
corps, of architects 60; of palace artisans 62
cotton 12, 16, 79–80, 102, 137–8, 161, 167, 173, 175, 177, 186; cloth 50, 51, 189, 193; dyers 175; mills 198; weavers 183; yarn 50, 161, 167
court, of Cairo 68; of the qadi xvi, xxvi, 40, 66–7, 70, 122; of the sultans xxvii, 83, 88, 146, 155
cover of the Ka'ba see kisve
credit 177
Crete, Cretan 54, 137, 165
çuha see wool/woollens
cushion covers 170; from Bursa 96
custom(ers) xx, xxv, 13, 39, 43, 87, 96, 99, 105, 120, 122

Dalsar, Fahri 9
Damascus, Damascene xiv, xviii, 10, 15, 20, 38, 46, 102, 130, 141, 148, 159, 173–4, 188, 204–5, 208, 214, 219
damga 38
dârâyâ (textile) 102
Daux, A. 195
decentralization xvii
defter-i sur-ı humayun 146
Denizli 41, 123
Dernschwam, Hans 89, 91–2, 105, 230
Derviş Mehmed Zıllî, goldsmith 58
dervishes 2, 4, 122, 152, 154
dervish lodges 28, 46, 124, 173
design office (nakkaşhane) 59
Despoineta, needlewoman and embroiderer 123
devşirme 59
differentiation, social in Balkan towns 162
Diyarbakır xxvi
Dubrovnik 48
dye-houses 42, 102, 182, 183, 191
dyers 6, 102, 174, 176

Edirne xviii, xxi, 30–1, 34–5, 38, 42, 46–7, 94, 101, 148, 154, 236
Egypt(ian) xv, xxi, xxiii, 16, 18, 22, 26, 30, 58, 60, 70, 79, 80, 86, 102, 108, 110–11, 117, 128–34, 136, 139–40, 145, 180, 187, 189, 200, 203–7, 214
ehl-i hibre 31–2, 37, 52
ehl-i hiref 56
ehl-i hirfet 31
emin 38, 70–1
Emine bint Mahmud 170–1
England, English 48, 238
entari 170–1
equality, of earnings, among guildsmen 201; supposed, among guildsmen 12–13, 36, 75, 85, 130, 169, 177, 185, 213
Ereğli (Karadeniz Ereğlisi) 193
Ergin, Osman Nuri 6
esnafia (from esnaf) 177
Evliya Çelebi xxii, 2, 9, 15, 30, 54–6, 58, 62, 65–6, 70–2, 74, 80, 82–4, 90, 93, 99–100, 102, 112, 123, 125, 128–30, 149

factories 21, 165, 167, 186, 195–8; in Egypt 137–8; Ottoman 190, 204
factory-made goods 5, 160, 203
faiences 56, 97, 99–100
family labour 184, 187
Fazıl Ahmed Paşa, Köprülüzade 84
festivities 46, 73
festive processions 145; see also guild elders: pageant (1582)
fetvas see juris-consult
fezzes 90, 168–9, 197
First World War xiii, 6, 190, 196, 206; see also Great War
fiscalism xviii

flower-sellers 62–3
food prices, in Cairo 131, 133
francala 112
France, French 45
furriers 72, 132
furun-ı tuc 56
*fütuvvetname*s 2, 3, 29–30, 43, 73

gardeners 178
gaytan 164–6, 174
Gaziantep/'Ayntâb 32–3, 192
*gedik*s 10, 18–19, 119–21, 126–27, 130, 140–1
Genç, Mehmet 8, 104
Gerber, Haim 8, 10–12
Ghazaleh, Pascale 17
gifts, to the sultan 146
Ginio, Eyal 3
glass-makers' ovens 62
gold 56, 130, 170, 175
goldsmiths xxii, 27, 33, 73, 132, 172
Gölpınarlı, Abdülbaki 2
Great War 191, 197, 205; *see also* First World War
Greece, Greek(s) 54, 84, 91, 94, 110, 112–13, 137, 160–1, 170, 177, 196, 199, 201, 203
guarantors, guarantees 139, 144–5; *see also kefil*
guild elders xxvi; in Cairo 72; in Istanbul 74; pageant (1582) 62, 64; sheikhs 180, 203–4; wardens xxvii, 19, 34–5, 107, 127; *see also kethüda*; headman/headmen of guilds
gum lac (*lök*) 34
Gümüşgerdan firm 165, 187, 196, 204

Habsburgs 45–6, 55, 109, 121, 155, 157, 161, 167–9, 184, 210, 218
halife, kalfa 73
halva conversation 31
Halvetis 153
Hamā 102
Hammer, Joseph von 170–1
handicrafts, survival of in the nineteenth century 186
Hanna, Nelly 103
Hasan b Abdülcelil, artist 57
Hasan Paşa, Nakkaş 59
Haunolth, Nicolaus 63
headman/headmen of guilds 19, 25, 35, 63, 115, 121–2, 139, 143, 169, 201, 203–4; *see also kethüda*, guild elders: wardens
helâlî (textile) 102
ḥimāya 132–3
hirfet 32, 43, 125, 219
Hızır b Ahmed, Hacı 40
Hitzel, Frédéric 21
horse gear, manufacture of 35
Hungary, Hungarian 14, 27, 45, 83, 94–5,
99, 101

Ibn Baṭṭūṭa 27–8, 41
İbrahim Paşa 151, 155
ibrik 178
İhtisab Nezareti 191
ihtiyarlar 149
ikat 173–4
immigration, into Istanbul 76, 113–16, 127, 156; of refugees to Tunis 168
Inalcik, Halil 11, 14, 104
incorporation, into European world economy 186, 188
indigo 174, 176, 183, 193
informal sector 206
Iran(ian) xxi, 26, 39, 57, 59, 83, 89, 96, 151, 219
ironworkers, part-time 195
İskenderun/Alexandretta 193
Ismā'īl Abū Taqiyya 84
Ismā'īl, khedive 189, 203
Ismā'īl I, Shah of Iran 39, 58
Istanbul, areas and structures: Âhi Çelebi 67; Balat 67; Beşiktaş 67, 192; Beyoğlu 83; Eyüp 66–7, 115; Feshane 197; Galata 66–7, 83–4, 169, 201; Hasköy 67, 115; Kadıköy 156; Kasımpaşa 67; Kızkulesi/Leander Tower 180; Mısır Çarşısı 84; Odun kapısı 146; Pera 83; Saraçhane 42, 118–19, 149; Sultan Ahmed mosque 59, 77, 125, 180; Süleymaniye 60, 61, 76, 80, 195; Tophane 67; Unkapanı 70, 111, 125; Üsküdar 66–7, 156; Yedikule 42; Yeni Cami 84; Yenikapı 146
Izmir 49, 93, 114, 181–2, 190
İzmit 197
İznik/Nicea 14, 27, 97, 99–100, 178

janissaries 19, 48–50, 70–2, 97, 118, 132, 134, 165; janissaries, candidate (*acemi oğlan*) 61
Jerusalem xiv, 10, 28, 32–3, 35–6, 50, 93, 160, 178, 180, 208
jewellery, jewellers xxv, 33, 50, 56, 130
Jews/Jewish xx, xxvi, 16, 26, 48–50, 58, 67, 92, 112, 115, 124, 132, 148, 152, 179, 181, 198–201
journeymen 204, 211, 214
juris-consult xx, 154

Kadızadeliler 155
kaftan 80, 174
kapan tüccarı 111
Kara Ferye/Verroia 49–50, 161
Karaçelebizade, chronicle writer 150
Kasım b Abdullah, manufacturer of 'paste' 42
kâşicibaşı 100
kassabbaşı 71
kaymakam 70, 142

Kayseri 59, 113, 123
kedek 119, 141
kefil bilmal, kefil binnefs 144
kefil, nezir (surety) 113, 115, 145; see also guarantors, guarantees
kethüda 43, 73–4, 79, 100, 121–2, 139, 169; see also guild elders: wardens; headman/headmen of guilds
kethüdalık avaidi see purchase, of headmen's positions
Khān al-Khalīlī 84
khans 49, 64, 84–5, 92, 118, 143, 148, 181
Kırlı, Cengiz 19, 217
Kırşehir 28, 123–4, 153
kisve 82, 102
Kösem Sultan 84
Kurds 201
küreci 53
Kütahya 51, 97, 99–101, 137
kutni 171
Kütükoğlu, Mübahat 14

labour market 199; organizations 205–7
labour-squeezing 20, 187
labourers, unskilled 157
law, of the market inspector/supervisor (*ihtisab kanunnamesi*) 31, 35, 37
Laz 201
Le Play, Frédéric 195
leather 12, 14, 35, 108, 161, 213, 218
Lebanon xx, 173, 191
leğen 178
legitimacy, of low-paid family labour 187; of a magnate family 182; of state intervention 208; of the sultan 116–19, 127, 142, 157–8, 183
legitimization, attempted, of British rule in Egypt 189
Levni, painter of miniatures 145–6
linen 108
Lis, Caterina 210
lonca 125, 219
London 77, 105
looms 62
Lucassen, Jan 210
Lyons 195, 214, 217

madder (*rubbia tinctorum*) 93, 167
Maghrib 169
Mahmud II 110, 114, 158, 168
makrama 79, 171
Mamluk 35, 79, 129–31, 133–4, 141, 151–2, 158
Manisa 28, 46, 49, 182
Mantran, Robert 9, 19, 21
markets xv, xviii, xxvii, 4–5, 14, 21, 38, 49, 61, 70, 77, 79, 83, 86, 88, 90, 105, 111, 145, 148, 156, 166, 168, 169, 177, 184, 189, 197, 202, 207, 212, 218; covered 64, 90, 197; domestic 14; inspectors 37, 67, 72; interregional 20; supervisors 36, 43, 107, 112, 133, 191–2; see also *muhtesib*; tax 51; values 216
marketplace 67, 150, 191
Marseilles 14, 168
Mecca 46, 82, 102, 169
Mehmed Ağa, architect of the Sultan Ahmed mosque 58–9
Mehmed II, the Conqueror 21, 38, 42, 51–2, 60
Mehmed IV 84, 150, 155
Mehmed, Seyyid b Seyyid 'Alâ' eddîn 29
Mehmet Ali Paşa 17, 110, 117, 128–9, 131, 137, 139, 140–1, 189; monopolies of 137–8
mercantilism 14
Mevlevi şeyh, entrepreneur in copper refining 178
Mevlevis 2, 153, 173, 178
mi'mārbāshā 71
Michel, Nicolas 16
Mihayil, maker of watch-cases 84
militarization, of artisan guilds 185, 219; of guilds 85, 132–3, 173
military men xviii, 72, 132–3, 159; see also soldiers
millers, milling, mills 13, 32, 70, 111, 116
mines, miners 187, 190, 194–5
mining, part-time 194
Mintzuri, Hagop 192
mohair 14, 91–3, 167; see also angora
Moldovia(n) 109–10
moneylenders, moneylending 161, 177
mosques 46
Mosul xxiv, 208
mu'temed adamlar 52
muhabbet cemiyeti 202
muhattam (textile) 102
muhtasib 72, 228
muhtesib 37, 71, 219, 225; see also markets: supervisors
mulawwan 173
municipality, Istanbul 201
muqarnas 62
Murad I 26, 28
Murad IV 58, 66, 73, 83
musicians 202
Muslims xix, 19–20, 26–7, 30, 37, 61, 67, 92, 100, 106, 109, 112–13, 116, 124–5, 127, 135, 144, 146–8, 151, 159, 161, 163, 173, 177, 180–1, 188, 194–6, 198
Mustafa II 150, 154, 157
Mustafa 'Âlî 57
Mustafa Naima 175
Mustafa Paşa 152
Mustafa Paşa, Kara 179, 181

Nablus 177, 208
nakkaş 57, 59

Nakşbendis 153
narh 32, 37–8, 108, 212; see also administrative prices; price fixing
Natanyan, Boğos 202
Nazım, Dr. 205
nizam 143
nomads, of the Balkans 53; see also *yürük*

ocak yaşmağı 170
olive oil 90, 177, 202
orducus 47, 63
Orthodox xxv, 41, 88, 96–7, 103, 161, 172, 177–8
Osman, Nakkaş 62
Osman, Seyyid Atpazarı 150
Özcan, Tahsin xx
Özmucur, Süleyman 75

painters, decorative 15, 60, 69, 71, 176
Palairet, Michel 184
Pamuk, Şevket 75
pazarbaşı 146–7
peripheralization 184
petitions, petitioners, petitioning xvi, 117, 142–3
pious foundations 7, 18, 41, 105, 120, 124, 128, 144, 176, 181, 185; guild-based 172–3
Piri b Abdullah 40
plague 48, 66, 85, 113–14
Plovdiv/Filibe 165
Poland, Polish 14, 92–3, 106
policemen 192, 200
population, of Bursa 97; of Cairo 66; of Istanbul 65, 113; of Iznik 100
porcelain, Chinese 100–1
porters xxv, 125, 192, 201
potters 100
Poulopos, Theodosia 41
price fixing 213; see also administrative prices; *narh*
prisoners 47; of war, as producers 61; of war, working in the arsenal 54
property 19, 121
protection money see *ḥimāya*
proto-industry 185
provisionism xviii
purchases, of headmen's positions 121–2, 127, 139; in common, of raw materials 74
putting out 11, 12, 165, 185, 187, 204

qadi registers xix–xxi, 9–10, 17, 23, 25, 32, 68, 92, 140, 177, 215, 217
qadis 19, 31, 33, 35–7, 43, 47, 51–2, 61, 63, 67, 69–71, 107, 111, 119–20, 122, 154
qāḍī' askar 69
qisma 'arabiyya 68
qisma 'askariyya 69
Quataert, Donald xxiii, 15, 20–1

Rachkov, Hristo 170
Rafeq, Abdul Karem 10
Raşid Bey 195
raw wool 50; cotton 188; silk 89, 192, 195–6; silk from Bursa 96; silk from Iran 96
Raymond, André 15–17, 21
real wages 156–8; slight increases in 199
reaya 142
red dye (*kızıl boya*) 34, 161
registers, of important affairs (*Mühimme Defterleri*) 9; of (sultanic) commands xx; see also *Ahkâm defterleri*
rents, owed to pious foundations 18–19, 143
reponsa, of rabbis xx
revolts, urban 148–52, 154, 156, 158–9, 200
rowers 47
rufetia (from *hirfet*) 177
Rumayla 151–2, 158
Rumeli 68, 76, 235

Sa'id, khedive 189
sabīl-kuttāb 134–5
saddlers 35, 42, 118–19, 126, 173
Safavids xvi, 45, 151, 209
Şah Muhammed, painter 58
sahan 178
Şahkulu, painter 57
Saliha bint Hacı Mustafa 171
Salonika 48–50, 108, 114, 172, 198–9, 205
Sarajevo xxvi, 173
Sariyannis, Marinos 3
scholars, religious xviii, 10, 28, 36, 154
Second World War 5, 7, 195
segregation by religion, within guilds 20, 147
self-exploitation 20, 188
Selim I 39, 57, 80, 83
Selim III 19, 110, 112, 114–16, 118, 156–8, 164, 175, 183, 212
Serbia(n) 27, 51
Sestini, Domenico 113, 171
şeyh 33; see also sheikh
şeyhülislam 31, 68, 149
sheikhs 43, 69, 71, 73, 124, 130, 139–40, 152–4, 178, 181; see also *şeyh*
shoemakers, shoemaking 6, 32, 35, 38, 41, 50, 202, 213
Sibiu/Hermannstadt 94, 103, 106
sicil see qadi registers
silk xv, xxiv, 10, 13–14, 23, 34, 38, 39, 41, 70, 79, 82, 92, 95, 102, 147, 161, 170, 173, 175, 183, 186, 197, 216; cloth for ecclesiastical use 96–7; industry 105, 214, 216–17; merchants 217; silk-cotton mixtures 193; spinners 34; weavers 79, 95; winders 215
silver 56, 88, 128, 130–1, 170, 175; in ecclesiastical use 177; silver-gilt 178
silversmiths xxv, 33, 73, 178
Sinan, architect 59–61
singers 136; see also *'alima*

Sivas 197, 202–3
slaughterhouses 152, 200, 202
slaves xv, xxiv, 40; as producers 95–6, 105
Sliven 196–8
soap 89–90, 174, 177
Society for the Prevention of Cruelty to Animals 200
soldiers, soldiery 45–7, 56, 70–2, 86, 122, 126, 132–3, 152, 157, 185, 190, 197, 219; pay (*mevacib*) 56; *see also* military men
solidarity, of guildsmen xxvi
Soly, Hugo 210
Spain, Spanish 48, 77, 90, 103
spice-sellers (*attar*) 148
spinners, spinning 168, 204
stamp taxes 176, 200
state intervention, in urban production xv, xviii, xxv, 6–8, 17–18, 106–7, 111–12, 114, 116, 139, 160, 179, 185, 203, 207–8, 214, 217–18
strikes 199–200, 205, 207
subaşı 72
Süleyman I, the Magnificent 39, 55, 57–8, 60, 62, 73, 76, 83, 89, 92
sur-ı humayun emini 147
sürgün 57–8, 65
Synadinos, Papa, of Serres 161
Syria(n) xx–xxi, xxiii, 22, 26, 38, 60, 89, 90, 102–3, 175, 189, 191

Tabriz 57–8
Taeschner, Franz 2, 9
tailors 32, 132, 174, 215–17
tanners, tannery, tanneries 28, 32, 35, 38, 42, 123–4, 126, 149, 213–14
Tanzimat xiii, 190, 200, 202
tavern keepers 2, 30
tax, collectors, collection 72, 107, 144, 219; farmers, farming 38, 74, 88, 91, 116, 121, 144, 160–1, 167, 176, 191, 202, 218; payers, paying 133, 142, 151; tax farms/farmers, lifetime (*malikâne, malikâneci*) xxii, xxiii, 8, 117, 121, 175
taxation 18, 88, 104, 180, 185, 203
teferrüc 73
Tekirdağ, in Ottoman Rodoscuk 32–3
Thessaly, Thessalian xiv, 13, 51, 95, 167–8
Thévenot, Jean 82, 125
Todorov, Nikolai 184
Tokat 28, 175–6, 178–9
tophane 55
trades, disreputable 2, 30
traditionalism xviii
transition, to capitalism 3
Transylvania 14, 94–5, 103
Tucker, Judith 17
Tunis(ian) 87, 89–90, 103, 106, 160, 168–9
Turhan Sultan 84
Turin 216–17, 219

Turna, Nalan 19, 217, 221
Tyrnavos 168

ulema 154–5, 157
Ülgener, Sabri 3–5, 222
Urfa/Şanlıurfa 12, 176, 181, 192
Uşak 93, 103
usûl 143
Uzunçarşılı, İsmail Hakkı xix

Vani Efendi 155
varak 51–3
Vatter, Sherry 20
velençe/velense 49–50
velvet makers 40
Venice, Venetian 14, 45, 48, 54, 89, 92, 100, 106, 109, 113, 163, 165
Votzi, Heidemarie Doğanalp xxiii
Vovelle, Michel 3

wage labour 41, 75
wages, of builders labourers, unskilled 76
Walachia 109–10, 170
Wallerstein, Immanuel 4, 184
watch-makers, from Geneva 84
weavers, weaving 6, 30, 136, 204
Weber, Max 3
weighing scales 202
Wilkins, Charles 13
women, as earners of cash xv–xvi, xxiv–xxv, 9, 12, 17, 20–1, 41, 89–91, 135–6, 163, 177, 187, 196, 198, 203–4, 214
wood-sellers 178
wool/wollens 12–13, 48, 93, 137, 161, 165, 167, 177, 218–19; rough (*aba*) 49–50, 164–5; woollen cloth (*çuha*) 50, 146, 174
workers, non-guild xv, xxvi

Yahya b Hacı Kasım, Hacı 40
Yahya b Halil, al-Burgâzî 29, 30, 43
yamak 146
yarn dealers 79
yeşil yaprak 124
Yi, Eunjeong 12
Yıldırım, Onur 20
yiğitbaşı 73, 79, 122, 233
Young Turk regime/period 190–1, 199, 205–6
yürük 47

Zeljazkov, Dobri 196
Zonguldak 53, 193–5, 206
zorba 150